EXPERIENCING THE STATE

'In this enterprising volume Rudolph and Jacobsen assemble a galaxy of South Asian, European and American stars who illuminatingly analyze the varieties of subjective experience of the state.'

—Brendan O'Leary, University of Pensylvania

'A bold invitation to stretch our imagination. These wide-ranging essays explore the state from below—exposing a subversive, alienating, oppressive leviathan as well as flashes of liberation, empowerment and transformation.'

—James A. Morone, Brown Universitty

'An excellent volume...bringing a rich and diverse collection of essays on how the state is experienced. The field will be the richer for its publication.'

—Niraja Gopal Jayal, Jawaharlal Nehru University

'Rudolph and Jacobsen's collection of studies on what the state is when it's at home is a brilliant fusion of theoretical acuity and an appreciation of the ordinary.'

—Anne Norton, University of Pensylvania

Experiencing the State

Edited by

LLOYD I. RUDOLPH
JOHN KURT JACOBSEN

UNIVERSITY PRESS

OXFORD
UNIVERSITY PRESS

Oxford University Press is a department of the University of Oxford.
It furthers the University's objective of excellence in research, scholarship,
and education by publishing worldwide. Oxford is a registered trademark of
Oxford University Press in the UK and in certain other countries

Published in India by
Oxford University Press
YMCA Library Building, 1 Jai Singh Road, New Delhi 110001, India

First Edition published in 2006
Oxford India Paperbacks 2009

ISBN-13: 978-0-19-806354-4
ISBN-10: 0-19-806354-7

Typeset by Sai Graphic Design, New Delhi 110 055

Contents

Introduction
Framing the Inquiry:
Historicizing the Modern State

LLOYD I. RUDOLPH AND JOHN KURT JACOBSEN

This is a book about experiencing the state—not the state as thing, a bureaucracy, an army, a police force, not something, as Wittgenstein would have it, one can define ostensibly by pointing to it, and not the state as an idea, an abstraction, what Hegel seems to have had in mind.[1] We and the authors in this volume mean to engage state and stateness as it is encountered in everyday life. Still, the question remains, what is being experienced in the essays that follow? In each case it is some kind of a construction that arises out of language and practice in context. Where the language and practice came from is a question that returns us to 'the literature'.

Much of the literature in political science and the social sciences more generally treats 'the state' as an abstraction by universalizing and standardizing what the state is, does, and means. States are discussed as if they were the same through time, space, and circumstance, a practice that often results in analyses and narratives that suffer from being anachronistic or being presentist. Sometimes the opposite happens; state analyses and narratives suffer from what Whitehead called the fallacy of misplaced concreteness.[2]

For starters, we try to avoid naturalizing the term 'state' by historicizing the term. By locating states in time, place, and circumstance, as most of the authors in this book do, we can be contingent and evocative rather than definitive and essentializing. We write in the first years of the twenty-first century, a time when it is frequently said that states are being compromised at home and abroad by globalization and terrorism, processes that challenge their sovereignty and capacities domestically and internationally. In the nineteenth century, the heyday of the modern state, states were assumed to be the means to solve problems and to realize progress. As the twentieth century gave way to the twenty-first, states were more often than not spoken of as the problem rather than as the solution.

Turning from what we may think or say about the state, what images, what hopes and fears, what expectations and anticipations does the word state evoke in the minds of our fellow scholars and potential readers? To unpack the baggage the word state may carry in their minds, we turn to the story of Europe's invention of the modern state. We start with absolutism as it was invented and practiced in seventeenth century France and Prussia.[3] We summon an image of Cardinal Richelieu (Armand-Jean du Plessis, duc de Richelieu) as it was recently portrayed in Montreal's Museum of Fine Art's 2002 exhibition, 'Richelieu: Art and Power' to help us imagine absolutism construction and career. From 1624 until his death at the age of 57 in 1642, Richelieu was the imaginative and ruthless prime minister of France. He moulded the unlikely and unpromising Louis XIII[4] into his conception of a divinely sanctioned absolute ruler, tamed the feudal aristocracy, reigned in post-reformation religious conflict, created, in Norbert Elias' phrase, a 'court society'[5], and brought into being one state governed from Paris that dominated Europe culturally and politically until 1789.[6] His campaign 'to invent the state' started with French culture; he built the first theatre in Paris, established the Académie Française to codify and elevate the language and became the protector of the Sorbonne. To exalt his state, 'Richelieu tapped the mythical glories of ancient Rome as well as the mystical faith of Christian Rome.' 'It was Richelieu's genius', Deborah Weisgall says, 'to transfer to politics the Counter-Reformation's tools—dramatic, immediate and often breathtaking images emphasizing the mystery, the compelling irrationality, of faith. For Richelieu, the state and the king, with their God-given authority, shared these mystic qualities. And he was the worldly priest, the master of mysteries.' Richelieu knew himself, Weisgall says. 'In his bedroom he hung a painting by George de la Tour: *The Penitent St. Jerome.* The saint, clad only in loincloth, holds his cardinal's robe and a crucifix in his left hand. In his right, he grips a scourge. Its knot drips blood onto the floor. Jerome's sin was intellectual pride.' Richelieu's pride, achievements, and wars with Spain and the Hapsburgs 'cost the common man heavily. When he died . . . he was immensely wealthy and almost universally hated.'[7]

We fast forward in our story of the formation of the modern state a century and half, from the era of absolutism to the era of the French revolution. The revolution had the effect of translating Rousseau's concept of the general will into a claim that the people, not the king, was sovereign. Popular sovereignty displaced the absolutist notion of monarchical sovereignty by embedding sovereignty in the nation. The modern state became a nation state. The era of high stateness[8] had begun. The career of the modern state, Stephen Toulmin argues, runs roughly from the Peace of Westphalia (1648)[9] to the First World War[10] when, *inter alia*, its claims to monopolize sovereignty and the legitimate use of force and to provide security inside and outside[11] began to prove ineffective, counter-productive or self-destructive.[12]

From feudal to modern to postmodern times we see an inverse relationship between attention to stateness and attention to civil society: the more attention to civil society the less attention to stateness; the more attention to stateness, the less attention to civil society. Starting with the early modern ideas advanced by Machiavelli, Bodin, and Hobbes in the sixteenth and seventeenth centuries and supplemented by Rousseau in the eighteenth, the claims for state sovereignty and the legitimacy of state institutions rose even as the claims for the legitimacy of the feudal institutions of medieval civil society, such as estates, parliaments, the church, guilds, and towns associated with parcellated and contested sovereignty, declined. Machiavelli made reason of state a ruler's supreme consideration.[13] Bodin advanced monopoly claims for state sovereignty. For Hobbes' concept of Leviathan and Rousseau's of the general will, associations were anathema, at best worms in the entrails of the body politic, a source of competing values, interests, and identities that threatened state sovereignty, individual security, and the public good.

In our effort to situate perceptions of the modern state prevalent in the essays that follow, we turn from the story of the rise of the modern state to the story of the modern state in decline. The First

World War was an important turning point. The meaningless death of 10 million soldiers and expenditure of vast amounts of national wealth in the First World War marked a watershed in the modern state's reputation as a vehicle for civilization and progress. That decline was re-enforced by the rise of violent and racist fascist states before the Second World War and the collapse of the Soviet empire at the close of the Cold War.

Increasing awareness towards the end of the twentieth century of state pathology and failure directed attention to the possibilities of civil society. The success or failure of ex-colonial states after the Second World War and of transitions to democracy and market economies after the end of the Cold War and the collapse of the Soviet Union began to be attributed to aspects of civil society such as the viability of associational life and public spheres and the availability of social capital and trust. In Poland during the 1980s, Solidarity's, and the Catholic Church's, ability to challenge, then help to topple, and displace a Communist state and to contribute to jump-starting a market economy were used to support arguments for the centrality of civil society for transitions to democracy and state and market viability. As states stumbled, foundered, and failed, the attractiveness of the civil society alternative grew. Renewed attention to Tocqueville's argument that democracy in America depended on the strength of its associational life and to Habermas' argument (in a book first published in 1962) for the civilizing effects of a public sphere[14] were forerunners for a spate of academic writing about civil society and its cousins, social capital and trust, that emerged in the closing decade of the twentieth century. Robert Putnam, a political science professor at Harvard, struck celebrity pay dirt in 1995 with a jeremiad about civic disengagement in America entitled 'bowling alone.'[15] But if, at the turn of the twentieth century, the state was being challenged by civil society as a means for collective action, a source of identity and security, and the realization of public goods, the state's decline was relative. Its decline did not herald its demise.

At the close of the twentieth century, citizens still turned to the state not only for security at home and abroad but also as a vehicle for societal self-protection from market forces. Karl Polanyi in his 1944 classic, *The Great Transformation*, spoke of a double movement. On the one hand, there was the relentless and ubiquitous drive by market forces to commodify human beings and nature as wages and rent and, on the other, there were the efforts by organized societal forces such as parties and trade unions acting through the state to save forms of life and the biosphere from the dehumanizing and destructive effects of market forces. As Joseph Stiglitz put it in his introduction to the 2001 edition of Polanyi's 1944 book, 'self-regulating markets never work; their deficiencies, not only in their internal workings but also . . . in their . . . [societal] consequences are so great that government intervention becomes necessary.'[16] The context for these observations was Stiglitz' observation that Polanyi wrote *The Great Transformation* before 'modern economists clarified the limitations of self-regulating markets. Today, there is no respectable intellectual support for the proposition that markets, by themselves, lead to efficient, let alone equitable outcomes.'[17]

The essays in this volume explore how citizens at the turn of the millennium are affected by the double movement. How do state policies, actions, and speech affect their everyday lives? Do they find the state supportive, impartial or hostile? Is it perceived as benign and helpful, a clumsy behemoth, a malevolent source of Orwellian surveillance or 'a committee for managing the common affairs of the whole bourgeoisie'?[18] Rashomon-like, the truth of each essay is shaped by its location in time, space, circumstance, and epistemic community.

The essayists have produced situated knowledge about experiencing the state in a variety of arenas, regional planning, local and urban government, the colonial, welfare and developmental state, literature, cinema, education, and psychotherapy. Combining personal experience or observation with careful analysis, they tell us about how state forms and manifestations are experienced by themselves or by citizens and explore the consequences of those experiences for politics and society.

In an era of downsizing and relentless technological change, market solutions by private corporations are being presented as better suited than state bureaucracies to provide the services citizens require. This was the message of the 1980s that British Prime Minister Margaret Thatcher and US President Ronald Reagan brought to their people.[19] They revived an American version of Lockean liberalism that called for a distrust of state power; the least government was said to be the best government.[20] Thatcher and Reagan redistributed income in ways that favoured the rich by cutting taxes and trying with some success to dismantle their respective country's version of the welfare state.[21] Yet states, for all their limitations and abuses, remain the means through which citizens as consumers and investors can attempt to regulate and perfect markets, protect their rights, and seek security.[22]

In so far as states, like nations, are 'imagined communities', it matters who does and who does not do the imagining. Stuart Hall argues that it is important to ask who does the imagining because there are many 'ways in which meaning about this world can be construed . . . it matters profoundly what and who regularly and routinely gets left out; and how things, people, events, relationships are represented. What we know of society, depends on how things are represented to us and that knowledge in turn informs what we do and what policies we are prepared to accept.[23] Henry Giroux takes a somewhat different tack when he argues that we should 'be conscious of how power and authority are secured in the language through which individuals speak and are spoken.'[24] But people are not trapped in material structures or linguistic prison houses either— at least not always. Margaret Archer reminds us that although the prior development of ideas (from earlier interactions) conditions the current context of action, the 'reflective ability of human beings to fight back against their conditioning [gives] them the capacity to respond with originality to their present context—either taking advantage of inconsistencies within it and generating new forms of syncretism or pluralism from it, or by exploring novel combinations of compatible elements.'[25]

In this volume we have asked writers from diverse disciplines and callings to look at, in Focualt's phrase 'how meanings are produced within relations of power.' They have done so by addressing a wide array of topics and using their preferred modes of analysis. Commencing from different vantage points and arenas, they explore how they or those whose story they tell have experienced some aspect of differently situated states. Their stories address overt policy aspects of the experience as well as the images and presuppositions built into the way a state is perceived. Readers will find that state policies are differentially enforced. Race, class, creed, and place matter. States are experienced in radically different ways by homeless persons offering tabloids for sale, poor peasants displaced by big dams, slum dwellers in Karachi, cultivators in north Indian villages, hospitalized mental patients, exhibitors dealing with philistine state sponsors, and a mahatma on trial for subversion of the colonial state in India.

The state, Polanyi argued, is the site where political communities decide where commodification ends (or is extended), where business has no business imposing a profit criterion. Neither firms nor citizens can accomplish much without the instruments and symbols of the modern state on their side.[26] The question then is, to what political purposes are such instruments and symbols put? Even if the scope and sovereignty of the modern state has been limited by the challenges that multi-lateral and international organizations, NGOs, and 'transnational civil society'[27] have posed, it is premature to compose its epitaph. For the foreseeable future the modern democratic state remains the leading institutional alternative for citizens to exert direct and compelling influence over those who govern them. Witness the rather intense concerns today over the 'democratic deficit' inside the European Union. As the struggle over globalization processes and their consequences make clear, transnational civil society and world public opinion are growing in importance and states' capabilities, functions, and strategies are being modified accordingly. But as we have argued and as the essays that follow illustrate, it would be wrong to suggest the imminent demise of the modern state. For the foreseeable future, experiencing the state will continue to occupy an important place in most peoples lives.

Having placed the state in a historical perspective and suggested the kinds of challenges it faces inside and outside, we turn to how the essays presented in this volume address our theme of experiencing the state. We have organized the essays in four thematic sections: I. Experiencing High Modernist States in America, India, and the Soviet Union; II. Experiencing the State from Below in Village Germany and India and Urban Karachi; III. Experiencing the State from the Outside: Psychiatry, Film, and Art; and IV. Emancipatory Resistance. The thinking that went into the writing of James Scott's opening essay in Section I, 'High Modernist Social Engineering: The Case of the Tennessee Valley Authority', helped shape his influential 1998 book, *Seeing Like a State: How Certain Schemes to Improve the Human*

Condition Have Failed.[28] The Tennessee Valley Authority (TVA) essay keynotes our volume in the sense that it makes a case for the potentially oppressive nature of the modern state. It does so as a vehicle for what Scott characterizes as high modernism, not only its a priori, abstract, contextless rationality[29] but also its increasingly ubiquitous surveillance[30] and control that limits human freedom and threatens citizens' rights. Scott's reading of the modern state as a potentially oppressive institution catches echoes from nineteenth century anarchist thinkers, Proudhon, Kropotkin, and Bakunin,[31] Weber's metaphor of modernity, the iron cage, and Foucault's (via Bentham) of the panopticon. High modernists shun politics because it can challenge the rationality of their abstract schemes.[32]

The state-sponsored 'high modernism' of the Tennessee Valley Authority, a 'multi-purpose' regional development scheme meant to transform Appalachia from rags to riches, is paradigmatic of the a prioristic, axiomatic character of high modernist thinking and practice.[33] TVA programmes and policies needed 'grass roots' support if they were to work. Instead TVA was 'co-opted and domesticated by local power holders.' The state was the crucial site in which these battles were waged because only 'the state could represent the interests of the poor, of blacks, or of the larger society.' Scott examines the high-modernist reformers dilemma; a vision of a more just society confronting democratic institutions controlled largely by the 'beneficiaries of these inequalities.' The TVA reflected internal tensions between its benign democratizing aims and short-term pragmatic accommodations. What people on the ground experienced were good intentions but ultimately not policies and actions that incorporated their knowledge, needs, and aspirations.

Arundhati Roy's 'The Cost of Living' picks up America's TVA story half a century later. Soon after winning the Booker Prize in 1997 for *The God of Small Things*, Roy joined forces with Medha Patkar's Narmada Bachao Andolan to resist the Narmada Valley Development Project,[34] a prodigious effort that continues to this day. Her excoriating essay challenges the worldview and practical claims of those bent on imposing big dams on unwilling citizens and a vulnerable environment.

Jawaharlal Nehru, India's first prime minister (1947–64) shared the TVA high modernist vision. Notoriously, he called big dams the 'Temples of Modern India'; the phrase, Arundhati Roy says, 'has made its way into primary school text books in every Indian language. Every school child is taught that Big Dams will deliver the people of India from hunger and poverty.' The Indian state's high modernist ambitions have imposed big dams upon local people in ways that sacrifice their way of life and livelihood. They become displaced persons whose promised 'rehabilitation' consistently fails to materialize. Like the TVA's Appalachia region and like the record of earlier big dam multipurpose river valley development authorities in India (and elsewhere), most of the benefits seem destined to go to distant, affluent city dwellers.[35]

In the third essay of Section I the focus shifts geographically to the former Soviet Union. In his essay on 'Reverse Double Movement', Hyung-min Joo links the collapse after 1929 in Western Europe and the United States of laissez-faire market capitalism and the collapse in the Soviet Union at the end of the 1980s of the Communist state, society, and planned economy by reconceptualizing the 'double movement' that Karl Polanyi featured in *The Great Transformation*. As a self-regulating market system, laissez-faire capitalism produced massive social dislocations and reduced man and nature to commodities that could be bought and sold. Various actors organized and intervened to protect themselves from destructive market forces. The unfettered expansion of the market economy is ultimately countered, and to some degree harnessed, by the self-protective actions of societal forces such as trade unions, labour and socialist parties, and agrarian and environmental movements.

Joo uses Polanyi's double movement concept to develop a corollary concept, what he calls a 'reverse double movement'. As the Marxist high modernist Soviet state proceeded implacably to appropriate or subjugate every aspect of civil society, the public sphere, and the economy, the pressure on ordinary life became increasingly unbearable. Like protective action by organized social forces in the face of market-induced commodification, Soviet subjects unwilling to accept what was being forced on them by the Soviet party-state apparatus began a process of constituting a 'parallel society'. As a result almost every aspect of the official system came to be accompanied by corresponding shadow formations, including thriving underground markets and lively intellectual and cultural networks. Deinied 'voice' and 'loyalty', the intrepid subjects of the Soviet system, Joo argues, chose internal 'exit'.[36] They migrated en masse to various manifestations of a parallel shadow society and economy where they could invest their talents and energies. What citizens could not openly laugh at, they stealthily evaded. Much like Tocqueville's account in *The Old Regime and the French Revolution*, the foundations of the Soviet state, society, and economy were hollowed out leaving the structures with no support. The reverse double movement was not the only cause of the collapse of the Soviet Union, Joo cautions, but without it our understanding of the collapse would be radically incomplete.

Paul Brass's article, 'How Political Scientists Experienced India's Development State', takes us into the realm of meta-experience; he writes about how political scientists based in American universities experienced the high modernist developmental state in India. He finds that, at best, they were complicit in legitimizing it. Like a growing number of political scientists dismayed by failing and failed states and economies and by the dark side of globalization, Brass finds this a wholly unsatisfactory state of affairs. The high modernist state that Jawaharlal Nehru, India's first prime minister, brought into being and bequeathed to his country was, for Brass, a poisoned chalice. Its innovators and acolytes not only worshiped the false god of big dams that Scott and Roy depict, they also made themselves powerful and prosperous in the name of helping the poor.

In addition to establishing himself as a leading scholar of Indian politics through a series of path-breaking and influential books, Brass has also cultivated a role as the *enfant terrible* of his fraternity. He enacts the role in this volume, scolding and berating his colleagues not so much for being taken in by the powers that be (he too admits to having been taken in for a time) but for failing to recognize as the 1980s gave way to the 1990s the developmental state's false assumptions and dire consequences.

His text proceeds at two levels, one a scholarly level where he deploys inner and outer critiques of his colleagues work, the other a self-conscious and deliberate polemical level. He deplores the fig leaf of neutrality behind which scholars who rely on the trope of science hide. Explanations, he argues, are situated in assumptions and have consequences. But Brass has trouble keeping his levels apart and under control. There are no shades of gray, no up sides to go with the down sides of the developmental state. 'I have been accused', he writes, 'of being a prophet of doom and gloom, of painting a picture

of an India heading seamlessly towards catastrophe . . . What I want
to say here and now . . . is that India is not heading for catastrophe:
India is a living catastrophe and its people, including its intellectuals,
know it.' So too, he implies, should the leading scholars of the
American establishment whom he criticizes. Instead of recognizing
the disaster wrought by the developmental state in India leading
American scholars of India have been complicit in legitimizing it.
Brass singles out the late Myron Weiner for most attention, attends
as well to two other senior figures, the co-authors, Lloyd Rudolph
and Susanne Rudolph, and Atul Kohli, and puts a number of other
political scientists feet to the fire of his critique of scholarship on the
developmental state in India.[37]

Helmuth Berking's essay 'Experiencing Reunification: An East
German Village after the Fall of the Wall' opens Section II,
'Experiencing the State from Below'. Berking writes about the moral
economy of an East German village in the decade after the fall of the
Berlin wall. Once again, an interventionist high modernist state, this
time a western capitalist one, evokes a protective response to its
market capitalist efforts at revolutionary change. The rich, powerful,
triumphant West German state sets out to reunify Germany by
making over the character and ideology as well as the economy of
the newly reunited nation's poor relatives, the *ossis* (East German
people). In West German eyes the East German state was evil, its
economy—even worse—antiquated, its people dupes. The East
Germans, many of whom were proud of their exemplary standing in
the erstwhile Soviet empire, experienced the sudden makeover as
degrading. The reunification process opened rather than closed the
perceptual gap that separated West from East Germany and laid the
groundwork for a smouldering politics of resentment.

Berking describes how newly minted Germans experienced their
ambivalent embrace by the West German state. They were, it seems,
like natives being ruled by a colonial power; the ossis were depicted
as backward and benighted natives who needed to be civilized by
being assimilated into the superior West German social character
and symbolic order. For the decade after the wall fell, the cultural
and symbolic orders occasionally clashed but more often passed as
ships in the night.

Berking found the village's institutional order embedded in
routines and expectations that made life not only comprehensible

but also morally intelligible. Such intangible presuppositions were not visible, not part of a public sphere, but sometimes akin to what James Scott calls hidden transcripts. Unlike the physical and monetary assets that flowed from West to East, the embedded routines and expectations could not be easily uprooted. Berking reveals the 'microcosms of life', a lingering 'really existing socialism', networks based on close personal relationships governed by norms of reciprocity, inconspicuous but shared modes of resistance, and pervasive power games. Such relationships avoided or evaded more formal and grating relationships based on edicts or cash. Berking's effort to find the macro in the micro in an East German village suggest that in the decade following reunification former East Germans more often experienced the high modernist West German state as subversive and alienating than as liberating and transformative. Not surprisingly, according to villagers, politics, as they conventionally understood it, played little role in everyday life.

Tasneem Siddiqui's 'personal view' of 'Dynamics of Bureaucratic Rule in Pakistan' carries forward Section II's account of 'experiencing the state from below'. His heterodoxical bureaucratic career, first as an agent of Pakistani high stateness, than as agent of Pakistani civil society, equips him with a double reflexivity. He is an adept and purposeful juggler, at once a self-conscious, alienated bureaucrat and a self-conscious civil society activist. He narrates two stories, one about 'corrupt and inept' developmental administration with respect to housing in Pakistan's largest city, Karachi, a sprawling, chaotic port-city on the Arabian Sea, and a second about a successful bottom-up people's alternative.

Karachi is a city where 40 per cent of the population lives in squatter settlements and another 20 per cent in sub-standard housing. Siddiqui's account exposes the adverse consequences for housing policy of high modernist assumptions and centralized, top-down administration (which he once championed). He then shows why and how a 'pro-people, bottom-up approach' succeeded. The do-it-yourself approach to housing which he propagated engaged the energies and ingenuity of the poor and foiled predators even while enlisting some state aid. The proliferation of *katchi abadi*s (squatter settlements) in the urban 'informal sector' became 'the peoples' response to the government's inability to provide shelter.' He demonstrates how citizens, once a few resources are made available to them, can identify needs, design projects, and implement and maintain housing schemes. 'If the government is freed from providing the basic services on individual basis (which it can't do anyway)', he argues, 'it can take care of bigger projects and external development.' NGOs and popular movements are necessary ingredients for making sure housing schemes work. But they cannot do it alone', Siddiqui says. 'The state, spurred on by civil society, must remain serious about its social responsibilities for housing and about revitalizing local governments that support and facilitate housing schemes'.

Like Tasneen Ahmed Siddiqui's essay about the Kachi Abadi Authority in Karachi, Philip Oldenburg's 'Face to Face with the Indian State: A Grass Roots View' locates the state experience locally in everyday life. Oldenburg provides vivid and telling thick descriptions in the context of analytic inquiries whose answers explain even as they describe. Oldenburg's essay shows us a state that is ubiquitous and embedded, even natural, but one that is also autonomous and often serviceable. 'Village teachers and doctors are figures', Oldenburg reports, 'who must look half public/half private in the eyes of citizens, employed by the state part-time and thus included in government but also using their government employment as base from which to build a private enterprise.' Corruption is common but often functional.

His story about the state as it is experienced at the local level in Ghazipur, a district in eastern Uttar Pradesh, in the early 1990s, has a certain timeless quality. *Sarkar* (the Hindi/Urdu word for state in the sense of government) for the locals has been, is, and will be. Yet new functions are added; the face of the developmental state that Brass warns us against in Oldenburg's telling seems more likely to be locally co-opted than it is to command and control the locals. 'The various programmes for rural development that have been implemented make an impressive list', Oldenburg writes. '. . . The community development programme of the 1950s . . . visible in Ghazipur in the form of a very large government tube well/water tank installation . . . food for work programmes and intensive; [or integrated] agricultural development programmes, etc., in the next decades and, in recent years, the Jawahar Rozgar Yojana [Jawaharlal

Nehru Employment Plan] (JRY) and the IRDP [Integrated Rural Development Programme] . . . Rural roads', Oldenburg continues, 'have been . . . a major portion of the 'assets' created by the JRY, along with housing for the 'weaker sections'. . ., and wells under the 'Million Wells Scheme.' Other 'assets' include trees planted under social forestry programmes, school buildings, sanitary latrines, 'works benefiting scheduled castes and scheduled tribes. . . . The major difference [in the early 1990s] . . . was that 'the major portion of the financial allocation is given to the gram panchayat [elected village councils] for planning and execution.' Oldenburg found that while the elected local government officials responsible for implementing development programmes siphon off as much as 30 per cent of the funds, 'corruption has not overwhelmed development programmes; the benefits outweigh the corruption.' 'There is no doubt', Oldenburg concludes, 'that the state reaches into the furthest corners of Ghazipur and touches the lives of large number of Ghazipur's people in significant ways.'

In Section III, 'Experiencing the State From Outside', three essays expose readers to how the state is experienced in the realms of psychotherapy, cinema, and art. Nicholas Temple, a psychiatrist and administrator, describes how perceptions and attitudes at the Tavistock Centre, a National Health Service facility in North London, were transformed by the 'organizational upheavals' that followed policy shifts by Conservative and then (new) Labour governments. Market radicalism was brought to bear on what was the core element of the Welfare State established in 1948 by Clement Attlee's Labour government. With a psychoanalyst's eye, Temple sees in Tory behaviour and New Labour's acquiescence a worldview that needs to 'attack dependency to fulfill greedy wishes while, at the same time, attributing badness and weakness to those who are vulnerable or needy.' This transformed worldview informs and pervades changes at the Tavistock Institute and in the NHS more generally. It often takes the form of blaming NHS staff for wasteful or indulgent use of resources, with the result that NHS staff are treated as if they, like the patients they care for, are dependent and needy. Professionals at Tavistock found that they experienced the state in the antagonistic attitude of the ministerial staff with whom they were in regular contact.'

John Kurt Jacobsen's essay, 'In Cahoots?: Experiencing The State in American Cinema', explores the ways in which recent Hollywood films about the state cultivate a cynical attitude in the viewing public. The cultivation of a cynical response occurs whether the films engage in critiques or in Capraesque treatments of politics (*JFK, Clear and Present Danger, Nixon, Dave, The American President*, and so on). Both arouse cynical responses by questioning the purposes of the American state—particularly whether it controls or is controlled by interests in the wider society and economy. The ambiguity latent in this dual possibility raises in turn another question, to what degree do films shape or are they shaped by the cultural expectations and political understandings of cinema-goers. How do films affect conversations in the public sphere? What lessons or views do they impart to a country's civic culture and moral reasoning? The ubiquitous framing of political legerdemain in terms of 'conspiracies' stems partly from Hollywood narrative conventions requiring identifiable heroes and villains, partly from an underlying cultural distrust of centralized public organizations, and partly from the personalized (and occasionally idiosyncratic) expressions of these preferences and attitudes by film-makers themselves. Jacobsen highlights the special characteristics of American film conventions and their public consequences by comparing them with those characteristic of European cinema. The contrast highlights differences between America and Europe with respect to how cinema reflects and inflects how citizens experience the state.

The last essay in this section by Patricia Bickers examines the relations between state funding and the nature and content of the art that results. Her narrative features the British Arts Council, dispenser of national lottery money. She highlights the British case by drawing comparisons with France and the United States. Her essay addresses the question, how do differences in forms of state mediation—particularly the source, amounts and conditions of funding—affect how citizens experience art.

The theme of Section IV, 'Emancipatory Resistance,' is first explored in an essay by Sudipta Kaviraj on Gandhi's trial for sedition in 1922. Kaviraj re-examines Gandhi's 1922 trial in ways that reveal how the man whom Winston Churchill once dismissed as a 'half naked fakir' managed to turn his trial for sedition into a vindication of his resistance to colonial rule. 'Trials are spectacles of power', Kaviraj argues, 'and thus bring to representation not only material aspects of political power, but also ideal, symbolic, and representational ones.'

Three major audiences who observed the trial 'tried to fit this new event into their narratives of colonial rule: the Raj administrators and British public at home, the Indian middle class and educated elites, and the Indian peasantry.' Kaviraj shows how Gandhi's rhetorical strategy contained skillful implicit messages for each audience: to the British audience, prevailing notions of 'justice' and fair play; to the Indian middle class audience, the prospect of nationhood; and to the peasants of village India for whom 'everything was invested with meanings . . . [an] ineradicable aura of mysteriousness . . . [about] the small and finite acts of ordinary people.'

Gandhi appreciated the theatricality of the law, its high drama in which both sides are obliged to stage an 'unprepared play' whose exchanges are 'not fixed, but strategic.' Kaviraj's essay illuminates how Gandhi was able to dramatize his experience in a courtroom of the colonial state in India in ways that transformed the consciousness of both the rulers and the ruled.

Bruce Cumings' essay, 'Experiencing Repressive States in America and the Koreas', offers a riveting 'subjective knowledge'[38] account of experiencing the American and Korean states as a result of his personal involvement in the conduct of US relations with the Korean peninsula. He carefully underlines how the American, South Korean, and North Korean states are repressive in a number of senses.[39] One is in the James Scott's sense of 'high modernism.' 'Among the many virtues of James Scott's recent work, *Seeing Like a State*, Cumings writes, 'is his unwillingness to distinguish between types of modern states. The industrial states were all gripped by "high modernist ideology"', yielding state practices that are best conceived as a strong, one might even say muscle-bound, version of the self-confidence about scientific and technical progress, the expansion of production— the mastery of nature [including human nature], and, above all, the rational design of social order commensurate with the scientific understanding of natural laws.' There is an 'elective affinity', he continues, 'between high modernist ideology and the interests of state officials—whether they hark from formal democracies, like the United States . . . totalized colonial states' like the Japanese colonial state in Korea or the American military occupation regime in Korea. What unites the behaviour of officials in such states, Cumings argues, 'is a self-confident certainty that they implement a seamless 'rational design' of 'social order' amid a heterodox reality.'

Cumings begins his account of the repressive face of the American state by resuscitating what he suggests are deliberately buried historical records of several American atrocities in Korea, including a particularly cold-blooded massacre at Nof'n-ri of Korean civilians in July 1950.[40]

But his most telling accounts are of his own experiences over 25 years as a dissenting policy voice on Korea to mostly Republican administrations—'telling what he knows' about FBI efforts to intimidate him in his University of Chicago office, gum-shoe CIA surveillance in Korea, seemingly punitive IRS audits, and the hostility displayed at the inauguration of Kim Dae Jung as president of South Korea by top US officials with CIA provenances who served as US ambassadors in Korea, James Lilley and Donald Gregg, and by former Reagan National Security Advisor Richard Allen.

Cumings concludes his gripping narratives of experiencing the American and Korean states by a playful but astringent critique of the scientific pretensions of Kenneth Waltz's neo-realist theorizing. Cumings then wryly denigrates what he has to say about the doyen of neo-realism and the scientific trope by 'confessing' to his readers that his spirited account 'would be chucked out of any "refereed" or "discipline conscious" journal of political science ... on the ground that . . . my "experience" of the Korean and the American state is personal, "anecdotal", and ad hoc . . . or that what I have said is not "theoretical". . . . Yet the experiences that I have related are true, they all happened.'

After a critical exegesis of Waltz' scientific claims Cumings concludes that Americans may filter their experience of the state through founding-father, Tudor-policy myths but 'rarely if ever experience the American state in the . . . arbitrary way' Waltz posits, that is in which state action flows from unmarked, empty structure. Their experience of the state can best be explained 'by arbitrary power or *force-majeure.*'

NOTES

1. Hegel's theory of the state can be found in his *Philosophy of Right*, trans. T. M. Knox (Oxford: Oxford University Press, 1942). According to Shlomo Avineri, 'On no account can Hegel's theory be so construed as to refer to any existing state; it is the *idea* [emphasis in the original] of the state with which Hegel is dealing and any existing state cannot be anything but a mere approximation.' Shlomo Avineri, *Hegel's Theory of the Modern State* (London: Cambridge University Press, 1972,1974), p. 177.

2. For the fallacy of misplaced concreteness, see 'Lecture Three: Understanding', in Alfred North Whitehead, *Modes of Thought* (New York: Capricorn Books/G. P. Putnam and Sons, 1958), pp.58–87.

3. For an effective and succinct historical overview of early modern state formation see Eugene Rice and Anthony Grafton, *The Foundations of Early Modern Europe, 1460–1559* (New York: W. W. Norton, 1994). Brian M. Downing's *The Military Revolution and Political Change: The Origins of Democracy and Autocracy in Early Modern Europe* (Princeton, NJ: Princeton University Press, 1992) and Perry Anderson's *Lineages of the Absolutist State* (London: New Left Books, 1974) provide differing versions of the formation of the absolutist version of the modern state. Downing shows how variations in circumstances such as geographical location and class structure opened the way for constitutional alternatives to French and Prussian absolutism in Britain and the Netherlands.

4. Son of Henry IV of Navarre and Marie de Medici. Having been raised a Protestant and led the Protestant (Huguenot) cause in France, he became a Catholic as a condition of becoming king of France in 1589. (Henry is believed to have said that Paris was well worth a mass.)

5. See Norbert Elias (trans. by Edmund Jephcott), *The Court Society* (New York: Pantheon Books, 1983).

6. Carl Friedrich credits Richelieu and Louis XIII with giving birth to the modern state in the following anecdote, 'I am more obligated to the state', Louis XIII declared on the famous 'Day of Dupes', 11 November 1630, when he rejected the Queen Mother [Marie de Medici, wife of Henry of Navarre or Henry IV] and her claims for family in favour of Cardinal Richelieu and his claims for the state. Friedrich says that 'More than any other single day, it may be called the birthday of the modern state.' Carl J. Friedrich, *The Age of the Baroque: 1610–1660* (New York: Harper, 1962), pp. 215–16.

7. Deborah Weisgall, 'A Hard Man Who Saw Art as Power and Vice Versa', the *New York Times*, 20 October 2002. Weisgall's article reviews 'Richelieu: Art and Power', an exhibit curated by Hillard T. Goldfarb at Montreal's Museum of Fine Art, October 2002 through 5 January 2003.

8. We take this term from Peter Nettl's seminal article, 'The State as a Conceptual Variable', *World Politics*, vol. 20, no. 4, (July) 1968. High

stateness was given new meaning and new life in James Scott's *Seeing Like A State; How Certain Schemes to Improve the Human Condition Have Failed* (New Haven: Yale University Press, 1998).

9. Although he died in 1642, six years before the Peace of Westphalia, it represented the success of Cardinal Richelieu's policies and concepts.

10. This is the view taken by Stephen Toulmin in *Cosmopolis: The Hidden Agenda of Modernity* (New York: The Free Press, 1990).

11. Processes, institutions, and organizations that limit state sovereignty 'inside' and 'outside' were theorized and examined early on by R. B. J. Walker in *Inside/Outside: International Relations as Political Theory* (Cambridge: Cambridge University Press, 1993).

12. Arguments that support the view that thinking about sovereignty and modern state have become obsolescent or anachronistic can be found in a wide variety of works only a few of which can be mentioned here: Vaclav Havel, 'The End of the Modern Era', the *New York Times*, 1 March 1992; John Dunn, 'Introduction: Crisis of the Nation State?'; Istvan Hont, 'The Permanent Crisis of a Divided Mankind: "Contemporary Crisis of the Nation State" in Historical Perspective', in *Contemporary Crisis of the Nation State?*, John Dunn (ed.), (Oxford, UK and Cambridge, MA: Blackwell, 1995); Susanne Hoeber Rudolph, 'Introduction: Religion, States and Transnational Civil Society', in *Transnational Religion and Fading States*, Susanne Hoeber Rudolph and James Piscatori (eds), (Boulder, CO: Westview Press, 1997); and David Held, 'The Decline of the Nation State', in *Becoming National; A Reader*, Geoff Eley and Ronald Grigor Suny (eds), (New York: Oxford University Press, 1996). Alarmed by the consequences for economic development of failing states and state collapse, The World Bank devoted its 1997 World Development Report to *The State in a Changing World* (New York: Oxford University Press, 1997).

13. For our purposes here, the literature on Machiavellism, most often read as the theory and practice of reason of state, is more salient than the literature by and on Machiavelli. For reason of state, Freidrich Meinecke's *Machiavellism: The Doctrine of Raison D' Etat and Its Place in History* (Boulder, CO: Westview Press, 1984) remains the authoritative work. Three chapters in Ernest Cassirer's *The Myth of the State* (New Haven: Yale University Press, 1946), 'Machiavelli's New Science of Politics', 'The Triumph of Machiavellianism and Its Consequences', and 'Implications of the New Theory of the State' update and add valuable historical and analytic insights to Meinecke's work. The essays in a book edited by Jules Kirshner, *The Origins of the State in Italy, 1300–1600* (Chicago: University of Chicago Press, 1996) puts Machiavelli's transformatory thinking in historical context.

14. Jurgen Habermas (trans. Thomas Burger and Frederick Lawrence), *The Structural Transformation of the Public Sphere: An Inquiry into a Category of Bourgeois Society* (Cambridge, MA: MIT Press, 1989 and 1991). First

xxvi *Introduction*

published in German under the title *Strukturwander der Offentlicheit* (Darmstadt and Neuwied, FRG: Herman Luchterhand Verlag, 1962). Similar argument were made in Lloyd I. Rudolph, 'The Origin of Party: From the Politics of Status to the Politics of Opinion in Eighteenth Century England and America', PhD diss., Harvard University, 1956.

15. In an end piece to his 2000 book, *Bowling Alone: The Collapse and Revival of American Community* (New York: Touchstone, 2001), Robert Putnam recounts how his January 1995 article about 'bowling alone' in *The Journal of Democracy* made him famous. 'Until January 1995', he writes, 'I was . . . "an obscure academic". . . . Although I had published scores of books and articles in the previous three decades . . . none had attracted the slightest public attention. Now I was invited to Camp David, lionized by talk-show hosts and . . . pictured with my wife, Rosemary, on the pages of *People*. The explanation [lay] . . . in the simple fact that I had unwittingly articulated an unease that had already begun to form in the minds of ordinary Americans'(p. 506). It seems that what Americans sensed they were losing or lacking, for example, social capital, trust, civic engagement, was what American academics, policy intellectuals, and domestic bureaucracies and international organizations thought developing and transitional countries needed for state formation and economic growth.

16. Karl Polanyi, *The Great Transformation: The Political and Economic Origins of Our Time* (Boston: Beacon Press, 2001), pp. vii–viii.

17. Ibid., p. viii.

18. Robert Tucker, *The Marx-Engels Reader* (New York: W. W. Norton and Company, 1978), p. 475.

19. See *inter alia* Joel Krieger, *Reagen, Thatcher and the Politics of Decline* (New York: Oxford University Press, 1986).

20. See Louis Hartz' generative analysis, *The Liberal Tradition in America* (New York: Harcourt Brace Jovanovich, 1955) and the critical considerations in Michael Paul Rogin, *The Intellectuals and McCarthy: The Radical Spectre* (Cambridge, MA: MIT Press, 1967).

21. Regarding Reagan and after in America, see Edward N. Wolff, *Top Heavy: A Study of the Increasing Inequality of Wealth in America* (New York: Twentieth Century Fund, 1995); Thomas Ferguson and Joel Rogers, *Right Turn* (New York: Hill and Wang, 1992); and David Stockman, *The Triumph of Politics* (New York: Harper & Row, 1986).

22. In December 2003 when we were re-writing this introduction, the story of collusion between Boeing, the Pentagon, and Senator Stevens [R-Alaska] with respect to an $18 billion order for 100 refueling tankers for the Air Force was being publicly told. See the *New York Times*, 19 December 2003.

23. Stuart Hall, 'Media Power and Class Power' in Jim Curran and Jake Eccleston (eds), *Bending Reality: The State of the Media* (London: Pluto Press, 1986).

24. Henry Giroux, *Disturbing Pleasures: Learning Popular Culture* (London: Routledge, 1994), p. 113. Pierre Bourdieu reminds us that the 'most successful ideological effects are those which have no need for words and ask no more than complicitous silence.' *Outline of A Theory of Practice* (Cambridge: Cambridge University Press, 1977).

25. Margaret Archer, *Culture and Agency: The Place of Culture in Social Theory* (Cambridge: Cambridge University Press, 1988), p. xxiv. See also the Introduction to Lloyd I. Rudolph and Susanne Hoeber Rudolph's *The Modernity of Tradition* (Chicago: University of Chicago Press, 1967, 1983), pp. 3–14.

26. See Karl Polanyi, *The Great Transformation: The Political and Economic Origins of Our Time,* (Boston: Beacon Press, 1944, 1957). See particularly chapter 19, 'Popular Government and Market Economy', pp. 231–44.

27. For an interpretation and application of the concept transnational civil society, see Susanne Hoeber Rudolph's 'Introduction: Religion, States and Transnational Civil Society', in *Transnational Religion and Fading States,* Susanne Hoeber Rudolph and James Piscatori (eds), (Boulder, CO: Westview Press, 1997), pp.1–24.

28. James Scott, *Seeing Like a State: How Certain Schemes to Improve the Human Condition Have Failed* (New Haven: Yale University Press, 1998).

29. An important aspect for contextless rationality is the invocation by high modernists of the science trope. For a critique of this view see Paul Feyerabend, *Science in a Free Society* (London: Verso, 1978).

30. Even before 9/11 Anthony Giddens, like James Scott, noted that the 'expansion of surveillance in the modern political order, in combination with the policing of "deviance," radically transforms the relations between state authority and the governed population. Administrative power now increasingly enters the minutiae of daily life and the most intimate personal actions and relationships.' Anthony Giddens, *The Nation-State and Violence* (Cambridge: Polity Press, 1985), p. 309. See also the essays in the more recent Kristie Bell and Frank Webster (eds), *The Intensity of Surveillance* (London: Pluto Press, 2003).

31. For an overview of anarchist thought and action and of its leading personalities see Barbara Tuchman's Chapter 2, 'The Idea and the Deed. The Anarchists: 1890–1914', in her *The Proud Tower: A Portrait of the World Before the War, 1890–1914* (New York: Ballantine Books, 1996), pp. 63–113.

32. Bernard Crick, *In Defence of Politics* (London: Penguin Books, 1982), pp. 92–110.

33. This is what Dahl and Lindblom call 'social engineering optimism' in high gear. See Robert Dahl and Charles Lindblom, *Politics, Economics and Welfare: Planning and Politico-Economic Systems Resolved into Social Processes,* 2nd ed. (Chicago, University of Chicago Press, 1967).

34. The Narmada Valley Development Project (NVDP) envisages building 3200 dams that will reconstitute the Narmada River. There will be 30 big dams, 135 medium dams, and the rest small. Two of the major dams will be multi-purpose mega-dams. The Sardar Sarovar in Gujarat and Narmada Sagar in Madhya Pradesh are nearing completion. Their height is still in dispute. The two dams will, between them, hold more water than any other reservoir in the Indian subcontinent. According to informed estimates, the NVDP will affect the lives of 25 million people who live in the valley and alter the ecology of an entire river basin.

35. For an evaluation of who has and who has not benefited from multi-purpose river valley development in the US and India see Daniel Klingensmith, *One Valley and a Thousand: Indian and American Developmentalism in the Making of India's Large Dams* (New Delhi: Oxford University Press, forthcoming), a study of the TVA idea in America and India. Gail Omvedt and Sharad Joshi support the NVDP, arguing that Narmada irrigation water will benefit commercial agriculture in Maharasthra. See Robert Jensen, 'Large Dams in India: Temples or Burial Grounds?', 21 September 2004, for an update on the Narmada story. Jensen, a professor of journalism at the University of Texas at Austin, writes that 'The violence of the everyday defies comprehension, as the state's mistreatment of the poor is intensified by hierarchies of caste, tribe, religion and gender'.

36. Joo draws on Albert O. Hirschman's *Exit, Voice and Loyalty* (Cambridge, MA: Harvard University Press, 1970).

37. For example, Brass says that the Rudolphs argued that the state in India was strong enough to prevail against the organized interests of capital and labour but does not mention the Rudolphs' further argument that the state, as a more powerful 'third actor' with respect to capital and labor, increasingly became self-interested, a 'state for itself', and the problem rather than the solution to economic development. And he has the Rudolphs writing about modernity *and* tradition as if they were dichotomous and opposed. They wrote about 'the modernity *of* tradition' by characterizing the relationship of modernity and tradition as dialectical and by de-essentializing modernity and tradition *inter alia* by finding elements of tradition in modernity and elements of modernity in tradition.

38. For a theoretical account of the place of subjective knowledge in political science and the social sciences more broadly see Lloyd I. Rudolph and Susanne Hoeber Rudolph, 'Engaging Subjective Knowledge: How Amar Singh's Diary Narratives of and by the Self Explain Identity Formation', *Perspective on Politics*, vol. 1, no. 4 (December 2003), pp. 681–94. Note also Bernard Crick's observation that 'Every purported methodology of how to study the activity of government objectively, that is, every prefabricated set of rules for the discovery of knowledge in advance of experience is itself a doctrine.' Crick, *In Defence of Politics*, p. 102.

39. South Korea's recent repressive political experience left in its wake multitudes of walking wounded to whom Cumings pays tribute—ordinary citizens of extraordinary courage who confronted the state and paid a price for it, but who manage to remain admirably human in their higher capacity for resistance, grit, and regeneration.

40. This leads Cumings to quote a sentence from Barrington Moore's *Social Origins of Dictatorship and Democracy: Lord and Peasant in the Modern World* (Boston: Beacon Press, 1966). Moore wrote that to sustain state power, people are 'put up against a wall, beaten, shot, and sometimes taught sociology.'

EXPERIENCING HIGH MODERNIST STATES
IN AMERICA, INDIA AND THE SOVIET UNION

1

High Modernist Social Engineering
The Case of The Tennessee Valley Authority

JAMES C. SCOTT

> Modern science which displaced and replaced God, removed that obstacle [limits on freedom]. It also created a vacancy: the office of the supreme legislator-cum-manager, of the designer and administrator of the world order, was now horrifyingly empty. It has to be filled or else. . . . The emptiness of the throne was throughout the modern era a standing and tempting invitation to visionaries and adventurers. The dream of an all-embracing order and harmony remained as vivid as ever, and it seemed now closer than ever, more than ever within human reach. It was now up to mortal earthlings to bring it about and to secure its ascendancy.
>
> Zygmunt Bauman, *Modernity and the Holocaust*

ARTIFICIAL SOCIAL ORDER

Not content merely to describe the world, homo faber seems impelled, paraphrasing Marx, to redesign it as well. The earliest cadastral surveyors were inclined to 'tidy up' the irregular boundaries of the property they encountered to make it more geometrically regular. Such shortcuts, while they distorted the social facts on the ground, greatly simplified the surveyors' work and the maps they produced. In the realm of forest management, the increasingly sophisticated efforts to map woodlands led to programmes of felling and replanting that more closely approximated the schematic map of scientific foresters. State initiatives to map cities and enumerate their inhabitants in order to rationalize tax collection and conscription led inexorably to attempts to re-design settlement patterns and personal designations to make them more legible. Schematic descriptions, backed by state power, had a habit of becoming positive prescriptions of how nature, space, and people ought to be rearranged. Where a fresh start was possible, on clearcut forest land, on open frontiers, or with sites for new cities, these prescriptions were more nearly realized, as they encountered less resistance.

The path from description to prescription was not so much the inadvertent result of some deep psychological tendency as a deliberate move. The point of the Enlightenment view of legal codes was not so much to mirror the distinctive customs and practices of a people but to help create a cultural community by codifying and generalizing the most rational of those customs and suppressing the more obscure and barbaric.[1] Establishing uniform standards of weight and measurement across a kingdom had a greater purpose then just making trade easier; the new standards were intended both to express and promote a new cultural unity. Well before the tools existed to make good on this 'cultural revolution', Enlightenment thinkers such as Condorcet were looking ahead to the day when the tools would be in place. He wrote in 1782,

Those sciences, created almost in our own days, the object of which is man himself, the direct goal of which is the happiness of man, will enjoy a progress no less sure than that of the physical sciences, and this idea so sweet, that our descendants will surpass us in wisdom as in enlightenment, is no longer an illusion. In meditating on the nature of the moral sciences, one cannot help seeing that, as they are based like physical sciences on the observation of fact, they must follow the same method, acquire a language equally exact and precise, attaining the same degree of certainty.[2]

The gleam in Condorcet's eye became, by the mid-nineteenth century, an active utopian project. Simplification and rationalization previously applied to forests, weights and measures, taxation, and factories were now applied to the design of society as a whole.[3] 'Industrial strength' social engineering was born. While factories and forests might be planned by private entrepreneurs, the ambition of engineering whole societies was almost exclusively a project of the nation state.

This new conception of the state's role represented a fundamental transformation. Until then, the state's activities were largely confined to those that directly contributed to the wealth and power of the sovereign as the example of scientific forestry and 'cameral science' illustrated. The idea that one of the central purposes of the state was the improvement of the whole society—its health, its skills and education, its longevity, its productivity, its morals, and its family life—was quite novel.[4] There was, of course, a direct connection between the old conception of the state and this new one. A state that improved its population's skills, vigour, civic morals, and work habits would increase its tax base and field better armies. It was the policy that an enlightened sovereign would pursue. And yet, in the nineteenth century, the welfare of the population came increasingly to be seen as an end in itself, not merely a wise means to national strength.

One essential precondition of this transformation was the 'discovery of society' as a reified object separate from the state that could be scientifically described. In this respect, the production of new statistical knowledge about the population, its age profile, its occupations, its fertility, its literacy, its property, its law-abidingness (for example, criminal statistics) allowed state officials to characterize the population in elaborate new ways in much the same fashion as scientific forestry permitted the forester to carefully describe the forest. Statistical facts were shortly elaborated into social laws. Hacking, for example, explains how a certain rate of suicide or homicide came to be seen as characteristic of a people, such that one could speak of a 'budget' of homicides that would be 'spent' each year, like clockwork, although the particular murderers and their victims were unknown.[5] It was but a short step from a simplified description of 'the social' to its design and manipulation with improvement in mind. If one could reshape nature to design a more suitable forest why not reshape society to create a more suitable population?

The scope of intervention was potentially endless. Society became an object that the state might manage and transform with a view towards perfecting it. A progressive nation state would set about engineering its society according to the most advanced technical standards of the new moral sciences. The existing social order that had been more or less taken by earlier states as a 'given', reproducing itself under the watchful eye of the state was, for the first time, the object of active management. It was possible to conceive of an artificial, engineered society designed, not by custom and historical accident, but according to conscious, rational, scientific criteria. Every nook and cranny of the social order might be improved upon: personal hygiene, diet, child-rearing, housing, posture, recreation, and family structure. The working poor were often the first subjects of scientific social planning along these lines.[6] Schemes for improving their daily lives were promulgated in model factory towns, in newly-founded welfare agencies, and in progressive urban and public health policy. Sub-populations found 'wanting' in ways that were potentially threatening—indigents, vagabonds, the mentally ill, and criminals— might be made the object of more intensive social engineering.

The metaphor of gardening, Bauman suggests, captures much of the new spirit of social engineering. The gardener—and perhaps a formal, landscape gardener is the most appropriate parallel—takes a natural site and creates an entirely designed space of botanical order. Although the organic character of the flora set some limits to what can be achieved, the gardener has enormous discretion in the overall arrangement, in training, pruning, and weeding the plants selected. As an untended forest is to a long-managed scientific forest, so is untended 'nature' to the garden. The garden is one of man's attempts to impose his own principles of order, utility, and beauty on nature.[7] What grows in the garden is always a very small consciously selected sample of what might be grown there. Social engineers, similarly, set out consciously to design and maintain a more perfect social order. An enlightenment belief in the self-improvement of man became, by degrees, a belief in the perfectibility of social order.

One of the great paradoxes of social engineering is that it seems at great odds with the experience of 'modernity' generally. The idea of gelling a social world, the most striking characteristic of which seems to be flux, is rather like trying to administer a whirlwind. Marx was hardly alone in claiming that the 'constant revolutionizing of production, uninterrupted disturbance of all social relations, everlasting uncertainty and agitation, distinguish[es] the bourgeois epoch from all earlier times.'[8] The experience of modernity (in literature, art, industry, transportation, and popular culture) was, above all, the experience of disorienting speed, flux, movement, and change that self-proclaimed 'modernists' found exhilarating and liberating. Perhaps the most charitable way of resolving this paradox is to imagine that what these designers of society had in mind was roughly what designers of locomotives had in mind with 'streamlining'. Rather than arresting social change, they hoped to design a shape to social life that would minimize the friction of progress. The difficulty with this resolution is that state social engineering was inherently authoritarian. In place of multiple sources of invention and change, there was a unitary planning authority; in place of the plasticity and autonomy of existing social life there was a fixed social order in which positions were designated. The tendency to what Jane Jacobs would have called 'social taxidermy' was unavoidable.

It seems appropriate at this juncture to enumerate, however briefly and schematically, some of the more ominous features of high modernism. They derive, for the most part, from the claim of high modernism to speak with the authority of scientific knowledge about the improvement of the human condition and to disallow other competing sources of judgement. First, high modernist ideology, by itself, tends to devalue or banish politics. Political interests and values can only frustrate the solutions to social problems devised by specialists with the scientific tools adequate to their analysis. Second, the greater the claim to social knowledge, the greater the range of potential interventions into social life. Particular high modernists might well hold democratic views about popular sovereignty or classical liberal views about the inviolability of a private sphere that would restrain them, but such convictions were external to their high modernist convictions. A third consequence of the scientific self-assurance that high modernist beliefs encourage is an Olympian ruthlessness towards the victims of their interventions. If they are utterly convinced that their social engineering is in the long-run interest of (most of) those who are affected, this conviction provides them with the iron will to impose their schemes in the face of the howls of those most immediately victimized. Le Corbusier and Lenin exhibited this ominous side of high modernism in abundance.

Three further facets of high modernist discourse bear emphasis. All three reflect a refusal to recognize sources of legitimation for social practices other than those that derive from its own assumptions. High modernism is truly radical in the sense that it rejects the authority of history and customary practice so central to conservatism. At its most radical, high modernism imagines wiping the slate utterly clean and beginning from zero. The Jacobins intended just such a fresh start, starting the calendar again at 'year one' and renaming the days and months according to a new, secular system. To signal its intention to create a wholly new Cambodian nation, the Pol Pot regime began with 'year zero'.

A second corollary of high modernism's scientific contempt for the past is a suspicion of all those social arrangements that are created autonomously and spontaneously by ordinary people. The informal social structures and practices that are integral to the experienced social order of daily life have no claim to high modernist legitimacy. On the contrary, they are presumably the more-or-less accidental result of unreflective and unscientific habits. The basic assumption of high modernism is that any social order designed along rational, scientific lines would necessarily be superior to the random contingencies of ordinary practice.[9] Finally, the logic of high modernism implicitly discounts the skills, knowledge, and insight of those whose future is being socially engineered.[10] Virtually nothing is to be learned from those who are, after all, destined to be the pupils, the trainees, in a scientifically designed social order. High modernist planning is required precisely because their existing habits are primitive, wasteful, and inefficient. The contribution they make to social order is mostly confined to fulfilling a designated role in a vast plan whose shape is vouchsafed only to the master planners.

This unsympathetic account of high modern audacity—aided by hindsight—is, in one important respect, grossly unfair. If we put the development of high modernist beliefs in their historical context, if we ask who the enemies of high modernism actually were, a far more sympathetic picture emerges. Doctors and public health engineers did possess new knowledge that could save millions of lives if they were not thwarted by popular prejudices and entrenched political interests. Urban planners who could, in fact, re-design urban housing in ways that were cheaper, more healthful, and convenient, were blocked by real estate interests and existing tastes. Inventors and engineers who had devised revolutionary new modes of power and transportation faced opposition from industrialists and labourers whose profits and work the new technology would almost certainly displace. For high modernists, the scientific domination of nature (including human nature) was emancipatory. It 'promised freedom from scarcity, want and the arbitrariness of natural calamity.' 'The development of rational forms of social organization and rational modes of thought promised liberation from the irrationalities of myth, religion, superstition, release from the arbitrary use of power as well as from the dark side of our human natures.'[11] Before we turn to some notable high modernist failures, it is well to recall that we are also beneficiaries, in countless ways, of various high modernist schemes.

TWENTIETH CENTURY HIGH MODERNISM

The idea of the root-and-branch, rational, social engineering of entire social orders as a realizable utopia was largely a twentieth century phenomenon. As a faith, it was shared across a wide spectrum of political ideologies. Its main carriers and exponents were an elite avant-garde of engineers, planners, technocrats, high administrators, architects, scientists, and visionaries. If one were to imagine a pantheon or 'Hall of Fame' of high modernist figures, it would almost certainly include names such as Le Corbusier, Lenin, Trotsky, Walter Ratnenau, Romain Roland, David E. Lilienthal, Robert McNamara, Jean Monnet,[12] the Shah of Iran, Julius Nyerere, Hyman Rickover, and Robert Moses. The intimate association of all these figures with state power is no coincidence.

There is, I believe, a range of historical soils that seem particularly favourable to the flourishing of high modernist ideology. Those soils include crises of state power—war and economic depression—and circumstances in which a state's capacity for relatively unimpeded planning is greatly enhanced—the revolutionary conquest of power and colonial rule. The industrial warfare of the twentieth century has required unprecedented steps toward the total mobilization of the society and the economy. Even quite liberal societies such as those of the US and Britain became, in the context of war mobilization, directly administered societies. The worldwide depression of the 1930s similarly propelled liberal states into vast experiments in social and economic planning in an effort to relieve economic distress and to retain popular legitimacy. In the cases of war and depression, the rush towards an administered society has an aspect of force majeure to it. The post-war rebuilding of a war-torn nation might well fall in the same category.[13]

Revolution and colonialism, however, are hospitable to high modernism for different reasons. A revolutionary regime and a colonial regime each dispose of an unusual degree of power. The revolutionary state has defeated the ancien regime, it often has the mandate of its mobilized partisans to remake the society after its image, and it faces a prostrate civil society whose capacity for active resistance is limited.[14] The millennial expectations so commonly associated with revolutionary movements give further impetus to high modernist ambitions. Colonial regimes—particularly late colonial regimes—have often been the site of extensive experiments in social engineering.[15] An ideology of 'welfare colonialism' combined with the authoritarian power inherent in colonial rule have encouraged ambitious schemes to remake 'native' society.

If one were required to pinpoint the 'birth' of high modernism to a particular time, place, and individual—inevitably a rather arbitrary exercise given its many intellectual wellsprings—a very strong case could be made for German mobilization during the First World War and the figure most closely associated with it, Walter Rathnenau. German economic mobilization was the technocratic wonder of the war, especially to her enemies. That Germany kept her armies in the field and adequately supplied long after most observers thought she must collapse was in large part due to the planning of Walter Rathenau. An industrial engineer and head of the great electrical firm, Allgemeine Elektricitats-Gesellschaft (AEG) founded by his father Emil, Rathenau was placed in charge of the Office of War Raw Materials (Kriegsrohstoffabteilung). He realized that the planned rationing of raw materials and transport was the key to sustaining the war effort. Inventing, as it were, a planned economy step-by-step, Germany achieved feats of industrial production, munitions and armament supply, transportation and traffic control, price controls, and civilian rationing that had never before been attempted. The scope of planning and coordination necessitated an unprecedented mobilization of conscripts, soldiers, and war-related industrial labour. Such mobilization fostered the idea of creating 'administered mass organizations' that would encompass the entire society.[16]

Rathenau's pervasive faith in planning and the rationalization of production had deep roots in the intellectual connection being forged between the physical laws of thermodynamics on the one hand and the new applied sciences of work on the other. For many specialists, a narrow and materialist 'productivism' treated human labour as a mechanical system that could be decomposed into energy transfers, motion, and the physics of work. The simplification of labour into an isolated problem of mechanical efficiencies led directly to the aspiration to a quasi-total, scientific control of the labour process. Late nineteenth century materialism had, Rabinbach emphasizes, an equivalency between technology and physiology at its metaphysical core.[17]

This 'productivism' had at least two distinct lineages: one North American and the other European. The American contribution came from the influential work of Frederick Taylor, whose minute decomposition of factory labour into isolatable, precise, repetitive motions had begun to revolutionize the organization of factory work. Particularly on new assembly lines, it permitted the use of unskilled labour, the control of the pace of production, and the assertion of control over the whole labour process by the factory manager or engineer.[18] The European tradition of 'energetics', focusing on questions of motion, fatigue, measured rest, rational hygiene, and nutrition also treated the worker, notionally, as a machine, albeit a machine that must be well-fed and kept in working order. In place of workers, there was an abstract, standardized worker with uniform physical capacities and needs. Seen initially as a way of increasing wartime efficiency at the front and in industry, the Kaiser Wilhelm Institut fur Arbeitsphysiologie was, no less than Taylorism, based on a scheme to rationalize the body.[19]

What is most remarkable about the perspective of both traditions is, once again, how widely they were believed by educated elites who were otherwise poles apart politicaly. Taylorism and technocracy were the watchwords of a three-pronged idealism: the elimination of economic and social crisis; the expansion of productivity through science; and the re-enchantment of technology. The vision of society in which social conflict was eliminated in favour of technological and scientific imperatives could embrace liberal, socialist, authoritarian, and even communist and fascist solutions. Productivism, in short, was politically promiscuous.[20]

The appeal of one or another form of productivism across much of the right and centre of the political spectrum was largely due to its promise as a technological fix for class struggle. If, as its advocates claimed, it could vastly increase worker output, then the politics of re-distribution could be replaced by class-collaboration in which both profits and wages could simultaneously grow.[21] For much of the left, it promised the replacement of the capitalist by the engineer or the state expert/official. There could, on productivist premises, only be a single optimum solution or 'best practice' for any problem of work organization. The logical inference was some form of slide-rule authoritarianism in the interest, presumably, of all.

A combination of Rathenau's broad training in philosophy and economics, his wartime experience with planning, and the social conclusions he thought were inherent in the precision, reach, and transforming potential of electric power allowed him to draw the broadest lessons for social organization.[22] In the war, private industry had given way to a kind of state socialism; 'gigantic industrial enterprises had transcended their ostensibly private owners and all the laws of property.' The decisions required had nothing to do with ideology; they were driven by purely technical, economic necessity. The rule of specialists and the new technological possibilities, particularly huge electric power grids, made possible a new social-industrial order that was both centralized and locally autonomous. In the necessary coalition between industrial firms, the state, and technocrats forged by war mobilization, Rathenau discerned the shape of a progressive peacetime society. Inasmuch as the technical and economic requirements for reconstruction were obvious, and required the same sort of collaboration in all countries, Rathenau's rationalist faith in planning had an internationalist flavour. He characterized the modern era as a 'new machine order ... a consolidation of the world into an unconscious association of constraint, into an uninterrupted community of production and harmony.'[23]

The World War was the high watermark for the political influence of engineers and planners. Having seen what could be accomplished in extremis, they imagined what they could achieve if the identical energy and planning were devoted to popular welfare rather than mass destruction.[24] They, together with many political leaders, prominent intellectuals (for example, Philip Gibbs in England, Ernst Junger in Germany, Gustave Le Bon in France), labour leaders, and industrialists concluded that only a renewed and comprehensive dedication to technical innovation and the planning it made possible could rebuild the European economies and bring social peace.

Lenin himself was deeply impressed by the achievements of German industrial mobilization and believed that it had shown how production might be socialized. Just as Lenin believed that Marx had discovered immutable social laws akin to Darwin's laws of evolution, so he believed that the new technologies of mass production were scientific laws and not social constructions. Barely a month before the October 1917 Revolution he wrote that the war had 'accelerated the development of capitalism to such a tremendous degree, converting monopoly capitalism into state-monopoly capitalism, that neither the proletariat nor the revolutionary petty-bourgeois democrats can keep within the limits of capitalism.'[25] He and his economic advisors drew directly on the work of Rathenau and Mollendorf in their plans for the Soviet economy. The German war economy was for Lenin 'the ultimate in modern, large-scale capitalist techniques, planning and organization'; he took it to be the prototype of a socialized economy.[26] Presumably, if the state in question were in the hands of representatives of the working class, the basis of a socialist system would exist. Lenin's vision of the future looked much like Rathenau's, provided, of course, we ignore the small matter of a revolutionary seizure of power!

Lenin was not slow to appreciate the advantages of Taylorism on the factory floor for socialist control of production. While he had earlier denounced such techniques, calling them the 'scientific extortion of sweat', he had, by the time of the Revolution, become an enthusiastic advocate of systematic control as practiced in Germany. He extolled 'the principle of discipline, organization, and harmonious cooperation based upon the most modern, mechanized industry, the most rigid system accountability and control.'

The Taylor system, the last word of capitalism in this respect, like all capitalist progress, is a combination of the subtle brutality of bourgeois exploitation and a number of its great scientific achievements in the fields of analysing mechanical motions during work, the elimination of superfluous and awkward motions, the working out of correct methods of work, the introduction of the best system of accounting and control, etc. The Soviet Republic must at all costs adopt all that is valuable in the achievements of science and technology in this field... We must organize in Russia the study and teaching of the Taylor system and systematically try it out and adapt it to our purposes.[27]

By 1918, with production falling, he was calling for rigid work norms and, if necessary, the reintroduction of hated piecework. The first All-Russian Congress for Initiatives in Scientific Management was convened in 1921 and featured disputes between 'Taylorism' and 'energetics' (also called ergonomics). At least twenty institutes and as many journals were, by then, devoted to 'scientific management' in the Soviet Union. A command economy at the macro-level and Taylorist principles of central coordination at the micro-level of the factory floor provided an attractive and symbiotic package for an authoritarian, high-modernist, revolutionary like Lenin.[28]

RATHENAU'S WESTERN PRECURSORS AND SUCCESSORS

High modernism, as we noted earlier, has had especially destructive consequences when it has become the faith of authoritarian state elites who are able to impose that faith on their subjects. The former Soviet Union and a good many recently independent nations in the Third World have fit this description. And yet the doctrine was born and elaborated almost exclusively in the West. The idea of progress through rational, technocratic rule was a natural ideological byproduct of the rapid development of science and industry in the West.[29] As a public philosophy, it was related to earlier public philosophies in roughly the same way that the new genre of science fiction was related to earlier utopian fiction. Literature and the fine arts, on the strength of imagination, see clearly what might be looming on the horizon. Thus it is that Goethe, in *Faust*, captures the protean promise and cost of high modernism long before Rathenau's birth.

He outlines great reclamation projects to harness the sea for human purposes; man-made harbours and canals that can move ships full of goods and new dams for large-scale irrigation; green fields and forests, pastures and gardens, a vast and intensive agriculture, water power to attract and support emerging industries, thriving settlements, new towns and cities to come—all to be created out of barren wasteland where human beings have never dared to live.[30]

Goethe was particularly alert to the authoritarian temptations inherent in this sort of modernism. 'Use every possible means/to get crowds of workers here/spur them on with enjoyment, or be severe./ Pay them well, allure or repress.'[31] To borrow the title of a later play by Henrik Ibsen, Goethe was aware that the whole scheme depended on 'the master builder' in whom complete power was vested:

What I have thought, I hasten to fulfill
The master's word alone has real might
To consummate the greatest work.
One mind for a thousand hands will do.[32]

For most high modernists, the organizational and technical imperatives of the new scientific knowledge clashed directly with both traditional habits and popular sovereignty. It seemed preposterous that the vast improvements in welfare and efficiency now within grasp should be blocked by inertia or prejudice. A sector of the political right, heir to a strong tradition of 'enlightened tyranny', found the political implications of high modernism easily palatable, once they had embraced the revolutionary potential of new forms of social and economic organization. Thus, nineteenth century conservative thinkers such as de Maistre and de Bonald imagined that a new social science could become the bulwark of an orderly, deferential society.[33] Saint Simon, nominally a 'progressive', however, was the representative figure. He believed that what we now knew about technology and social organization made possible a society that was no longer governed by 'men' (that is, arbitrarily) but would be regulated 'by principles'.[34] The new union of science and industry provided the model for 'the necessary and organic' social bond.

This implied an overall directing intelligence who would divide tasks according to a rational plan, establish a hierarchy of tasks, and enforce the new order. Saint Simon recognized that the logic of industrial organization was at odds with the egalitarian promise of the Revolution. Hierarchy and subordination could be justified, he argued, in two ways. First, the subordination in question was a technically necessary subordination 'absolutely independent of the human will'.[35] Second, once the material rewards of this subordination were manifest, the populace would voluntarily cede their claim to an equal hand in shaping society.

Saint Simon was hardly alone. His perspective was largely shared by Prudhon, Fourier and other utopian socialists (Engel's term), and anarchists. It was, in fact, the newly discovered 'natural' laws of industrial and social organization that made government in the traditional sense, obsolete; what replaced the state was what Fourier called '*la science du mecanisme societaire*'.[36] As we saw in the case of Walter Rathenau, such beliefs have survived and been replenished by further industrial progress and social planning. Karl Mannheim, the emigre socialist, writing at least a decade after Rathenau's assassination in 1922, believed that ever greater sectors of human life were now the legitimate object of rational planning.

With the gradual integration of unplanned events into a planned society an important stage in the technical control of nature is reached. The newly controlled provinces of nature lose their original character and become functional parts of the social process.[37] The language, implying the colonial conquest of 'wild' provinces that are finally tamed and domesticated into the techno-structure, is diagnostic. There is no politics here, only the growing scientific mastery of man's natural and social environment.

The temporal emphasis of high modernism is almost exclusively on the future. Although any ideology with a large altar to 'progress' is bound to privilege the future, high modernism carries this to great lengths. The past is an impediment, a history that must be transcended; the present is the platform from which the aspirations to a better future will be launched. An aesthetic characteristic of discourses of high modernism, and of the public pronouncements of those states which have embraced it, is a heavy reliance on images of heroic progress toward a totally transformed future.[38] The strategic choice of the future is freighted with consequences. To the degree that the future is known and achievable—a belief which the faith in 'progress' encourages—the less future benefits are discounted for uncertainty. The practical effect is to convince most high modernists that the certainty of a better future justifies the many short-term sacrifices required to get there.[39] The ubiquity of 'five-year plans' in socialist states are an example of that conviction. Progress is objectified by a series of pre-conceived goals—largely material and quantifiable—which are to be achieved through savings, labour, and investments in the interim.

There may, of course, be no alternative to planning, especially when the urgency of a single goal (such as winning a war) seems to require the subordination of every other goal. The immanent logic of such an exercise, however, implies a degree of certainty about the future, about means-ends calculations, and about the meaning of human welfare that are truly heroic. How often such plans have had to be 'adjusted' or abandoned is an indication of just how heroic the assumptions behind them are.

Despite the authoritarian temptations of twentieth-century high modernism, they have often been resisted. The reasons are not only complex; they are different from case to case—but the particular importance of liberal democratic ideas and institutions deserves emphasis. Three factors seem decisive. The first is the existence, and belief in, a private sphere of activity in which the state and its agencies may not legitimately interfere. To be sure, this zone of autonomy has had a beleaguered existence as, following Mannheim, more previously private spheres have been made the object of official intervention. Much of the work of Michel Foucault was an attempt to map these incursions into health, sexuality, mental illness, 'vagrancy', sanitation, etc., and the strategy behind them. Nevertheless, the idea of a private realm has served to limit the ambitions of many high modernists, either out of their own political values or else a healthy respect for the political storm that such incursions would provoke.[40]

The second, and closely related, factor is the 'private sector' in liberal political economy. As Foucault put it, 'political economy announces [unlike absolutism and mercantilism] the unknowability for the sovereign of the totality of economic processes and, as a consequence, the impossibility of an economic sovereignty.'[41] The point of liberal political economy was not only that a 'free' market protected property and created wealth; it was also that the economy was far too complex for it ever to be managed in detail by a hierarchical administration.[42]

The third, and by far most important, barrier to thoroughgoing high modernist schemes has been existence of working, representative institutions through which a resistant society could make its influence felt. Such institutions function to thwart the most draconian features of high modernist schemes in roughly the same way the publicity and open opposition of an open society, as Amartya Sen has argued, typically avoids famines. Rulers, he notes, don't go hungry and are unlikely to learn about and respond readily to famine unless their institutional position provides strong incentives. Freedom of speech, of assembly, and of the press ensure that widespread hunger will be publicized, while freedom of assembly, elections, and representative institutions ensure that it is in the 'self-preserving' interest of elected officials to prevent famine when they can. In the same fashion, high modernist schemes in liberal democratic settings must accommodate themselves sufficiently to local opinion to avoid being undone at the polls. A twentieth century episode of high modernist ambition will make this clear.

THE TENNESSEE VALLEY AUTHORITY (TVA): US HIGH MODERNISM UNDONE

The TVA, mostly remembered for its work during the Great Depression in building dams that prevented floods and generated great quantities of hydro-electric power, was initially a far more visionary project. It was, surely, the most ambitious attempt in American history to improve the general welfare of millions of people on the basis of plans laid by a vast regional public authority and directed by a technical intelligentsia. The importance of the TVA extended well beyond American politics.[43] The agency became a model for regional development, first in the reconstruction of Europe following the Second World War and, later, in developing countries.

A brief historical diagnosis of this high modernist episode in American history can serve several purposes. Perhaps the most important is to show the extent to which the faith in a technocratically planned future was shared across much of the political spectrum in the early twentieth century. The centre of gravity of high modernist faith following the carnage of the First World War, it might be said, had shifted from Western Europe to the US and Russia: the former's faith in technological progress relatively unscathed by the war and the latter, under the Bolsheviks, now planning a revolutionary future. In the context of a democratic political culture, an examination of the TVA will also serve to illustrate how the authoritarian temptations of such a faith might be reconciled with a belief in popular sovereignty. Finally, because the high modernist aspirations of the TVA soon came to grief, along with their most fervent backers, the episode helps explain how representative institutions, coupled with economic inequalities, manage to derail such 'revolutions from above'.

The point of departure for the concept of a TVA was the dilemma of what to do with the Muscle Shoals munitions plant that had been built with the First World War's needs in mind. Now, in the middle of the depression, President Roosevelt, relying heavily on the trusted advice of Arthur E. Morgan and Senator Norris of Alabama, chose to launch a bold development agency that would cover the entire Tennessee river watershed and its people. The scale was un-precedented. The river passed through eight states on its course from Virginia to western Kentucky where it emptied into the Mississippi, draining—and frequently flooding—a basin of 40,000 square miles, in which more than two million people lived. They were among the poorest in the US. Much of the watershed was badly eroded farmland and over-exploited forests (many owned by absentee owners); much of the population was illiterate and one of every three farmers was a tenant or sharecropper. Like Appalachia as a whole, the largely rural population of the region lived in relative isolation from big urban markets. The classic response to poverty and subsistence-level incomes in the Tennessee Valley had been out-migration to industrial centres. With the onset of the world depression, however, this safety valve was closed.

One does not have to look far behind the rhetoric and the propaganda for the TVA to stumble across the conviction that much of the population of the valley urgently required transformation from above. Part of this conviction was the desire to take a backward region and bring it 'into the twentieth century'. The other part was the desire to take a backward population and provide them the means for economic and cultural citizenship.[44] Not far behind this last aspiration lay the stereotype of the 'hillbilly'. When Roosevelt spoke in 1934 of making 'a different type of citizen' of this rural people he added, 'Now that applies not only to the mountaineers—we all know about them—but it applies to the people around Muscle Shoals.'[45] Comprehensive development from above was more plausible and defensible for a population that was seen as poor, exploited, and above all, too benighted to know what was good for them.

The TVA was originally conceived as a development project that would be comprehensive in every sense of the term. It would build dams (thereby preventing floods and promoting navigation), generate cheap electricity, encourage industry, start cooperatives, train workers, build schools and clinics, conserve topsoil, replant denuded forests, teach modern agriculture, personal hygiene and sanitation, improve the diet, and, in general, transform a static, underdeveloped subsistence society into a dynamic, growing, productive society.[46] It was *the* original, comprehensive, integrated development scheme. The high tide of TVA's comprehensive planning phase was comparatively brief, roughly from 1933 when the Act founding it was passed by Congress until 1938, when Arthur Morgan, the leading exponent of the broadest possible role for TVA was dismissed. By then, if not by 1936, the political forces hoping to confine the TVA to a much narrower sphere had gained the upper hand. Any residual hopes for broad social planning were dashed by the outbreak of the Second World War, when the TVA was valued chiefly as a supplier of electricity for the aluminum industry and later for the nuclear labs in Oak Ridge.[47]

There is no doubt that President Roosevelt and Arthur Morgan had expansive ideas about what TVA might portend for the development of the country as a whole. Roosevelt had long been an active partisan of regional planning.[48] In a note he attached to his address to Congress on TVA, Roosevelt explained his particular passion for land use planning and its relation to the legislation he was proposing. It is worth quoting in some detail.

As Governor of New York, I had sponsored and brought about a statewide planning movement to be based on a study of the proper use of the 30,000,000 acres of land in the State, in which each ten-acre square would be separately studied and classified. Up to that time although many cities, weary of 'growing up like Topsy,' had begun to plan their future growth and development, little on a very large scale had been done for country areas. Before coming to Washington, I had determined to initiate a land use experiment embracing many states in the watershed of the Tennessee River. It was regional planning on a scale never before attempted in history . . . by means of a public authority similar to public authorities created in New York while I was Governor.[49]

Three months earlier, during a political reconnaissance trip to Muscle Shoals, Roosevelt spoke informally about 'setting an example of planning, not just for ourselves, but for generations to come' by uniting hitherto separate concerns for industry, agriculture, forestry, and flood prevention under a single authority.[50] Having become familiar with the 'piney woods' South from his long convalescence at Warm Springs, Roosevelt had a larger vision than just raising incomes; he wanted to raise people to real citizenship. 'Power,' he said, 'is really a secondary matter.' 'What we are doing there is ... trying to make a different type of citizen out of them from what they would be under their present conditions.'[51] 'They have never had a chance.' 'All you had to do was to look at the houses in which they lived.'

Given what we know about Roosevelt, the report of Arthur Morgan, the primary designer and first chairperson of the TVA, on his first conversation with the president about the plans, is perfectly credible. Roosevelt, he said, did not talk at all about electricity, dams, or fertilizer but rather about the chance to create 'a designed and planned social and economic order'. The president lamented that virtually all of his programme was devoted to dealing with emergencies and that the TVA was the only opportunity he had to do any 'deliberate social planning for the future.' The founders of TVA hoped that it would become a model for regional development that would be eventually applied throughout the nation.

ARTHUR E. MORGAN

Arthur E. Morgan was the most thoroughgoing exponent of high modernism within TVA, an advocacy that eventually cost him his political backing. Morgan was a remarkable, self-educated engineer. He rose to become the supervising engineer for many flood control and reclamation projects, and drainage schemes throughout the south and west. The water and drainage codes he wrote or revised were adopted as policy by many states. The fact that he had no college education did not deter Antioch College from naming him its president in 1922, and it was through his writings in 'Antioch Notes' that he came to Roosevelt's attention.

Morgan was a utilitarian 'improver', convinced that the application of science and technology, including eugenics, could immeasurably improve the human condition.[52] As an engineer, Morgan was appalled at the 'waste', a term he used constantly, of 'hit-or-miss' development compared to what could be achieved through systematic planning. Viewing the waste, as it were, from the vantage point of the world depression, he claimed that the TVA was 'part of the major program to try and find a way out of the industrial chaos into a designed social and industrial order.'[53] Nor was he unaware of similar experiments in large-scale social planning being carried out in other countries. Treading lightly, he said,

For instance, there is the great undertaking in Russia. I think we have ceased to make sport of Russia. We have come to realize that something important is happening there. I dislike to think of a program in this Country which might be a duplicate of that in Russia. I believe that program tends to destroy initiative and the freedom of personality which gives color and richness to life.[54]

Morgan's reference to Russia had less to do with doctrinaire Marxism than with the conviction that, everywhere, the future lay with large-scale organization and planning. His ideology of planning doubled as a theory of culture: differences in levels of human culture being 'primarily differences in the amplitude, inclusiveness, foresight, and thoroughness of planning.'[55] The epoch of the lone inventor or laboratory scientist, the individual entrepreneur or the pioneer was giving way to 'highly organized' commercial and/or public institutions. Similarly, local generation of electric power was no longer efficient. 'More effective organization and administration,' he wrote, 'are as necessary as improved technology in the elimination of small stations and the building up of great systems.' 'Now consider what would be accomplished by a single unified system, thoroughly interconnected by transmission lines and controlled from a single office.'[56] The very size of the endeavour predisposed Morgan in favour of public ownership and administration, inasmuch as placing such monopolistic power in the hands of 'self-appointed' business people would be unthinkable.

Morgan, with Roosevelt's initial backing, believed he was creating the model for national industrial and social planning. As huge as the Tennessee Valley was, Morgan could still see it as an experimental miniature, 'as a laboratory of the nation.'[57] As soon as the details were ironed out, the model could be applied generally. In the meantime, there might be inconveniences and dislocations; 'we must ask the patience and forbearance of the American people while the great project is taking shape.'[58]

The 'great project' was to be primarily the work of a small elite of professionals and engineers whose importance Morgan thought should be given greater recognition and honour. He lamented the fact that vital administrative offices in the US were treated as political positions. If, instead, such administrators of demonstrated talent could be forged into a nationwide profession and judged by their peers rather, he implied, than by politicians, 'we could revolutionize the character of Government'.[59] He knew that successful planning in the Tennessee Valley would require 'stepping on people's toes' and going up against an 'existing order ... made up of vested interests.'[60] He came as close as anyone in TVA's leadership to calling for giving the planners and technicians full power to bypass the politicians and apply their scientific knowledge.

In keeping with his experience and interests, Morgan was in charge of engineering construction, social and economic planning, forestry, and the integration of all planning elements into a whole.[61] The first step was, of course, a vast data gathering and mapping exercise necessary to any subsequent planning. Once the relevant 'facts' were ascertained, Morgan produced a truly comprehensive regional plan project (RP1) which classified and located all natural resources, specified population movements, transportation and communications improvements, a detailed land use plan, and a full plan for economic development.[62] The implications for the kind of power TVA would necessarily require to realize this plan were not lost on local propertied interests or on Morgan's opponents within the Authority.

Morgan was a social planner as well as a physical planner. In the first large construction project, the Cove Creek Dam, the work force was divided in two. While half worked, the other half and their spouses were trained in hygiene, sanitation, home management, and a new job skill. The objective was not simply a working dam, but a transformed population. As Morgan put it, 'After three or four years spent in building this great dam, these young men and their wives should be far better adapted to the new order.'[63] The organizational life of TVA itself was to be minutely planned. Morgan's proposed code of ethics required all TVA employees to answer a searching questionnaire about their private life and public views. The code itself warned against intemperance, lax sexual morality, gambling and other vices. Perhaps exposed by colleagues who resented this intrusion into their private lives, the code and the questionnaire became a small cause celebre and damaged Morgan's standing. They were abandoned.

DAVID E. LILIENTHAL

The name of Lilienthal and the TVA became practically synonymous, not only because he prevailed in the political struggle with Arthur Morgan, who was fired by Roosevelt in 1938, but also because he went on to write about the TVA and to serve as the head of another large public agency, the Atomic Energy Commission. Lilienthal was trained as a lawyer and had made a name for himself in Wisconsin, in the Progressive LaFollette tradition, as a defender of public interests against private utilities.

Lilienthal's high modernist commitments were evident but, unlike Morgan's, they were greatly tempered by political realism. As TVA's most articulate spokesperson, Lilienthal constantly expressed his faith that the combination of science, technology, and organizational skills could accomplish miracles. He also believed that, through what he called 'grass-roots democracy', the threat of centralized, technological authoritarianism could be averted.[64] Part of the reconciliation of democracy with technical authority consisted in removing much of what TVA did from the realm of politics altogether. A river had no 'politics'; the comprehensive development of a great river's watershed was not a political matter, though it certainly required popular cooperation. He was an enthusiastic promoter of 'valley authorities' elsewhere in the US and, for that matter, throughout the world. Like

Morgan, he believed that the future belonged to huge public authorities and was not shy about touting their accomplishments. The very comprehensiveness of a 'valley authority', he argued, was the source of its superiority as a planner. Rather like Le Corbusier's planner or Lenin's revolutionary field marshal, the authority could see the entire watershed and reconcile the potentially conflicting advice of hundreds of different specialists in soils, finance, dam construction, training, sanitation, etc. Comprehensiveness was the basis of an integrating vision.

References to sheer size, to production statistics, and to the taming of nature also recur throughout his writing and speeches. This passage from a 1940 speech, coloured a bit by the desire to diminish Mussolini, is typical:

... a mighty river system has been harnessed by a series of mammoth dams, and in three years it will be the first great river in America to be completely within the power of man ... I am proud of the fact that the largest, the most costly structure ever built by man is on the American continent- the Grand Coulee Dam; I am proud of the fact that the greatest bridge ever thrown across a barrier ... is an American accomplishment [compares these favourably to Mussolini's draining of the Pontian marshes] ... I have no apologies to make to anyone that we do things in a big way ... Why shouldn't we be proud that America has as many miles of highway as the whole of Europe, has half the world's trucks and three quarters of its automobiles ... that this country accounts for more than half the consumption of energy on this planet.[65]

The rhetoric is, of course, not at all exceptional for the time. One imagines his listeners' heads nodding approvingly, not only at the nationalism, but also at the aspiration to master nature. As the winner in the struggle with Arthur Morgan to define the shape of the TVA, Lilienthal's account is generally accepted. Lilienthal portrayed himself as the 'democrat' and Morgan as the 'authoritarian planner'. There is surely an element of truth in this. Morgan's plans were novel and far reaching. He envisioned forcing the sale of 'misused' land, creating a miniature federally-supervised planned economy, consolidating existing counties, and founding large handicraft cooperatives. With Morgan in mind, Lilienthal condemned any 'Alexander-the Great complex' and warned against 'the danger of regimentation, pouring human beings and communities into a model fashioned from above.'

The struggle between Lilienthal and Morgan is better understood, however, as a choice between a 'revolution-from-above',[66] which would require the mobilization of a new political base, or the alternative of working through the existing local power structures. Neither route was particularly compatible with a democratic conception of citizenship.[67]

REVOLUTION-FROM-ABOVE AND 'GRASS ROOTS DEMOCRACY'

Lilienthal's astute political practice may have given the TVA the local 'cover' it needed to survive, but it did not conform to his theory of 'grass roots democracy'. He wanted the TVA officials and technicians to be close to the people, to 'speak their language', to understand their needs and circumstances in detail, and to always operate with their best interests in mind. What was involved, however, was a kind of participatory autocracy. A local official needed to know those whose habits he was transforming in the same way that a sculptor needs to know the grain of the stone or wood he is fashioning. It set limits to what might be achieved. But there is not much more doubt who is transforming whom here than there was in the case of Lenin's professional revolutionist, though the means were far different.

Lilienthal envisioned a kind of working coalition between the experts and 'the people' which would protect the expert from the politicians and ensure that his advice was practical. 'The experts ... have a central role to play ... in every facet of modern living. The people and the experts: the relations between them is of the greatest importance in the development of the new democracy. For the people are now helpless without the experts.'[68]

Much of Lilienthal's writing was an attempt to reconcile what was, I think, a genuine democratic faith with the imperatives of technocratic planning. His democratic convictions did not permit him to simply impose a plan on people, even if it was in their best interests. Although 'the well-being of the people of the region' was the criteria of planning, the people could not be left out. 'A man wants to feel that he is important. He wants to be able not only to express his opinion freely, but to know that it carries some weight; to know that there are some things he decides, or has a part in deciding, and that he is a needed and useful part of something far bigger than he is.'[69]

Lilienthal's twofold resolution of this dilemma represents what I have come to regard as the populist technocrat's creed. The first element is, of course, persuasion and education. Lilienthal believed that patient explanation and demonstration would bring the wants of the population into alignment with the plans of the experts. 'They [farmers]', he wrote, 'wanted to have a say-so about changes, they had to be "shown"; but when their confidence had been earned they were enthusiastic, and they were generous of spirit.'[70] If, however, the specialists behaved arrogantly or impersonally—always a danger given their knowledge and position—they would fail to earn people's confidence. The second part of the creed, therefore, required the experts to 'live with the people.' To the degree that they shared the life of the people, they would come to understand their wants and needs better; the symbiosis between experts and the people would become so close that their interests would be automatically harmonized. Lilienthal imagined that this symbiosis would not only provide the experts with a popular shield against partisan political attacks, but that it would eliminate the need for public hearings and other formal ways of representing opinion. He was not concerned, as was Lenin, that proximity to the people would 'contaminate' the experts. Still, the relationship of teacher to student was very asymmetrical; what the expert could chiefly gain was a finer and more sensitive grasp of how he might 'serve the people'. And the chief satisfaction of the people was to know that the experts were attentive to their needs and wishes and that, above all, they had a role in something 'far bigger', that is, the plan.[71]

A crucial part of Lilienthal's 'participatory autocracy' was what he called 'administrative democracy'. He understood that central policies had to be adjusted locally and that TVA needed 'grassroots' support if these policies were going to be implemented. He argued for the decentralized administration of central authority,[72] not for a moment to be confused with the decentralization of political power. The logic of both Morgan and Lilienthal envisaged a mobilization of the 'grassroots' which would support the TVA's plan against its enemies, bypassing both the normal political process and the private sector.[73] It was to be a 'revolution-from-above' which created its own popular base. As Thorsten Veblen described it, the premise of TVA was that a 'technical intelligentsia allied with workers and farmers could create a garden of beauty and well being; capitalists and financiers would be relegated to a marginal role.'[74] Given the general failure of the capitalist market in the depression and the enormous legitimacy of the federal government under the New Deal as a guarantor of economic security, this vision was not preposterous.

A certain amount of mobilization from above did take place in the first three years of TVA's existence, when its revolutionary elan was still high. New local associations of labourers, farmers, members of cooperatives, and sharecroppers, working for the TVA or using its services, were formed by the Authority on its terms, typically bypassing existing structures. They played no role in determining policy; instead, their participation entailed 'mere administrative involvement', a 'pattern which simply transforms an unorganized citizenry into a reliable instrument for the achievement of administrative goals and calls it "democracy".'[75] Their presence was, however, sought less for their opinions than as a makeweight for the agency. All projects were TVA initiated and there was no significant, 'bottom-up' decision-making.

THE DOMESTICATION OF THE TVA BY EXISTING POWER STRUCTURES

The fact is that the TVA, by 1938 at the very latest, far from being a revolutionary presence in the Tennessee Valley, had been coopted and domesticated by a variety of local power holders. The institutions of a powerful and resistant civil society (including its competing bureaucracies and entrenched interests), had succeeded in limiting both its power and its aspirations. The story of how this high modernist scheme was brought to ground is complex; we abbreviate it in keeping with our particular interests.

Many of the key reasons why the TVA's wings were clipped had more to do with politics along the Potomac than with politics along the Tennessee. The coalition that, in 1932, had made possible the radical federal initiatives of the New Deal had been renegotiated, for electoral reasons, in favour of an accommodation with the states.[76] The struggle over the Social Security Act and other key policies in this period led to the disillusioned departure of many high modernist planners. One of them was, of course, Arthur Morgan who, among other things, discovered that Lilienthal was making political patronage appointments within the TVA despite regulations to the contrary.[77] In addition to challenges to the TVA's authority in the courts, there were a host of bureaucratic competitors who had always resented what they saw as usurpation of their administrative territory—the Department of the Interior, Department of Conservation, the Forest Service, the Bureau of Reclamation, the Army Corps of Engineers, etc. They had a collective interest in curbing the planning ambitions of the Authority. At the local level, a variant the same question was posed. Should the TVA create its own constituency from zero, as the 'revolution-from-above' model would suggest, or should it work through existing groups and institutions, reflecting their interests in the process? By 1938, the pattern of working through local institutions clearly prevailed.

The issue of how the TVA would deal with its largest constituency, farmers, was diagnostic. Harcourt A. Morgan (no relation to Arthur), the third man in the TVA triumvirate, was an agricultural research scientist with state experimental stations, head of the Association of Land Grant Colleges and Universities, and president of the University of Tennessee. The land-grant system of experimental stations and extension services was closely linked to larger, well-to-do farmers through the American Farm Bureau Federation (AFBF). The AFBF was a curious hybrid. It had formal representation in extension services and, thus, in the disbursement of funds through these services. On the other hand, it had a private dues paying membership, which often included local business persons, and a strong lobby in Washington. This was the institutional linkage to farmers that Harcourt Morgan was accustomed to and inclined to perpetuate. The large farmers in the AFBF were, given their resources and market-orientation, often the most innovative and progressive as well.

Lilienthal, perhaps as a part of his alliance with Harcourt Morgan against Arthur Morgan and also not wanting to affront a powerful organization which had already shown its muscle opposing Roosevelt's Secretary of Agriculture, Henry Wallace, acquiesced. The consequences for TVA's agenda for rural social change were enormous. It meant an end to TVA's alliance with the Farm Security

Administration (FSA) which was, unlike the AFBF, directly concerned with the sharecropper and the small farmer. Fertilizer supplies and soil conservation payments were monopolized by the large farms. It meant that virtually nothing was done for the black farming population or for the black agricultural colleges.[78] It led to the abandonment of plans for federal control of misused, sub-marginal land, of comprehensive land-use planning, and support for national wildlife conservation policy. It meant the canceling of ambitious plans for local education, and of plans to found and assist cooperative enterprises. In short, the effective price for the tacit backing of the AFBF was a renunciation of virtually all of TVA's ambitions for a 'social revolution' in welfare and class relations. One disappointed reformer claimed that, by 1936, its scope had been so drastically curtailed that 'the TVA should have been called the Tennessee Valley Power Production and Flood Control Corporation.'

THE OPTIONS

Working through local institutions, when those institutions reflect great inequalities in property, education, income, and political access, means accepting and reinforcing those inequalities. The high modernist reformers of the New Deal understood this very clearly. They believed that the combination of the depression and the popular legitimacy of the New Deal offered them a unique political opportunity to remake American society. The changes they did initiate were unprecedented in peacetime but reflected, ultimately, the limits of a 'revolution-from-above' in a liberal democratic society.

Rexford Tugwell was a representative figure of the radical New Dealers. He believed that in coopting existing elites in the Tennessee Valley to build its political base, the TVA foreclosed a chance to democratize the local society in a more profound sense. Grass roots democracy, if it meant coopting local elites, meant capitulation to an aristocracy of class and race.

In the South grass-roots democracy can only mean the exercise of the powers of government by the white planters; elsewhere it must mean control by and for the prosperous farmers who have hired men to do their work while they go to committee meetings. The plain fact is that if most farm communities are to have democratic administration they will have to import it from Washington.[79]

Social and economic conditions in the Tennessee Valley were, he argued, 'grossly undemocratic' and it was the obligation of the national state to eliminate those conditions.[80] Only the state could represent the interests of the poor, of blacks, or of the larger society. It was foolhardy to imagine that those who had a vested interest in the current inequities would make way peacefully. '... what is needed is a mechanism to assert the interest of the whole people against the local interest and to coerce the local interest when necessary.'[81] 'Democratic administration' at the local level would only be conceivable after a period of centralization during which comprehensive planning would lay the social and economic basis for real democracy. 'Nothing can be decentralized properly which has not first been centralized.'[82] The revolution-from-above he had in mind would require, he insisted, large planning bodies, a dedicated administrative elite, and, above all, the political power to see the plans through.

Tugwell eloquently captured the high modernist reformer's dilemma. A vision of a more just, equitable, prosperous, progressive, and educated society was effectively blocked by democratic institutions now controlled largely by the beneficiaries of these inequalities. He realized that to break these inequalities decisively would require coercion from the centre. He justified this move by appeal to a larger, national, and presumably democratic, interest, and by appeal to the benefits—including a more inclusive democracy—it would bring to the locality. The possibility of a coercive revolution-from-above which might lay the socio-economic groundwork for a subsequently wider democracy locally is not far-fetched. One thinks of the early period of Reconstruction after the Civil War—a revolution which foundered on similar political rocks—and of the land reforms, under occupation regimes, in Japan and Taiwan. It is not coincidental that these are all examples of martial law powers.

Eliminating such inequalities while working through local democratic institutions are nearly impossible. Tugwell appealed to the president to 'struggle with Congress' to achieve the necessary power. But this is precisely what Roosevelt, operating with an unprecedented mandate and quasi-emergency conditions, had failed to do. Lilienthal and Arthur Morgan had hopes that the TVA could mobilize its own popular constituency from above, which could then defeat the vested interests at the polls. This, in turn, was precisely what local power-holders and large farmers feared and were able, finally, to prevent. Short of a genuine, autonomous populist movement from below which won local political power (and various agrarian movements in American history have periodically done just that!), a locally democratic path to root-and-branch reform was very unlikely.

Documenting the high modernist faith of much of the political elite under the New Deal would not be difficult. It was part of the zeitgeist in the US and elsewhere. Despite claims to the contrary, high modernism came in all political shades; it was never confined exclusively to socialist ideology.[83] That the depression and the war should have been a high-water mark for this faith, is perfectly understandable given the unavoidable reliance on the state to provide for the unemployed and, later, to mobilize for war. The institutional legacy of the TVA can still be found the continued creation of huge public authorities. They are founded to accomplish tasks of great complexity and technical sophistication which require state funding and power to realize. The Atomic Energy Commission, the National Aeronautical and Space Agency, the large metropolitan transportation and planning agencies, and the post-war European Coal and Steel Community are only a few examples.

The TVA episode serves to remind us that reformist democrats were drawn to state high modernism as a means to the equality and prosperity that promised a more democratic society. Their goals were not merely widely admired; they were also among the social conditions associated with stable democracy. Compared to their enemies, who included private power monopolies, landed interests, and white supremacist politicians, the reforming high modernists seem positively edifying. The crucial distinction among the high modernists in the New Deal was how far they were willing to circumvent local democratic institutions to achieve their vision. None of them were as frankly authoritarian on behalf of a 'scientific vision of the future' as were Le Corbusier and Lenin. Arthur Morgan, and certainly, Tugwell, were willing to override local oligarchies, even if they were entrenched in democratic institutions, in the name of social reform and comprehensive planning. Harcourt Morgan worked through the large farmers, as he always had, and hoped for the best.

Lilienthal worked hard, initially, to reconcile high modernism with democracy via a popular mobilization from above. This popular mobilization, as we saw, was in practice as authoritarian as the local interests were oligarchic. Ever the political realist, Lilienthal gradually accommodated himself to enough local and regional interests to preserve those elements of the TVA he thought most vital—especially public power. In the end, the Tennessee Valley was almost certainly more prosperous, economically diverse, and flood free than it would have been without the TVA, but nearly all its plans for social reform had been discarded. What happens when high modernist planners of rural society can have their way? In *Seeing Like A State* we explored episodes of authoritarian high modernism in contexts where state elites are determined to force change, where civil society is weak and lacks many institutional resources to resist, and where the elites doing the planning are even more convinced that the subjects of development 'don't know what is good for them'.

THE SETTING FOR SOVIET ULTRA HIGH MODERNISM

To borrow an analogy from city planning, the master-builders of the TVA were rather like Baron Hausmann trying to retrofit Paris. The moment was propitious for bold strokes but, at the same time, each had to contend with an existing social structure, with powerful vested interests and with competing institutions. The master-builders of Soviet society were, by contrast, rather more like Niemeyer designing Brasilia. A combination of defeat in war, economic collapse, and a revolution had provided the closest thing to a bulldozed site that a state builder ever gets. The result was a kind of ultra-high modernism that, in its audacity, recalled the utopian aspects of its precursor, the French Revolution.

This is not the place—nor am I knowledgeable enough—for a full blown discussion of Soviet high modernism.[84] What I aim to do, instead, is to emphasize the cultural and aesthetic elements in Soviet high modernism. This will, in turn, pave the way for an examination of an illuminating point of direct contact between Soviet and American high modernism: the belief in huge, mechanized, industrial farms. Soviet high-modernism is, in some vital respects, not a sharp break from Russian absolutism. Ernest Gellner has argued that of the two facets of the Enlightenment: the one asserting the sovereignty of the individual and his interests, the other commending the rational authority of experts; it was the second facet that spoke to the desire of rulers of 'backward' states to catch up. The Enlightenment arrived in Central Europe, he concludes, as a 'centralizing rather than a liberating force'.[85]

Strong historical echoes of Leninist high modernism can thus be found in what Stites calls the 'administrative utopianism' of the Russian Tsars and their advisors in the eighteenth and nineteenth centuries. This administrative utopianism found expression in a succession of schemes that would organize the population (serfs, soldiers, workers, functionaries) into institutions 'based upon hierarchy, discipline, regimentation, strict order, rational planning, a geometrical environment, and a form of welfarism'.[86] Peter the Great's Petersburg was the urban realization of this vision. It was laid out according to a strict rectilinear and radial plan on completely new terrain. Its straight boulevards were, by design, twice as wide as the tallest building which was, naturally, at the geometric centre of the city. The actual buildings reflected function and hierarchy; the facade, height, and material of each corresponded to the social class of its inhabitants. Its physical layout was, at the same time, a legible map of its intended social structure.

Petersburg had many counterparts, urban and rural. Under Catherine the Great, Prince Gregory Potemkin established a whole series of model cities (for example, Ekaterinoslav) and model rural settlements.[87] The next two Tsars, Paul and Alexander I (1796–1855) inherited Catherine's passion for Prussian order and efficiency. Their advisor, Alex Arakcheev, established a model estate on which peasants wore uniforms and followed elaborate instructions on upkeep and maintenance, to the point of carrying 'punishment books' with a record of their violations. This estate was then made the basis of a far bolder plan to create self-sufficient military colonies all over Russia. By the late 1820s these authoritarian, military colonies included 750,000 people. This attempt to create a new Russia, in contrast to the disorder, mobility, and flux of a frontier society, quickly succumbed to popular resistance, corruption, and inefficiency. Long before the Bolsheviks took power, in any case, the historical landscape was littered with the wreckage of many miscarried experiments in authoritarian social planning.

Lenin and his confederates could implement their high modernist plans starting from nearly zero. The war, the revolution, and the subsequent famine had gone a long way toward dissolving the pre-revolutionary society, particularly in the cities. A general collapse of industrial production had provoked a vast exodus from the cities and a virtual retreat to a barter economy. The ensuing four-year-long civil war further dissolved existing social ties as well as schooled the hard-pressed Bolsheviks in the methods of 'war communism'—requisitions, martial law, coercion.

Working on a 'levelled' social terrain and harbouring high-modernist ambitions in keeping with the distinction of being the pioneers of the first socialist revolution, the Bolsheviks thought big. Nearly everything they planned was on a monumental scale—from the design of cities, individual buildings (the Palace of Soviets), construction projects (the White Sea Canal), and, later, the great industrial projects of the first Five-Year-Plan (Magnitogorsk), not to mention collectivization. Sheila Fitzpatrick has appropriately called this passion for sheer size, 'gigantomania'.[88] The entire economy itself was conceived as a 'well-ordered machine' where everyone would simply produce goods of the description and quantity specified by the central state's statistical bureau as Lenin had foreseen.

A transformation of the physical world was not, however, the only item on the Bolshevik agenda. It was a cultural revolution they sought, the creation of a new person. The secular intelligentsia were the most devoted partisans of this aspect of the revolution. Campaigns to promote atheism—and to suppress Christian ritual life—were pressed in the villages. New 'revolutionary' funeral and marriage ceremonies were invented amidst much fanfare and a ritual of 'Octobering' was encouraged as an alternative to baptism.[89] Cremation—rational, clean, economical—was promoted. Along with this secularization came enormous campaigns to promote education and literacy which were widely popular. Architects and social planners invented new communal living arrangements designed to supersede the bourgeois family pattern. Communal food, laundry, and child care services promised to free women from the traditional division of labour. Housing arrangements were explicitly intended to be 'social condensers'.

The 'new man', the Bolshevik specialist, engineer, or functionary came to represent a new code of social ethics—sometimes simply called *kultura*. In keeping with the cult of technology and science it emphasized punctuality, cleanliness, business-like directness, as well as polite modesty and good, but never showy, manners.[90] It is this specific kultura and the party's passion for the 'League of Time' that were so brilliantly caricatured in Eugene Zamiatin's novel *We*, and which became much later, the inspiration for George Orwell's *1984*.

What strikes an outside observer of this revolution in culture and architecture is its emphasis on public form—on getting the visual and aesthetic dimensions of the new world straight. One can perhaps see this best in what Stites calls the 'festivals of mustering' organized by the cultural impresario of the early Soviet state, Lunacharsky.[91] The revolution was re-enacted on a scale perhaps larger than the original, with 4,000 actors, cannons, bands, searchlights, ships on the river, and 35,000 spectators.[92] The re-enactment, unlike the original, called for military precision, with the various actors mobilized by platoon using semaphore and field telephones. Like 'mass exercises', the public spectacle gave, retroactively, an order, purpose, and central direction to the events which were designed to impress the spectator, not to reflect the historical facts. If one could see in Arakcheev's military colonies an attempt to pre-figure, to represent, a wished-for order, then perhaps Lunacharsky's staged revolution can be seen as a representation of the wished for relationship between the Bolsheviks and the proletarian crowd. Little effort was spared to see that the ceremony turned out right. When Lunachorsky himself complained that churches were being demolished for the May Day celebrations, Kaganivich replied, 'And my aesthetics demand that the demonstration processions from the six districts of Moscow should all pour into Red Square at the same time.'[93] In architecture, public manners, urban design, and public ritual, the emphasis on a visible, rational, disciplined social facade seemed to prevail. Stites suggests that there is some relationship between this public face of order and purpose and the near social anarchy that reigned outside.

As in the case of all such utopias, its organizers described it in rational symmetrical terms, in the mathematical language of planning, control figures, statistics, projections, and precise commands. As in the vision of military colonies, which the utopian plan faintly resembled, its rational facade barely obscured the oceans of misery, disorder, chaos, corruption, and whimsicality that went with it.[94] One possible implication of Stite's assertion is that, in some circumstances, what I would call the 'miniaturization of order' may be substituted for the real thing. A facade or a small, easily managed, zone of order and conformity may come to be an end in itself; the representation may usurp the reality. Miniatures and small experiments have, of course, an important role in studying larger phenomena. Scale model aircraft and wind tunnels are essential steps in new airplane design. But when the two are confused, when, say, the general mistakes the parade-ground for the battlefield itself, the consequences are potentially disastrous.

A JOINT SOVIET-AMERICAN HIGH MODERNIST FETISH: INDUSTRIAL FARMING[95]

The high tide of enthusiasm for applying industrial methods to agriculture in the US stretched roughly from 1910 to the end of the 1930s. Agricultural engineers, a new speciality, were the main carriers of this enthusiasm, influenced by currents in their parent discipline, industrial engineering, and most particularly by the doctrines of the prophet of time-motion studies, Frederik Taylor, they re-conceptualized the farm as a 'food and fiber factory'.[96] Taylorist principles of scientifically measuring work processes in order to break them down into simple, repetitive motions that an unskilled worker could learn quickly, might work well enough on the factory floor but their application to the variegated and non-repetitive require-ments of growing crops was problematic. Agricultural engineers turned, consequently, to those aspects of farm operation that might be more easily standardized. They tried to rationalize the layout of farm buildings, to standardize machinery and tools, and to promote the mechanization of major grain crops.

The professional instincts of the agricultural engineers lay with replicating on the farm, so far as possible, the features of the modern factory. This impelled them to insist on enlarging the scale of the typical small farm so that it could mass produce standard agricultural commodities, so that it could mechanize its operation and thereby, it was thought, greatly reduce the unit cost of production.[97]

As we will see later, the industrial model, which the agricultural modernizers were intent on applying was applicable to some, but not all, of agriculture. It was nonetheless applied indiscriminately as a creed rather than a scientific hypothesis to be examined sceptically. The modernist faith in huge scale, centralization of production work, standardized mass commodities, and mechanization was so utterly hegemonic in the leading sector of industry that it became an article of faith that the same principles would work *pari passu* in agriculture.

Many efforts were made to put this faith to the test. Perhaps the most audacious was the Thomas Campbell 'farm' in Montana, begun—or perhaps more appropriately, founded—in 1918.[98] It was an 'industrial farm' in more than one respect. Shares were sold by prospectus describing the enterprise as 'an industrial opportunity'; with the help of J.P. Morgan, the financier, two million dollars were raised from the public. The Montana Farming Corporation was a monster wheat farm of 95,000 acres, much of it leased from four Native American tribes. Despite private investment, the enterprise would never have gotten off the ground (no pun intended) without help and subsidies from the Department of Interior and the US Department of Agriculture (USDA).

Having proclaimed that 'farming was 90 per cent engineering and 10 per cent agriculture', Campbell set about standardizing as much of his operation as possible. He grew wheat and flax, two hardy crops that needed little or no attention between planting and harvest time.[99] The land he farmed was the agricultural equivalent of the bulldozed site of Brasilia. It was never-broken, virgin soil, the natural fertility of which would eliminate the need for fertilizer. The topography was also vastly simplified, perfectly flat with no forests, creeks, rocks, or ridges that would impede the smooth course of machinery over its surface. In other words, the selection of the simplest, most standardized crops and the leasing of something very close to a blank agricultural space was calculated to favour the application of industrial methods. In the first year Campbell bought 33 tractors, 40 binders, 10 threshing machines, four combines, and 100 wagons, employing 50 men normally and as many as 200 during the peak season.[100]

This is not the place to chronicle the fortunes of the Montana Farming Corporation, and, in any event, Fitzgerald has done this splendidly. Suffice it to note that a drought in the second year and the elimination of a government support price the following year led to a collapse that cost J. P. Morgan one million dollars. The Campbell farm faced other problems besides weather and prices; such as soil differences, labour turnover, finding skilled, resourceful workers who would need little supervision. Although the Corporation struggled on until Campbell's death in 1966, it provided no evidence that industrial farms were superior to family farms in efficiency and profitability. The advantages industrial farms did have over smaller producers were of another kind. Their very size gave them decisive advantages in access to credit, in political influence (relevant to taxes, support payments, and avoiding foreclosure) and marketing muscle. What they gave away in agility and quality labour, they often made up for in their sheer political and economic clout.

Many large industrial farms, managed along 'scientific' lines were established in the 1920s and 1930s.[101] Some of them were the stepchildren of depression foreclosures that left banks and insurance companies holding many farms they could not sell. Such 'chain farms', consisting of as many as 600 farmsteads, which were organized into one integral operation (for example, one farm to farrow pigs and another to feed them out, along the lines of contemporary 'contract farming' of poultry) were quite common and buying into them was a speculative investment.[102] They proved no more competitively superior to the family farm then did the Campbell Corporation. In fact, they were so highly capitalized that they were singularly vulnerable to unfavourable credit markets and lower farm gate prices, given their high fixed costs in payroll and interest. The family farm could, by contrast, more easily tighten its belt and move into a subsistence mode.[103]

The most striking proposal designed to reconcile the American small property regime with huge economies of scale and scientific, centralized management was that of Mordecai Ezekial and Sherman Johnson in 1930.[104] They outlined a 'national farming corporation' that would incorporate all farms.[105] It would be vertically integrated and centralized and could move raw farming materials through the individual farms of the country, could establish production goals and quotas, distribute machinery, labour and capital, and move farm products from one region to another for processing and use. Bearing a striking resemblance to the industrial world, this organizational plan was a sort of gigantic conveyor belt.[106]

Ezekial was no doubt influenced by his recent tour of Russian collective farms as well as by the plight of the depression-stricken economy. Johnson and Ezekial were hardly alone in calling for centralized industrial farming on a massive scale, not just as a response to economic crisis but as a matter of historical confidence in an ineluctable high modernist future. The following expression of that faith is fairly representative:

Collectivization is posed by history and economics. Politically, the small farmer or peasant is a drag on progress. Technically, he is as antiquated as the small machinists who once put automobiles together by hand in little wooden sheds. The Russians have been the first to see this clearly, and to adapt themselves to historical necessity.[107]

There was less specifically political ideology behind these admiring references to Russia than a shared high modernist faith. That faith was reinforced by something on the order of an improvised, high modernist exchange programme. A great many Russian agronomists and engineers came to the US which they regarded as the Mecca of industrial farming. Their tour of American agriculture nearly always included a visit to the Campbell's Montana Farming Corporation and to M.L. Wilson, in 1928 the head of the Department of Agricultural Economics at Montana State University (and later a high official in the Department of Agriculture under Henry Wallace). The Russians were so taken with Campbell's farm that they said they would provide him with a million acres if he would come to the Soviet Union and demonstrate his farming methods.[108]

Traffic in the other direction was just as brisk. The Soviet Union had hired thousands of American technicians and engineers to help design Soviet industrial production—including the production of tractors and other farm machinery. By 1927, the Soviet Union had also purchased 27,000 American tractors. Many of the American visitors like Ezekial were greatly impressed with Soviet State Farms and, by 1930, with the promise of collectivized agriculture on a massive scale. Americans who visited were impressed not just by the raw size of the state farms but also by the fact that technical specialists—agronomists, economists, engineers, statisticians—were, it seemed, developing Russian production along rational, egalitarian lines. The failure, in the West, of their own market economy in 1930 merely reinforced the attractiveness of the Soviet experiment.[109] Visitors in each direction returned to their own country thinking that they had seen the future.

As Deborah Fitzgerald and Lewis Feuer argue, the attraction of collectivization to American agricultural modernizers had very little to do with a belief in Marxism or in the attractiveness Soviet life. 'Rather it was because the Soviet idea of growing wheat on an industrial scale and in an industrial fashion was similar to American ideas about the direction American agriculture should take.'[110] Soviet collectivization represented, to these American viewers, a vast demonstration project without the political inconveniences of American institutions.

That is, the Americans viewed the giant Soviet farms as huge experiment stations on which Americans could try out their most radical ideas for increasing agricultural production and, in particular, wheat production. Many of the things they wished to learn more about simply could not be tried in America, partly because it would cost too much, partly because no suitable large farmsite was available, and partly because many farmers and farm labourers would be alarmed at the implications of this experimentation. The hope was that the Soviet experiment would be to American industrial agronomy more or less what the TVA was to be to American regional planning: a proving ground and a possible model for adoption.

Although Campbell did not accept the Soviet offer of a vast demonstration farm, others did. M. L. Wilson, Harold Ware (who had extensive experience in the Soviet Union) and Guy Riggin were invited to plan a huge mechanized wheat farm of some 500,000 acres on virgin land. It would be, Wilson wrote to a friend, the largest mechanical wheat farm in the world. They planned the entire farm layout, labour force, machinery needs, crop rotations, and lock-step work schedule in a Chicago hotel room in two weeks in December 1928.[111] The fact that they imagined that such a farm could be planned in a Chicago hotel room underlines their presumption that the key issues were abstract, technical interrelationships that were context-free. As Fitzgerald so perceptively explains:[112]

Even in the US, those plans would have been optimistic, actually, because they were based on an unrealistic idealization of nature and human behavior. And insofar as the plans represented what the Americans would do if they had millions of acres of flat land, lots of laborers, and a government commitment to spare no expense in meeting production goals, the plans were designed for an abstract, theoretical kind of place. This agricultural place, which did not correspond to America, Russia, or any other actual location, obeyed the laws of physics and chemistry, recognized no political or ideological stance ...[113]

The giant Sovhoz, named 'Verblud', they established near Rostov-on-Don, 1,000 miles south of Moscow, comprised 375,000 acres that were to be sown with wheat. As an economic proposition, it was an abject failure, although it did produce, in the first years, large quantities of wheat. The detailed reasons for the failure are of less interest for our purposes than the fact that most of them could be summarized under the rubric of context. It was the specific context of this specific farm that defeated them. The farm, unlike the plan, was not a hypothecated, generic, abstract farm but an unpredictable, complex, and particular farm with its unique soils, social structure, administrative culture, local weather, work skills and habits, repair yards, political strictures, machinery, roads, and personalities.

It was, like Brasilia, the kind of failure typical of large high modernist schemes, for which local knowledge, practice, and context is considered irrelevant or, at best, an annoyance to be circumvented.

NOTES

1. Witold Kula, *Measures and Men*, Princeton: Princeton University Press, p. 211.
2. Ian Hacking, *The Taming of Chance*, p. 38. A few years later, the Jacobins were, one could argue, the first to actually attempt to engineer happiness by transforming the social order. As Saint-Just wrote, 'The idea of happiness is new in Europe.' See Albert O. Hirschman, 'Rival Interpretations of Market Society: Civilizing, Destructive, or Feeble', *Journal of Economic Literature*, vol. XX (December), 1982, pp. 1463–84.
3. I am greatly indebted to James Ferguson whose perceptive comments on an early draft pointed me in this direction.
4. See, for example, Graham Burschell, Colin Gordon, and Peter Miller (eds), *The Foucault Effect: Studies in Governmentality* (London: Harvester Wheatsheaf, 1991), Ch. 4.
5. Hacking, *The Taming of Chance*, pp. 88–115. Hacking shows brilliantly how a statistical 'average' metamorphosed into the category 'normal', and 'normal', in turn, into a 'normative' standard to be achieved by social engineering.
6. See Gareth Stedman-Jones, *Languages of Class: Studies in English Working Class History, 1832–1982* (Cambridge: Cambridge University Press, 1983).

It is, I believe, important to recognize that virtually all the initiatives associated with the 'civilizing mission' of colonialism by Western powers in their empires were preceded by comparable programs to assimilate and civilize their own lower-class rural and urban populations. The difference, perhaps, is that, in the colonial setting, officials had greater coercive power over an objectified and alien population, thus allowing for greater feats of social engineering.

7. There is the interesting and problematic case of the 'wild' garden in which the precise shape of 'disorders' is minutely planned. Here it is a matter of an aesthetic plan, designed to have a certain effect on the eye—an attempt to 'copy' untended nature. The paradox is just as intractable as that of a zoo that mimics 'nature'—but rarely to the extent of allowing the critters to eat one another!

8. Marx, from the Manifesto, quoted in Berman, *All that Is Solid Melts into Air*, New York: Penguin, 1982, p. 95.

9. The literary 'spore' of this conviction is best seen in much of science fiction, the rise of which more or less paralleled the rise of high modernism generally.

10. An interesting, and diagnostic, exception would seem to be Taylorism which at least began its time and motion studies with a rigorous analysis of the movements of skilled workers. The ultimate purpose, of course, was to break down these skills into divisible units, each of which could be accomplished by workers with little or no training.

11. David Harvey, *The Condition of Post-Modernity* op. cit., p. 12.

12. Monnet, like Rathenau, had experience in economic mobilization during the First World War, when he helped organize the transatlantic supply of war material for Britian and France—a role he resumed during the Second World War. By the time he helped plan the post-war integration of French and German coal and steel production, he had already had several decades of experience in supranational management, See Francois Duchene, *Jean Monnet: The First Statesman of Interdependence* (New York: Norton, 1995).

13. For case studies of 'public entrepreneurs' in the US, see Eugene Lewis' study of Hyman Rickover, J. Edgar Hoover, and Robert Moses, *Public Entrepreneurship: Toward a Theory of Bureaucratic Political Power* (Bloomington, Indiana: University of Indiana Press, 1980).

14. A civil war, as in the Bolshevik case, may be the price of consolidating their power.

15. White-settler colonies (for example, South Africa, Algeria) and anti-insurgency campaigns (for example, Vietnam, Algeria, Afghanistan) have carried out huge population removals and forced resettlement. In most such cases, however, even the pretence of comprehensive social planning for the welfare of the affected population has been paper-thin.

16. Here, I am particularly indebted to the discussion of Yaney, The Urge to Mobilize, op. cit., pp. 448 et seq.

17. Anson Rabinbach, *The Human Motor: Energy, Fatigue, and the Origins of Modernity* (Berkeley: University of California Press, 1992), pp. 260 et seq. Long before the war, Rathenau, together with a number of architects and political leaders had participated in the Deutsche Werkbund, founded in 1907, which was devoted to fostering technical innovation in industry and the arts.

18. See Gregory J. Kasza, *The Conscription Society: Administered Mass Organizations* (New Haven: Yale University Press, 1995), especially Chapter 1, pp. 7–25.

19. Anson Rabinbach, *The Human Factor: Energy, Fatigue, and the Origins of Modernity* (Berkeley: University of California Press, 1992), p. 290.

20. Rabinbach, op. cit., p. 272. Rabinbach is here paraphrasing the conclusions of a seminal article on this subject by Charles S. Maier, 'Between Taylorism and Technocracy', *The Journal of Contemporary History*, vol. 6, no. 2 (1970), pp. 27–63.

21. Thorsten Veblen was the best known social scientist exponent of this view in the US while more literary versions of this ideology are apparent in Sinclair Lewis's *Arrowsmith* and in Ayn Rand's *The Fountainhead*, each from very different quadrants of the political spectrum.

22. Ibid., p. 452. For Rathenau's writings see, for example, 'Von kommenden Dingen' ('Things to Come') and 'Die Neue Wirtschaft' ('The New Economy'), the latter written after the war.

23. Rathenau, Von kommenden Dingen, [1916], quoted in Charles Maier, 'Between Taylorism and Technocracy: European Ideologies and the Vision of Industrial Productivity in the 1920s', *Journal of Contemporary History*, vol. 5, no. 2 (1970), p. 47. Maier (p. 46) notes that the aparent harmony of capital and labor in wartime Germany was achieved at the cost of an eventually ruinous policy of inflation.

24. Michael Adas, *Machines as the Measure of Men: Science, Technology, and Ideologies of Western Dominance* (Ithaca: Cornell University Press, 1989), p. 380. Wolin, *Politics and Vision*, op. cit., provides an extensive list spanning the political spectrum, starting from fascism and nationalism at one end and including liberals, social democrats and communists, in France, Germany, Austria-Prussia (for example, the Prussian Wichard von Moellendorf who was a close associate of Rathenau and a publicist for a managed post-war economy), Italy (for example, Antonio Gramsci on the left and fascists Masimo Rocca and Mussolini on the right) and Russia (Alexi Gastev, the "Soviet Taylor").

25. V. I. Lenin, *The Agrarian Programme of Social-Democracy in the First Russian Revolution, 1905-1907* (Moscow: Progress Publishers, 1954), Second revised edition, Epilogue, p. 195, written 28 September 1917. First emphasis, only, added.

26. Leon Smolinski, 'Lenin and Economic Planning', *Studies in Comparative Communism*, vol. 2, no.1 (January), 1969, p. 99. Lenin and Trotsky were explicit, Smolinski claims, about how electric centrals would create a farm population dependent on the centre and thus make state control of agricultural production possible. Ibid., pp. 106–7.

27. V. I. Lenin, *Works*, Vol. 27, (Moscow, 1972), p. 163. Quoted in Ranier Traub, 'Lenin and Taylor: The Fate of 'Scientific Management' in the (Early) Soviet Union', *Telos*, (Fall, 1978), pp. 82–92. Originally published in *Kursbuch*, vol. 43 (1976), translated by Judy Joseph. The 'bard' of Taylorism in the erstwhile USSR was Alexej Kapitonovik Gastev whose poetry and essays waxed lyrical about the possibilities of a 'union' between man and machine. 'Many find it repugnant that we want to deal with human beings as a screw, a nut, a machine. But we must undertake this as fearlessly as we accept the growth of trees and the expansion of the railway network.' Ibid., p. 88. Most of the labour institutes were closed and their experts deported or shot in the Stalinist purges of the 1930s.

28. V.I. Lenin, 'The Immediate Tasks of the Soviet Government', *Izvestia*, 28 April 1918, cited in Maier, op. cit., p. 51, fn 58.

29. A lot depends, in this statement, on exactly how one categorizes National Socialism in Germany. For two contrasting views, see Jeffrey Herf, *Reactionary Modernism: Technology, Culture, and Politics in Weimar and the Third Reich* (Cambridge: Cambridge University Press, 1984) and Zygmunt Bauman, *Modernity and the Holocaust*, op. cit.

30. Berman, *All that is Solid Melts Into Air*, op. cit., p. 50. I rely on Berman's astute analysis of Faust here.

31. Faust, quoted in Ibid. Goethe, *Faust*, trans. Theodore Martin, London: Sutton, 1908, part I, p. 24.

32. Ibid.

33. This and the next paragraphs follow, to a considerable degree, the intellectual history provided by Sheldon Wolin in *Politics and Vision: Continuity and Innovation in Western Political Thought* (Boston: Little Brown and Co., 1960), especially Chapter 10, 'The Age of Organization and the Sublimation of Politics', pp. 352–434.

34. C. H. de Saint-Simon, *Oeuvres Choisis* (Brussels, 1859), Vol. II, pp. 375–7. Quoted in ibid., p. 361. Prudhon, an individualist if there ever was one, agreed. 'It is always the government of man, the rule of will and caprice ... It ought to be the expression of fact.'

35. Ibid.

36. Charles Fourier, *Oeuvres complÈtes*, 3rd ed., 6 vols (Paris, 1846), Vol. III, pp. 18–19. Cited in Wolin, op. cit., p. 379.

37. Karl Mannheim, *Men and Society in an Age of Reconstruction* (London: Kegan Paul, 1940), p. 155, final, cited in Wolin, op. cit. p. 363. Emphasis added. Like Rathenau, Mannheim was committed to democracy; he thought that the 'objective' aspects of life could be regulated by planning

thereby freeing man's creative, artistic side. The problem , it would seem, was that the logic of his argument implied that more and more of human experience was being subsumed under the category 'objective'.

38. See, for example, Margaret M. Bullitt, 'Toward a Marxist Theory of Aesthetics: The Development of Socialist Realism in the Soviet Union', *The Russian Review*, vol. 35, no.1 (January), 1976, pp. 53–76.

39. See the suggestive paper by Baruch Knei-Paz, 'Can Historical Consequences Falsify Ideas? Or: Karl Marx After the Collapse of the Soviet Union.' Paper presented to Political Theory Workshop, Yale University, Fall 1994.

40. Graham Burchell, *The Foucault Effect . . .*, op. cit.

41. A point made forcefully and polemically in the twentieth century by Frederich Hayek, the darling of those opposed to post-war planning and the welfare state. See, especially, *The Road to Serfdom* (Chicago: University of Chicago Press, 1976).

42. I am very grateful for the astute commentary and plentiful sources provided for this section by Cassandra Moseley.

43. It would be hard to write an adequate history of the Food and Agriculture Organization (FAO), the International Labor Organization (ILO) the World Bank, or the US Agency for International Development (USAID), without understanding the virtual hegemony of the TVA as a model development scheme in their early years. For one of the earliest (before the end of the war!), and completely celebratory accounts, that helped launch the career of the TVA as template for development generally, see Herman Finer, *The T.V.A.: Lessons for International Application* (Montreal: International Labor Office, 1944). David E. Lilienthal, the head of the Authority for many years also wrote a book that would become formative in the 'international development career' of the TVA, *TVA: Democracy on the March* (New York: Harper and Brothers, 1944). The influence of the TVA model derives in part, as one might expect, from the fact that a good many of the actual founders of these agencies had been closely associated with the TVA and other New Deal development agencies, particularly the US Department of Agriculture (USDA). [Within the USDA the prevailing ideology was strikingly similar to the high modernist convictions described earlier in this chapter. In the midst of the depression, USDA planners believed that scientists and professionals could devise a rational public policy—a public policy which they believed they could persuade the citizenry to support at the polls.] For example, Howard Tolley, Chief of the Bureau of Agricultural Economics (The USDA was probably the largest single employer of economists in the western world at the time.) resigned in 1946 to become chief economist of the FAO which he had helped set up at a Hot Springs conference in 1943. Mordecai Ezekiel, Henry Wallace's main economic advisor and an admirer of the large-scale agricultural experiments in the USSR, moved to the FAO at the same time. Rexford

Tugwell, a major figure during the high-modernist days of the early New Deal, became governor of Puerto Rico in 1941 and implemented development programmes which would become models for later development schemes in Latin America and elsewhere. For some of the actual linkages between the TVA, the USDA, and development abroad, see the impressive analysis of Jess Gilbert and David Lachman, 'Democratic Ideology and Agricultural Policy: 'Program Study and Discussion' in the U.S. Department of Agriculture,' Jess Gilbert and Ellen R. Baker, 'Wisconsin Economists and New Deal Agricultural Policy: The Legacy of Progressive Professors'. For the linkages between TVA and the Food and Agriculture Organization (FAO), the International Bank for Reconstruction and Development (IBRD), and the first model, integrated development plan (for Columbia in 1949). For links between the Farm Security Administration and Nelson A. Rockefeller's American International Association for Economic and Social Development which urged comprehensive agrarian reform in countries like Venezuela after WWII, see Sidney Baldwin, *Poverty and Politics: The Rise and Decline of the Farm Security Administration* (Chapel Hill: University of North Carolina Press, 1968). See also for this period Arturo Escobar, 'Power and Visibility: Development and the Invention and Management of the Third World,' *Cultural Anthropology*, 1988, 3(4), pp. 428–43.

44. See, in this context, David Gelernter's study of the comprehensive faith in science and technology evident in the New York World's Fair of 1939, despite a long economic depression, *1939: The Lost World of the Fair* (New York: Free Press, 1995).

45. *The Public Papers and Addresses of Franklin D. Roosevelt* (New York: Random House, 1938), Vol. 3, *The Advance of Recovery and Reform*, 1934, p. 466. Emphasis added.

46. An early, polemical critic, whose concerns about ecological effects, local autonomy, and growing state power seem prescient today was Donald Davidson, in *The Tennessee*, Vol. II, *The New River: Civil War to TVA* (New York: Holt and Rinehart, 1948). See the comparison between his analysis and Lilienthal's in 'Images of TVA: The Clash Over Values', in *TVA: Fifth Years of Grass-roots Bureaucracy*, Erwin C. Hargrove and Paul K. Conklin (eds), (Urbana: University of Illinois, 1983), pp. 297–315. For all the condescension possibly implied in the TVA programme, it is worth pointing out that it avoided taking an 'essentialist' view that 'hillbillies' were 'just like that' and could never be changed. The premise behind the TVA was that if you could revolutionize the circumstances of those who lived in the valley, you would change them fundamentally.

47. *The Public Papers and Addresses of Franklin D. Roosevelt*, Vol. 2, *The Year of Crisis*, 1933. (New York: Random House, 1938), p. 123.

48. Ibid., vol. 1, *The Genesis of the New Deal, 1928–1932*, pp. 888–9.

49. Ibid., vol. 3, *The Advance of Recovery and Reform*, 1934, p. 466.
50. Arthur E. Morgan, 'Bench-marks in the Tennessee Valley'. Reprinted from *Survey Graphic*, (January, March, and May 1934), p. 8.
51. See his article 'A Prospect', *Atlantic Monthly*, CXXIX (March, 1922), p. 382 cited in Thomas K. McCraw, *Morgan vs Lilienthal: The Feud Within TVA* (Chicago: Loyola University Press, 1970), p. 11.
52. Morgan, 'Address' of Arthur E. Morgan Before the Kiwanis Club of Knoxville Tennessee, 31 August 1933. mimeographed, p. 9.
53. Ibid.
54. Morgan, "Bench-marks in the Tennessee Valley," op. cit., p. 16.
55. Ibid., p. 8.
56. Morgan, 'Planning in the Tennessee Valley', *Current History Magazine*, (September, 1933), p. 665.
57. Ibid., p. 668.
58. Morgan, "Address before the Kiwanis Club...," op. cit., p. 14.
59. Ibid.
60. The two other principals in TVA were David E. Lilienthal, in charge of electrical power and the legal department, and Harcourt Morgan (no relation to Arthur), in charge of agriculture, fertilizer production, and rural life planning. The three men made TVA decisions but, after an initial disagreement, Lilienthal and Harcourt Morgan had an informal pact to support one another against Arthur Morgan in case of disputes. Arthur Morgan, of course, was not told.
61. William Bruce Wheeler and Michael J. McDonald, *T.V.A. and the Tellico Dam, 1936–1979* (Knoxville: University of Tennessee Press, 1986), Chapter 1. Much of the forest land within the valley, often owned by absentee landowners, had been logged in a predatory way with predictable consequences for soil erosion and subsequent timber yields. One question discussed was whether such land ought to be placed under some kind of federal custodianship.
62. Morgan, 'Planning in the Tennessee Valley', op. cit., p. 668. Emphasis added.
63. Lilienthal, TVA: Democracy on the March, op. cit., 'Preface'.
64. David E. Lilienthal, Mimeo transcript of a speech given in San Francisco, 29 November 1940, 'Armament of a Democracy', p. 13.
65. Cited in McCraw, op. cit., pp. 34, 63–4.
66. Students of organizational theory will recognize my debt to the analysis of Philip Selznick, in *TVA and the Grass Roots: A Study in the Sociology of Formal Organization* (Berkeley: University of California Press, 1949). My purposes and analysis are rather different from Selznick's. Selznick went on to write what can only be described as a 'cold war classic', *The Organizational Weapon* (New York: McGraw Hill, 1952), an attack on Leninist techniques of subversion.
67. Lilienthal, TVA: Democracy on the March, op. cit., p. 120.
68. Ibid., p. 75.

69. Ibid., p. 78.
70. Ibid., p. 120.
71. Ibid., See Chapter 14, 'Decentralization: Antidote for Remote Control', pp. 139–51.
72. Cited in Richard Lowitt, 'The T.V.A., 1933-1945', Chapter 2 of Hargrove and Conklin, eds, op. cit.
73. Philip Selznick, *TVA and the Grass Roots*, op. cit., p. 220.
74. Richard Lowitt, 'The TVA, 1933-1945', op. cit., p. 56. Davidson, The Tennessee, op. cit., p. 301 claimed that from the perspective of local farmers, the head of T.V.A was 'like a king in the Middle Ages, crowned in some distant city. All his subjects could hope for was that he was a good king.'
75. Linked by many to the ascendancy of what many called the Brandeis-Frankfurter view of regionalism.
76. Patronage was an important means for the New Deal to gain the enthusiastic support of the representatives, senators, and governors of the states through which the river ran.
77. McCraw, op. cit., Chapter 4, also suggests that Lilienthal was primarily concerned with the public electric power and that this arrangement would neutralize a potentially powerful opponent to his own plans.
78. The National Association for the Advancement of Colored People (NAACP) accused TVA of consistently yielding to local racial attitudes: for example, hiring blacks only as unskilled workers and handing over its parks to local states and counties which segregated them. See Lowitt, 'The TVA, 1933-1945,' op. cit., p. 58.
79. R.G. Tugwell and E.C. Banfield, 'Grass Roots Democracy- Myth or Reality', *Public Administration Review*, vol. 10, no. 1, 1950, p. 50. This article is a review of Selznick's TVA and the Grass Roots, op. cit., published in 1949. American political scientists will be amused to find the name of Edward Banfield attached to this attack on the TVA for having not lived up to its high-modernist promise of socializing the Tennessee Valley.
80. Tugwell and Banfield, op. cit., p. 54.
81. Ibid.
82. Tugwell is quoting Paul Appelby here. *Big Democracy* (New York: Alfred A. Knopf. 1945), p. 104.
83. Adolph E. Berle, a New Deal official, went on to describe a social order in which the great capitalist corporations would do all the planning for the country as they had become, in their organizational form, the collective conscience of the society. See his *The Twentieth Century Capitalist Revolution*, and *The Modern Corporation and Private Property*, New York: Harcourt Brace, 1954.
84. The best source for this is probably Richard Stites, *Revolutionary Dreams: Utopian Vision and Experimental Life in the Russian Revolution* (New York: Oxford University Press, 1989). Its generous bibliography appears to cover most of the available sources.

85. This inference is not, we know, a distortion of the doctrines of liberalism. J.S. Mill, whose credentials as a liberal son of the Enlightenment are not in doubt, considered backwardness a sufficient condition to justify placing authoritarian powers in the hands of a modernizer. Ernest Gellner, 'The Struggle to Catch up', *Times Literary Supplement*, 9 December 1994, p. 14. For a more detailed argument along these lines, see, Bhikhu Parekh, 'The Cultural Particularity of Liberal Democracy', in David Held (ed.), *Prospects in Democracy*, Stanford: Stanford University Press, 1993.

86. Ibid., p. 19. Engels expressed his disdain for communist utopian schemes along these lines by calling them 'barracks communism'.

87. Being Prussian born and an avid correspondent with several of the Encylopaedists, including Voltaire, one could say she came by her mania for rational order honestly!

88. Sheila Fitzpatrick, *The Russian Revolution* (Oxford: Oxford University Press, 1982), p. 119. The term was, I believe, also in use in the USSR. The ultimate failure of most of the USSR's great schemes is in itself an important story. Its importance was captured epigramatically by Robert Conquest who observed that 'the end of the Cold War can be seen as the defeat of Magnitogorsk by Silicon Valley.' 'Party in the Dock', *Times Literary Supplement*, 6 November 1992, p. 7. For an industrial, cultural, and social history of Magnitogorsk, see Stephen Kotkin, *Magnetic Mountain: Stalinism as Civilization*, Berkeley: University of California Press, 1995.

89. Revolutionary campaigns in the French countryside following the Revolution—called 'dechristianization'—and their associated secular rituals offer an interesting parallel. Nor do the cultural parallels end there.

90. Stites, Revolutionary Dreamsy, op. cit., p. 119. See also Vera Sandomirsky Dunham, in *Stalin's Time: Middleclass Values in Soviet Fiction* (Cambridge: Cambridge University Press, 1976), for the transformation of this austerity into opulence under Stalin.

91. Ibid., Ch. 4. 'Festivals of the People', pp. 79–97.

92. Ibid., p. 95. Through Sergei Eisenstein's film, these public theatrical re-enactments are the visual images that remain embedded in the conscious of many of those who were not participants.

93. Ibid., p. 243.

94. Ibid., p. 242.

95. This entire section is based entirely on Chapters 2, 4, and 6 of a remarkable forthcoming book by Deborah Fitzgerald, *Yeoman No More: The Industrialization of American Agriculture* to whom I am greatly indebted. The chapter and page references which follow are to the draft manuscript.

96. Fitzgerald, op. cit., Ch. 2, p. 21.

97. As many commentators have emphasized, this re-designing of work processes served to wrest the control of production from skilled artisans and labourers and place it in the hands of management, whose ranks and prerogatives grew as the labour force was 'de-skilled'.

98. Around 1920, much of the market for the agricultural machinery made by US manufacturers was not in America where farm size was relatively small but international—Canada, Argentina, Australia, Russia—where the sale was larger. Fitzgerald, Ch. 2, p. 31.

99. For a more complete and fascinating account of the Campbell enterprise, see Fitzgerald, Ch. 5. 'The Campbell Farm Corporation'. It is worth adding here that the economic depression for agriculture in the US, began at the end of the First World War, not in 1930. The time was thus ripe for bold experimentation and the price of land or leases on land were cheap.

100. They are, in the terminology developed in the next chapter, 'proletarian' crops as opposed to 'petty-bourgeois' crops.

101. Fitzgerald, Ch. 4, pp. 15–17.

102. Supra, fn. 87.

103. Another such farm, and one with very direct links to later New Deal experimentation in the 1930s, was the Fairway Farms Corporation. Founded in 1924 by M.L. Wilson and Henry C. Taylor, both of whom were trained as economists at the University of Wisconsin in the John R. Commons and Richard Ely school of institutional economics, it was designed to turn landless farmers into scientific, industrial farmers. The capital for the new enterprise came, through intermediaries, from John D. Rockefeller. 'Fair-way' Farms would become the model for many of the New Deal's more ambitious agricultural programmes as Wilson, Taylor, and many of their Wisconsin Progressive, economist colleagues moved to influential positions in Washington under Roosevelt. For a more searching account of the connection, see Jess Gilbert and Ellen R. Baker, 'Wisconsin Economists and New Deal Agricultural Policy: The Legacy of Progressive Professors', op. cit. One reason why experimentation with new forms of enterprise took place in agruculture during the 1920s is simply that the economic slump for agricultural commodities began not long after the First World War, prompting a sectoral crisis and the policy initiatives designed to alleviate it.

104. Fitzgerald, Ch. 4, pp. 18–27. For an account of industrial farming in Kansas which is linked to the ecological disaster known as the 'Dust Bowl', see Donald Worster, *Dust Bowl: The Southern Plains in the 1930s* (New York: Oxford University Press, 1979).

105. Ibid., Ch. 4, p. 33. The plan's outline can be found in Ezekial and Johnson, 'Corporate Farming, The Way Out?', the *New Republic*, 4 June 1930, 63, pp. 66–8.

106. Michael Gold, 'Is the Small Farmer Dying?', the *New Republic*, 7 October 1931, 68, pp. 211. Cited in Fitzgerald, Ch. 2, p. 35.

107. Fitzgerald, Ch. 6, p. 13.

108. Enthusiastic visitors included the likes of John Dewey, Lincoln Steffens. Rexford Tugwell, Robert LaFollette, Morris Llewellyn Cooke (the foremost exponent of scientific management in the US at the time), Thurman

Arnold, and, of course, Thomas Campbell who called the Soviet experiment 'the biggest farming story the world has ever heard.' Typical of the praise for Soviet plans for a progressive and modern rural future was this appraisal by Belle LaFollette, wife of Robert M., 'If the Soviets could have their way, all land would be cultivated by tractors, all the villages lighted by electricity, each community would have a central house serving for the purpose of school, library, assembly hall, and theatre. They would have every convenience and advantage which they plan for the industrial workers in the city.' Cited (p. 129) in Lewis S. Feuer, 'American Travelers to the Soviet Union 1917-32: The Formation of a Component of New Deal Ideology', *American Quarterly*, vol. 14 (Spring), 1962, pp. 119–49.

109. Feuer, 'American Travelers to the Soviet Union', cited in Fitzgerald, Ch. 6, p. 4.
110. Ibid., p. 6.
111. Ibid., p. 37.
112. Ibid., p. 14.
113. Ibid., p. 39.

2

The Cost of Living
The Narmada Dam and
The Indian State

ARUNDHATI ROY

Fame is a funny thing. Apart from my friends and family and of course some old enemies (what is life without a few old enemies?), most people who know of me now, know of me as the author of that very successful book—*The God of Small Things*.

Success, of course, is a funny thing too.

Many are familiar with the public story that surrounds the publishing of *The God of Small Things*. As stories go, it has a sort of cloying, *Reader's Digest* ring to it—an unknown writer who spent secret years writing her first novel which was subsequently published in 40 languages, sold several million copies, and went on to win the Booker Prize.

The private story, however, is a less happy one.

When *The God of Small Things* was first published I truly enjoyed accompanying it on its journey into the world. I had a high old time. I spent a year travelling to places I never dreamed I would visit. I was exhilarated by the idea that a story written by an unknown person could make its way across cultures and languages and continents into so many waiting hearts. At readings, when people asked me what it felt like to be a writer who was published and read in so many languages, I would say, 'The opposite of what it must feel like to be a nuclear bomb. Literature hugs the world and the world hugs it back.' After a year of travelling, I decided I wanted to go back to my old life in what was now the New Nuclear India. But that proved impossible. My old life had packed its bags and left while I was away.

As the Indian government gears up to spend millions on nuclear weapons, the land it seeks to protect moulders. Rivers die, forests disappear, and the air is getting impossible to breathe.

Delhi, the city I live in, changes before my eyes. Cars are sleeker, gates are higher, old, tubercular security persons have made way for young, armed guards. But in the crevices of the city, in its folds and wrinkles, under flyovers, along sewers and railway tracks, in vacant lots, in all the dank, dark places, the poor are crammed in like lice. Their children stalk the streets with wild hearts. The privileged wear their sunglasses and look away as they glide past. Their privileged children do not need sunglasses. They do not need to look away. They have learned to stop seeing.

A writer's curse is that he or she cannot easily do that. A writer tends to keep those aching eyes open and bear witness to the obscenity. A writer is reminded everyday that there is no such thing as innocence. A writer has to think of new ways of saying old and obvious things. Things about love and greed. About politics and governance. About power and powerlessness. About war and peace. About death and beauty. Things that must be said over and over again.

While I watch from my window, the memory of the years of pleasure I had writing *The God of Small Things* has begun to fade. The commercial profits from book sales roll in. My bank account burgeons. I realize that I have accidentally ruptured a half-completed, Sardar Sarovar Dam on the Narmada river in central India. The court order came as a body blow to one of the most spectacular, non-violent resistance movements since the freedom struggle. A movement which, those of us watching from a distance thought, had more or less already achieved what it set out to. International attention had been focused on the project. The World Bank had been forced to withdraw from it. It seemed unlikely that the government would be able to cobble together the funds to complete the project. Then suddenly, with the lifting of the stay, the scenario changed. There was gloom in the Narmada Valley and dancing on the streets of Gujarat.

I grew interested in what was happening in the Narmada Valley because almost everyone I spoke to had a passionate opinion based on what seemed to me to be very little information. That interested me too, so much passion in the absence of information.

I substituted the fiction I intended to read in the coming months with journals and books and documentary films about dams and why they are built and what they do. I developed an inordinate, unnatural interest in drainage and irrigation. I met some of the activists who had been working in the valley for years with the NBA—extraordinary Narmada Bachao Andolan (NBA). What I learned changed me, fascinated me. It revealed in relentless detail, a government's highly evolved, intricate way of pulverizing a people behind the genial mask of democracy. I have angered people in India greatly by saying this. Compared to what goes on in other developing countries, India is paradise, I have been told. It is true, India is not Tibet, or Afghanistan, or Indonesia. It is true that the idea of the Indian Army staging a military coup is almost unimaginable. Nevertheless, what goes on in the name of 'national interest' is monstrous.

Though there has been a fair amount of writing on the Narmada Valley Development Project, most of it has been for a 'special interest' readership. Government documents are classified as secret. Experts and consultants have hijacked various aspects of the issue—displacement, rehabilitation, hydrology, drainage, water-logging, catchment area treatment, passion, politics—and carried them off to their lairs where they guard them fiercely against the unauthorized curiosity of interested laypersons. Social anthropologists have acrimonious debates with economists about whose jurisdiction resettlement and rehabilitation falls in. Engineers refuse to discuss politics when they present their proposals. Disconnecting the politics from the economics, from the emotion and human tragedy of uprootment, is like breaking up a band. The individual musicians do not rock in quite the same way. You keep the noise but lose the music.

In March I travelled to the Narmada Valley. I returned ashamed of how little I knew about a struggle that had been going on for so many years. I returned convinced that the valley needed a writer. Not just a writer, a fiction writer. A fiction writer who recognized that what was happening in the valley was perhaps too vulgar for fiction, but who could use the craft and rigour of writing fiction to make the separate parts cohere, to tell the story in the way it deserves to be told. I believe that the story of the Narmada Valley is nothing less than the story of Modern India.

The Narmada Valley Development Project is supposed to be the most ambitious river valley development project in the world. It envisages building 3,200 dams that will reconstitute the Narmada and her 419 tributaries into a series of step-reservoirs—an immense staircase of amenable water. Of these, 30 will be major dams, 135 medium and the rest small. Two of the major dams will be multi-purpose mega dams. The Sardar Sarovar in Gujarat and the Narmada Sagar in Madhya Pradesh, will, between them, hold more water than any other reservoir in the Indian subcontinent.

For better or for worse, the Narmada Valley Development Project will affect the lives of 25 million people who live in the valley and will alter the ecology of an entire river basin. It will submerge sacred groves and temples and ancient pilgrimage routes and archaeological sites that scholars say contain an uninterrupted record of human occupation from the stone age.

The Sardar Sarovar project belongs firmly in the era of the great Nehruvian dream. But before I come specifically to the story of the Sardar Sarovar, I would like to say a little about the raging Big Dam debate.

For half a century after independence, Nehru's foot soldiers sought to equate dam-building with nation-building. Not only did they build new dams and irrigation schemes, they took control of small, traditional water harvesting systems that had been managed for thousands of years and allowed them to atrophy. To compensate the loss they built more and more dams. Today, India is the world's third largest dam-builder. According to the Central Water Commission, we have 3,600 dams that qualify as big dams, 3,300 of them built after independence. A thousand more are under construction.

Nehru's famous statement about dams being the Temples of Modern India has made its way into primary school textbooks in every Indian language. Big dams have become an article of faith inextricably linked with nationalism. To question their utility amounts almost to sedition. Every schoolchild is taught that Big Dams will deliver the people of India from hunger and poverty.

But will they? Have they? Are they really the key to India's food security?

Today India has more irrigated land than any other country in the world. In the last 50 years the area under irrigation increased by about 140 per cent. It is true that in 1947, when colonialism formally ended, India was food deficient. In 1951 we produced 51 million tonnes of food grain. Today we produce close to 200 million tonnes. Certainly, this is a tremendous achievement. (Even though there are worrying signs that it may not be sustainable.) But surely nobody can claim that all the credit for increased food production should go to Big Dams. Most of it has to do with mechanized exploitation of groundwater, with the use of high-yielding hybrid seeds and chemical fertilizers.

The extraordinary thing is that there are no official figures for exactly what portion of the total food grain production comes from irrigation from Big Dams.

What is this if not a state's unforgivable disregard for its subjects? Given that the people of the Narmada Valley have been fighting for over 15 years, surely the least the government could do is to actually substantiate its case that Big Dams are India's only option to provide food for her growing population.

The only study I know of was presented to the World Commission on Dams by Himanshu Thakker. It estimates that Big Dams account for only 12 per cent of India's total foodgrain production! 12 per cent of the total produce is 24 million tonnes. In 1995 the state granaries were overflowing with 30 million tonnes of foodgrain, while at the same time 350 million people lived below the poverty line.

According to the Ministry of Food and Civil Supplies, 10 per cent of India's total food grain production—that is 20 million tonnes—is lost to rodents and insects because of bad and inadequate storage facilities. We must be the only country in the world that builds dams, uproots communities, and submerges forests in order to feed rats. Clearly we need better storerooms more urgently than we need dams.

Similarly, in the case of electricity, planners flaunt the fact that India consumes 20 times more electricity today than it did 50 years ago. Yet, over 70 per cent of rural households have no access to electricity. In the poorest states—Bihar, Uttar Pradesh, Orissa, and Rajasthan—over 80 per cent of Adivasi and Dalit households have no electricity. Electricity produced in the name of the poor are consumed by the rich with endless appetites.

Official estimates say that 22 per cent of the power generated is lost in transmission and system inefficiencies. Existing dams are silting up at a speed that halves and sometimes quarters their projected life-spans. It seems obvious, surely, that before the government decides to build another dam it ought to do everything in its power to maintain and increase the efficiency of the systems it already has in place. What happens in fact, is the reverse.

Dams are built, people are uprooted, forests are submerged, and then the project is simply abandoned. Canals are never completed—the benefits never accrue (except to the politicians, the bureaucrats, and the contractors involved in the construction). The first dam that was built on the Narmada is a case in point—the Bargi Dam in Madhya Pradesh was completed in 1990. It cost 10 times more than was budgeted and submerged three times more land than engineers said it would. To save the cost and effort of doing a survey, the government just filled the reservoir without warning anybody. Around 70,000 people from 101 villages were supposed to be displaced. Instead, 114,000 people from 162 villages were displaced. They were evicted from their homes by rising waters, chased out like rats, with no prior notice. There was no rehabilitation. Some got a meagre cash compensation. Most got nothing. Some died of starvation. Others moved to slums in Jabalpur. And all for what? Today, 10 years after it was completed, the Bargi Dam produces some electricity, but irrigates only as much land as it submerged. Only 5 per cent of the land its planners claimed it would irrigate. The government says it has no money to make the canals. Yet it has already begun work downstream, on the mammoth Narmada Sagar Dam and the Maheshwar Dam.

Why is this happening? How can it be happening?

Because Big Dams are monuments to corruption. To international corruption on an inconceivable scale. Bankers, politicians, bureaucrats, environmental consultants, aid agencies—they are all involved in the racket. The people that they prey on are the poorest, most marginalized sections of the populations of the poorest countries in the world. They do not count as people. Therefore the costs of Big Dams do not count as costs. They are not even entered in the books. What happens instead is that international consultants on resettlement (global experts on despair) are paid huge salaries to devise ever more sensitive, ever more humane-sounding, ever more exquisitely written, resettlement policies that are never implemented. Like the saying goes—there is a lot of money in poverty.

When I was writing 'The Greater Common Good'—my essay on the Narmada Valley project—wading through the fusillade of 'pro-dam' and 'anti-dam' statistics, what shocked me more than anything else was not the statistics that are available but the ones that are not. To me, this is the most unpardonable thing of all. It is unpardonable on the part of the Indian state as well as on the part of the intellectual community. The government of India has detailed figures for how many million tonnes of foodgrain or edible oils the country produces and how much more we produce now than we did in 1947. It can tell you what the total surface area of the National Highways adds up to, how many graduates India produces every year, how many men had vasectomies, how many cricket matches we have lost on a Friday in Sharjah.

But the government of India does not have a record of the number of people that have been displaced by dams or sacrificed in other ways at the altars of 'National Progress'. Is this not astounding? How can you measure Progress if you do not know what it costs and who has paid for it? How can the 'market' put a price on things—food, clothes, electricity, running water—when it does not take into account the real cost of production?

Unofficial estimates of the number of displaced people have swung from an unsubstantiated two million to an unsubstantiated 50 million, and everything in between. There is plenty of scope for bargaining.

When I wrote my essay, I thought it necessary to try and put a figure on how many people have actually been displaced by Big Dams. To do a back-of-the-envelope calculation. A sort of sanity check. The point was to at least begin to bring some perspective to the debate. As my starting premise, I used a study of 54 Large Dams by the Indian Institute of Public Administration (IIPA) based on field data from the Central Water Commission. Between them, the reservoirs of these 54 dams displaced about 2.4 million people. The average number of people displaced by each dam came to 44,000. Correcting for the fact that the dams the IIPA chose to study may have been some of the larger of the Large Dam projects, I pared down the average number of displaced people to 10,000 people per dam. Using this scaled-down average, the total number of people displaced by Large Dams in the last 50 years worked out to a scandalous 33 million people!

Recently N.C. Saxena, Secretary to the Planning Commission said he thought that the number was in the region of 40 million people. About 60 per cent of those displaced are either Dalit or Adivasi. Considering that Dalits account for 15 per cent and Adivasis only 8 per cent of India's population, this opens up a whole other dimension to the story. The ethnic 'otherness' of the victims takes some of the strain off the nation builders. What has happened to these millions of people? Where are they now? How do they earn a living? Nobody really knows. When history is written, they will not be in it, not even as statistics. When it comes to resettlement, the government's priorities are clear. India does not have a National Resettlement Policy. Displaced people are only entitled to a meagre cash compensation. The poorest of them, Dalits and Adivasis, who are either landless or have no formal title to their lands, but whose livelihoods depend entirely on the river—get nothing. Some of the displaced have been subsequently displaced three and four times—a dam, an artillery proof range, another dam, a uranium mine. Once they start rolling there is no resting place. The great majority is eventually absorbed into slums on the periphery of our great cities, where it coalesces into an immense pool of cheap labour (that builds more projects that displaces more people)—and still the nightmare does not end. They continue to be uprooted even from their hellish hovels whenever elections are comfortingly far away and the urban rich get twitchy about hygiene. In cities like Delhi they get shot for defecating in public places, like three slum dwellers were, only a few years ago.

On the whole there is a deafening silence on the politics of forced, involuntary displacement. It is accepted as a sort of unavoidable blip in our democratic system. In 1999, while the Indian Army fought in Kargil to regain every inch of territory captured by Pakistani infiltrators, hundreds of people in the Narmada Valley were being forcibly flooded out of their homes by the rising waters of the Sardar Sarovar Reservoir. The nation rose as one to support the soldiers on the front. Middle-class housewives held cooking festivals to raise money, people queued up to donate blood, they collected food, clothing, first aid. Actors, athletes, and celebrities swarmed to the border to bolster the morale of the fighting forces.

There were no such offers of help for the people in the Narmada Valley. Some of them had stood in their homes in chest deep water for days on end, protesting the Supreme Court's decision to raise the height of the Sardar Sarovar Dam. They were seen as people who were unwilling to pay the price for national progress. They were labelled anti-national and anti-development and carted off to jail. The general consensus seems to be, 'Yes it is sad, but hard decisions have to be made. Someone has to pay the price for development.'

I often wonder what would happen if the government was to declare that in order to raise funds to complete these mammoth projects, it was going to commandeer the assets and bank accounts of a hundred thousand of its richest citizens. I have no doubt that it would become an international scandal. Banner headlines would appear in newspapers announcing the death of democracy. Suddenly the ecological and human costs of Big Dams would be page one news.

In a flash there would be phenomenal, imaginative solutions for irrigation and power generation. Cheaper, quicker, more efficient. Nuclear hawks would suddenly realize they could drastically scale down the number of bombs they need for a minimum credible deterrent.

So far I have only discussed the human and social costs of Big Dams. What about the environmental costs? The submerged forests, the ravaged ecosystems, the destroyed estuaries, the defunct, silted up reservoirs, the endangered wildlife, the disappearing biodiversity, the millions of hectares of land that are either water-logged or salt-affected. None of this appears on the balance sheet. There are no official assessments of the cumulative impact Big Dams have had on the environment. What we do know is that a study of 300 projects done by an Expert Committee on River Valley Projects reported that 270 of them—that is 90 per cent of them—had violated the environmental guidelines laid down by the Ministry of Environment. The Ministry has not taken action or revoked the sanction of a single one of them.

The evidence against Big Dams is mounting alarmingly—irrigation disasters, dam induced floods, the fact that there are more drought-prone and flood-prone areas today than there were in 1947. The fact that not a single river in the plains has potable water. The fact that 250 million people have no access to safe drinking water. And yet there has not been an official audit, a comprehensive, honest, thoughtful, post-project evaluation of a single Big Dam to see whether or not it has achieved what it set out to achieve. Whether or not the costs were justified, or even what the costs actually were.

'This is exactly why the Sardar Sarovar Project is different,' its proponents boast. They call it the 'most studied project' in the world. One of the reasons the Sardar Sarovar is so 'studied' is because it is also so controversial.

In 1985, when the World Bank first sanctioned a 450 million dollar loan to fund the project, no studies had been done, nobody had any idea what the human cost or the ecological impact of the dam would be. The point of doing studies now can only be to justify what has become a fait accompli. So costs are suppressed and benefits exaggerated to farcical proportions.

The politics of the Sardar Sarovar Dam are complicated because the Narmada flows through three states—90 per cent of it through Madhya Pradesh, it then merely skirts the northern border of Maharashtra and finally flows through Gujarat for about 180 kilometres before it reaches the Arabian Sea. In order for the three states to arrive at a water sharing formula, in 1969 the Central Government set up a body called the Narmada Water Disputes Tribunal. It took 10 years for them announce their award. Geographically, the Sardar Sarovar Dam is located in Gujarat. Its reservoir submerges 245 villages, of which only 19 are in Gujarat. All the rest are in Madhya Pradesh and Maharashtra. What this means is that the social costs are borne by Maharashtra and Madhya Pradesh, while the benefits go to Gujarat. This is what has sharpened the controversy around it.

The cost-benefit analysis for the project is approached in a friendly, cheerful way. Almost as though it is a family board game. First, let us take a look at the 'costs'.

In 1979, when the Narmada Water Disputes Tribunal announced its award, the official estimate for the number of families that would be displaced by the Sardar Sarovar Reservoir was about 6,000. In 1987 the figure grew to 12,000. In 1992 it surged to 27,000. Today it hovers between 40 and 42,000 families. That is about 200,000 people. And that is just the official estimate. According to the NBA, the actual number of affected families is about 85,000. Close to half a million people.

The huge discrepancy between the government's estimate and the NBA's has to do with the definition of who qualifies as 'Project Affected'. According to the government, the only people who qualify as Project Affected are those whose lands and homes are submerged by the reservoir. But when one tears up the fabric of an ancient, agrarian community, which depends on its lands and rivers and forests for its sustenance, the threads begin to unravel in every direction. There are several categories of displacement that the government simply refuses to acknowledge.

For example, the Sardar Sarovar Project envisages bending the last 180 kilometres of the Narmada and diverting it about 90 degrees north, into a 75,000 square kilometres network of canals that planners claim will irrigate a command area of 1.8 million hectares. The government has acquired land for the canal network. 200,000 families are directly affected. Of these 23,000 families, let us say about 100,000 people, are seriously affected.

They do not count as project affected. Not in the official estimates.

In order to compensate for the submergence of 13,000 hectares of prime forest, the government proposes to expand the Shoolpaneshwar Wildlife sanctuary near the dam site. This would mean that about 40,000 Adivasi people from about 101 forest villages within the boundaries of the park will be 'persuaded' to leave. They do not count as project affected. In addition to the sanctuary, the other mitigating measure is the extraordinary process known as Compensatory Afforestation in which the government acquires land and plants three times as much forest as has been submerged by the reservoir.

The people from whom this land is acquired do not count as project affected.

In its plans for what it is going to do with its share of the Narmada water, the Gujarat government has allocated no water at all for the stretch of river downstream of the dam. This means that in the non-monsoon months there will be no water in the last 180 kilometres of the river. The dam will radically alter the ecology of the estuary and affect the spawning of the *hilsa* and freshwater prawns. 40,000 fisherfolk who live downstream depend on the river for a living. They do not count as project affected

In 1961, the Gujarat government acquired 1,600 acres of land from 950 Adivasi families for the infrastructure it would need for starting work on the dam, such as guest houses, office blocks, housing for engineers and their staff, roads leading to the dam site and warehouses for construction material. Overnight, the villagers became landless labourers. Their houses were dismantled and moved to the periphery of the colony, where they remain today, squatters on their own land. Some of them work as servants in the officers' bungalows and waiters in the guest house built on land where their own houses once stood. Incredibly, they do not qualify as project affected!

In its publicity drive, the other sleight of hand by the proponents of the Sardar Sarovar is to portray costs as benefits. For instance there is the repeated assertion that displacement is actually a positive intervention, a way of relieving acute deprivation. That the state is doing people a favour by submerging their lands and homes, taking them away from their forests and river, drowning their sacred sites, destroying their community links, and forcibly displacing them against their wishes. Anybody who argues against this is accused of being an 'ecoromantic', of wanting to deny poor and marginalized people the 'fruits of modern development'. Of glorifying the notion of the Noble Savage.

If the well-being of Adivasi people is what is uppermost in the planners' minds, why is it that for 50 years there have been no roads, no schools, no clinics, no wells, no hospitals in the areas they live in? Why is it for all these years they did not take any steps to equip the people they care so deeply about for the world they were going to be dumped in? Why is it that the first sign of 'development'—a road—brought only terror, police, beatings, rape, murder? Why must the offer of development be conditional: you give up your homes, your lands, your field, your language, your gods, and we will give you 'development'?

As part of 'the best rehabilitation package in the world', the Gujarat government has offered to rehabilitate all the officially 'project affected', even those from Madhya Pradesh and Maharashtra. The Madhya Pradesh government has filed an affidavit in court declaring that it has no land to rehabilitate people displaced by the Sardar Sarovar Reservoir. This means that all the displaced people from Madhya Pradesh have no choice but to move to Gujarat—not a state known for its hospitality towards 'outsiders'. Notwithstanding its feigned generosity, in point of fact the government of Gujarat has not even managed to rehabilitate people from the 19 Adivasi villages in Gujarat that are being submerged by the reservoir, let alone those from the rest of the 226 villages in the other two states. The inhabitants of Gujarat's 19 villages have been scattered to 175 separate rehabilitation sites. Social links have been smashed, communities broken up. Not a single village has been resettled according to the directives of the Tribunal. Some families have been given land, others have not. Some have land that is stony and uncultivable. Some have land that is irredeemably waterlogged or infested with pernicious *daab* grass. Some have been driven out by landowners that sold land to the government but had not been paid yet. Some who were resettled on the peripheries of other villages have been robbed, beaten, and chased away by their host villagers.

In several resettlement sites, people have been dumped in rows of corrugated tin sheds which are furnaces in summer and refrigerators in winter. Some of them are located in dry riverbeds which, during the monsoon, turn into fast-flowing drifts. I have been to some of these 'sites'. I have seen film footage of others: shivering children, perched like birds on the edges of *charpais*, while swirling waters enter their tin homes. Frightened, fevered eyes watch pots and pans carried through the doorway by the current, floating out into the flooded fields, thin fathers swimming after them to retrieve what they can. When the waters recede, they leave ruin. Malaria, diarrhoea, sick cattle stranded in the slush.

Forty households were moved from Manibeli in Maharashtra to a resettlement site in Gujarat. In the first year, 38 children died. In April 1999, the papers reported nine deaths from chronic malnutrition in a single rehabilitation site in Gujarat. In the course of a week. That is 1.2875 people a day.

Many of those who have been resettled are people who have lived all their lives deep in the forest with virtually no contact with money and the modern world. Suddenly they find themselves left with the option of either starving to death or walking several kilometres to the nearest town, sitting in the marketplace (both men and women), offering themselves as wage labour, like goods on sale. Instead of a forest from which they gathered everything they needed—food, fuel, fodder, rope, gum, tobacco, tooth powder, medicinal herbs, housing material— they earn between 10 and 20 rupees a day with which to feed and keep their families. Instead of a river, they have a hand pump. In their old villages, certainly they were poor, extremely poor, but they were insured against absolute disaster. If the rains failed, they had the forests to turn to. The river to fish in. Their livestock was their fixed deposit. Without all this, they are a heartbeat away from destitution.

For the people who have been resettled, everything has to be re-learned. Every little thing, every big thing: from relieving oneself (where do you do it when there is no jungle to hide you?) to buying a bus ticket, to learning a new language, to understanding money. And worst of all, learning to be supplicants. Learning to take orders. Learning to have masters. Learning to answer only when they are addressed. From being self-sufficient and free, to being further impoverished and yoked to the whims of a world they know nothing about—what must it feel like? In 15 years, the government has not managed to resettle people displaced by half a dam. What are they going to do about the remaining 3,199 dams? There is something wrong with the scale of the operations here. This is Fascist Maths. It strangles stories, bludgeons detail, and manages to blind perfectly reasonable people with its spurious, shining vision.

So much for project costs. Now let us take a look at the benefits. The stated benefits.

The whole purpose of the Sardar Sarovar, the government of Gujarat says, is to take water to the drought-prone regions of Kutchch and Saurashtra, which lie at the very end of the canal network. The Sardar Sarovar Narmada Nigam publicity campaign is full of pictures of parched earth and dying cattle. In the name of Kutchch and Saurashtra, it justifies using about 80 per cent of Gujarat's irrigation budget for the Sardar Sarovar. It says, categorically, that there is no alternative to the Sardar Sarovar.

To understand what is really going on, the first thing one must do is to look at a map of Gujarat, especially for two other rivers—the Mahi and the Sabarmati. Both are miles closer to Kutchch and

Saurashtra than the Narmada is. Both have been dammed and the water diverted to Ahmedabad, Mehsana, and Kheda, the Patel-rich, irrigation rich, politically powerful areas of central Gujarat. The people of Kutchch and Saurashtra have not seen a drop of water from these rivers. When the Sardar Sarovar Project was first planned, there was no mention of drinking water for the villages in Kutchch and Saurashtra. It was supposed to be primarily an irrigation project. When the project ran into political trouble, the government discovered the emotive power of thirst. Drinking water became the rallying cry of the Sardar Sarovar Project. Officially, the number of people whose thirst would be slaked fluctuated from 28 million (1983) to 32.5 million(1989) to 10 million (1992) to 25 million (1993). The number of villages that would get drinking water varied from zero in 1979 to 8,215 in 1991. When pressed, the government admitted that the figures for 1991 included 236 uninhabited villages.

Nobody builds Big Dams to take drinking water to remote villages. Of the one billion people in the world who have no access to safe drinking water, 855 million live in rural areas. The cost of installing an energy intensive network of thousands of kilometres of pipelines, aqueducts, pumps, and treatment plants to provide drinking water to scattered populations is prohibitive. When the members of the World Bank's Morse Committee arrived in Gujarat to do the Independent Review, they were impressed by the Gujarat government's commitment to take drinking water to the state's remote regions. They asked to see the plans. There were none. They asked if the costs had been worked out. 'A few thousand crores,' was the breezy answer. A billion dollars, is an expert's calculated guess. But of course, that is not a part of the cost-benefit analysis (the benefit-benefit analysis, shall we call it?)

As for the irrigation benefits, when the government of Gujarat argued its case before the Water Disputes Tribunal it pleaded for more than its proportionately fair share of water because it said it desperately needed water to irrigate 1,100,000 acres of land in the arid region of Kutchch. The Tribunal accepted the argument and allotted Gujarat 9 MAF of water. It did not specify how that water should be used. The Gujarat government then reduced the 1,100,000 hectares to less than a tenth of that. To 100,000 hectares. That is 1.8 per cent of the cultivable area in Kutchch. And that is on paper. On paper it irrigates only 9 per cent of the cultivable land in Saurashtra. If you ask what they are going to do about the rest of the drought-prone regions, they talk of 'alternatives'. Watershed management. Rainwater harvesting. Well-recharging. The point is that if there are alternatives which are good enough for 98.2 per cent of Kutchch and 91 per cent of Saurashtra, then why will they not work for the whole 100 per cent?

There are some other interesting caveats which make it unlikely that water from the Narmada will ever get to Kutchch and Saurashtra, situated as they are at the tail end of the canal. First, there is a lot less water in the Narmada than the government says there is. Before the Tribunal announced its water sharing formula, it had to assess how much water there actually was in the river. Since there was no actual flow data available at the time, they extrapolated it from what was even at the time thought to be faulty rainfall data. They arrived at a figure of 27.22 MAF. In 1992, actual flow data indicates that there is only 22.69 MAF of water in the river—that is a whole 18 per cent less!

Second, the Sardar Sarovar Dam was planned in conjuction with the Narmada Sagar Dam. In the absence of the Narmada Sagar, on which construction has temporarily been stopped, the irrigation benefits of the Sardar Sarovar drop drastically.

Third, the irrigation efficiency of the Canal has been arbitrarily fixed at 60 per cent when the highest irrigation efficiency ever achieved in India is 35 per cent.

Last, and perhaps most important of all, are the competing claims being made on the water. The authorities of the Sardar Sarovar Narmada Nigam declared that farmers would not be allowed to grow sugarcane in the command area because sugarcane is a water-guzzling cash crop and would use up the share of water meant for those at the tail end of the canal. But the government of Gujarat has already given licences to dozens of large sugar mills at the head of the canal. The chief promoter of one of them is Sanat Mehta, who was Chairperson of the Sardar Sarovar Narmada Nigam—the Dam Authority—for several years. The chief promoter of another was Chiman Bhai Patel, former chief minister of Gujarat, probably the most ardent promoter of the Sardar Sarovar Project. When he died, his ashes were scattered over the dam site.

Other than the politically powerful sugar lobby, to get to Kutchch and Saurashtra the canal has to negotiate its way past a series of golf-courses, luxury hotels, and water parks which, the government says, it has sanctioned in order to raise money to complete the project! Apart from all this, and in complete contravention of its own directives, the government has allotted the city of Baroda a sizeable quantity of water. What Baroda gets, can Ahmedabad bear to lose? The political clout of powerful urban centres will make sure they get their share.

So the chances of the farmers of Kutchch and Saurashtra benefiting from the Narmada get remoter by the day. Of late, the people of Kutchch and Saurashtra, who have endured water shortages for years, have begun to recognize government propaganda for what it is. Civil unease is stirring as realization dawns that the Sardar Sarovar is mopping up their money but is not going to solve their water problems. That the solution lies not with the government but with themselves. The Gujarat Land Development Corporation estimates that there is at least 15 to 20 million acre feet of rainwater that can be harvested by local watershed harvesting schemes in Kutchch and Saurashtra. (The Sardar Sarovar promises, on paper, three million acre feet to these areas.) In several villages, entirely through peoples' initiatives, successful water harvesting schemes are already under way. Hundreds of thousands of wells are being recharged with rainwater that was flowing away unused. So much for the government of Gujarat's claims that there are no alternatives to the Sardar Sarovar.

A people's organization has filed a case against the Sardar Sarovar Narmada Nigam, demanding an express canal to Kutchch, with no designer stops on the way. Another huge cost that does not figure in the benefit-benefit analysis of the Sardar Sarovar Project is the cost of installing drainage in the command area to prevent water-logging and salinization. The cost of installing drainage is about five times higher than installing the irrigation system. So, traditionally drainage costs are left out in order to make projects in developing countries appear viable. I am told this is an old World Bank practice.

Over the last 14 years, the NBA has pointed to these facts over and over again, and asked for the project to be reviewed. After the World Bank's Independent Review was published and the Bank stepped back from the project, the Gujarat government has systematically blocked every attempt at a review. It prevented the Five-Member Group Committee from entering Gujarat. It refused permission to the World Commission on Dams to visit the dam site. It prevented the Commissioner for Scheduled Castes and Tribes from visiting the dam site. It prevented the Union Welfare Ministry from assessing the Rehabilitation and Resettlement situation. It stood by and watched while the NBA office in Baroda was ransacked and its documents publicly burnt.

In May 1994, the NBA filed a petition in the Supreme Court in which it listed all the points I have talked about, and asked for a review of the project. In early 1995, on the grounds that the resettlement of displaced people was not satisfactory, the court ordered a halt to the construction. Over the years the court has managed to limit the whole issue to resettlement. It has cast itself in the role of a sort of Welfare Inspector of Resettlement Colonies whose jurisdiction is more or less restricted to Gujarat. It oversees the resettlement of only those who officially qualify as 'project affected'. Unfortunately, even here it hasn't distinguished itself.

In February 1999, despite the fact that nothing had changed radically in the resettlement scenario, despite the fact that families who were supposed to have been resettled had returned in despair to their original villages, the Supreme Court lifted the four-year long stay and allowed construction of the dam to continue. The people in the valley responded by declaring that they would drown rather than move from their homes. The NBA defied the gag imposed on them by the court. In a statement to the press, its leader, Medha Patkar, announced that she would drown herself in the river if the court permitted any further construction.

As a response to this, the Gujarat Government filed a petition asking that the NBA be removed as petitioners for committing contempt of court and that criminal action be taken against me for writing 'The Greater Common Good' which, they claimed, undermined the dignity of the court and attempted to influence the course of justice. In July and August, while the waters rose in the Narmada, while villagers stood in their homes for days together in chest deep water to protest the decision of the court, while their crops were submerged, and while the NBA pointed out (citing specific instances) that government officials had committed perjury by signing false affidavits claiming that resettlement had been carried out when it had not, the three judge bench in the Supreme Court met over three sessions. The only subject they discussed was whether or not the dignity of the court had been undermined. On 15 October 1999 they issued an elaborate order. Here are some extracts.

Judicial process and institution cannot be permitted to be scandalized or subjected to contumacious violation in such a blatant manner in which it has been done by her [me]. Vicious stultification and vulgar debunking cannot be permitted to pollute the stream of justice—we are unhappy at the way in which the leaders of NBA and Ms Arundhati Roy have attempted to undermine the dignity of the Court. We expected better behaviour from them. After giving this matter thoughtful consideration and keeping in view the importance of the issue of Resettlement and Rehabilitation—we are not inclined to initiate contempt proceedings against the petitioners, its leaders or Arundhati Roy—after the 22nd of July 1999. Nothing has come to our notice which may show that Ms Arundhati Roy has continued with the objectionable writings insofar as the judiciary is concerned. She may have by now realized her mistake.

So, shall I heed the warning or persevere with the contumely?

To heed the warning might be prudent, but in my opinion it would undermine the dignity of Art. And, as we all know, there is no excuse for bad art. Just as much as the valley needs a writer, I believe that writers need the valley. Not just writers—poets, painters, dancers, actors, filmmakers—every kind of artist. If we are to remain alive, if we are to continue to work, we need to reclaim the political arena which we seem to have so willingly abdicated. If we choose to look away now, at this point—somehow it does not say very much about our art. I am not suggesting that everybody must turn out a hectoring, political manifesto. I am all for Matisse and goldfish on a window sill. All I mean is that from time to time we could lift our eyes from the page and acknowledge the condition of the world around us. Acknowledge the price that someone, somewhere far away is paying, in order for us to switch our lights on, cool our rooms, and run our baths.

Today the Sardar Sarovar Dam is 88 metres high. It has submerged only a fourth of the area that it will when (if) the dam reaches its full height of 138 metres. It is true that the government has already spent a lot of money on the project. But continuing with it would mean spending about six times that amount—throwing good money after bad. There is a detailed engineering proposal in place for how the dam can be used at the current height in order to take water straight to Kutchch and Saurashtra, if that is indeed what the government wants to do. Restructuring the project with this lower dam height would mean saving hundreds of thousands of people from certain destitution. It would mean saving thousands of hectares of forest. It would mean saving some of the most fertile agricultural land in Asia from submergence. It would mean having enough money to fund local water harvesting schemes in every village in Gujarat. It would mean a victory for non-violence and the principles of democracy. It would mean that we still have hope.

Let me end with a quote from a speech Jawaharlal Nehru made in November 1958 at the Annual Meeting of the Central Board of Irrigation and Power.

For some time past however, I have been beginning to think that we are suffering from what we may call the 'disease of gigantism'. We want to show we can build big dams and do big things. This is a dangerous outlook developing in India—it is the small irrigation projects, the small industries and the small plants for electric power which will change the face of this country far more than half a dozen big projects in half a dozen places...

Needless to say, this speech never made it into the school books. I have made myself very unpopular in India by saying the things I say. Fortunately, I am not standing for elections. As a writer, I would rather be loved by a river valley, than by a nation state.

Any day.

3

Understanding the Collapse of the Soviet Union

Hyung-Min Joo

Reflecting upon the meaning of the French Revolution half a century afterward, Tocqueville opened *The Old Regime and the French Revolution* with the apt comment:

No great historical event is better calculated than the French Revolution to teach political writers and statesmen to be cautious in their speculations; for never was any such event, stemming from factors so far back in the past, *so inevitable yet so completely unforeseen* (1983, p. 1. Emphasis added).

It appears to be the fate of social scientists to be baffled repeatedly by great but 'unforeseen' events. Yet ultimately and ironically their academic goal is to devise a story or theory that will make such unforeseeable events appear, in retrospect, to have been 'inevitable'. The collapse of the Soviet Union is no exception. Scholars were caught completely by surprise by one of the most earthshaking events in modern history. Privilege is rarely appreciated while it is possessed. How many scholars wished to be present when the Bastille was attacked, when Lenin raised the red flag triumphantly, and so on? How many future scholars will wish that they witnessed (or watched contemporaneously on television) the fall of the Berlin Wall? We are in a rare historical moment, but this privilege has its price. Scholars face the daunting task of groping their way toward a theoretical framework by which to understand the relevant features of this remarkable event, just as so many sophisticated analysts have contended with the French and the Russian Revolutions, and with each other. Ready or not, we are obliged to open a long process of defining, redefining, interpreting, and reinterpreting the collapse of Soviet communism.

At first glance the decline of laissez-faire might seem the very last place to begin when theorizing about this collapse but my contribution will begin here in the belief that the two great system failures of the modern era—laissez-faire and Soviet communism—are related in a significant way. Following a brief overview I examine Karl Polanyi's 'double movement' explanation of the decline of laissez-faire. According to Polanyi, when the market expanded and nearly became (with the state's blessing) a self-regulating system, it placed unbearable centrifugal pressure on the fabric of the entire society. In response, social actors organized to protect themselves from the deleterious effects of blind and unchecked market forces. As a result, laissez-faire was countered by these social protective movement(s).

In this essay I develop the corollary thesis of a 'reverse double movement'. I argue that as the Soviet state became ever more powerful, it also put unbearable stress upon ordinary people, fraying the fragile fabric of society. In response, actors 'intervened' in suitably discreet ways to protect themselves. As a result, the deleterious effects of the domineering state were countered to an indispensible degree by a 'protective social intervention'. In sum, there was a reverse double movement.

In order to constitute a satisfactory explanation, the reverse double movement thesis must deal with several vital questions. Why did this communist state become so overbearing as to evoke such protective social activities? Moreover, was there really latitude for such social 'counter-movements', despite the evident iron grip of the Soviet state? When the Bolsheviks came to power they had a genuine revolutionary dream of building a worker's heaven on earth. Since the proletariat were few and the people as a whole were not yet 'awake', the party leaders, who were also under severe external attack, resorted to a strong state as a temporary expedient by which to reach long-term revolutionary goals. The temporary, alas, froze into the permanent. As revolutionary zeal evaporated in the face of hard realities and mundane passions for power, there remained only the sweeping power of the state in all formal spheres of Soviet (and Soviet-dominated) life. The revolutionary dream manifested itself as a crude and unresponsive 'dictatorship over human needs'.

I will analyse the response of the Soviet citizenry to this bleak situation. Though deficient in many activities, the Soviet state was indisputably successful in the maintenance of its monopolistic power. Soviet leaders were extremely antagonistic toward any hint of a direct challenge. Unable to confront the state, Soviet people intervened *indirectly* in order to protect themselves. Their indirect social interventions cumulatively stirred development of 'parallel societies', composed of the official society which the state imposed, and of a second society through which the needs forbidden under a dictatorship were channelled and met. In this way, the deleterious effects of the overarching state were reduced, neutralized, and reversed for the benefit of society and perhaps also, ironically, enabled the state to exist for as long as it did.

This reverse double movement, unlike Polanyi's double movement, is entirely defensive in nature. In the long run, however, the widespread effects of the growth of a parallel society are much more than defensive. To illustrate why, it is helpful to use Hirschman's *Exit, Voice, and Loyalty*. In the Soviet Union, 'loyalty' obviously was compelled where it was not willingly given. 'Voice', whether through routine processes like political parties and interest groups or through radical processes like revolution, was silenced. Under such circumstances, 'exit' occurred. People withdrew their time, energy, and emotion from the official society to redirect it into their own second society. That is, there was an *internal* exit. All the necessary external formalities were observed but as the withdrawal proceeded slowly but continuously, the official system became an empty shell that few truly believed and supported anymore. This helps explain why such an outwardly imposing fortress suddenly could tumble like a house of cards.

Finally, I will combine the two great failures of the modern era— the decline of laissez-faire and the collapse of communism—to evoke the guiding metaphor of 'the bicycle'. Steering between these two great ideational forces societies have moved somewhat like a faltering bicycle. It tends to lose its balance when skewed to one direction or the other. Whenever such swerving occurs, social actors intervene to protect themselves as a part of a double movement or a reverse double movement, by compensating for the existing imbalance. In this sense, the two movements display the spontaneous and resilient tendency of society to defend itself in times of trouble. Finally, in the conclusion, several issues are discussed to avoid likely misinterpretations of the reverse double movement thesis: specifically, the problem of agency, the potential forms of a reverse double movement, and the actual degree of separability of a parallel society within the official one.

MAPPING AND POSITIONING

'A specter is haunting Europe—the specter of Communism.' When Marx and Engels wrote these prophetic words, they never imagined that it would be realized in the opposite way that they foresaw. The spectacle of the Soviet Union disappearing into the dustbin of history is now 'the specter' that is haunting us. Among scholars today there exist roughly eight rival schools of thought as to why it happened: eclecticism, nationalism, ideology, Weberian scheme, the Gorbachev factor, state-centred institutionalism, totalitarianism, and social mobilization. The most common approach is eclecticism, which lists a series of factors and argues that all of them, if in differing combinations, contributed to the outcome. Proponents include Daniel Chirot, Alexander Dallin, and Seweryn Bialer. By contrast, Ronald Suny, Leszek Kolakowski, and Kazimerz Poznanski single out one dominant factor and develop it to an extreme in order to view the collapse of communism from that illuminating angle. Ronald Suny makes nationalism the core of his 'accentuation'—to borrow from Weber—whereas both Kolakowski and Poznanski do so with communist ideology. Ken Jowitt elaborates a full-blown Weberian scheme, arguing that in the beginning the communist party was an amalgam of Weber's three types of legitimate domination: traditional authority, charisma, and rational bureaucracy. Whereas charisma is a purely personal quality, Jowitt deems the communist party as an expression of 'impersonal charisma'. Charismatic or not, the party could not escape the grinding force of 'routinization' and slowly became a self-maintaining 'machine'. There was more than just bureaucratization to blame because the communist party not only lost its charismatic mission but also became deeply corrupted. As a result, 'corrupt routinization' set in like a virus and grew ever worse.

At a more personalized level John Miller and Angus Roxburgh emphasize the importance of the Gorbachev *factor*. This Soviet version of 'great-man-history' is, like all such theories, highly problematic. It is wiser to incorporate the Gorbachev factor into one's theory, instead of founding the latter exclusively on a single leader's behaviour. For Phillip Roeder, accordingly, what is crucial is not a single ruler but the entire ruling regime. The Soviet regime collapsed because it could no longer adapt to ever-changing society. To explain the long process of regime sclerosis, Roeder develops what he calls state-centred institutionalism. Yet even his fine work is incomplete because of the two important processes in his theory—the rigid regime and the changing society—Roeder focuses exclusively on the regime side.

The Totalitarianism approach has had great public appeal yet supplied surprisingly few academic insights. According to scholars like Zbigniew Brzezinski, Martin Malia, and Richard Pipes, party control over Soviet society was 'total'. As the notion of totalitarianism implies, there could not exist any significant social dynamics that could underlay the collapse. Rather, the totalitarian regime came to power without significant support from society; hence, communists lost power without significant challenge from society too. Clearly, a social vacuum looms behind the theoretical threads of totalitarianism. The key rival of totalitarianism is the social mobilization approach. According to Moshe Lewin and Jerry Hough, party control over society fell far short of being total. As the communist regime modernized a basically peasant society, the Soviet citizenry became increasingly urbanized and educated. In the end, the regime could not keep up with newly mobilized social forces and the gap between the two increased untenably in the final decades of the state. According to this model, the events of the late 1980s and early 1990s exhibited neither a failed revolution from above nor an externally generated collapse. Rather, it was a 'middle class revolt' within an 'emerging civil society'. Though the party dominated the first half of the Soviet experience, it was the society that later played the role of a 'powerful system maker' or unmaker, as the case may be.

This essay is theroetically situated between totalitarianism and social mobilization approach, though leaning toward the latter. The main boast of totalitarianism is its correct prediction of the sudden end someday of the Soviet Union. The problem is that this collapse did not occur in a social vacuum. Communists, whatever they intended, never achieved a totalitarian reality. The considerable gap evident between the intent and the reality provides significant room for the social autonomy approach. Still, even this approach does tend to overstep the evidence by describing the events of 1991 largely as a middle class revolt or revolution from below.

So the analytical objective—a tricky one, indeed—is neither to ignore social dynamics nor overestimate them. For this purpose, it is necessary to examine the Soviet system from within. This is not because domestic social factors are the only cause of the collapse but because without them, our understanding of the experience would be radically incomplete. To approach from the inside is to identify a long and subtle process of social dynamics that finally rendered a collapse possible—though not inevitable. To expose this subtle process, we need to see beyond what is apparent to locate complex undercurrents that are invisible on the calm surface.

POLANYI'S DOUBLE MOVEMENT

Adam Smith viewed laissez-faire as a natural result of the human tendency 'to truck, barter, and exchange' (Smith 1976, p. 17). Out of this tendency arose local markets, which expanded to national markets and eventually international trade. The laissez-faire view of expanding markets as both natural and beneficial was challenged by Polanyi. According to him, there originally were many 'local' markets covering small geographical areas, and which were sometimes connected internationally, thus constituting 'foreign' trade. These local markets and international trade were not linked through 'domestic' markets. Rather, they revolved around cities and towns which quite deliberately impeded the growth of national markets: 'Far from "nationalizing" German economic life, the Hanse deliberately cut off the hinterland from trade' (Polanyi 1957, p. 63). The premier economic goal of cities and towns was the maintenance of their noncompetitive trade. The rise of national market was achieved only when the centralized state subdued local particularism to its administrative structure. In this sense, 'regulation and markets, in effect, grew up together' (ibid. p. 68).

The logic of markets, once established, dictated that it should be unfettered. This logic was the driving force behind 'the change from regulated to self-regulating markets' in the eighteenth century (Polyani 1957, p. 71). Laissez-faire as a self-regulating system meant that the entire economy should be directed by nothing but the vagaries of market prices. This required that everything necessary for production be made available for sale. 'Everything' included labour, land, and money. The problem was that these were 'obviously *not* commodities' (ibid., p. 72). Human (labour), environment (land), and capital (money) were not 'produced' in the first place in order to be sold. To overcome this problem, the notion of 'fictitious commodity' was developed (ibid., p. 72). Labour, land, and money henceforth were to be treated as if they were real commodities; their prices called, respectivelym wage, rent, and interest.

Laissez-faire did not result in the magical cornucopia ruled by the 'invisible hand'. Instead, the invisible hand produced 'satanic mills' and enormous social suffering as fictitious commodities became treated as if they were *real* commodities. As workers were 'bought', employers treated them as being as dispensable as any other commodity. Abusive and exploitative labour relations became prevalent. Land was treated likewise. As it was 'bought' up, neighbourhoods were abolished, people who had lived there for generations were forced out, and landscape was treated as the owner pleased. Finally, as money became an object of speculation, the capital market periodically liquidated business enterprises in a series of shortages and surfeits of money. These inflationary and deflationary effects were as disastrous to many businesses 'as floods and droughts in primitive society' (ibid., p. 73).

In sum, laissez-faire settled for nothing less than 'the running of society as an adjunct to the market' (ibid., p. 57). Instead of economy being embedded in social relations, social relations are dictated by the capricious market system. What proponents of laissez-faire failed to grasp was the fact that production factors such as labour, land, and money were more than just 'economic' factors. They were social in nature. For instance, labour was not just an economic category identifying people only as workers; rather, it denoted no less than full human beings who take on many roles and guises in any given society. Likewise, land was a different name for nature and for the delicate environment in which every society existed. When these simple truths were overriden in the utopian dream of laissez-faire, the effects on the lives of the vulnerable majority were 'awful beyond description' (ibid., p. 76). In the end, 'no society could stand the effects of such a system for the shortest stretch of time unless its human and natural substance as well as its business organization was protected against the ravage of this satanic mill' (ibid, p. 73). As a result, the tumultuous social history in the nineteenth century was that of a 'double movement' (ibid., p. 76) On the one hand, the market spread continuously to incorporate every aspect of society under its omnivorous logic. On the other hand, this extraordinary development was countered by a network of protective counter-movements, such as socialist parties, trade unions, labour movements, factory laws, unemployment insurance legislation, land laws, agrarian tariffs, and central banking systems. In this way, the self-regulating market was tethered and at least somewhat tamed (ibid., p. 201).

REVERSE DOUBLE MOVEMENT

On the basis of Polanyi's logic, a corollary thesis can be developed to understand the collapse of communism. As the Soviet state overexpands, it generates such tremendous pressure that the very fabric of society threatens to tear apart.[1] In response, ordinary actors intervene in the process to protect themselves. Behind the rapid collapse of Soviet communism is the slow rise of a 'reverse double movement' initiated by the spontaneous tendency of a resilient society to reorganize itself in times of trouble. Obviously, the crude form in which this reverse double movement is laid out here raises questions. Why should the overarching state become so unchecked as to evoke a reverse double movement? Moreover, is it not true that the lack of such social resistance is one of the defining characteristics of the Soviet experience? If there really is a reverse double movement, who are its main agents and how do they go about it?

The most challenging question is probably that of agency. The agents of the classic protective colunter-movement are clear enough: trade unions, socialist parties, and voluntary associations like the Owenite movement arose to protect 'workers' and their familes and communities (ibid., pp. 165–76). In the case of 'land' there also was a feudally motivated opposition from aristocrats and the clergies because of their vested interests. Peasants likewise raised a strong voice to protect their cultivatable land (ibid., pp. 183–91). Finally, in the case of 'money,' the state was the key contributing agent as it developed a modern banking system to protect business enterprises from, in essence, themselves as well as the fluctuating value of money (ibid., pp. 192–6). It is not so easy to identify the main agents of a reverse double movement. The Soviet Union was 'one day, a mighty empire, the next, rubble' (Pipes 1994b, p. 25). One does not spot any significant agents in such a 'quiet death'. (Poznanski 1992, p. 2) How then are we to understand this apparently agent-free phenomenon? It is interesting to notice that Tocqueville once was baffled by a similar puzzle. As he reflected upon the Ancien Regime, Tocqueville observed:

Once the bourgeois had been completely severed from the noble, and the peasants from both alike, and when a similar differentiation had taken place within each of these three classes, with the result that each was split up into a number of small groups almost completely shut off from each other, the inevitable consequence was that, though the nation came to seem a homogeneous whole, its parts no longer held together. *Nothing had been left that could obstruct the central government, but, by the same token, nothing could shore it up. This is why the grandiose edifice built up by our Kings was doomed to collapse like a card castle once disturbances arose within the social order* (1983, pp. 136–7. Emphasis added).

What Tocqueville sensed is that extreme centralization of political power has destabilizing as well as stabilizing effects. As the central government eliminates potential rivals, it builds a stable system because 'nothing had been left that could obstruct the central government.' An impregnable castle is built, but the stability of such a system is deceiving in the long run. When government monopolizes political power, it eliminates not only those who 'could obstruct' but also those who 'could shore it up'. As a result, there is no one left to defend the system when crisis strikes.

The Soviet central state was notoriously ruthless toward political rivals and this was true even during the 'liberal' periods of the NEP (New Economic Policy, 1921–8) and Khrushchev's thaw. In those periods the state made certain that 'liberalization' was accompanied by a tight political control so that relaxation in some areas could not spill over to politics—rather like China today (Fitzpatrick 1994, pp.

96–102). As a result, even those liberal periods were part of 'the false Thermidor' (Pipes 1994a, p. 369). What Soviet leaders did not realize, however, was that this apparent stability came at a steep price that they themselves had suppressed any awareness of. It was a process with which Tocqueville was familiar. A seemingly agent-free collapse can happen whenever and wherever there is extreme centralization.

Two questions linger. First, is it really possible to have an agent-free political collapse? Are we not missing something going on behind the scenes? The fundamental question is 'Who brought down the system?' Second, Tocqueville's thesis is applicable to any form of centralized rule. This brings up another question. Is communism just another instance of political dictatorship? Or is there more to it than that? This second question is discussed in the next section. The question of agency is dealt with in the fifth section.

DICTATORSHIP OVER HUMAN NEEDS

It is common to describe communism as just a modern instance of political dictatorship. Obviously, communism was a political dictatorship and probably one of its cruelest forms. There was, however, more to it. The Party dictatorship went well beyond political matters. Indeed, party control over society was meant to be all-encompassing (Malia 1994; Pipes 1990). Some scholars explain the Soviet period as part of the patterns of the tsarist omnipotent state. That is, the Russian tradition continued (Pipes 1990). Others develop more elaborate theories. For instance, Lindblom argues that elimination of the market necessarily leads to the rise of a powerful state (1977). As the 'invisible hand' is replaced by the 'iron fist', the state grows, performing functions that used to be or could be done by market.

There is no doubt that 'the Russian tradition' and 'elimination of market' help to explain the rise of the Soviet state, but their impact should not be overemphasized.The development of the strong state was not peculiar to the Soviet Union: it was a common characteristic of all communist countries. As for 'elimination of market', the facts simply do not fit the theory. According to the thesis, the Soviet state became powerful as it eliminated markets. That is, the state became powerful after markets were abolished. Such an understanding is to read history backwards. In reality, the 'effect', the growth of a strong state, preceded the 'cause', the elimination or subordination of markets. In 1922, Lenin intensified political control with the establishment of *Glavlit*, which censored 'not only the printed word but also all cinemas, theatres, musical performances, and even the circus' (Pipes 1994b, p. 63). This occurred even as Lenin was permitting markets through the launch of the NEP. In fact, the market system was maintained but political control tightened. That is, the state grew stronger while there were still markets. When the state became powerful enough under Stalin, it finally abolished the market system.

The Soviet state was not just another instance of tsarist Russian tradition. It was truly revolutionary. When they came to power, Bolsheviks did not just want to 'rule' their society. Instead, they had a revolutionary dream of 'creat[ing] a new society' (Hoskings 1993, p. 499). As early revolutionary zeal eroded, what remained was the iron grip of the state on all spheres of life. The principle was gone but the tool remained—or became the new principle. In this way, the 'iron cage' was born in a different sense from Weber's, yet through a similar process (Weber 1991, p. 181). Through such a tragic transformation the noble dream of communism manifested itself as an ironic self-betrayal.

Anyone who demonstrated the slightest will to challenge the Soviet system was harshly persecuted. Such political dictatorship went hand in hand with the command economy. The state decided what was to be produced and consumed. From the viewpoint of people, this meant it was not they themselves but the state that determined what goods and services they could and could not enjoy. For instance, even a cook in a restaurant could not make something special—that is, something unplanned—for customers 'without hard-to-get permissions' from the state (Havel 1985, p. 73). Though the customer had a capability to buy his 'special' meal and the cook had all the necessary materials, the meal could not be legally made unless it was 'approved' by the state.

In cultural areas the state maintained the right to determine what was to be allowed. In literature, the state required that only the members of the state-controlled writers' union could publish. As a result, literary expression was severely circumscribed. Similarly in music only 'approved' contents were to be composed and performed publicly. Any genre that displayed a 'corrupt spirit of bourgeois' such as jazz and rock-and-roll had to suffer from the whims of the Soviet leadership (Starr 1983). State control was no less severe in painting and cinema. The state censorship in painting ranged 'from the individual canvas to matchbox labels' (Alexeyeva 1985, pp. 3-4). Accordingly, everyone in all aspects of life was caught in the 'regulatory tangle of red tape' (Havel 1985, p. 73). It reached well into the tight regulation of politics, economy, literature, music, art, cinema, education, leisure, religion, sports, and so on. As a result, communism degenerated into a 'dictatorship over human needs'.[2]

PARALLEL SOCIETY

The predictable result of this 'Babuvian violent homogenization' was the prevalence of unsatisfied, ignored, and repressed needs (Feher et al. 1983, p. 227). In a democratic polity these forbidden needs of society would form the basis of organized social resistance, either to change the policies of the state through routine political channels like interest groups and political parties, or to change the very nature of the polity through revolutionary activity. None of these options were available to the Soviet people.

So then, 'was the glass totally empty?' (Di Palma 1991, p. 67) Historical evidence suggested otherwise. When official routes were closed, unsatisfied, ignored, and repressed needs eventually found their *own* ways to express and gratify themselves. Herein lay the origin of a 'curious and paradoxical feature of Soviet society' (Hoskings 1993, p. 219). The official efforts of the state to build a politically, economically, and culturally correct society were paralleled by cumulative social responses that gave rise to the 'second' society. Like Janus, the Soviet Union became a two-faced society—or 'parallel polis' (Benda 1988, p. 214).

Because the second society is unofficial (and formally non-existent), its activities are illegal or semi-legal. So legality could be used as a first indicator to distinguish the second society. Legality alone, however, does not exhaust the possibilities. For instance, legal activities such as 'garden plots' or 'private housings' were alien to or even contradictory to a Soviet communist ideology that suspected private property. Though these private activities were features of the second society, they were legalized by the Soviet state as it was forced to compromise with hard realities which its ideological zeal alone could not overcome. In those cases the first society could be said to be 'invaded' successfully by the second society insofar as the latter's activities are legalized. But legality alone is not sufficient to distinguish the two faces of Soviet society. A better way is to combine legality with ideology.

When the state became too powerful, it engaged in 'mounting a total assault on humans', upon their needs and desires (Havel 1985, p. 67). Such a system could not exist for long without developing forms of protective adjustment or evasion. Since direct challenges to the state were futile, protective social interventions were made indirectly by the widest assortment of affected actors. In this section, the parallel society is analysed in the realms of economy and culture (although they are not the only areas where the parallel society prospers).

SECOND ECONOMY

Rise of the Official Economy: When the Bolsheviks came to power, and the country plunged into a civil war abetted by foreign invaders, their initial economic policies were that of War Communism (1917–21) which placed the economy under state control through nation-alization of the means of production, introduction of compulsory labour, and the abolition of money. The zeal of the time was nowhere more evident than in the audacious but ill-fated attempt to create a moneyless economy. This was a result of a hyper-inflation that rendered money worthless. If the price of a particular good in 1917 was one ruble, the corresponding figure in 1923 was 100 million (Pipes 1990, p. 687). When the civil war ended, Lenin launched a more conventional set of policies under the New Economic Policy. The NEP (1921–8) was a compromise in which the state maintained control over heavy industries and finance while the rest was delegated to the market. Such a compromise was short-lived. When Stalin consolidated power, he abolished the NEP and launched the First Five Year Plan (1928–32) to pursue rapid industrialization and rural collectivization. The state-orchestrated planning system remained the core of the 'official' economy ever since.

The central planning system was a truly distinctive economic framework in which the 'laws of supply and demand did not apply' (Rutland 1994, pp. 132–3). *Gosplan*, the State Planning Committee, made a plan with specified output targets and drew up a grid chart, matching available resources with desired targets. The plan was then disaggregated into pieces. Some 60 to 70 economic ministries under Gosplan allocated these disaggregated targets to appropriate production units. Finally, Gossnab, the State Committee on Supplies, allocated necessary resources to production units so that they could fulfil targets. In this process, the role of market was minimal. This was demonstrated by the fact that prices remained practically 'unchanged' (Lindblom 1977, p. 292). Since markets were not employed in determining what was to be produced and thus consumed, consumer preference found little resonance. Instead, the state, or Party, alone determined what was produced, consumed, and invested (Binyon 1983, p. 15).

Problems of the Central Planning System: The command economy had other serious problems. Managers of production units learned early on that promised input materials often 'did not arrive on time or in the right amounts' (Verdery 1996, pp. 20–1). Knowing this, they responded in two ways. First, managers relied on expediters who employed various means to acquire the necessary materials. What was important in this process was *blat*, meaning 'personal influence', 'connections', or 'string-pulling'. Second, managers also demanded more investments and raw materials than they actually needed. Underlying such a response was what Kornai called the 'soft budget constraint' (1990, p. 20). That is, managers knew that the state would bail them out and so became increasingly insensitive to economic efficiency. Extra resources were hoarded and this hoarding had two crucial functions. The reserved materials could be kept for the next production cycle since shortages were chronic or they could be exchanged with other resources that the firm lacked. The result was widespread shortages.The paradox of the 'shortage economy' (Kornai 1980) was that shortages went hand in hand with waste of resources. Resources were not efficiently utilized even though they were desperately needed. In this sense, shortage and waste did 'necessarily presuppose and mutually condition each other' (Feher et al. 1983, p. 84). From the viewpoint of Soviet society, this meant that the same production resource was both underutilized through hoarding-up process and in short supply through shortages, the latter causing further waste of resources as it evoked another round of hoarding-up.

In the market system, competitive pressures weed out poor products. Lacking such guidance, central planners elect that the target should be *quantity* such as length, weight, volume, and so on. Literalness produced serious problems. For instance, the target assigned to one factory manufacturing sunglasses was the 'number' of sunglasses. The factory met its target of 13,000 pairs which, however, were 'so dark that you could not see the sun through them even when looking directly at it' (Binyon 1983, p. 15). This illustrated nicely the problem of quality control that tormented all communist economies. Even Khrushchev complained of 'the tradition to produce not beautiful chandeliers to adorn houses, but the heaviest chandeliers possible since its output is calculated in tons' (Lindblom 1977, p. 71). Similar phenomena were found in services. Restaurants had a fixed number of meals to serve, taxi drivers a fixed number of journeys to make, and so on. This produced such bizarre situations as 'empty trains rattl[ing] round the network to achieve the requisite monthly mileage' or 'tanker trucks prowl[ing] around the big cities washing the streets—and continue doing so even during a thunderstorm' (Binyon 1983, pp. 15–17).

Second Economy: People suffered from chronic shortages and poor 'quality' control meant that goods and services were produced that no one *really* wanted. These shortcomings form the basis on which the 'shadow' economy prospered. Instead of eliminating the market, Lenin's drastic measures ended up splitting the system into an official sector and 'alongside it, an illicit private sector, which followed the laws of supply and demand' (Pipes 1990, p. 700; Fitzpatrick 1994, p. 95). The second economy remained the indelible shadow of the official economy. As a result, the official economy was superimposed, and predicated upon, the huge shadow economy that followed the market.

There are always 'black markets' in any society. What is so special about the Soviet case? Consider the shadow economy of drugs in the US. What is problematic is the 'content' of the product, that is, drugs. Otherwise, there is little wrong with the way this second market operates. After all, it follows the laws of supply and demand. Almost the opposite is true in the Soviet case. What matters there is not the content. Indeed, most goods and services dealt in the shadow economy are legal in the Soviet Union. Instead, what troubles the state is the very existence of this second economy because it underlines, symbolically and physically, the serious faults of the command economy.

Invasion of Second Economy: In some cases the role of the second economy was so crucial that the state incorporated it into the official system. The garden plot could be cultivated by everyone. People grew agricultural products in the tiny 'garden' around their houses. Garden plots should not matter much because in total they represented only 2–3 per cent of the cultivated land (Shlapentokh 1989, p. 191). What troubled the state was the fact that they yielded private properties. That is, people grew and sold things outside the central planning system. From the very beginning, Soviet leaders had been a consistent enemy of private property. After all, Karl Marx declared 'the theory of Communism may be summed up in the single sentence: Abolition of private property' (Marx 1978, p. 484)—although what Marx actually meant by 'private property' was wealth-generating property such as factories and large farming estates, not private households. But even garden plots were reluctantly tolerated by early Soviet leaders as 'a temporary and unavoidable evil' (Fitzpatrick 1994, pp. 139, 153; Shlapentokh 1989, p. 160) As a result, a grudging relationship continued through the Soviet period. With only 2-3 per cent of the arable land they produced 22–40 per cent of the meat, 32–40 per cent of the milk, 60 per cent of potatoes, and 67 per cent of eggs in the Soviet Union (Shlapentokh 1989, p. 191; Hoskings 1993, p. 395). In the end, the state incorporated garden plots into the official system. During the mid-1970s, Brezhnev gave them enthusiastic support. The history of garden plots demonstrated how the state became disempowered by the ubiquitous social response to the official system. It was one of the moments when 'the power of the powerless' prevailed (Havel 1985, p. 23).

Considerable private activity was to be found in the housing sector. When the state failed to deliver adequate housing individuals built their own. The state yielded again by accepting such properties as legal and as a result, 60 years after the Revolution, approximately half the population resided in private housing. As late as 1975 about 30 per cent of new housing was completed by non-state *shabashniki* or 'moonlighters', who did the job in the evening or over weekends, using tools and materials illegally diverted from their regular jobs in the official economy (Grossman 1981, p. 73). Though legitimate, they were anathema to the Soviet communist ethos.

Who were the involved actors? There are three economic actors: state enterprises, collective farms, and individual households. Since they are involved in both production and consumption, we can draw a three-by-three matrix that maps nine types of economic interactions. The shadow economy is present in all nine interactions. It is especially 'rampant' in the 'state enterprise (producer)—state enterprise (consumer) interaction' and the 'household (producer)—household (consumer) connection'. Scholars contend that some are illegal 'black' markets whereas others are more or less allowable 'gray' or 'brown' markets (Katsenelinboigen and Levine 1981, pp. 64–8). 'Millions of Soviet people take part in the second economy as producers' (Shlapentokh 1989, p. 191). Specifically, the official Gosplan estimated the second economy involved 1.7–2 million people as full-time producers in the late 1970s. When part-time workers were included the figure rose to 17–20 millions (Rutgaizer 1992, pp. 40–1). Consumers of the second economy 'include practically the entire Soviet population' (Shlapentokh 1989, p. 191). That people from all walks of life were involved was demonstrated in survey data. Grechin found that 17 per cent disapproved of stealing of state property but 77 per cent were extremely hostile to violation of private property (ibid., pp. 90–1). The dominant feature of second economy activities was that it was apolitical in nature, with motives ranging from desperate need to naked greed. The vast scope of the second economy testified that the official doctrine never shaped what people *really* thought nor how they behaved.

How large was the second economy? Data about the official Soviet economy are unreliable and therefore estimating the size of the shadow economy can be extremely difficult. Even 'an educated guess' is difficult (Grossman 1981, p. 82). But there have been serious efforts. For instance, in his survey of the *Current Digest of the Soviet Press* for 1982–3, Feldbrugge found that (1) most crimes reported in the Soviet press were related to second economy activities and (2) that reported crimes covered the entire Soviet Union (1984, pp. 532–41). It seemed the entire Soviet society 'fell into the zone of the dominant second economy' (Shlapentokh 1989, p. 71).

One of the most popular second economy goods was automobiles. The official auto-industry had shown so poor a performance that the waiting list period usually was several years. In response, the black market grew larger. Since building cars within the second economy was practically impossible, many automobiles built in the official economy began to slip into the shadow market. It was reported that in Rostov oblast in a two-year period, 1,000 out of 3,500 cars held for the rural population were, in fact, sold to 'non-rural' people. In this case, the second economy constituted about 30 per cent of the official automobile industry (O'Hearn 1980, p. 220). Interestingly, although car ownership increased, it was not accompanied by a corresponding surge in 'official' gasoline sale (Alexeev 1987, p. 1). This was because so much official petrol slipped into the shadow economy. Only 13.5 per cent of the 8.5 million rubles of fuel in Omsk was officially purchased in 1971. The remaining 'unofficial' consumption was from the second economy based on pilfered petrol. 'Even by the most conservative estimates,' however, the official *Izvestiya* reported, 'more than a third of private motorcars drove on state petrol' (O'Hearn 1980, p. 221). Probably, the national average lay somewhere between those two extreme figures, 'perhaps in the 45–50 per cent range' (Alexeev 1987, p. 14).

A large second economy also arose in agriculture and fishing. Gravryhyod estimated that the annual 'private' catch in internal waters was 1.5 million centres while the total industrial catch was 4.5 million. So the second economy constituted about 33 per cent of the fish industry. The state-enforced low official price combined with an insufficient supply in the widespread shadow economy produced a parallel price-structure. For instance, trout, officially 1.5 rubles per kilo, could usually fetch 7 rubles on the shadow market. Also, in the case of saiga, the *real* price could get 10 times as much as the official price (O'Hearn 1980, p. 222).

The shadow economy flourished in the repair industry 'for quite simple reasons' (Hoskings 1993, p. 382). For instance, a Soviet driver who needed to replace his wiper or fan belt knew that official suppliers were unable to help him, at least not without long delay.

As a result, he went to an 'unofficial' supplier who met his need immediately at much higher prices. In this way, the second economy generated a burgeoning repair industry. In the late 1970s, it was estimated that about 58–60 per cent of private cars, 50–55 per cent of shoes, 30–67 per cent of electrical appliances, and 84 per cent of furniture were repaired in the shadow economy (Neuhauser and Gaddy 1989, p. 29; Shlapentokh 1989, p. 192). As in the case of foods, shadow production of clothing was usually on a small scale and distribution so informal that a quantified estimation was difficult. But there were ways. Consider muskrat pelts used for hats. As official supplies were short, most people resorted to the second economy. As a result, about 80 per cent of the total muskrats were caught privately (O'Hearn 1980, p. 223). About 55 per cent of clothes were repaired in the shadow economy in the late 1970s (Neuhauser and Gaddy 1989, p. 29).

Out of the severe housing shortage rose the shadow housing industry, dominated by workmen called *shabashniki* who always had more and better materials than official enterprises like Zarya (O'Hearn 1980, p. 225). Indeed, Zarya may well have had inadequate supplies because shabashniki had a complete selection. It was estimated that every year, about 120,000 flats were built in Moscow, totaling 14.4 million rubles. Official builders, however, took only four to five million rubles. 70 per cent of the money spent on housing went to shadow builders and 40–76 per cent of houses were repaired in the shadow industry (Neuhauser and Gaddy 1989, p. 29; Shlapentokh 1989, p. 192). In some cases, not only some branches of economy but the whole republic fell into the second economy. This was true of the trans-Caucasian and Central Asian republics. Even the officials admitted that of the total sum spent by Georgians on housing repair and decoration, 98–99 per cent went to the shadow economy (O'Hearn 1980, p. 225). Though such an extremely high level of private activity was not normal, the unbelievably huge shadow sector in Georgia was indicative of the ease with which individuals could deal with the ineffective and inefficient official system by developing their own parallel society.

The second economy was no less permanent than the official economy itself. Also, it covered not remote regions but the entire Soviet Union. Furthermore, it included 'almost all kinds of goods and services' (Simes 1975, p. 48). All these points added up to the conclusion that the shadow economy was a fact of life just like the official economy, if not more so. As it mirrored problems integral to the central planning system, the shadow economy was echoing the voice of 'the silent, or rather silenced' (Lukes 1985, p. 13).

Second Culture: Samizdat in Literature

'The creation of a new culture' was one of the foremost goals of the revolutionary leaders (Rywkin 1989, p. 183). The new culture was supposed to be 'proletarian' though what that meant was never clear. What did become ominously clear was that it should be 'an area of ideological work' (White 1990, p. 1). That is, culture was to be an instrument of the state. As Sandor Boros, a former Hungarian deputy culture minister, recollected, 'We used to really impose culture on people: we told them what they were interested in and needed' (ibid., p. 118). As a result, the official culture was 'a culture constructed, promoted, and even financed by the state' (Stites 1992, p. 5). The state alone decided what kind of books people could read, what kind of songs people could hear, what kind of movies people could see, and even what kind of dances people could dance. Actors with unsatisfied cultural needs responded by expressing themselves in their *own* way outside the rigid framework of official culture. People wrote, read, sang, and danced 'the way they wanted' whenever possible. As a result, the state found that its people 'loved what they were supposed to laugh at' (ibid., p. 133) Such social resistance formed the basis of the 'second culture'. In this section, the establishment of the official culture and the resulting social response with the second culture are analysed in the case of literature.

The Establishment of the Official Culture: The NEP encouraged reconciliation with the peasantry and the bourgeois. The compromise commenced during the civil war when military specialists and technical experts were desperately needed. In the 1920s, it extended to other branches like science, education, literature, and arts. Such relaxation led to the formation of 'fellow travelers' who were neither for nor against the proletariat. Instead, they wanted to promote their own specialties and careers. While there were Bolsheviks who favoured strong state intervention in culture, their voice was muted because the party kept aloof from direct involvement in cultural matters. As Trotsky summed up, 'the party is not called upon to command' there (McCauley 1993, p. 73).

The situation changed with the rise of Stalin. The defeat of Bukharin, long known as the protector of the non-party intelligentsia, was the death-knell of a flexible cultural policy. The proponents of the proletarian culture (*proletkult*) now asserted themselves with the establishment of the state-sponsored Russian Association of Proletarian Writers (RAPP). These proponents of 'cultural revolution' claimed to speak on behalf of the proletariat, condemned fairy tales, folk music, jazz, and science movies as the spillover of decadent bourgeois intellectuals, produced for the 'unhealthy appetites' (Stites 1992, p. 64). These proponents of proletarian culture won the day. Their victory was, however, temporary. This was because the RAPP was 'genuinely concerned' about revolutionary ideals and so believed that it had a responsibility to tell the whole truth including 'warts and all' (McCauley 1993, p. 97). Obviously, the RAPP failed to understand Stalin. In 1932 the party disbanded it to set up its replacement, the Union of Soviet Writers, which all those who wished to publish had to join. This was aligned with what was happening in other fields such as music, painting, cinema and so on. The goal was to have just one organization under its control, catering for all involved in a particular pursuit with the party directing its activities. 'Warts' were not literary material. The intention of the state was spelled out at the First Congress of the Union of Soviet Writers in 1934. Speaking for Stalin, Andrei Zhdanov called for a new framework inside which all cultural actors must work. This new framework was 'socialist realism'. In principle, socialist realism meant the comprehensive depiction and interpretation of life by art from the viewpoint of approved social relations. Any cultural expression was allowed only 'so far as it was in accordance with the goals of the Communist Party' (ibid., p. 98). Everything else was 'to be barred' (Rywkin 1989, p. 185). The solution reached by Stalin was to direct cultural actors to produce 'correct' works (Stites 1992, p. 72).

Samizdat—The Second Culture in Literature: Writers who would not bend were expelled from the Union of Soviet Writers. This meant that they could not publish anything officially. People responded by what was called *samizdat* (self-publication). Samizdat referred to the phenomenon of widely circulated clandestine publications without censorship. Those secret publications were produced, reproduced, and circulated 'through self-generated, improvised networks', in which involved actors were single individuals (Di Palma 1991, p. 71). The author typed his uncensored work with four or five carbons, which he then passed to other people in his samizdat group. If others found his work interesting, they also made more copies to distribute them further. Through this snowballing, samizdat continued to spread to various regions, 'overcoming Gutenberg' (Feldbrugge 1975, p. 3). Samizdat was, of course, inefficient in terms of time and energy but the message was clear, 'if the bureaucrats won't print it, we'll get it around *ourselves*' (Saunders 1974, p. 8).

Samizdat was composed of spontaneous small-scale unofficial publications. Indeed, many individuals involved in the samizdat movement considered themselves as its originator. For instance, the memoirs of Anatoly Krasnov-Levitin, Andrey Amalrik, Vladimir Bukovsky, and Pyotr Grigorenko showed that each was convinced that samizdat was born in his circle (Alexeyeva 1985, p. 14). Though each of those groups was unaware of other samizdat activities beyond its own, each in the end responded to the official culture in a strikingly similar way. This illustrated the spontaneous, yet inevitable, response of society to a dictatorship over human needs.

Samizdat in Early Years: Samizdat originated in the 1920s. In their struggle against Stalin, some Left Oppositionists used the same method that was later called samizdat (Saunders 1974, p. 8). Samizdat at the time was, however, not a mass phenomenon. Rather, it was a factor in power struggles among ruling factions. In the 1950s, poetry was dominant, probably because it was easier to reproduce. As one noted, there was 'overflowing with poetry of the censored, forgotten, and persecuted poets' (Alexeyeva 1985, p. 13). By the early 1960s essays, short stories, and even novels began to circulate. Novels circulated at the time were usually translations of foreign works, including Hemingway's *For Whom the Bell Tolls*, Koestler's *Darkness at Noon*, Orwell's *1984*, and Milovan Djilas' *The New Class* (Shlapentokh 1989, p. 198). Boris Pasternak's *Doctor Zhivago* (1958) was one of the first original works distributed in samizdat. This whole process gave rise to the term *tamizdat,* meaning 'publishing over there'. Other than its beautiful story, *Doctor Zhivago* revealed the tragic message of Soviet society.[3] According to the official social realism, books like *Doctor Zhivago* reflected the decadent bourgeoisie mentality. The resulting state repression did not decrease even after the novel received the Nobel Prize. In fact, not until the late 1980s was *Doctor Zhivago* officially published (Rywkin 1989, p. 187). Soviet people, however, knew and read the book *somehow.* That 'somehow' part was what samizdat was all about. Many original books appeared in samizdat during the late 1960s. These included famous works like Vasily Grossman's *Forever Flowing,* Venidikt Yerofeyev's *Moscow to the End of the Line,* and Vladmir Maksimov's *Seven Days of Creation.* Also, the most influential works at the time such as Solzhenitsyn's *Cancer Ward,* Amalrik's *Will the Soviet Union Survive until 1984?,* and Sakharov's *Thoughts on Progress, Peaceful Coexistence, and Intellectual Freedom* appeared in samizdat in the late 1960s (Feldbrugge 1975, pp. 110--11).

Politicization of Samizdat: The authorities responded quickly and harshly. The state knew very well what was at stake. After all, the success of Lenin was also facilitated by his own version of samizdat: *Pravda* and *Iskra* (Shlapentokh 1989, p. 198). As state repression increased, the whole phenomenon became less a cultural matter and more a political one. A good example that testified this new trend was the rise of the *Chronicle of Current Events* in 1968. As its name implied, the *Chronicle* intended to report violations of human rights. Not surprisingly, the *Chronicle* received the brunt of the attack. Due to severe repression the *Chronicle* stopped functioning in 1972.

The state might take out some samizdat here and there but the phenomenon was so spontaneous and widespread that the state could never rub it out (Alexeyeva 1985, p. 319). Instead of explicitly political contents like the *Chronicle,* poems and novels became the main menu of samizdat as in the early years. There was, however, an important difference. Even poems and novels that appeared during this period contained political messages. A good example was Solzhenitsyn's *Gulag Archipelago.* which was introduced to Soviet people through a tamizdat-samizdat process (Feldbrugge 1975, pp. 180–1). Like *Doctor Zhivago,* it also won the Nobel Prize in spite of, *or* because of, state repression. Like Pasternak, Solzhenitsyn was attacked as a 'traitor'. As in the case of *Doctor Zhivago*, Soviet people read *Gulag Archipelago*, though the book was never officially published until 1989. In this way, people showed who the *real* traitor was.

The whole incident of *Gulag Archipelago* prompted another round of repression. In response, samizdat again became political. This trend of politicization was nicely illustrated by two events. Sakharov wrote his *Thoughts on Progress, Peaceful Coexistence, and Intellectual Freedom* in 1985. The *Thoughts* was one of the most popular items in samizdat, and Sakharov became the third Russian involved in samizdat to receive a Nobel Prize. Unlike his predecessors, his field was not literature. Instead, he won a Nobel 'Peace' Prize. That is, the third Nobel that samizdat reaped was blatantly political in nature, not cultural. The *Chronicle of Current Events* resumed publication—though the editors of the *Chronicle* never really stopped their work after no. 27 appeared. They continued to collect materials and in early May 1974, nos 28, 29, and 30 appeared simultaneously. Ten days later, no. 31 was also published (Alexeyeva 1985, p. 327; Feldbrugge 1975, p. 50).

The politicization of samizdat went a step further with *Memory* and *Quest*. From 1976 to 1983, six collections of *Memory* (*Pamyat*) were issued. In the foreword, the editors of *Memory* declared that their underground journal was 'to be the collection of historical testimony and its publication' (Alexeyeva 1985, p. 353). The importance of such a task was emphasized because history was constantly distorted. As a result, *Memory* gave special attention to the Soviet period to find and preserve what *really* happened. This was a vital need of Soviet society because as the editors' foreword read, 'whenever social memory is destroyed, the possibility for all kinds of misfortune and adversity exists'. The coming of *Memory* demonstrated that now people denied the 'official' version of history which had been taught repeatedly throughout their life. Instead, they tried to 'correct' it by investigating the past by themselves. The politicization of samizdat in the late 1970s and early 1980s proceeded to such a level that even history itself became a parallel structure.

In 1979, *Quest* (*Poiski*) appeared as a literary-publicist journal, averaging 200–300 pages per issue. At the time, *Quest* bore the legend 'a free Moscow Journal'. As the legend revealed, *Quest* offered a nonpartisan forum for *all* points of ideas. This was shown clearly in its first issue with the 'invitation':

Bitterness and enmity between those seeking different solutions have made the general impasse even deeper and more aggravating. The editors of Quest appeal for *give-and-take and patience* in the interests of looking for a way out of *our general misfortune* (Alexeyeva 1985, p. 354. Emphasis added).

First, the journal clearly identified the contemporary situation of Soviet society with 'general misfortune'. Second, the origin was traced to the ideological rigidity of communism. As a result, the suggested solution was 'give-and-take and patience'. The ideological monopoly of communism was finally challenged. In its place, ideological pluralism was 'invited'. Obviously, such a direct challenge could not escape repression. Due to arrests of its editors, *Quest* ceased in 1980. In the same year, however, a new samizdat called *Quest and Thought* appeared. As the name implied, the journal was the children of *Quest*. In fact, the editors admitted that their journal was 'a direct continuation of *Quest*' (ibid., p. 375). Clearly, the situation was such that when Menocchio was executed, 'Marcato, or perhaps Marco' soon appeared with different names but similar ideas (Ginzburg 1984, p. 128).

Large and Growing: Considering the primitive methods involved, however, the most notable samizdats were produced and distributed with remarkable effectiveness. Even lengthy works which required extensive typing often found their way to readers at distant regions in spite of 'the weak connection or absence of connection between the source and the reader' (Feldbrugge 1975, p. 18). How widespread was the samizdat movement? Ironically, data for the answer came from the state itself. During the 1970s and early 1980s, the attack on samizdat was conducted not only in Moscow but also in Leningrad, Kaluga, Obninsk, Sverdlovsk, Voronezh, Bobrov, Smolensk, Rostov, Sochi, Tomsk, Novosiirsk, Krasnoarsk, Irkutsk, other provincial areas, and non-Russian republics. The extensive attacks demonstrated how widespread the samizdat movement was in Soviet society. Moreover, in spite of increasing state repression, samizdat was in fact growing as time went on (Alexeyeva 1985, p. 377). Samizdat was not a peculiar phenomenon found only in remote places for short periods. Many people were involved in samizdat as its author, distributor, or reader.

This did not mean, however, that the phenomenon had a single overarching view. What samizdat reflected was views, not the view. In fact, that was the whole point of the samizdat movement. It echoed various voices silenced by *the* single voice of the dictatorship over human needs. Like an undercurrent, it was 'expressing what was probably the deepest layer of values' of Soviet people (Stites 1992, p. 144). As a result, some sang beautiful poems in a world of bleakness. Some sought for forbidden stories of love. Some despaired of the horror of the Stalin years. Nobody in samizdat, however, praised the official system. After all, that was a job done faithfully by socialist realism.

EXIT, VOICE, AND LOYALTY

The focus in the previous section was on economy and literature, but the parallel structure was prevalent throughout the entire sphere of Soviet society, including music, cinema, dance, history, education, ideology, religion, medical system, and so on. The shadow society was as widespread as the official one. In fact, the second society was prevalent *because* the first society was prevalent. A phenomenon so widespread and deep could not exist for long without affecting the Soviet system. The effects of the shadow society are both material and mental. First, consider the 'material' side. As many have noticed, the shadow economy fulfils the indispensable function of filling in the holes of the official command economy. The rigidity of the central plan and the resulting shortages are considerably eased by the second economy. That is, the shadow economy was inadvertently an important force of stabilization for 'lubricating the system' (Altman 1980, p. 60). Some scholars even argue that 'the planned economy is held together by the baling wire and chewing gum of the parallel markets' (O'Hearn 1980, p. 231) Indeed, one wonders whether the official command economy could have existed for so long without its 'shadow'. In this sense, the second economy is 'supplementary' to the official sector (Feher et al. 1983 p. 99).

In spite of its supplementary function, the shadow economy introduced disturbing obstacles to the central planning system because of its 'depletive' nature (O'Hearn 1980, p. 230). Like a double-edged sword, it both helps and hurts the official command economy.

The shadow economy can function only if it successfully siphons off the real or potential resources of the official economy to its arena. The shadow economy must be depletive or parasitic in the first place to be supplementary later. Like a strange medicine, it cures only after infecting first. When the shadow economy in housing had a better selection of building materials than official Zarya, it was due to illegal transfer from the official sector. This 'pilfering' is not limited to the housing sector. Indeed, stealing from the state is prevalent in 'the food and light industries, their outlets, cafeterias and restaurants, hospitals, kindergartens, rest homes, as well as the industries producing electrical appliances, watches, car parts' (Shlapentokh 1989, p. 215). Simply put, it is 'practiced by virtually everyone' (Grossman 1981, p. 75). For instance, out of 1.6 million car parts produced by WAZ, the car plant on the Volga River, 1.1 million were stolen (Shlapentokh 1989, p. 215). The prevalence of 'pilfering' was nicely demonstrated by the survey of Soviet people that reveals their 'complacency towards theft from public concerns' (Altman 1980, p. 60). In fact, they strongly 'disapprove of those who do not engage in it' (Grossman 1981, p. 75). As one puts, 'it's a crime *not* to steal' (Bushnell 1980, p. 187. Emphasis added).

Time and energy of Soviet people are also affected. That is, the shadow economy depletes *labour* itself. The existence of the second economy means that there now exists a parallel wage system: the official wage from the command economy and the shadow wage from the second economy (Feher et al. 1983, p. 100). Under such circumstances, people have a clear incentive to 'relax' during working hours to reserve more energy for their 'moonlighting'. Also, moonlighting is sometimes done during official working hours. Treml finds that 12.1 per cent of official working hours were actually spent on various shadow economy activities in the 1970s (Treml 1992, pp. 37–9). In this case, the term 'daylighting' is more appropriate. When 'relaxation', 'moonlighting', and 'daylighting' are combined, the result is obvious. The shadow economy depletes labour, thus reducing the productivity of the official sector.

Being supplementary, the second economy helps to integrate production with consumption in Soviet society and is the lubricant that smoothes out the worst dysfunctions of the rigid central planning system. This is, however, done only at the price of disintegrating production itself. As various resources and labours of the official economy are appropriated, the shadow economy depletes the official sector. There are some elements of truth in the argument that the first economy could not have functioned for so long without the shadow economy. The other side of the story is that the first economy did not function in its full strength because of its overarching shadow.

Second, consider the 'mental' impact of the shadow society. Indeed, what is involved is more than just material sides because the essence of the parallel society is the 'spirit of defiance' (Lyons 1967, p. 317). People refuse to accept what is imposed upon them by force. This does not necessarily mean that they challenge the official system directly. As mentioned several times, the state is strong enough to punish explicit dissent. Instead, people try to create a structure in which 'the voice of the ruling power is heard only as an insignificant echo from a world that is organized in an entirely different way' (Jirous 1988, p. 227). The parallel society is not about a revolution. Rather, it is a manifestation of the spontaneous tendency of society to reorganize itself for protection in times of stress.

People withdrew their resources, time, energy, and emotion from the official society and entered the shadow society. As 'loyalty' and 'voice' were not available in any meaningful sense, people made an 'exit' from the official system to the shadow society. That is, there was an internal exit. As the withdrawal proceeded slowly but continuously, the official system eventually became an empty shell no one truly believed or supported. Behind the sudden and rapid collapse of communism was this slow, yet continuous and ubiquitous, rise of the parallel society that constituted a long and subtle process of social dynamics that finally rendered the collapse possible. In this sense, although the parallel society was not a revolution per se, its impact was truly revolutionary.

As Vaclav Havel pointed out, the situation was similar to that of the emperor without clothes. It was a world of empty 'appearances trying to pass for reality' (1985, p. 30). It falsified the past. It falsified the present. It falsified the future. It pretended that repression was not there. It pretended that socialist utopia was real. It pretended that the emperor was not naked. In response, people pretended to believe it was so. Most importantly, everyone in this process 'pretends to pretend nothing' (ibid., p. 31). Probably the most destabilizing incident under such circumstances was for the emperor *himself* to cry out loud that he was in fact naked. This Gorbachev did. Once this was done, the unraveling process began with rapidity and to completion. What Gorbachev really had in mind was to change the rule of the game so that the game could continue. It was, however, soon clear that people had more than that in their mind. They refused to play the game itself. As a result, the centre could no longer hold. A rapid and complete collapse ensued. In this way, the parallel society revealed 'the power of the powerless' (ibid., p. 23).

THE BICYCLE

The main goal of this essay is to understand the collapse of communism from *inside*, that is, from domestic social dynamics that rendered the sudden collapse possible. This goal is pursued with a rather odd move in the sense that we began to theorize a reverse double movement by first looking at nineteenth-century England. This approach, however, enables us to recognize a counter-intuitive parallelism between the failure of laissez-faire and the collapse of communism. As a result, to approach from inside in the end yields a theoretical framework that goes indeed beyond the 'inside'. That is, it is both possible and necessary to locate the Soviet experience in a longer trajectory of modern history. This point needs more elaboration.

According to Etzioni, there are three major sources of control, of which allocation and manipulation account for the foundations of social order: 'coercive, remunerative, and normative' (1975, p. 5). Lindblom identifies three organizing principles of society: 'exchange, authority, and persuasion' (1977, p. 12). The market corresponds to 'exchange' mechanism whereas the state corresponds to 'authority' relation. 'Persuasion' is dominant in what Lindblom calls 'the preceptoral system' in which the role of unilateral indoctrination is maximized (ibid., p. 54). A good example is Maoist China during the Cultural Revolution. It is, however, questionable whether Maoist China had a fundamentally distinctive system. Rather, it seems that China during the Cultural Revolution was basically a communist state based on the iron grip of the party. It is true that the role of 'persuasion' was emphasized to the extreme. That was, however, done by the state. As a result, the preceptoral system seems to be a branch of 'authority' relations. Also, note how essential 'persuasion' is to the market. The commercialization of a capitalist society with the increasing role of advertisement illustrates the implicit yet fundamental function of persuasion in the market system. As a result, persuasion is not really a 'third' principle. Rather, it is integral to the market and the state as both attempt to maintain themselves. As a result, there are not three but two organizing principles of society in the modern era: the market and the state.

When those two fundamental principles are overemphasized, they often end up with utopian ideals. Laissez-faire is the extreme case of the market principle and communism is that of the state principle. Applied to a real world, however, those utopian ideals have not produced utopian realities. Instead, the most thoroughgoing destruction of society is carried out . Instead of 'invisible hand' and 'worker's heaven', they have produced a 'satanic mill' and a 'dictatorship over human needs'. As such, they represent the two great failures of our time.

Having observed the first great failure, Polanyi developed the double movement thesis. Laissez-faire meant that everything should adapt to the self-regulating market. Simply put, the entire society must be marketized. This included labour, land, and money. The problem was that those production factors were more than just economic resources. They were the very fabric of society. As a result, laissez-faire proceeded only at the direct expense of social cohesion. In response, various social actors including the state intervened as a double movement to protect society from the blind forces of the market. The self-regulating market was regulated.

We have recently observed the second great failure of the modern era: the collapse of communism. When communists came to power in Russia, their dream eventually ended up with a dictatorship over human needs which brought about a great human tragedy. Unable to challenge the strong state directly, people intervened in the process to protect themselves by developing a parallel structure through which their forbidden needs were channelled. In this way, the deleterious effects of the overarching state were reduced. This defensive social intervention was the origin of a reverse double movement. As people withdrew their time, energy, and emotion from the official system, it became eventually an empty shell no one truly believed or supported. As a result, power became powerless in the end. Although the dictatorship over human needs assumed that people were passive objects of manipulation, their very thoughts, dreams, aspirations, hopes, frustration, anger, and sorrow profoundly influenced the evolution of Soviet society.

The invaluable lesson of the two great failures is that anything extreme is extremely dangerous. On the one hand, radical liberals still praise the magical touch of the 'invisible hand'. Arguably, the self-regulating market system was once effective during the Manchesterian era. As Taylor points out, however, 'those days are gone forever' (1990, p. 97). On the other hand, stubborn Marxists still argue that the collapse of the Soviet Union does not mean much because it was not really communism. The argument is true but pointless. The genuine communism they want is unlikely to be realized in this earthly world. That is the whole point the failure of many 'communisms' has demonstrated repeatedly in the last century. It is time to stop criticizing existing capitalism in favour of imagined communism that exists only in Marx's writings. As the 'invisible hand' illustrates, imagined capitalism is no less heavenly than imagined communism.

The painful experiences of eighteenth-century England and the Soviet Union warn that neither of the two organizing principles of society, whether the market or the state, can be blindly applied to the exclusion of the other. A safe path, if there is any, is probably somewhere between those two with 'some mix of market and state orchestration'. In this sense, the two great failures represent the two poles between which society has moved in the modern era. At one end of this political economy continuum is laissez-faire with the maximized role of the market. At the other end lies communism with the overarching state. Between these two extremes, society of our time has behaved somewhat like riding a faltering bicycle. Often, it tends to lose its balance, being skewed to one direction or the other. When such imbalance occurs, however, various actors intervene to protect themselves as a double movement or as a reverse double movement, to correct a dangerous imbalance. Of course, this does not mean that balance will always be maintained. The bicycle sometimes falls. Even in that case, however, the collapsing process is a radical means of correcting an existing imbalance. Through that painful process, the bicycle starts anew with and for a new balance.

No one knows how the balance will be maintained or how it will be lost. Only time will tell. The only comfort history bestows on us is the lesson of the two great failures of our time. Whatever formula society develops, extreme ones will be eventually countered by social actors who attempt to correct the resulting imbalances through a painful process of a double movement or a reverse double movement. In this sense, the two movements are the expression of the spontaneous and resilient tendency of society to reduce, neutralize, and reverse dangerous imbalances successfully or unsuccessfully so that 'the bicycle' can go on or, if necessary, start anew.

CONCLUSION

It is probably a general tendency of scholars to overread or under-read other's work. This is not necessarily bad because through that process, innovation often comes. In some cases, however, overinterpretation and underinterpretation become extreme to such a degree that the implications of the original work are distorted. To avoid that, it is necessary to clarify a few points. First, consider the question of agency. As communism exerted an unbearable control over the entire society, almost the whole of it suffered from a dictatorship over human needs. In response, social actors intervened as a part of a reverse double movement to protect themselves by developing the parallel society. Who was the agent in this process? Everyone was. Virtually everybody in the Soviet Union was involved in various second society activities in one way or another. In fact, just because almost everyone was the agent of a reverse double movement, we have the agency problem in the first place. 'Visibility' is reduced by 'multitude'.

Second, why was it that the parallel society became the form of a reverse double movement in the Soviet Union? Unable to challenge the state directly, various actors tried to express themselves by developing a parallel society. That is, the rigidity of the state was crucial to the origin of the parallel society. When the state is flexible enough, however, a reverse double movement may take a different form. It is quite plausible to have a scenario in which the state itself recognizes existing imbalances. In that case, the state can be an agent of a reverse double movement as it tries to correct the imbalance through reforms. An obvious reference point is the experience of post-Mao China. As the British state in the nineteenth century was a crucial agent of a double movement, contemporary China demonstrates that the state can also play an important role in a reverse double movement. In this sense, the state is one of the crucial social actors, a point often missed by the 'civil society' argument.

Finally, the official society and the second society are not two separate entities. Such is never possible. Like Janus, Soviet society had two faces but the point is that those two faces were intermingled. There was no such thing as two Soviet *societies*. Two examples should be enough to demonstrate this point. A first case is from Altman's example of a biscuit factory (Altman 1980, p. 62). In this case, a Soviet biscuit factory produced 'official' biscuits and 'informal' biscuits side by side. In fact, the official biscuits and the shadow biscuits were completely identical, made of the same ingredients by same workers, even packed under identical labels. The only difference was that at the end of the process, the two biscuits were sent to different places: the official biscuits to the state and the second biscuits to shadow consumers. A second example is the 'garden plot'. As argued, the private plot was legalized by the state as it could not successfully deal with food shortages. The legality of the garden plot was, however, spurious because the garden plot could function only with 'illegally obtained' seed, fertilizer, fodder, and manure (Grossman 1981, p. 72). As a result, the legal part of the garden plot appeared only as 'a visible tail wagging an invisible dog' (Feldbrugge 1984, p. 530). It might well be the case that the typewriter used for samizdat during the night was, in fact, used during the day to type an official decree that denounced samizdat (ibid. 1975, p. 17). The conceptual dichotomy of the parallel society does not divide the *real* Soviet society into two distinctive groups completely shut off from each other (Hankiss 1988, p. 21; Di Palma 1991, p. 66). Rather, they coexist simultaneously, overlapping each other in complex ways.

NOTES

1. This point is emphasized by totalitarianism. For the old totalitarian model, see Arendt, 1951 and Friedrich Brzezinski, 1956. For the neo-totalitarian model, see Malia 1994 and Pipes, 1990.

2. I need to clarify two points. First, 'dictatorship over human needs' is borrowed from Feher et al.'s book *Dictatorship Over Needs*. Second, when I describe communism as dictatorship over human needs, my intention is not to accept totalitarianism. As will be shown, Soviet society does not just accept what is imposed by a 'dictatorship over human needs.' Instead, various actors intervene in the process to protect themselves from the overarching state. As a result, even neo-totalitarian theorists like Martin Malia admit that totalitarian *intent* of Soviet leaders does not realize into totalitarian *consequence* (Malia 1990, pp. 300–1 and 1992, p. 102). The gap between the intent and the consequence provides a crucial evidence of social autonomy, which is not recognized by theorists of totalitarianism.

3. For the record, Ivan Bunin (1870–1953) was the first Russian to receive the Nobel Prize for literature in 1933. When the Revolution occurred, however, Bunin escaped to Paris where he spent the rest of his life. Since he maintained 'stateless' status during his Paris years (1920–53), the Nobel Foundation still regards his Nobel Prize in 1933 as 'stateless'.

REFERENCES

Alexeev, Michael V., 'Underground market for gasoline in the USSR', *Berkeley-Duke Occasional Papers in the Second Economy in the USSR*, 9, 1987.

Alexeyeva, Ludmilla, *Soviet Dissent: Contemporary Movements for National, Religious, and Human Rights* (Middletown: Wesleyan University Press, 1985).

Altman, Yochanan, 'Second Economy Activities in the USSR: Insights from the Southern Republics', in *Corruption, Development and Inequality*, Peter M. Ward (ed.), (London: Routledge, 1980).

Arendt, Hannah, *The Origins of Totalitarianism* (New York: Harcourt, Brace, 1951).

Benda, Vaclav, 'Parallel Polis, or An Independent Society in Central and Eastern Europe: An Inquiry', *Social Research*, vol. 55, nos. 1–2), (Spring/Summer) 1988.

Bialer, Seweryn, 'Domestic and International Factors in the Formation of Gorbachev's Reforms', *Journal of International Affairs*, vol. 42, no. 2, 1989.

Binyon, Michael, *Life in Russia* (New York: Pantheon Books, 1983).

Brzezinski, Zbigniew, *The Grand Failure* (New York: Collier Books, 1989).

Bushnell, John, 'The "new Soviet man" turns pessimist', in *The Soviet Union since Stalin*, Stephen F. Cohen, Alexander Rabinowitch, and Robert Sharlet (eds), (Bloomington: Indiana University Press, 1980).

Chirot, Daniel, *The Crisis of Leninism and the Decline of the Left: The Revolutions of 1989* (Seattle: University of Washington Press, 1991).

Commisso, Ellen, 'Crisis in Socialism or Crisis of Socialism', *World Politics*, vol. XLII, no. 4, 1990.

Dallin, A. and G. W. Lapidus (eds), *The Soviet System from Crisis to Collapse*

(Boulder: Westview, 1995).

Di Palma, Giuseppe, 'Legitimization from the Top to Civil Society: Politico-Cultural Change in Eastern Europe', *World Politics*, vol. 44, no. 1, (October) 1991.

Erickson, Richard E., 'On an allocative role of the Soviet second economy', in *Marxism, Central Planning, and the Soviet Economy*, Padma Desai (ed.), (Cambridge: The MIT Press, 1983).

Etzioni, Amitai, *A Comparative Analysis of Complex Organizations* (New York: The Free Press, 1975).

Feher, F., A. Heller, and G. Markus, *Dictatorship Over Needs* (New York: St Martin's Press, 1983).

Feldbrugge, F. J. M., *Samizdat and Political Dissent in the Soviet Union* (Leyden: A. W. Sijthoff, 1975).

———, 'Government and Shadow Economy in the Soviet Union', *Soviet Studies*, vol. XXXVI, no. 4, (October) 1984.

Fitzpatrick, Sheila, *The Russian Revolution* (New York: Oxford University Press, 1994).

Friedrich, Carl J. and Zbigniew Brzezinski, *Totalitarian Dictatorship and Autocracy* (Cambridge: Harvard University Press, 1956).

Ginzburg, Carlo, *The Cheese and the Worms* (New York: Penguin Books, 1984).

Grossman, Gregory, 'The "Second Economy" of the USSR', in *The Soviet Economy: Continuity and Change*, Morris Bornstein (ed.), (Boulder: Westview Press, 1981).

———, 'Economies of virtuous haste: a view of Soviet industrialization and institutions', in *Marxism, Central Planning, and the Soviet Economy*, Padma Desai (ed.), (Cambridge: The MIT Press, 1983).

Hankiss, Elemer, 'The "Second Society": Is There an Alternative Social Mode Emerging in Contemporary Hungary?', *Social Research*, vol. 55, nos. 1–2, (Spring/Summer) 1988.

Havel, Vaclav, 'The Power of the Powerless', in *The Power of the Powerless: Citizen against the State in Central Eastern Europe*, John Keane (ed.), (London: Hutchinson, 1985).

Hirschman, Albert O., *Exit, Voice, and Loyalty* (Cambridge: Harvard University Press, 1972).

———, *The Passions and the Interests* (Princeton: Princeton University Press, 1977).

———, *Rival Views of Market Society* (New York: Viking, 1986).

Hoskings, Geoffrey, *The First Socialist Society: A History of the Soviet Union from Within* (Cambridge: Harvard University Press, 1993).

Hough, Jerry, *Russia and the West* (New York: Touchstone, 1990).

Jirous, Ivan M., 'Parallel Polis, or An Independent Society in Central and Eastern Europe: An Inquiry', *Social Research*, vol. 55, nos. 1–2, (Spring/Summer) 1988.

108 *Experiencing the State*

Jowitt, Ken, *New World Disorder: The Leninist Extinction* (Berkeley: University of California Press, 1992).

Katsenelinboigen, Aron and Herbert S. Levine, 'Market and Plan, Plan and Market: The Soviet Case', in *The Soviet Economy: Continuity and Change* Morris Bornstein (ed.), (Boulder: Westview Press, 1981).

Kolakowski, Leszek, 'Mind and body: Ideology and economy in the collapse of Communism', in *Constructing Capitalism: The Reemergence of Civil Society and Liberal Economy in the Post-Communist World*, Kazimierz Poznanski (ed.), (Boulder: Westview Press, 1992).

Kornai, Janos, *Economics of Shortage* (New York: North-Holland, 1980).

———, *Vision and Reality, Market and State: Contradictions and Dilemmas Revisited* (New York: Routledge, 1990).

Lewin, Moshe, *The Gorbachev Phenomenon* (Berkeley: University of California Press, 1991).

Lindblom, Charles E., *Politics and Markets: The World's Political-Economic System* (New York: Basic Books, 1977).

Lukes, Steven, 'Introduction', in *The Power of the Powerless: Citizen against the State in Central Eastern Europe*, John Keane (ed.), (London: Hutchinson, 1985).

Lyons, Eugene, *Workers' Paradise Lost: Fifty Years of Soviet Communism, A Balance Sheet* (New York: Funk & Wagnalls, 1967).

Malia, Martin, 'To the Stalin Mausoleum', *Daedalus*, vol. 119, no. 1, 1990.

———, 'From under the rubble, what?', *Problems of Communism*, vol. XLI, 1992.

———, *The Soviet Tragedy* (New York: The Free Press, 1994).

Marx, Karl, 'Manifesto of the Communist Party', in *The Marx-Engels Reader*, Robert C. Tucker (New York: W. W. Norton & Company, 1978).

McCauley, Martin, *The Soviet Union1917–1991* (London: Longman, 1993).

Millar, James R., *The Soviet Economic Experiment* (Chicago: University of Illinois Press, 1990).

Miller, John, *Mikhail Gorbachev and the End of Soviet Power* (New York: St Martin's Press, 1993).

Neuhauser, Kimberly and Clifford Gaddy, 'Estimating the size of the private service economy in the USSR', *Berkeley-Duke Occasional Papers on the Second Economy in the USSR*, 15, 1989.

O'Hearn, Dennis, 'The Consumer Second Economy: Size and Effects', *Soviet Studies*, vol. XXXII, no. 2, 1980.

Pipes, Richard, *The Russian Revolution* (New York: Alfred A. Knopf Inc., 1990).

———, *Russia Under the Bolshevik Regime* (New York: Alfred A. Knopf Inc., 1994a).

———, *Communism: The Vanished Specter*, New York: Oxford University Press, 1994b.

Polanyi, Karl, *The Great Transformation: The Political and Economic Origins of Our Time* (Boston: Beacon Press, 1957).

Powell, Raymond P., 'Plan execution and the workability of Soviet planning', in *The Soviet Economy: Continuity and Change*, Morris Bornstein (ed.), (Boulder: Westview Press, 1981).

Poznanski, Kazimierz Z., *Constructing Capitalism: The Reemergence of Civil Society and Liberal Economy in the Post-Communist World* (Boulder: Westview Press, 1992).

Roeder, Philip, *Red Sunset: The Failure of Soviet Politics* (Princeton: Princeton University Press, 1993).

Roxburgh, Angus, *The Second Russian Revolution* (London: BBC Books, 1991).

Rutgaizer, Valeriy M., 'The Shadow Economy in the USSR', *Berkeley-Duke Occasional Papers on the Second Economy in the USSR*, 34, 1992.

Rutland, Peter, 'The Economy: The Rocky Road from Plan to Market', in *Developments in Russian and Post-Soviet Politics*, S. White, A. Pravda, and Z. Gitelman (eds), (Durham: Duke University Press, 1994).

Rywkin, Michael, *Soviet Society Today* (New York: M. E. Sharpe Inc., 1989).

Saunders, George, *Samzdat: Voices of the Soviet Opposition* (New York: Monad Press, 1974).

Shlapentokh, Vladimir, *Public and Private Life of the Soviet People: Changing Values of the Soviet People* (Oxford: Oxford University Press, 1989).

Simes, Dimitri K., 'The Soviet Parallel Market', *Survey*, vol. 21, no. 3) (96), (Summer) 1975.

Smith, Adam, *The Wealth of Nations* (Chicago: University of Chicago Press, 1976).

Starr, S. Frederick, *Red and Hot: The Fate of Jazz in the Soviet Union, 1917–1980* (New York: Oxford University Press, 1983).

Stites, Richard, *Revolutionary Dreams* (New York: Oxford University Press, 1989).

——, *Soviet Popular Culture* (Cambridge: Cambridge University Press, 1992).

Suny, Ronald, *Revenge of the Past* (Stanford: Stanford University Press, 1993).

Taylor, Charles, 'Modes of Civil Society', *Public Culture*, vol. 3, no. 1, (Fall) 1990.

Tocqueville, Alexis de (trans. by Stuart Gilbert), *The Old Regime and the French Revolution* (London: Anchor Books, 1983).

Treml, Vladimir G., 'A study of labor inputs into the second economy of the USSR', *Berkeley-Duke Occasional Papers on the Second Economy in the USSR*, 33, 1992.

Verdery, Katherine, *What was Socialism, and What comes next?* (Princeton: Princeton University Press, 1996).

Weber, Max (trans. by Talcott Parsons), *The Protestant Ethic and the Sprit of Capitalism* (London: HarperCollins, 1991).

White, Anne, *De-Stalinization and the House of Culture: Declining State Control over Leisure in the USSR, Poland, and Hungary, 1953–89* (London: Routledge, 1990).

4

How Political Scientists Experienced India's Development State

PAUL R. BRASS

Political and other social scientists who have done research and written about Indian politics during the past half century, including North American, European, and Indian scholars, have mostly shared the developmentalist perspective of western policy planners and India's political elites. Whatever the individual differences in scholarly approaches, the political science of development, as a subdiscipline of the profession, has been implicated in the developmentalist framework. Further, despite the rhetoric of socialism that accompanied that framework, both the practice in India and the development theory that justified it, were fundamentally conservative. The conservative elements in the developmentalist framework comprised an ideology of state-exaltation, arising out of a 'fear of disorder' that I have analysed elsewhere (see note 34). So implicated were we in the developmentalist goals of India's elites that we failed to provide an independent basis for critique that has become increasingly necessary as it has become more and more obvious that those goals have failed to transform India into the modern, industrial state of its elite's imaginings, have failed at the same time to provide for the basic minimum needs of its peoples, have failed to eliminate 'the causes of unrest' (Inden 1995; see note 55, p. 263) and have instead drawn India into the ugly morass of state terrorism in the Northeast, Punjab, and Kashmir, and have failed to provide a basis for accommodation between the Hindu and Muslim populations of the country. My purpose herein is to illuminate the ways in which the discipline has been implicated in the developmentalist framework and to show how we may move away from it and modify the methods that we have used to analyse Indian society and politics in order to better comprehend what is happening in India today.

The essay is divided into four sections. In the next three, I provide examples from the literature that demonstrate the theoretical hold that the developmentalist perspective has held over most of us during the past several decades. The examples are, in part, arbitrary; many other examples could have been provided. I have chosen for purposes of illustration three sets of examples. The first section on 'Political Development and Organized Demands' discusses statements about Indian politics that refer to the relationship between organized demands and political development. In the second section on 'Democratic Development', I consider what democratic development means for India and what it means to scholars who have written on the subject. In the third section on 'Governance and Governability' I discuss how these terms have been used by political scientists of India. The fourth section, 'Conclusion', summarizes my arguments with a plea for a substitution of a stance of critique of Indian society and politics for—and outside of—the developmentalist position.[1]

POLITICAL DEVELOPMENT AND ORGANIZED DEMANDS

The conservative, institutional-organizational bias in the political development studies framework has been reflected in the works of several of the leading scholars of Indian politics, including, among others, Myron Weiner, the Rudolphs, and Atul Kohli. For example, among Weiner's principal concerns in his second book, *The Politics of Scarcity*, those that persisted into his later works to some extent as well, were the consequences for 'the modernization process' and for 'public order and economic development' of demands made by 'organized interests'.[2] In the political development framework, organized interests made demands that might endanger modernization, public order, and economic development unless they were aggregated by the political parties and by 'party systems'. These demands constituted 'problems' for the polity that required proper 'handling'[3] or 'managing',[4] which was another way of referring to this aggregative-filtering process. Such demands could become quite 'serious' when they took 'an ethnic form'.[5]

In 1987, in their book, *In Pursuit of Lakshmi*, the Rudolphs took a somewhat different view of these matters from Weiner. They examined more closely the internal functioning of organized groups or, put another way, groups in the organized sectors of the economy, particularly organized labour and organized capital, and minimized their potential threat to the processes of modernization, public order, and economic development. They argued to the contrary that the trade unions were so divided, 'fragmented', and competitive with each other that they lacked the ability to have a major impact on 'national policy'. On the other side, 'organized capital', operating in a restricted, but protected economic environment, was largely dependent upon government and could not and, in fact, did not oppose the thrust of the economic development strategy of import substitution.[6] Both organized labour and organized capital, in the Rudolphs' reckoning, emerged as the weaker parties in a triangular relationship with the Indian state, which had the capacity to prevail over these and other organized interests not only because the state was the strongest party, but also because it had 'won wide acceptance for its claim that it has a special responsibility for nation building and economic development',[7] in other words, that it had legitimacy that overrode the interests of organized groups such as labour and capital. In short, the Rudolphs, while coining the term 'weak-strong' for the Indian state, took the view that the state was strong enough to prevail against such interests.[8]

As I have pointed out elsewhere,[9] Atul Kohli a few years later took a less sanguine view of Indian state capacities, which he thought had been severely eroded during Indira Gandhi's tenure in office to such an extent that India was now confronted with a crisis of governability. Using Samuel Huntington's framework and terminology, he argued that there had been, in effect, a political decay of Indian institutions and an unwillingness on the part of government under Indira Gandhi's hegemony, to incorporate the 'growing demands of power blocs in the polity'. Although his book constitutes a considerable indictment of Indira Gandhi and her policies and practices, he nevertheless takes the position that she 'perceived—not without some justification—that such moves would weaken the Center and thus both national integrity and the state's capacity to steer economic development'. She opted instead for strategies that involved the 'undermining of democratic institutions',[10] including the weakening of her own party, the Indian National Congress, the premier institution in Indian political life. Adhering closely to Huntington's argument, while denying any 'normative suggestion' implied by it, he deplored this dismantling of the Congress and the weakness of other political parties in India. 'Widespread politicization,' he remarked, 'does put a high premium on a polity's institutional capacity simultaneously to accommodate the resulting demands and to promote socioeconomic development. Well-organized political parties thus become especially crucial.'[11]

We have here, despite the differences in emphasis, an essentially congruent set of arguments about what is important in Indian political development and how that development may be endangered. Interest groups, organized or not, present demands that naturally proliferate in a heterogeneous society such as India's that is also undergoing extensive politicization. These demands are presented to the state which, throughout most of this period, made the crucial decisions affecting organized interests. Between the interests and the Indian state stood the Indian National Congress, which had the capacity for two decades to aggregate, accommodate, and incorporate such demands and the power to deflect and resist them when necessary. After the death of Nehru and during the long period of rule by Indira Gandhi, the balance shifted in such a way that the institutions, particularly the Congress, that had performed these functions, had weakened and now lacked the capacity to deal effectively with them, thus producing a 'crisis of governability'. That crisis in turn cast doubt on the ability of the Indian state 'to promote socioeconomic development.'

Now, what is wrong with all this? As a broad summary statement of what has happened in India during the past half century, it cannot be said that it is wrong. Neither for that matter can it be said to be true. It is, however, a framework for attaching meaning, significance, and value to sets of processes abstracted from political happenings. Beginning first of all with values, it is transparent—all protestations denying normative preferences to the contrary notwithstanding— that the state and its capacities to promote modernization, maintain public order, and promote socio-economic development constitute the apex value for political scientists of India as well as for the elites who have (mis)governed the country for the half century. Second, it is sufficient for political scientists of India simply to mention those processes of modernization and socio-economic development to be understood by their colleagues and vaguely understood by their students, despite the actuality that neither these terms nor their sub-referents, such as secularization, restratification, urbanization, and the like have any kind of concrete reality other than those produced by manipulating census data. One can talk, for example, of urbanization as an aspect of modernization and cite census figures to show its rate, the sources of the migrating populations, and some of the political results produced by migration of ethnically distinct migrants into an urban metropolis. One then also attaches some significance or value to these processes for which summary terms are also used, such as 'rapid' or moderate for the rate of change, 'rural' for the source of migrants, interethnic conflict for the consequences of migration, and the like.

What is wrong with all this is that it is without doubt a conservative, state-supporting politico-moral framework that ignores the lived realities of the Indian people. These concepts are all misguiding. These old concepts and terms not only mislead us, but they are of no predictive value, which is so highly valued in the modern social sciences. These concepts start from the top. We need to start from the bottom to look at relations between people, which for us as political scientists means especially relations of power. The vast majority of the Indian people have no idea of what is meant by modernization, socio-economic development, state capacity, and the like. They have specific needs and wants and have to interact with persons in positions of authority in order to attain them. But does not Indian 'democracy' provide the means for those at the bottom to gain influence, respect, resources, and power? Is not 'democracy' in fact working in India to the increasing advantage of the lower orders? Let us see how this question has been taken up in one type of answer to this question of democratic development in India.

DEMOCRATIC DEVELOPMENT

While denying that their developmental model contained a built-in, ethnocentric bias towards Anglo-American political practices as the end result of political development, there can be no doubt that most of the developmentalists favoured such a result. Further, among India specialists, both democratic development and the relationship between democratic practices and 'socio-economic' development have been the central concerns of our research. Here, as elsewhere, there was a consensus among practitioners in India—the politicians, on the one hand, and political scientists, mainly American, on the other hand—concerning 'the desirability of a secular, democratic state dedicated to economic development and national unity'.[12] That consensus, especially on the role of a democratic state in directing economic development, in fact was formed in India as early as the late nineteenth century, at the beginnings of nationalist thought and political organization.[13] While this consensus might seem admirable from a liberal democratic perspective, it is further evidence of the absence of distance between intellectuals and politicians, a distance that is necessary for critique.

In place of critique, India specialists warned, preached, and cautioned the political elites in India after independence. Following Shils, our writings were supposed to 'enlighten' the political elites about the meaning of democracy, its practices, and its dangerous shoals.[14] Thus, Weiner pointed to the 'danger' that India's political elites might, in their search for utopian solutions to India's vast problems, 'fail to recognize' the inevitability of conflict, the arousal of 'ethnic loyalties', 'the struggle for patronage and power', and the essential presence of both 'political parties and pressure groups' in the 'democratic process'. They might feel their plans threatened by all these elements and opt instead for authoritarian solutions.[15] While Weiner phrased these points in neutral terms, they amounted nevertheless to advice to India's political elites. But, at the time Weiner wrote these lines, India's political elites did not need such advice, for they had their own preacher and tutor, Jawaharlal Nehru, who understood all these points and was himself committed to the values and practices of contemporary democracy and democratic development.

Nehru himself, however, largely escaped critical analysis. He was by far, among all the leaders of the post-colonial world, the darling of liberal academic political scientists in the West. Only during the last decade have his ideals and policies come in for increasingly sharp intellectual critique, mostly from Indian social scientists of the post-modernist persuasion. However, during virtually the entire period of his political dominance after the death of his rival, Sardar Patel, until the fiasco of his handling of the war with China in 1962, Nehru faced no serious opposition to his rule and his ideals either from within the Indian political process or from intellectuals, though there was subterranean sentiment amongst the then politically weak militant Hindu nationalists against him.

The current critique of Nehru's ideals and policies derives from two sources, one indigenous, the other once again western. The first is the political thought, ideas, and practices of Mahatma Gandhi, the second is the contemporary post-modernist critique of the intellectual apparatus as well as the ideals derived from the Enlightenment and its enshrinement of Reason as the solution for all social problems, which Nehru embodied. I will return to the second critique of both Nehru and the development perspective later. Here, however, it needs to be noted that Gandhi anointed Nehru as India's prime minister despite the fact that he certainly knew that Nehru's political goals and practices were utterly incompatible with his own. Gandhi's thought, ideals, and practices were anti-statist, anti-party, and anti-industrialist. He proposed the disbanding of the Indian National Congress and the creation of a new political order based on village self-government and rural development. The makers of the Indian Constitution ignored the total incompatibility of the two approaches to India's political future and ignored Gandhi's hopes.[16] In the nearly 400 articles of the exceedingly long Constitution of India, there is only one brief article that refers to the favoured form of Gandhian political organization, the village panchayat. Article 40 in the Directive Principles of State Policy—that, in fact, have no directive power— says only that 'the State shall take steps to organise village panchayats and endow them with such powers and authority as may be necessary to enable them to function as units of self-government'.

This is not the place to discuss the history of the organization of such panchayats in India. For purposes of this essay, it is sufficient to note only that they posed no obstacle whatsoever to the centralization of power, the development of the command economy, and the proliferation of political parties and interest groups that Gandhi opposed. There can be no doubt that here also political development specialists shared the same views as the members of the Indian Constituent Assembly, namely, that a strong state structure was essential to India's development—political, economic, and social—and that it was the Gandhian alternative, not the Nehruvian approach, that was utopian and unrealistic, not to say obscurantist.

Although Ralph Retzlaff published a book on Indian village government in 1962[17] and others of us have from time to time commented on the functioning of those systems of *panchayati raj* (village self-government) that have been introduced in several states in India,[18] the bulk of our writing has focused on the institutions associated with the modern state and with its democratic development. Weiner and LaPalombara raised questions such as whether or not 'mobilist single-party systems' could be compatible with 'democratic political values'[19] or whether or not, 'from the standpoint of long-range democratic political development a bureaucracy subject to party patronage, even to a certain amount of political corruption, is to be preferred to one in which, while it nicely conforms to the Weberian requisites of a legal-rational authority system, is also by this very reason in a position to distort the development of political parties and interest groups and even to subject them to bureaucratic domination.'[20] Once again, though stated in neutral academic terms, it is obvious that Weiner at least preferred the development of a multiparty system for India that aggregated group interests and that he was, in effect, saying to India's political elites that it was more important to nurture these institutions than to worry overmuch about political penetration of, and corruption in, the bureaucracy. Here too India's political elites needed no such advice as they transformed the Indian polity into what I have called a corrupt bureaucratic state.[21]

Specialists in Indian political development have also repeatedly expressed their sympathies with the problems faced by Indian political elites in pursuing the various aspects of the development process. Once again, these sympathetic statements have been made in impeccably neutral social scientific terms, but they cannot be interpreted otherwise than as sympathetic. The special overall problem that India and its political elites are said to have faced from the start is the necessity of confronting all the development problems at once instead of in a gradual sequence, as in the West. As Das

Gupta has put it, echoing the earlier theoretical development literature on sequences of political development,[22] 'democratic systems in developing countries have the *unenviable* [my italics] task of simultaneously and rapidly developing the polity, economy, and society.'[23] The phrasing is important. It is not only an *unenviable* task, but it is a *task*, that is, a duty, or, as the American Heritage dictionary puts its, 'a piece of assigned work', 'a difficult or tedious undertaking'.

Who assigned to India's political elites this unenviable task? Well, they assigned it to themselves, and political development specialists on India also assigned it to them. The consensus remains intact here as well and any critique of the undertaking itself was for long absent, though there has been ample critique of measures taken along the way to implement it or deviate from it. We all reacted with shock and anger, reflecting our deep commitment to the democratic development process in India, when Indira Gandhi temporarily gave up 'combined development' on the plea that the democratic part of that development was undermining social stability and economic development goals and when she, instead of pursuing the unenviable task, 'set out to dismantle the democratic system of persuasion and replace it with an authoritarian mode of creating and enforcing public assent'.[24] But we did not criticize the whole enterprise, not to mention its increasing association with another form of development, namely, military development that led to India's first 'peaceful' nuclear explosion under Indira Gandhi in 1974, and in the May 1998 nuclear explosions at Pokhran, to its further development under a militant Hindu government. That this striving for great power status was inherent in the development process from the beginning was, for the most part, neglected,[25] along with its implications for the well being of the Indian peoples.

Far from criticizing the whole enterprise of India's 'simultaneous development of social, economic, and political resources',[26] we heaped praise upon its elites—always expressed in neutral social scientific terms—for adhering to the path of 'democratic political development'. Das Gupta remarked in 1989, for example, how India's democratic political development had 'not been constrained by the slow development of the so-called social and economic requisites of democratic being'. Indeed, 'Indian democracy' in this respect stood 'as a deliberate act of political defiance of the social and economic constraints of underdevelopment'.[27] The adverbs and adjectives are missing from these statements, but they are nonetheless apparent; they were commendably 'not . . . constrained' and the act of defiance was commendable.

Those who have criticized and worried more about India's political future and have seen present circumstances as less commendable have, nevertheless, done so from within the same developmentalist perspective. I refer once again to Kohli—with whom I have also been bracketed[28]—who coined in 1990 the term 'crisis of governability' for India's political condition in the late 1980s, and asked the question whether 'India's democratic government [can] simultaneously accommodate conflicting interests and promote socioeconomic development.'[29] It is, once again, the unenviable task that India's political elites may not, after all, be able to bring off.

Well, more than 56 years have passed. Have they brought it off or not? Whenever we India specialists are asked to give an answer to this type of question of assessment of the results of India's 'experiment' in so-called simultaneous development, we have what I have called elsewhere[30] a canned speech or a canned paper in which we recite the achievements of the Nehruvian planning process, mostly in aggregate or abstract terms such as the creation of a broad and diversified industrial base, the maintenance of the 'Hindu rate of growth', the absence of famines, the rise of a new urban middle class, and most of all the maintenance of democratic practices. We then recite the deficiencies: failure to cross the 50 per cent literacy line, absence of clean drinking water, absence of sanitation and hygiene in most of the country, absence of anything that can be called medical treatment in most of the country and very little that can be called antiseptic, proliferation of urban slums the like of which the world has never before seen, increased communal violence, dowry deaths, and gender discrimination that takes the form of extremely low literacy rates for women, victimization of females in the family with regard to provision of food and medical facilities, persistence of caste disabilities, and so. As the reader will note, I wax more eloquently on the latter set of issues than on the former, but most of my colleagues manage to maintain a more perfect equilibrium in their canned articles and speeches.

In fact, I have been accused of being a prophet of doom and gloom, of painting a picture of an India heading seamlessly towards catastrophe, as one of my critics recently put it. What I want to say here and now, however, is that India is not heading towards catastrophe: India is a living catastrophe and its people, including its intellectuals, know it. But that line will get us nowhere but into endless, unsolvable arguments. More important, from an analytical rather than a polemical point of view, I want to say that this developmentalist perspective, this endless talk about simultaneous development, this grand celebration of Indian democracy is an intellectual dead end that has us going round in circles like this all the time. We have all been caught in it and cannot seem to get out of it.

I want to propose how to get out of it or, at least, how we may begin to find a way out and how other kinds of questions may be asked that will lead us out of this dead end. However, I want first to consider another set of terms that I have spotted trotting along beside us that have led us still further astray.

GOVERNANCE AND GOVERNABILITY

Much of the writing about India by India specialists has been concerned with the question of 'governance'. It is a curious word to apply to a state deemed democratic. It was not much used in the US until a recent flood of political science literature fixed on this term and began to use it in the titles of books and articles. Before this upsurge, mostly the more common term government was used, sometimes called 'good' as in good government, though the opposite term, bad government was rarely used. When the term good government was used, it usually meant a government free of the taint of corruption, that 'governs'—that is, administers—the government efficiently and convinces a majority of the people that it does so in 'the public interest', whatever its specific policy goals. The term 'govern' was more often used with reference to multiparty systems, where the question was sometimes raised whether or not a particular combination of parties was able to govern effectively or not. That usage of the term also became quite prominent in India after—and ever since—the results of the 1967 General Elections, as a consequence of which the Congress lost its majority at the centre[31] and in half the Indian states, introducing a period of unstable coalition governments in many of them. It has also been used by political analysts in India with reference to Congress rule at the centre both before and after the 1967 elections. For example, one writer, remarking upon the diversity of interests contained within the Congress, thought it explained 'why the Congress Party cannot adopt rational policies or govern effectively; it has to contend all the time against itself'.[32] Finally, it has also been used in the sense of 'self' versus 'other' forms of governance, as in self-government for India after British rule and, in India itself after independence, in the sense of restoration of self-governance to federal units whose government has been taken over by the centre for a time, that is, restoration of 'its own governance'.[33]

When talking about India, however, the terms governance, govern, and governability convey a much broader range of concerns. It is used more often in the conventional meanings of the term, that is, to rule, control, direct, steer, regulate, determine, and/or restrain. Thus, Indians use the term govern and governance to refer to British rule in India, which did all of those things. However, like so many other things that were carried over from British authoritarian rule, the idea of governance was also carried over into the new Indian democracy along with its opposite, namely, the possibility that the country or its parts, that is, the former provinces—now states—of the country might be misgoverned or mismanaged. This possibility was very much in the minds of members of the Constituent Assembly, among whom the fear of disorder was very prominent and who associated the notion of disorder with these terms, mismanagement and misgovernance. As I have shown elsewhere, that fear was used to justify the inclusion in the Indian Constitution of the right to make use of extensive emergency powers, including the imposition of what is called President's Rule upon any state whose government failed to maintain 'law and order'.[34]

Dua, among others, has noted that India's political leaders in the Constituent Assembly in fact 'borrowed the concept of emergency governance from the Government of India Act of 1935.'[35] But it was not just disorder that these political elites feared, but especially a particular type, that which might threaten 'the integrity and unity of the Indian Union.'[36] Provisions for emergency governance were justified because disorder or misgovernance might lead to such a breakdown of order that India's territorial statehood itself might be endangered. Such concerns about misgovernment and mismanagement could only have reflected another kind of continuity between the new governing elites and the former British rulers, namely, an attitude of distrust of the ordinary politicians of the country and a lack of faith in the ability of a mostly newly franchised population to check the misbehaviour of their elected governors.

There is also built into the concept of governance in India the underlying fear that India itself is so big and heterogeneous that it might in fact be impossible to govern effectively at all, a fear unstated but presumably felt by its Constitution-makers and asserted openly by foreign specialists on Indian politics. It is sometimes argued also that several of India's states are themselves too large and heterogeneous to be governed effectively and efficiently by a single government and should, therefore, be split up into much smaller units.[37]

The most striking assertion of the question of whether or not India as a whole could be governed at all was made by Selig Harrison in 1960.[38] It has been reasserted most recently by Kohli who has remarked that 'the area that is now identified as India was never easy to govern' and has in recent years, in fact, 'become difficult to govern'.[39] However, unlike Harrison, who was raising the underlying fear of early Indian nationalists that the country might disintegrate, Kohli means by govern, 'the state's capacity ... simultaneously to promote development and to accommodate diverse interests',[40] the simultaneous development question once again. He argues even more strongly that the great fear of disorder of the Indian constitution-makers has materialized, that 'political order in contemporary India' has, in fact, broken down.[41]

It needs to be noted also that the way in which the term 'governance' is used in the literature on Indian politics separates it from democracy. Thus, Manor refers to the 'political awakening' that has occurred in recent years among India' s 'disadvantaged groups', which he argues has 'made India both a more genuine democracy and a more difficult country to govern'. Manor means by the latter that conflicts have become more difficult 'to manage'. What has made matters especially difficult is that, as this democratic awakening has taken place, political decay of India's principal 'political institutions', those of the state as well as the Congress, has taken place.[42] Huntington's shadow is here again, obviously, with his formula for democracy as a regime defined by the autonomy of its institutions from social forces and, as well, his formula for disaster arising from the imbalance between participation/social mobilization and institutionalization.[43] This formula, of course, eliminates the 'self' from 'governance', ignores the possibility that self-governance may only become possible through political disorder, the dismantling of institutions, the displacing of old political elites by new ones, and the articulation of a new 'political formula' that better reflects the aspirations of the formerly disadvantaged.

This formula also eliminates the 'human' and the 'humane' from governance, as Kothari has put it in a poignant and powerful essay. Kothari argues in a paradoxical formulation that not only in India, but globally, 'governance has been usurped by governments' and further that 'governments have been taken over by corporate interests and the military–technocratic order, and by the ideology of national interest and national security.'[44] Although the first part of the statement sounds paradoxical, it is as clear as can be and means what I have just said, that the self, meaning 'the people', has been taken out of the term governance, and, further, that governments no longer rule humanely in the interests of the people but in the interests of multinational corporations in which the good society has become one in which happiness is identified with possession and utilization of the latest technological devices, in a world made safe for those who posses and use them, by a state whose primary concern is not even governance but the mere protection of the interests and safety of its citizens, especially of its privileged citizens. India, of course, was not part of the inner circle of such states when Kothari wrote these lines, but rather was at once a victim of the new global order and an increasingly eager participant in it, creating its own internal victims among the poor and disadvantaged, that is, the vast majority of its own citizens. In this new world order, it seems, there are really no citizens, only beneficiaries and victims, those with influence and those with none.

Kothari's call is for a 'return to humane governance', including a concern for 'human rights and ethical imperatives', for the 'recovery

of the human, the good, and the just'.[45] In restoring such a conception
and form of government, the intellectuals have a role to play, which
includes 'exposing misgovernance and oppression', creating a
'knowledge base for transformative politics and democratic
governance', and identifying themselves 'with the victims of history
and with the democratic movement waged on their behalf'. Instead
of playing 'the role of rationalisers and legitimisers' of existing
political forms, presenting a vision of the future derived from
developmentalist perspectives for the benefit of the people, their role
should be to listen to the people and build that knowledge base from
what they themselves hear from the people.[46]

I will come back to the issues raised by Kothari in a moment, but
will say now only that Kothari too has been caught in the discursive
framework of the term, governance, which presumes an abstract
entity above the people that will somehow govern better, that is,
more humanely, in the interests of the people. For reasons that will,
I hope, become clear in a moment, I do not believe that there can be
any such form of governance.

However, I want to refer first to another source for the
contemporary usage of the term, 'govern', namely elite theory and
the arguments that have surrounded it. In classical elite theory
associated with Mosca, Michels, and to a considerable extent Lasswell
as well, democracy cannot exist in reality. The idea of democracy
itself is merely a political formula in the modern age that hides the
reality that all large-scale organizations, including the state and
political parties that vie for power within it, are oligarchies controlled
by elites who govern in the name of the people. Those elites cannot
be replaced by 'the people', by any genuine form of self-rule, but
only by counter-elites. Even when the ruling elites are overthrown in
the course of a mass revolutionary movement, the end result can
only be the re-establishment of some form of elite rule or governance.
The reigning democratic theory in contemporary American political
science associated with the name of Robert Dahl departs from this
theory only to the extent of denying the inevitability and the reality
in the US of the argument that a single elite always rules. Dahl instead
argues that the struggle of interests and parties in the US 'produces a
"pluralist" rather than an "elitist" distribution of power'.[47] But Dahl's
polyarchal democracy remains itself an elitist form of rule in which

the participation of the people consists primarily in the act of voting.[48] It is fully consistent with the Schumpeterian redefinition of modern democracy as rule by elected elites.[49]

Elite theory in its early phase constituted a sharp critique of then existing regimes that claimed to be democratic. In its contemporary form, however, it constitutes a justification for such regimes. In neither form is elite theory fully adequate to comprehend the functioning of contemporary regimes of symbol manipulation in societies whose lives are controlled and disciplined in great detail by multinational corporations rather than by governments, such as the US,[50] or of corrupt bureaucratic developmentalist regimes such as India's. There remain nevertheless several aspects of early—not late elite theory—that remain superior to the developmentalist paradigm as well as to critiques of it such as Kothari's. First is the very recognition that there is an inevitable tendency for elites to emerge in all societies, in all social movements, in all formal organizations, and in the agencies of the state themselves. Second is the recognition that elites and governments rule, govern under the guise of a 'political formula' in which they may or may not themselves believe, but which provides a justification for their rule that sustains them in power as long as most of the people believe in it. Third is the notion that political struggle in modern regimes that operate under the political formula of liberal democracy is a continuous engagement of social forces.

If we apply this scheme in its bare bones to India, one can say with a fair degree of summary accuracy that, in the early years after independence—throughout the Nehru period, in fact—India was ruled by an upper class, upper caste elite whose political formula was the very developmentalist ideology that I have been discussing so far in this essay. During those years, the struggle of social forces was contained primarily within a 'ruling class' of westernized professional persons, commercial and industrial elements, and ex-landlord and upper peasant groups. Under the cover of the political formula, persons from these classes gained control over most of the instruments of governance at the centre and in the states, particularly the ministries, departments, and public sector undertakings, which they gradually converted into increasingly bountiful sources of corrupt income. In the meantime, as all India specialists know, what is called the basic human needs of the people were disregarded, the institutions that sustained this plunder began to collapse, and the funds to continue to sustain them were depleted.

As the state and its agencies and agents became more and more corrupt and self-serving, gradually also new social forces, containing in their midst new sets of elites, began to challenge the old order, but not its corrupt foundations, in which they all wish to share or control themselves or divide more equitably. Simultaneously also, as the old institutions declined and the old elites lost their bases of power, so did the political formula under which they governed, whose key terms were modernization, development, secularism, and socialism. In their place, the ascendant political formula contains the terms Hindu nation, respect for the (Hindu) faith of the people, unification of the (Hindu) nation, abandonment of policies of appeasement of minorities, honesty and integrity in government, law and order, and respect for India in the world of nations. Some of these terms are carry-overs that were contained within the old political formula, some are distortions of it, some are outrageously false in their implications, though widely believed (for example, that militant Hindu politicians in the Bharatiya Janata Party [BJP] are less corrupt than others). But those who have articulated the new political formula themselves come predominantly from the elites that dominated India during the Nehru period. On the other side, the rising social forces and the elites within them adhere to elements of the old political formula to which they have added the demands for equality, economic betterment of the lower castes and classes, and rule by the real majority (the *bahujan* in the party called the Bahujan Samaj Party [Party of the Majority]).

These rising castes and classes and social forces are challenging in India a part of the wider notion of governance: 'who can govern; what governing is; what or who is governed'.[51] The militant Hindus, however, are challenging all three parts of this particular statement of governance. The rising backward and lower caste movements are saying: you Brahmans and other upper castes are not going to govern us any longer; we are now going to govern. But they have no notion of 'what governing is' or 'what or who is governed'.[52]

The militant Hindu politicians, on the other hand, are saying: you pseudo-secularists and appeasers of minorities are not going to govern any longer; only those who declare themselves to be Hindus are going to govern. They are also saying that we know better 'what governing is', that is, 'how to govern',[53] we will rule honestly, impartially, without discrimination among persons and groups, all of whom are to be included in the great Hindu family, and we will maintain law and order, in respect to all of which you others have failed, at the risk of critically endangering the country and the nation. They are also redefining 'what or who is governed'. The what is a united India, free from the conflicts and disorders among its peoples that have divided it till now. The 'who' is the undivided Hindu nation that is to include under the designation 'Hindu', Muslims, Sikhs, Buddhists, all Hindu castes and classes and sects, not that composite mixture of cultures that formed the nation of the 'pseudo-secularists'.

It should be obvious, by the very fact that it contains answers to all three questions while the lower and backward caste parties and movements do not, that the militant Hindu response is potentially the more powerful and persuasive one. The former offers only the spoils from the existing state apparatus to those previously denied access to them. The latter offers a vision of a future great India— never mind how dishonest, pathological, and dangerous to some social forces in India, to its neighbours, and to others it may be— that has a considerable appeal to the still-dominant classes in society, the upper classes and castes, and to a part of the middle classes and castes as well.

Both movements in contemporary India, that of the lower classses and castes, and that of the militant Hindus, however, are participating in a critique of the political order that was created by Nehru and the Congress in the first two decades of Indian independence and that has been falling apart for the past 30 years. They are joined in this critique by several of the most respected intellectuals in India as well, such as Ashis Nandy and T. N. Madan. This critique responds to another question, namely, 'how not to be governed', that is to say, 'how not to be governed *like that* [italics in original], by that, in the name of those principles, with such and such an objective in mind and by means of such procedures, not like that, not for that, not by them.'[54]

The answers to the 'how not to be governed' questions are again different from the side of the lower classes and castes and from the militant Hindus. That from the former has already been partly noted above: we will not be governed by you upper caste people as if we were inferior beings; we will not accept the leavings from your tables any longer; we will have our share and our rights. And, we will not have our share and our rights as benevolent gifts from you; we will take them through our own efforts and we will take them from you, if necessary. However, the parties representing these social forces are not rejecting the old political formula of developmentalism and secularism. They cannot reject developmentalism because there is no other way open to them in this land without opportunities for the disadvantaged outside of government. They cannot reject secularism because it is only through coalition among diverse castes and communities, including especially Muslims, that they can achieve control over government and government resources.

The militant Hindu response to the question 'how not to be governed' is more encompassing. It is in some ways also more 'radical', not in the Left's sense of radical, but in the sense of distancing from the old political formula. Militant Hindus share many, if not most, of the original objectives of Nehru and the Congress. They want to build a new India that is industrialized, technologically modernized, and militarily powerful enough to overawe its neighbours in South Asia, to equalize its position in relation to China, and to gain the respect of the western industrial powers. They even claim to be secular—and they are in a different, sophistical way: once all Indians declare themselves to be politically Hindu, all will be treated in the same way. Those who do not accept the political Hindu designation (particularly Muslims and Christians) are to be treated as, in effect, non-Indians, non-citizens, who should go somewhere else, to Pakistan or to England.

But there is also a more radical critique of the old political formula that comes from some of India's intellectuals and has been articulated also by Ronald Inden.[55] That critique rejects lock, stock, and barrel the entire developmentalist perspective and the secular political framework as well. However, while the critique is powerful, the prescriptions are ineffectual. It offers no sensible political alternatives beyond such phrases as 'the recovery of religious tolerance',[56] respect for the indigenous values and faiths of the people, and the like. Such intellectual constructions have no power to confront the militant Hindu ideology, whose leaders are as much or more in touch with the indigenous values and faiths of the people and who know how to manipulate them to their political advantage.

For those who wish to challenge the old order and the old political formula without falling into the net of the BJP and its family of militant Hindu organizations, something more is needed. Neither pleas for 'humane governance' nor for respect for the values and beliefs of the ordinary people of India can offer much of political substance. Resistance is called for, but resistance to what? Against whom? How? And what should be the role of intellectuals in India and the West who are sympathetic to the need for resistance.

The greatest failing of the developmentalist/institutionalist approach is that it utterly lacks any basis for critique. Its last vestiges need to be utterly disowned and discarded. It has contributed in its own way to the catastrophe that is India today.

Nor does the classical elite theory outlined above take us far enough. We need a framework for the analysis of the relations of power in Indian society and of the interrelations of state and society. We need to build a political ethnography, that is, an ethnography of power relations in Indian society and an ethnography of the Indian state. Such an ethnography can be built only from empirical observation of Indian realities, not from developmentalist or anti-developmentalist abstractions.[57] We need to begin with the other side of our canned speeches about Indian development and Indian democracy.

So, let me present a list of starters. Poverty is first, but not poverty as an abstraction, not poverty as a counting of the numbers of people below an imaginary line—even if that line is constructed and commented upon by a radical theorist such as Amartya Sen—but poverty as a way of life that one cannot escape and that dramatically constrains one's abilities and relations with the non-poor. Second, and associated with poverty, comes illiteracy: continuing, increasing illiteracy that makes a mockery of the idea of equality in Indian society, especially for women whose illiteracy rates are very high indeed. Third, comes inequality itself: the persistence at all levels of Indian society—outside the most westernized—of relationships that emphasize difference between, and deference of, the low to the high. Fourth, comes violence: from the violence of everyday life against women in the family to the violence against the poor and other unprotected persons perpetrated by the police in police stations and in the countryside to the criminal violence of so-called Hindu-Muslim riots, which are often in fact pogroms against Muslims in which the police are participants or quiet bystanders. Fifth, comes corruption: pervasive, systematic, graded, corrosive of all institutions and agencies in Indian society in which all are implicated, in which all participate from the lowest to the highest in Indian society. Sixth, and related to all the above, the continued diversion of the resources of the country from any serious attempt to satisfy the basic human needs of the population to big dams, nuclear power plants, military projects, and nuclear weapons and delivery systems.

One needs also to open one's eyes to what denial of the basic human needs of this population approaching one billion means. One has to keep before one's eyes what one sees every day in India and that one tends to forget almost instantly as soon as one settles into the seats of the departing flights: people living in garbage dumps on the outskirts of cities from which they scavenge their food and clothing; children lying listlessly on the ground outside rural medical dispensaries where they have come because they have a flu or stomach ailment or perhaps something more serious and life-threatening, their bodies covered with flies from head to toe and no one there or interested in or capable of attending to them; peasants tilling tiny plots of land insufficient to feed their families, some of them still tied in relations of bonded labour to those with larger landholdings; police raising their lathis against bicycle rickshaw drivers sweltering in unbearable heat to beat them because they have made some minor traffic error; old Muslim men walking up a hill to tell the mufti at the end of riot curfew how they were beaten by police, their beards grabbed and pulled, how they have lost sons in the riots; women telling their stories of husbands, sons, and brothers killed in the same riots; men sitting listlessly in government offices doing absolutely nothing hour after hour, day after day; the rich, privileged, and powerful sitting comfortably in their new bungalows, their five-star hotel suites, their restaurants, oblivious to all the above and prepared to deny that any of it actually exists in their country; politicians moving about with guns in their holsters beneath their *kurtas* (long shirts), with shadows and bodyguards; ministers in the government moving about in retinues of cars, accompanied by smart-stepping

Black Cats who rush out to open their doors and surround them with their automatic rifles until they are safely inside their huge bungalows. I have many other such images in my mind's eye gathered over 43 years of personal observation, some of them too noisome to mention in print, which the phrase 'absence of sanitation' does not capture even euphemistically. To refer to such things in a scholarly paper is to immediately elicit the following responses: 'Mother India', drain inspector's report, what about conditions in the USA? You have spent too much time in Uttar Pradesh.[58] Or simply silence.

But I am not interested in the shock value of these images for their own sake, but rather as a spur to new research, but without the intellectual baggage of development theory, the institutional approach to Indian politics, and the fulsome praise of Indian 'democracy', all of which ought to be banished from the field or at least to some reservation where it may be preserved as an example of an outmoded practice.

CONCLUSION

All of us who have been writing about Indian politics since the 1950s and 1960s were aware of the existence of something like what Shils called 'the gap' between political cultures, political idioms, political discourses in India and other developing countries. This notion of the gap has been stated and restated in different ways during the past half-century up to the present, though often qualified by the argument that there was intercommunication across the boundaries. Weiner called it a gap between elite and mass political culture. The Rudolphs wrote about modernity and tradition. Morris-Jones added a third 'idiom', as he called them, to the modern and traditional, namely, the 'saintly', derived from the discourse and practice of Gandhi and his followers. Indian scholars, anthropologists as well as political scientists, developed other dichotomous modes of analysis of processes of change in Indian society. M.N. Srinivas and others argued that there was a double gap in contemporary India that was mediated through two distinct processes, Sanskritization and westernization. Others have argued that British rule introduced a dichotomy between 'a modern secular state' and traditional ethnic, status-based, religiously derived, and caste-based forms of political mobilization, which were stimulated by the very secular institutions that they were designed to ignore or transcend. Sudipta Kaviraj has formulated yet another version, comprising 'an upper discourse', (elite and modernizing) and a 'lower discourse' that is indigenous. Most articulators of these various dichotomies and trichotomies were also aware that the gap did not constitute an impenetrable barrier to communication between levels in Indian society, that there was a certain amount of interpenetration between/among them as well as discontinuity. What we were not so aware of, or did not know quite how to articulate, was that this very gap was reflected in the distance between the prevailing theoretical framework and our confrontation with the mass political culture, the traditional and saintly idioms, the 'lower discourse'. What some of us did and said was simply that we had to discard the framework when we arrived in the field and find other ways to relate our empirical work and our discoveries about Indian political behaviour to generalizations at the middle and lower ranges of theory in the discipline.

But that framework, the developmentalist framework—whether in its Almond and Coleman guise or in the guise of Shils or the Social Science Research Council Studies in Political Development or Samuel Huntington—has shadowed us for half a century.

What has been greatly missing in most of our work throughout the past 50 years has been an intellectual foothold—I will not call it a theory—from which to launch a critique of Indian politics and the functioning of the Indian polity. We have been weak at critique because we ourselves have been implicated in the propagation of the developmentalist framework that is at the root of the developing crises in India and in many other developing countries. It is not that many of us have not done good ethnographic work that is relevant to theory. But, for the most part, we have ended by fitting our empirical work and our theories into a framework that continues to implicate us in the great celebration of the wonder that is called Indian democracy.

In his last book on India, Weiner launched a biting critique of one among the many blots on this Indian democracy: the persistence of illiteracy and child labour in that country and the nearly total disinterest of policy makers, party leaders, educationists, and others in doing anything about it. Weiner aked why this was the case and answered his question through careful comparative analyses of how and when illiteracy and child labour were eliminated in other countries, including many countries more poorly situated than India. His ultimate answer to the 'why' question in this case was outside the developmentalist framework. It was, in effect—and to put it in my words—that the persistence of illiteracy and child labour contributed to the reproduction of the hierarchical social order of Indian society. So, we learn something thereby about the relationship between the social order and the Indian state, how the state controllers have maintained a myth, a political formula of democracy, while the great mass of the people lack the elemental basis for political and social equality.

In my own recent work on communal violence in India, I have been quite critical of Indian political behaviour. [59] I have used different methods and a different analytical perspective from Weiner, but there is a kind of family resemblance in the conclusions that we have reached by different methods. I say that violence is endemic in north Indian society, that it takes many forms and has many political uses. I say that it persists, though it may appear to ebb and flow, *because*—if you will—there is a communal discourse that sustains it and institutionalized riot systems in particular sites that promote it. Further, I argue that the persistence of communal riots is not a function of a developmental problem, but of a lack of will or interest (in both senses of the word, interest) in stopping them. In fact, on the contrary, most political parties have many times benefited from the persistence of riots and many local political leaders have thrived on them. I say finally that this is another fundamental blot on what we call Indian democracy, not only because of the violence itself, which is, of course, a great evil, but because of the power relations that are sustained by the maintenance of systems of communal violence and communal talk. I refer especially to the fact that communal riots are mostly in fact pogroms against Muslims.[60] The consequence is that Muslims constitute in many parts of the country, in effect, a huge body of second-class citizens.

I mentioned above several other subjects that need more attention outside the developmentalist framework: poverty, the myriad inequalities of caste and gender that persist and sustain relations of deference and obedience in Indian society, corruption. To that list should be added state terrorism, the intensification of a militarized form of nationalism, and the virtual absence of any dissent in Indian society over 56 years concerning India's basic policies on the maintenance of Kashmir as part of the Indian union no matter the cost. The political aspects and implications of the wretched university system in India and its consequences for the lives of students aspiring to improvement of their life chances. The continuing victimization and displacement of tribal peoples and the expropriation of their lands and livelihoods by corrupt state officials in cahoots with local businessmen, police, and politicians in the name of construction of great dams or the creation of 'forest reserves'. The ongoing criminalization of politics, business relations, and police practices and the consequences thereof for present and future political, social, and economic life in India.[61] The existing and possible forms of resistance—not 'participation' or turnout in elections—to the forms of power expressed in all the relations between persons and social forces involved in all the above. The appearance in India from time to time of a very curious, ugly, and disconcerting form of resistance, namely, suicide deaths, for example, of upper caste students in 1998 in response to the decision of the V.P. Singh government to reserve 27 per cent of jobs in public sector enterprises controlled by the Government of India for backward castes and, more recently, the suicide deaths of more than 300 cotton farmers in the state of Andhra Pradesh, reported in 1999, and 275 poor farmers in Karnataka in 2003.[62] In each of these cases and many others that might be conjured up as worth investigation and that appear in one form or another in the pages of that great Indian journal, the *Economic and Political Weekly*, such as, for example, 'the stinking criminal justice system',[63] in such cases the method of choice remains detailed, first-hand, empirical research through in-depth interviewing, asking—as you choose—either 'why' or 'how', but from a standpoint of critique rather than of development.

NOTES

1. This is a somewhat revised and shortened version of my essay, 'India, Myron Weiner, and the Political Science of Development' originally prepared for the *festschrift* conference, India and the Politics of Developing Countries: Essays in Honor of Myron Weiner, held at the Kellogg Institute

for International Studies, University of Notre Dame, 24–6 September 1999.
A longer version was published in the *Economic and Political Weekly*, 20–6
July, 2002, pp. 3026–40, and is available online at *epw.org.in* and through
my own website, *paulbrass.com*.

For a comprehensive and invaluable review of the vast literature on
developmentalism, see Jan Nederveen Pieterse, *Development Theory:
Deconstructions/Reconstructions* (New Delhi: Sage, 2001). This essay is not
meant to offer an alternative theoretical construction nor any new
deconstruction, but simply to emphasize the extent to which the work of
most political scientists of India has been framed within what Nederveen
Pieterse would call an overwhelmingly 'non-reflexive', uncritical,
developmentalist perspective.

2. Myron Weiner, *The Politics of Scarcity: Public Pressure and Political Response in India* (Bombay: Asia Publishing House, 1962), p. 11.
3. Myron Weiner and Joseph LaPalombara, 'The Impact of Parties on Political Development', in *Political Parties and Political Development*, Joseph LaPalombara and Myron Weiner (eds), (Princeton, N.J.: Princeton University Press, 1966), pp. 399-400.
4. Ibid., pp. 351–2.
5. Myron Weiner, '"Congress Restored: Continuities and Discontinuities in Indian Politics', *Asian* Survey, vol. XXII, no. 4 (April), 1982, pp. 351–2.
6. Lloyd I. Rudolph and Susanne H. Rudolph, *The Modernity of Tradition: Political Development in India* (Chicago: University of Chicago Press, 1967), p. 25.
7. Rudolph and Rudolph, *In Pursuit of Lakshmi*, p. 273.
8. The Rudolphs also discussed at length the roles of unorganized groups in Indian politics, what they called 'demand groups' that rely more 'on symbolic and agitational politics', ibid., pp. 252–3. But, their argument about the strength of the Indian state is not affected by this distinction.
9. Paul R. Brass, 'Political Scientists' Images of India', *South Asia*, vol. XXI, no. 1, 1998, pp. 26, 29–30.
10. Atul Kohli, *Democracy and Discontent: India's Growing Crisis of Governability* (Cambridge: Cambridge University Press, 1990), p. 16.
11. Ibid., p. 30.
12. Myron Weiner, 'The Politics of South Asia', in Myron Weiner, *Political Change in South Asia* (Calcutta: Firma K.L. Mukhopadhyay, 1963), p. 39.
13. Jyotirindra Das Gupta, 'India: Democratic Becoming and Combined Development', in *Democracy in Developing Countries*, Larry Diamond, et al. (eds), vol. III: *Asia*, (Boulder, Col.: Lynne Rienner, 1989), p. 59.
14. Edward Shils, 'On the Comparative Study of the New States', *Old Societies and New States: The Quest for Modernity in Asia and Africa*, in Clifford Geertz (ed.), (New York: The Free Press, 1963). See e.g., pp. 7–8 where Shils envisaged this process of enlightenment as involving direct transmission from scholars engaged in the comparative study of the new

136   *Experiencing the State*

states to the students from the new states studying in American universities 'to the enlightenment of opinion and policy there as well'.

15. Myron Weiner, 'India's Two Political Cultures', in Myron Weiner, *Political Change in South Asia* (Calcutta: Firma K.L. Mukhopadhyay, 1963), pp. 150–1.

16. Instead, they took the position that the two sets of goals were not incompatible; Granville Austin, *The Indian Constitution: Cornerstone of a Nation* (Oxford: Clarendon Press, 1966), pp. 48–9.

17. Ralph Retzlaff, *Village Government in India: A Case Study* (New York: Asia, 1962).

18. See especially in this regard James Manor's strongly favourable and hopeful assessment of the new panchayat system recently introduced in Madhya Pradesh in his 'Madhya Pradesh Experiments with Direct Democracy', *Economic and Political Weekly Commentary*, 3 March 2001 (online edition).

19. Weiner and LaPalombara, 1966, p. 425.

20. Ibid., p. 434.

21. Paul R. Brass, *The Politics of India Since Independence*, 2nd ed. (Cambridge: Cambridge University Press, 1994).

22. Leonard Binder et al., *Crises and Sequences in Political Development* (Princeton, N.J.: Princeton University Press, 1971).

23. Das Gupta, 1989, p. 66.

24. Ibid., p. 73.

25. An early exception on this matter was Baldev Raj Nayar, *The Modernization Imperative and Indian Planning* (Delhi: Vikas, 1972).

26. Das Gupta, 1989, p. 93.

27. Ibid, p. 95.

28. Stuart Corbridge, 'Federalism, Hindu Nationalism and Mythologies of Governance in Modern India', in *Federalism: The Multiethnic Challenge*, Graham Smith (ed.), (London: Longman, 1995), pp. 102, 111–12, 116.

29. Kohli, 1990, p. ix.

30. Brass, 1998, p. 30.

31. This term is common usage in India to refer to the central government in New Delhi.

32. J. D. Sethi, *India in Crisis* (Delhi: Vikas, 1975), p. 55.

33. Harold A. Gould, 'A Sociological Perspective on the Eighth General Election in India', *Asian* Survey, vol. XXVI, no. 6 (June), 1986, pp. 634, 637.

34. Paul R. Brass, 'The Strong State and the Fear of Disorder', in *Democracy and Social Transformation*, Francine Frankel (ed.), (New Delhi: Oxford University Press, 2000). For example, in the debate on these issues, one of the very few opponents in the Assembly of the adoption of extreme emergency powers in the Constitution remarked: 'Articles 275 and 276 give the Central Executive and Parliament all the power that can reasonably be conferred on them in order to enable them to see that law and order

do not break down in the country, or that *misgovernment* [my italics] in any part of India is not carried to such lengths as to jeopardise the maintenance of law and order. It is not necessary to go any further.' Pandit Hirday Nath Kunzru in India, *Constituent Assembly Debates: Official Report*, vol. IX (30 July 1949 to 18 September 1949) New Delhi: Government of India Press, 1967, p. 156.

35. B. D. Dua, *Presidential Rule in India, 1950–1984: A Study in Crisis Politics*, revised ed. (New Delhi: S. Chand, 1985), p. 5.
36. Ibid., p. 11.
37. For example, see V. M. Dandekar, 'Unitary Elements in a Federal Constitution', *Economic and Political Weekly*, vol. XXII, no. 44 (31 October) 1987, p. 1870.
38. Selig S. Harrison, *India: The Most Dangerous Decades* (Princeton, N. J.: Princeton University Press, 1960).
39. Kohli, 1990, p. 3.
40. Ibid., p. 5.
41. Ibid., p. 14.
42. James Manor, 'Ethnicity and Politics in India', *International Affairs*, vol. LXXII, no. 3, 1996, pp. 471–2.
43. Samuel P. Huntington, *Political Order in Changing Societies* (New Haven: Yale University Press, 1969).
44. Rajni Kothari, *State Against Democracy: In Search of Humane Governance* (Delhi: Ajanta, 1989), p. 1
45. Ibid., p. 2.
46. Ibid., pp. 13–14.
47. Citation is from the characterization of Dahl's concept of power in Stewart R. Clegg, *Frameworks of Power* (London: Sage, 1989), p. 53.
48. Robert A. Dahl, *A Preface to Democratic Theory* (Chicago: University of Chicago Press, 1956).
49. Joseph Schumpeter, *Capitalism, Socialism, and Democracy*, 3rd ed. (New York: Harper, 1950).
50. I would go a step further insofar especially as the US is concerned, and assert that, along with the dismantling of the domestic functions of the American state and the increasing power of the global corporations, governance of our daily lives has been increasingly taken over by the corporations, seducing us, as Baudrillard would put it, limiting us, identifying us, refusing even basic services to us unless we agree to provide our social security number and other of our most personal, private information, no matter what so-called laws are passed to deny them the right to do so, herding the 'economy' class like cattle into cramped seats on airplanes, submitting us to mechanized formalistic treatment from telephone answering systems to the infernal blasting of wretched music and advertising in our ears, and on and on, but that is another story that

is yet far from India's future and its march towards 'development', this 'have a good day' condition in which the populace of the 'developed states' live.

51. Colin Gordon, 'Government Rationality: An Introduction', in *The Foucault Effect: Studies in Governmentality: With Two Lectures by and an Interview with Michel Foucault*, Graham Burchell, et al., (London: Harvester, 1991), p. 3.

52. As many observers have noted, it is 'state power' that these movements wish, access to the same resources and privileges that the upper castes have monopolized for so long, but they have no alternative conception of governance. See, for example, Sudha Pai, 'The State, Social Justice, and the Dalit Movement: The BSP in Uttar Pradesh', in *Democratic Governance in India: Challenges of Poverty, Development, and Identity*, Niraja Gopal Jayal and Sudha Pai (eds), (New Delhi: Sage, 2001), pp. 201–20.

53. Gordon, 1991, p. 7.

54. Michel Foucault, 'What is Critique?', in *The Politics of Truth*, SylvPre Lotringer and Lysa Hochroth (eds), (New York: Semiotext [e], 1997), p. 28.

55. Ronald Inden, 'Embodying God: from imperial progresses to national progress in India', *Economy and Society*, vol. XXIV, no. 2 (May), 1995, pp. 245–78.

56. The phrase comes, of course, from Ashis Nandy, 'The Politics of Secularism and the Recovery of Religious Tolerance', in *Mirrors of Violence: Communities, Riots, and Survivors in South Asia*, Veena Das (ed.), (Delhi: Oxford University Press, 1990), pp. 69–93.

57. A notable move in this direction has been made by Akhil Gupta, *Postcolonial Developments: Agriculture in the Making of Modern India* (Durham: Duke University Press, 1998).

58. This last one needs to be answered here once and for all. My answer is as follows. First, UP does, in fact, stand for India in several respects: 1) it is in India and could not be anywhere else; 2) it is the largest political unit in India; 3) the living conditions of most of its people are at approximately the same level as the rest of North India and parts of eastern India as well; 4) although living conditions in some other parts of India are somewhat better in some respects, they are not so much better anywhere as to set them so far apart from UP as to place them in some other world. Further, I have done research and travelled in other parts of India as well, especially Bihar where I did research off and on for about 10 years, Punjab, Gujarat, Madras, Assam, Kerala, and, of course, Delhi, where I have interviewed politicians and other persons from all parts of the country.

59. Paul R. Brass, *The Production of Hindu-Muslim Violence in Contemporary India* (Seattle: University of Washington Press, 2003; and Delhi: Oxford University Press, 2003).

60. A fact egregiously and fatuously denied by Ashutosh Varshney in 'Understanding Gujarat Violence', *conconflicts.ssrc.org/gujarat/varshney*.
61. Many of these practices that are part of everyday life in India, and their consequences for the poor, are very effectively brought out in an exemplary work by James Manor, *Power, Poverty, and Poison: Disaster and Response in an Indian City* (New Delhi: Sage, 1993).
62. For the Andhra suicides, see C. Shambhu Prasad, 'Suicide Deaths and Quality of Indian Cotton: Perspectives from History of Technology and Khadi Movement', *EPW*, vol. XXXIV, no. 5 (30 January) 1999; for Karnataka, see Parvathi Menon, 'From Debt to Death', *Frontline* (27 September –10 October 2003), online at www.flonnet. com/fl2020/stories/2003101003810800.htm
63. *Economic and Political Weekly*, vol. XXXIV, no. 12 (20 March) 1999, p. 647.

EXPERIENCING THE STATE FROM BELOW IN
VILLAGE INDIA AND GERMANY AND
URBAN KARACHI

5

Experiencing Reunification
An East German Village
After the Fall of The Wall

Helmuth Berking

The process of unification has meant that Germany must come to grips with new and contradictory predicaments. The last fourteen years have demonstrated that the standard strategy of modernization is simply not succeeding in restructuring Eastern Germany's economy and that the much-touted locational appeal of the East for industry does not now and may never exist. Above all, more than a decade of unification indicate that, far from having achieved the desired degree of social integration, the process seems only to have aggravated the cultural gap between East and West citizens. How do citizens of one state experience and cope with their sudden and permanent envelopment by another, much more powerful one?

As the euphoria of the celebrations subsided, disenchantment quickly set in, and today the scene is dominated on both sides by strong resentments that have hardened into such stereotypical figures of fun as the *Besser-Wessi* ('know-it-all' West German) and the *Jammer-Ossi* ('woe-is-me' East German). Today the 'Ossies' bitterly complain about the Westerners' unbridled arrogance and presumptuousness, suffer from severe competitive pressures and the tender mercies of the profit motive, and want their Wall back, only this time a bit higher. The characterizations by West Germans are not much kinder, labelling as they do their new brothers and sisters as lazy, unreliable, and—measured in terms of Western behaviour—somewhat slow and therefore stupid. A commonplace slur by the West Germans is that Ossies 'want to live like capitalists, but when it comes to work they prefer socialism.' There seems to be no getting used to one another's profoundly irritating ways.

Cultural otherness—experienced here as superiority, there as collective degradation—not only impairs social interaction between the two groups, it inevitably obstructs the necessary structural adjustment processes and heightens the social distortions stemming from reunification. In the East there has long been sarcastic talk of the naked colonization of their provinces, and, when you come right down to it, in the blink of an eye a whole society, with its 40-year history, was indeed made to vanish, customary ways of life were insulted and assaulted, vocational qualifications often gained at great cost were summarily invalidated, and ingrained ideological certainties disappeared—not all of which, of course, need be mourned.

Once the walls behind which the poor relations subsisted had finally crumbled, a new, hitherto unknown, ethnic group suddenly emerged, and with it a new kinship-oriented racism that did little to encourage normal everyday encounters based on at least a modicum of mutual respect. The initial phase of unification even saw some brawls break out. Take these exemplary scenarios: an indignant West-woman scolds a surprised East-woman who, quite innocent of the Western taste for liberal child-rearing practices, has slapped her own child in public; or, at a supermarket checkout a West woman roundly denounces the East father for stealing a candy bar for his child, noting gruffly about this miscreant, 'otherwise you'll never learn'; or the avid East woman grabs the last available TV dinner from her West compatriot's shopping cart and goes into the ensuing fray with, for her, the clinching argument that after all, for 40 years she has had to do without. By now, on the other hand, and after minor casualties, each wary group is doing its level best to steer clear of the other.

The expectations of the East German population have, despite some significant improvements in income and living standards, taken a turn for the worse. Whereas in 1990 82 per cent of East Germans believed that the federal government was doing too little to bring about parity in the living conditions in both parts of the country, in 1994, after transfer payments amounting to a not inconsiderable 600 billion marks, this figure still dropped to 76 per cent. If in 1990 84 per cent of East Germans saw themselves as 'second-class citizens', today 83 per cent continue to see this self-description as well justified.

71 per cent would welcome the election of PDS—the successor-party of the former communists—to the Bundestag which actually happened. By now (2004), the PDS electorate outnumbers all other parties in most of the Eastern states. When asked to comment on the distribution of social qualities between East and West, the East Germans awarded themselves a rating of 77 to 4 for '[socially responsible] attitudes', 63 to 8 for 'honesty', while a score of 77 to 4 was easily conceded to the West Germans for the less coveted quality 'arrogance' (Spiegel 33/1994, p. 111).

Other polls underline the trend toward a deep depoliticization of East German society, whose inhabitants saw the introduction of democracy more as a call to break with a long-standing tradition of overpoliticization than as an opportunity to take a responsible and effective hand in reshaping German social realities. The second structural challenge—transformation of a socialist planned economy into one based on private ownership and the free market—has not garnered mass support. If in 1990 77 per cent still accepted the bright and shiny notion of a market economy, a mere 35 per cent still favoured this disappointing model by the end of 1993 (Srubar 1994, p. 216). At least in 2004, contemporary political debate had to aknowledge that the 'Aufbau Ost' failed. Regional disparities deepened, Westbound migration resulted in a significant population decrease in the contryside as well as in the cities in the East, unemployment is skyrocketing, and the very effects of this ongoing brain-drain do not offer any hope for a turnaround in the near future.

How can these divergent yet deeply interrelated patterns of perception and interpretation be explained? What cultural background assumptions and stocks of tradition, what norms and values determine perception and action orientation, imparting to the everyday dialectic of intrinsic and extrinsic attributions this specific, resentment-laden expression?

I will start by describing structural problems bearing on the 'unique German journey' (Offe) from socialism to capitalism, and its problems and unintended consequences in terms of the new constraints which a wholesale transfer of Western-style state and market institutions implied for the reorganization of everyday life in the East. In the next section, significant narratives will be identified and used to address the nature of discrepant expectations that seem so clearly to dominate individual and collective actors in modern Germany. My underlying thesis is a simple one: 40 years of cultural modernization in the West—slotted under the laudatory keywords: individualization, detraditionalization. and pluralization of life-forms—have generated a West German social character and a symbolic order which coldly gazes, with a complete lack of under-standing, upon those whose personal identities, socialization, and sociation were formed by 40 years of life in a bygone socialism depicted as inferior in absolutely *every* way.

So these cultural codes and symbolic orders cannot help but bypass each other or clash when they do meet. The specific mode of unification tended to reinforce the Western model, indeed, it amounted to the enforced allocation by state institutions of the experiences—if not, formal statuses—of inferiority and superiority in a highly skewed manner. Today it is the complete invalidation of the East German population's biographical experience that appears as the institutional presupposition, the prime condition and admission ticket, that constitutes the *sine qua non* for full participation in the new order. I begin with a brief description of German unification and the social and cultural consequences it entailed.

In contrast to the developmental paths taken by western industrial societies where, as a rule, nation, market, and democracy emerged step by step, the societies of Eastern and Central Europe face the daunting problem of achieving concurrently all the structural aims of modernization: especially, to square a rocky transition to a capitalist economy with the development of working democratic institutions, and to establish conditions for the creation of a class in possession of the means of production with the consent of a majority of those who, at least initially, will not profit from it. In this configuration of 'political capitalism' (Max Weber), market and democracy appear fated to obstruct one another. Here is the 'dilemma of simultaneity', of which Offe aptly speaks. Historically, a market economy has been 'set in motion only under predemocratic conditions. In order to promote it, democratic rights must be held back in order to allow for a healthy dose of original accumulation.... But the introduction of a market economy in the postsocialist societies is a "political" project, which has prospects of success only if it rests on strong democratic legitimation. And it is possible that the majority of the population finds neither democracy nor a market economy a desirable perspective' (Offe 1991, p. 872).

The 'specific German course' at least appears to have been successful in circumnavigating this structural problem. The complexity of the transformation process was eased rather peremptorily by grafting the entire system of West Germany's institutional order onto the civil society of the former German Democratic Republic (GDR). Market and democracy came from the outside. What therefore constitutes the most severe challenge in the German case is not the concurrent creation of democracy and market economy in some sort of equilibrium but the adaption of a society to an institutional order as yet alien to it.

To function successfully, institutions, whether private or public, require a broader foundation of social and cultural structures and understandings that broadly correspond to their own goals and procedures. Every institutional order is embedded in a whole set of norms and cultural values, adequate action orientations, routines, expectations and assessments which help to make things comprehensible. This essentially cultural framing is what is meant by the need to attend to the noninstitutional presuppositions of any institution, and these intangible elements can by no means be transferred easily and unproblematically along with physical devices and equipment. One of the crucial dimensions of the ongoing institutional transfer from West to East and its forced transformation of the latter from notions of collective to private interest, from homogeneity to plurality, from autocratic decision-making to bureaucratic procedures is therefore that of 'extrinsic roles' (for a detailed analysis see Berking and Neckel 1992).

The everyday life problems of 'extrinsic roles' can be observed in a very graphic form in East German communities today. First of all, one needs to train and create personnel, and citizens, capable of fleshing out this strange new institutional framework. But how are East Germans to be able to grasp these often perplexing rules—many of which are informal or misleading or extremely subtle—of the game, which they are compelled to act as if they can learn in a trice? In their shaky but ongoing lives as politicians or businessmen, as civil servants or traffic offenders, as voters or welfare clients, their biographical experience and personal identities often chafe against the new conceptions of their roles hauled in by Western institutionalizers.

What, seen from a distant and imperious institutional perspective, presents itself as a stubborn lack of adaptability is experienced by the East German population as an impugning of their competence, a coerced self-invalidation and institutionally prescribed inferiority. This friction-laden situation was intensified by the fact that the institutional transfer to the East was accompanied by a bevy of ambitious Western managers. West German politicians, administrators, lawyers, managers, and professors today hold the positions formerly held by the old socialist establishment. It is these Western experts, financially cushioned by a so-called 'bush allowance', who are busy building the new administrations, advising the municipalities in legal matters, running the banking and credit sector, and, all in all, intrepidly transforming the strategic advantages afforded them by their familiarity with the new reigning institutional profile into symbolic and, not rarely, economic capital too. It is witnessing activities of this kind that helps substantiate the self-perception of East Germans as second-class citizens in their old haunts. Following the dramatic downturn in career curves after 1989, one of the few constants of life in East Germany—aside from the otherwise totally unknown phenomenon of mass unemployment—is that higher rungs on the social ladder are blocked, that those Easterners scrambling upward get shunted off into the second or third echelon, and that each individual is forced to reconstitute his professional life under the ubiquitous supervision of not so frequently sympathetic Western experts.

MISCONCEPTIONS AND 'THE MICROCOSMS OF LIFE'

One way to understand structural incompatibilities in East-West identity constructions and patterns of perception is to focus on the contours of those habitual customs and cultural traditions which emerged in part during the 40-year history of socialist society but in part also in open rebellion or secret opposition against the behavioural coercion of East Germany's didactic-dictatorial state. We know hardly anything, a few exceptions notwithstanding (see Niethammer et al.1991), about the 'microcosms of life', the daily forms of relationships, the unspectacular reserves of resistance, the assimilation pressures and the power games at play in what was 'really existing' socialism.

The dominant social science views are characterized by a structuralist-theoretical fixation on forms of hegemony, repressive state apparatuses, and mechanisms of system integration which see the GDR as 'bureaucratic socialism', an 'organization society' (Pollack 1990), a politically overdetermined 'monosubject' (Adler 1991), a 'niche society' (Gaus, critiqued in Mayer 1993). According to these views the key structural markers are: systematic homogenization of social life through central planning bodies, monopolizing of structures of power through party leaders in line with the 'principle' of democratic centralism, and the eradication and/or subordination of intermediary organizations and civil bodies. In short, it was the transformation of state and society into a 'working body' and 'Head Plant'(see Niethammer 1990; Thaa 1991; Neckel 1992) structured hierarchically under the supervision of the SED (Socialist Unity Party of Germany) which in turn was propped up on the outside through the Soviet army, and on the inside through barbed wire, the wall, and a gigantic apparatus of surveillance and repression. Accordingly, in retrospect, the stability of the GDR seems to have been a direct effect of two intertwined political forces: the state mechanisms governing 'protection and obedience' plus 'assimilation and reward' for the acquiescent in the population, and an all-encompassing, apparatus of coercion widely known, and not loved, as 'Stasi.' Moreover, as Pollack describes

all institutions, all companies, all parties, and all citizens aspired for decades to show good behavior because that was their only chance to get a piece of the centrally-administrated cake. Only insofar as one was prepared to assimilate, which meant, in fact, to cede one's freedom to the system and thus to strengthen the system with one's labor power, could one expect to receive system-administrated benefits, for example, social security, a career, or consumer goods, or even personal freedom. In order to profit one participated. And since one had to participate/collaborate in order to profit, the system remained stable over decades (1990, p. 226).

Hence, the abrupt breakdown of East German socialist society is often interpreted, among other things, as a pure consequence of economic dysfunctionality, which could no longer guarantee the balance between gratification and conformity necessary for the survival of the power elite. Why the Stasi, in spite of its intimidating omnipresence, failed so miserably to hold the structure together anyway remains a puzzle. To this oversimplified picture of socialist organization realities is usually added a likewise oversimplified theory wherein those Eastern subalterns appear, depending on the political inclination of the observer, either as a collective of victims or as eager conformists.

However, beside the official power structures and formal politicized forms of organization, a second and equally important but informal sphere of influence had evolved. This crucial network was based on close personal relationships in an arena in which it was neither planning edicts nor hard cash but norms of reciprocity that ultimately regulated intimate social interaction. The often neglected or overlooked fact that everyday life in East Germany could have been forged only with an astonishing investment of energy, imagination, and many personal risks beyond the ideologically permissible (and often verging on political crime) must contradict the usual dismissive portrayal of a systemically disenfranchised population enmired in passivity and impotence (Mayer 1993, 47f).

Life in this 'divided reality' is in itself a vital marker of socialist society, or as Piotr Sztompka puts it: 'the most fundamental and lasting cultural code organizing thought and action in the conditions of real socialism is the opposition of two spheres of life: private (personal) and public (official)' (1993, p. 90). What results is not only a whole series of binary oppositions, like 'society' versus 'state', 'we' versus 'them', etc. These attributions at the same time imply a 'dual morality' (Srubar 1994, p. 208). The private is the sphere of the good, of virtue, of a personally upright conduct of life in which reliability and solidarity are solidly at home, while the public sphere, characterized by power, corruption, and oppression, is diametrically opposed to the domain of private life. The self-perception of these actors as being morally bound to one another is in no way altered by the additional aspect that at all levels, including the sphere of state action, personal networks and 'tied parties' provided for the redistribution of scarce goods and sought-after positions, and nepotism, clientelism, and patronage that constituted the actual action orientations. Yet a strong sense of moral self-obligation and solidarity were reserved exclusively for these personal networks and by no means extended to the legal-rational realm.

Since no state can wholly neglect the mobilization of loyalty and legitimacy, but rather is dependent on voluntary allegiance and inner consensus, the question remains how the problematic of social integration and conflict really had unfolded in this split construction of reality, and what effects this dual morality had on everyday interactions between true believers, loyal citizens, conformists, opportunists, oppositionals, and cultural dissidents.

COMMUNITY AND STRATEGY

To illustrate the day-to-day meaning of the informal, moral economy of socialism, I look at a small Brandenburg village which will give us an opportunity to meet the diverse social figures, characterized here as representative types, who offer in their entirety some insights into the banal yet very tricky interplay of politics and morality, adaption and resistance—all of which militate against the commonplace schematic view of omnipotent power and repression.

The ensuing portrayal is based on a project 'Forty years of Socialism', undertaken in a local 'history workshop' (*Geschichtswerkstatt*) in this community from 1991 until 1993. Within the confines of the project 28 interviews concerning the relationship between politics and everyday life with persons who had mostly beeen selected because of their representativeness due to their individual combinations of position and reputation in the old or the new local establishment. The narratives of these key agents and several group interviews with both teachers and students form the basis for the following account.

Grunthal, situated about 70 kilometres to the northeast of Berlin in the midst of forests and lakes, is a village of 502 inhabitants rich in traditions. Connected loosely with the district's central town via a third degree rural route and a sideline of the German Reichsbahn, its inhabitants live a quiet, rural life. Big politics nevertheless threaded through the fabrics of their lives for at least a century. The last German emperor used to hunt here, followed by Hermann Goering who built Karinhall here, and finally both little and big Erich commandeered the state hunting grounds which resulted in certain welcome privileges for the local hunting club but also in quite irksome limitations of freedom of movement for the local population.

At the political-organizatorial level Grunthal constitutes a miniature edition of official GDR society. The SED was the strongest party with 55 members. One finds, unsurprisingly, that the large block parties, with the exception of the liberal party, were the socialist mass organizations — the 'Young Pioneers', the 'Free German Youth', 'the Free German Leage of Trade Unions', the 'Society for German-Soviet friendship', the 'Society for Sports and Technology', and the 'Democratic League of Women.' In addition, we also find the 'National Front' jostling for membership numbers beside the local athletic, fishing, and hunting clubs. In short, given the actual number of inhabitants, Grunthal had an intermeshed, overlapping, and hierarchically organized network of social control and command of political loyalty firmly, if rather diffusely, in place. Membership in any of these organizations provided coveted privileges. Those who wanted to elude the pressure tactics of SED party canvassers but were not willing to surrender all hope for a good career would get involved with the block parties, and thus expressed, at least officially, their basic consent in the most innocuous way possible.

Membership in the 'Free German Youth' was usually a prerequisite for access to higher education and universities, and the minimum requirement for work in the primary pedagogical positions—for example, kindergarten teachers—was at the very least to join the 'Society for German-Soviet Friendship'. Membership in the 'Society for Sports and Technology' was the easiest route to obtaining a driver's license. In the local administrative council, each organization had seats and votes. The mayor's office was always occupied by the SED cadre, except during a short CDU spell. Hence, this organization model of systematic over-politicization dominated by the local SED, and higher up on the administrative level controlled by the area council, regulated the interplay of inclusions and exclusions concerning the distribution of advantages and disadvantages.

The economy of the village centred on forestry and agriculture. For centuries owned by the von Ahlimbs family, the community is marked by the East Elbian 'Gutsherrschaft' which, until the first decades of the twentieth century, provided a living for farm workers and their dependants though not for free peasants and independent craftsworkers. This situation changed only in 1934 with the land reform of the feudal estate, which created some 60 private agricultural and forestry enterprises. By the late 1940s, Grunthal reached its top populace with over 1000 new inhabitants, including refugees and urban Berliners, willing to try their luck as farmers. When the polytechnic high school was built in 1963, the socio-structural and political situation shifted. From this point on we behold two feuding organizations of the SED: the agricultural communes formed by agricultural workers in 1953 that continued to struggle economically until their disastrous final collapse; and the collective of teachers who were so very different in habitus and biography from farmers. The 24 teachers introduced 'socialist culture' in the village and began to dominate local politics, honing the fine points of ideological education, and not only of the students. Devout Christians or vote-dodgers became labelled as 'enemies of the peace' and the political fight for the souls of the children provoked drastic family conflicts.

In this locality we also find, besides a overpoliticized organizational structure, a well-organized opposition in the Protestant church and particularly in the person of the local minister. This was a religiously motivated and morally integrated milieu in which we find vibrant remains of the traditional bourgeoisie and master craftsmen class which continued to rub salt in the wounds of the envisioned socialist unitary society.

K., the Protestant minister, arrived in Grunthal in 1953 and quickly came into conflict with the local organs of state. The main topic then and now is religious versus atheist youth education. The so-called 'Youth Initiation Ceremony' (*Jugendweihe*) had been invented as a socialist substitute for the 'confirmation of faith' ceremony (in Protestantism) and had long been an acrimonious bone of contention. For the party committee and the teachers any new induction thereby into their camp meant a little star in their records; for the dissenting families this ideological quarrel meant they somehow had to cross a threshold beyond the public expression of loyalty to the state in such a way as to preserve an educational future of their children. This state requirement became an 'infernal imposition' for active Christians, to which some did eventually submit under the pressure of promised rewards. It was not only in his role as minister but also as father of five children that K. experienced the

extent of perfidiousness of the local state power. The conflict erupted
when his second-born boy was refused admission to higher education
because of his religious world view and his refusal to participate in
the 'Youth Initiation Ceremony.'

Minister K., perturbed, wrote thus to the central board of education: 'I can still remember the day when Jewish classmates were
removed from our school, not because they could not live up to the
standards, but because they were, in quotes, "different". At that point
they had not been gassed yet. That came later; so where, if you please,
lies the difference between someone being refused for racist or now
for ideological reasons?' Whoever questioned the basic anti-fascist
consensus—a political-moral orientation which was of fundamental
integrative meaning for the citizenry—in such a sensationally open
fashion had to expect the worst. Yet, despite some threats and an
interrogation by the Stasi, nothing much happened. Nevertheless,
his son was refused admission to higher education and Minister K.
chose private education for his other sons in order to make them
largely independent from state mechanisms of repression. In any case,
at least in the last decade of the GDR's existence, the number of
cases involving personal demotion and persecution was surprisingly
low. Those who openly expressed dissent were left in peace at some
point, except if they tried to become politically active and organize.

Over the years the minister was able to find more support in the
community for his non-statist vision of moral authority. His cause
was further fuelled by an unseemly fuss over the funeral for the night
watchman and parish clerk. Because he had been both a Communist
and a church member a bitter quarrel arose over the proper disposal
of his corpse. Against the resistance of the party a full church funeral
finally got under way but not without taking flak. When the SED
delegates refused to remove their hats at the open grave the minister
refused to continue the ceremony. This tension-laden showdown only
ended when the comrades at last agreed to bare their heads. From
this point on a highly personalized, as well as ideological, war was
declared between the respective sides.

But who were the members of the parish? Next to a few who had
a foot in both camps—seeking paradise on earth and in heaven
equally, so to speak—the members were primarily the victims of
forced collectivization. The first wave of collectivization in Grunthal

in the early 1950s affected primarily the so-called 'hunger victims', people who during the land reform had become peasants and farmers, and who joined the collective LPG because they had realized after years of unsuccessful toil that they could not survive economically. The 'real' farmers, though, insisted on their independence. This situation only changed at the beginning of the 1960s under massive threats—such as 'if you don't sign, we will fence in your plot, close up your chimney, and then you'll see where you go'—and a ruinous policy of increased taxes on private agriculture.

This coercive form of recruitment for the LPG cooperative also coincided with the 'inner resignation' of the farmers, expressed in local sayings like 'I know better, but if that's the way they want it . . .' There were nonetheless frequent occurrences of strikes and of violent threats against the impassive local administration. In addition, up until the breakdown of the GDR, there was no one in the local peasantry who had been willing to take up leadership positions in the cooperative. Administrative leadership was an extremely unpopular position that one chose only to perform a service to the party (and oneself), not for one's constituency. Since none of the former independent farmers joined the party, all in all, no one had much left to lose anyway, and these people found it possible to declare their religious faith as openly as they pleased.

The local true believers, on the other hand, were comprised by the SED leadership cadre, especially a majority of teachers. These people disproportionately represented those segments of society born in 1935–48, and those belonging to two generations whose political socialization happened solely within the horizon of GDR experience. 'We were raised to execute orders given to us', said a former mayor and party secretary. Both generations were active in building the GDR, graduated from 'peasants and workers faculties' and obtained positions that would not have been open to them so readily under capitalist conditions. Those who got support from political mass organizations and delegated by the party helped to close the worrying gaps in the functional apparatus of state and society caused by the emigration of millions of highly qualified people to the West. One should not belittle this phenomenon. This overarching mechanism of collective social advancement, beside the ideological reassurance it offered to serve a better and anti-fascist Germany, formed one of the key conditions of the winning voluntary inner consent to the 'system' (see Engler 1992a, 88f). In these circles socialism and inner consent were genuinely at home.

THE OLD STATE AS OUTSIDER

If one carefully examines 'belonging' as defined within the local community, we find in Grunthal a politically and ideologically fixed configuration of 'the established and the outsiders' (Elias and Scotson 1990) as opposed to the publicly voiced communal rhetoric. All 15 cooperative leaders and a majority of teachers—almost 90 per cent of those who represent the local power of the state and about 70 per cent of SED members—came from outside the community. Socialism was brought to Grunthal and kept alive through 'campaign biographies' quite typical for GDR careerists following the overt state ideological projects sloganized as, 'cadres to the northern regions' or 'teachers to the villages'.

When a 'new' phenomenon, which is not seldom associated with evil *per se*, is insinuated from outside and, moreover, wields considerable power, its agenda must account not only the normatively guided internal and external differential of the local community but also include a scheme for carrying out an adequate redefinition of 'frames' for cooperation and interest-led arrangements.

From the point of view of established local residents the available social space appears as a hierarchical structure of different levels of integration and the accompanying power differential appears as a kind of topographical order. A community-centred 'morality of proximity' based on a sociology of intimacy and shaped by norms of egalitarianism and recognition marks out the inner circle while the outside margins are populated by the devout deputies of socialism who fight both for their own recognition in the community and to secure loyalty for the state socialist goals. But the bigger the social differential between state groups and everyone else, the weaker the normative standards of the local group becomes especially with respect to authorities. Outsiders, after all, can be treated differently and with less probity than one's own people.

Hence, the community-centred 'morality of proximity' starts fraying at these margins. This applies in particular to the third concentric circle, the outermost one which, in this case, refers to the regional council with its own lurking Stasi department. The local state representatives thus share with the inner circle of established residents a wary perception of that outermost circle on which, however, they remain dependent for their own power and whose system goals they are required to implement.

To resolve this nagging dilemma—that social acceptance remains the *sine qua non* for realizing socialist state goals on the local level even as a community 'moral of proximity' works fundamentally to contradict the party-line—we have to distinguish between three ideal types of interactive strategies. First, there is a politics which intrudes from the outermost ring and ignores the local situation completely; a stilted politics that is conditioned to order and obedience and which in the long run fails because the sanctions with which it threatens offenders could not in the end be executed. This politics is personified in the first school principal: 'With him', says an old Grunthaler, 'dictatorship arrived in the village.' Among other typical examples of this behavioural pattern are the black leather coated folk in the back pews of the church and the handful of party secretaries who eagerly report any sort of compromise or discouraging words immediately as ideological deviation to the regional state power.

Second, there is the 'all for our people, all for our village' strategy— an enormously work-intensive style of fraternization and graft within the local community, for which trust and social acceptance depend on local benefits and the proven distance of each individual from influence of the outermost ring. Hans E., born 1933, for instance, was mayor in Grunthal from 1957 to 1990 and now local leader of the PDS, frequently is depicted by enemies—of which he possesses far fewer than other local functionaries—as a 'red angel'. He represents the kind of the mediator who knows all the tricks of the trade and who is not overly bothered by a double standard. His motto 'together with and for humankind' gains its resonant community meaning through his locally responsive but rhetorically conciliatory framing of activities for consumption by the outermost ring, as is evident in his enunciations of 'But everything as absolutely legal' and 'Always cleverly covered up', and so forth.

'I could risk certain things because the community always stood behind me and because I could show results', he admits. 'I just departed a little bit from the narrow path, but it has never caught up with me.' Quite the contrary. The regional council's investigative unit would visit the village because of concerns such as unlawfully erected single family homes or questionable billing practices, but actually strengthened the position of the mayor who cheerfully organized his community in the spirit of the state directives—never mind that he paid volunteers from the municipal purse or billed more hours than were actually worked. 'That's how we fleeced them' though, as mentioned, it was 'always cleverly covered up.' Money designated as handouts for loyalty to the system instead formed the monetary lifeblood for the local realm of social interaction as it was diplomatically overseen by the mayor, which in turn, made it possible for him to represent himself to the people above as a loyal and successful functionary.

The third strategy of interaction can be characterized as a peculiar mix of know-how, authoritarian behaviour, and a morality based on principles modelled on the idea of justice and fairness. 'Don't get the wrong impression here, I do have the Party membership insignia. In my own case, I was never under the thumb of anyone, but the idea of socialism seems still quite rational', says Eva A. Born in 1940, she is a farmer and agricultural economist who administered the local agricultural cooperative for over a decade. Her self-perception as a person with valued expertise and moral integrity is largely shared by the townspeople. She ended the state of war between party and church by permitting horsecarts belonging to the LPG to be used for religious festivities and by allowing 'her' workers to participate in church activities while the collective paid them.

In short, Eva is in every respect the prototype of a 'good Communist', which we find quite often at work on this local level. The good Communist, just like the good Christian, is somebody who can sacrifice his own immediate interests for the cause without appearing doctrinaire and who does not simply pass on the straight jacket of state directives to his underlings but rather tries to ease up, find gaps, make room for play, knowing life and also its tricksters, and thus gets along well with everybody. The respect that anyone earns in such a social position, of course, is based exclusively on the person, never on his or her function. It is the good person, who accidentally also is a Communist, that one values and respects, while one keeps in mind how one could use this person's access to positions of power to one's own benefit.

If I somehow have created the impression of an utterly over-politicized local community riddled with internal strife, this image has to be vigorously challenged, at least from the wilier and savvier perspective of the villagers themselves. For, surprisingly, according to a majority of interviewees there was no politics in the village; politics, as they understood it, played no role at all in everyday life. Politics was the business of the local state power and its fraught connection to the regional council. This interpretation does not seem as erroneous or obtuse as it sounds. Falsified reports and sundry advantages based on personal loyalties, private conflict solutions, and clandestine arrangements strengthened the trust in individual talent and everyday coping strategies to the same degree as they undermined the legitimacy of the socialist institutions and of their representatives. The feeling of powerlessness alluded to earlier turned out on examination to refer only to centralized, not local, politics.

All such actors were 'reachable', could be open to argument and persuasion. Votes were often bartered with rare commodities such as housing, building permits, and so forth. The political cadres punished well-known non-voters with the denial of social advantages/rewards: 'You did not vote so therefore I cannot meet your request.' Besides the so-called 'Buckle-down-wares'—services and goods attainable exclusively through political channels—all economic exchange was connected to person-oriented networks of relationships not accessible through money or position, but exclusively through closeness to the issue itself. Rural life, in fact, offered quite a few advantages since every family possessed some objects of exchange, originating usually from some agricultural sideline or private small stock raising. They know each other and they know how to show their gratitude.

THE NEW STATE AS OUTSIDER

Wolfgang Engler has called this underlying structural mechanism of socialist real life 'de-objectivization (Engler 1992b)', which means, first, the disappearance of all objective social structures, the mixing of law and both public and private morality, that is, a reduction of functionally differentiated forms of societation to unmediated relationships; second, the de-economization of economic action, the destruction of market rationalism through state planning, and the reduction of allocation and distribution to unmediated relationships; and third, the de-bureaucratization of administrative action, the superiority of ideological knowledge over expertise, and the loss of predictability and legitimate administrative action, and thus the reduction again of all these to unmediated relationships.

It is the political economy of socialism that bestirs these formally unacknowleged (and unnoticed) economic communities which, however precariously, are forced into personalized alliances in which traditional forms of habitus become preserved and an exclusive solidarity is nurtured. And it is precisely the identity constructions resulting from such economic communities for which the bi-polar codings of socialist solidarity and capitalist self-interst, GDR-style '*GemÅtlichkeit*' and West German-style social incompetence, which rule both self definition and the defining of others, now seem indispensable. The person-based distribution networks were solitary communities of a very singular kind, whose operational logic, of course, disappeared when the encompassing system became altered after the fall of the Wall. There is little that remained of the moral orientation of these self-help groups apart from the nostalgic invocation of community spirit. Whereas the village community had already been multiply divided during the socialist period, unification politics creates new lines of conflict which diminish the potential social-integrative power of the community-based 'moral of proximity.'

At first it was the hour of the minister and his clientele. He called to life a local citizen's interest group which won the first local elections by riding a CDU-ticket. Political change has gone hand in hand with abrupt generational change. Today, it is the 25 to 35-year olds who represent the new local state power. German unification was greeted with church bells and the national anthem, a ceremony which the attending SED members greeted with disgust. The culture of village festivities, dominated for decades by outsiders, seemingly returns to— or takes refuge in—its traditional bosom.

Change, as before, is largely driven by external factors which have taken on drastically different forms. It starts with the new institutional order that throws people off well-worn paths and disrupts the customary organization of daily life. Consequently, the local agricultural cooperative (employing 125 workers) was disbanded; the polytechnic secondary school was cut to the size of a village school; ideologically suspect teachers were dismissed or transferred to other districts. Although real estate values, as well as a 'rural economy of modesty' (see Inhetveen 1994) connecting communities bound by years of common economic shortages, soften the blow of financial losses, they can hardly compensate for the existential loss of meaning in people's lives inflicted by unemployment. The privatizing of formerly cooperative-owned land (see Bergmann 1992) motivated a mere trio of peasants to strike out as private farmers. Others, who regained ownership of their land deeds, succumb to a fascination with personal power, which results in a politics oriented solely towards their own benefit. A village meadow, for example, that was used for decades as the shortcut between a single family dwelling neighbourhood and the village centre, is now fenced in and off limits. Outrageous price tags are attached to parcels of land that used to be readily available to those building houses with the support of friends and neighbours. In legal matters, courts rather than personal negotiations are now settling disputes between neighbours.

The New appears on the scene also in the guise of a West Berlin cultural entrepreneur who settles in the former gate buildings of the feudal estate and established here, with charitable contributions of the mayor and the regional employment office, a development company which eventually employed 120 state-sponsored temporary workers. They clean up, carve new trails, dream of an ecologically sound agriculture and thus start to shape cultural life in the village just as the teachers did in the mid-1960s. With people subscribing to a romanticized image of rural life, village festitvities are again organized from outside, a local newspaper was founded and the initial funding for the history workshop also came out of this effort. The majority of the villagers, however, participate today without really being engaged. Socio-structural differentiations steadily become more visible while the hazy memory of socialist everyday life beckons in the stubborn egalitarian formula that proclaims that 'back then, all had little but nobody had nothing.'

The only group that survived the transformation process as a collective actor is the old ideological community, largely drawn from the old establishment. (When the local parish priest retired in 1992, the political influence of the parish also declined.) Although the PDS lost almost half of its membership—including such local heroes as the leader of the National Front—it finally succeeded in achieving what the SED never managed in all its decades of power. After being initially ostracized, party representatives now encounter the kind of social, if not political, acceptance that they had struggled for but never achieved in the previous regime. The PDS now takes credit for embodying the continuity of a stable (if monstrously spied-upon) life once led by millions and the party's policy of invoking anti-capitalist resentments also resonates with the disappointments suffered by the former East German population.

Further and paradoxically, loyalty to a party that can no longer bestow personal advantage in return, is now honoured. Trust in the new/old party establishment has become sugar-coated with the seductive optimism of nostalgia. It is heavily coloured by the collective suspicion that unification, as the project of a patently 'foreign' elite, permanently has pushed everyone into an inferior position and consequently robbed everybody of their own biographies, of the worth of their own experiences. Demands for justice, including from the PDS, form the normative basis for dispelling old enmities and replacing them with a collectively shared resentment against the West. An invasive form of politics that aimed to exclude the cultural and political elite of an entire country, is now forced to deal with many unintended consequences. In the short run, any attempts at dis-crimination—from which not only East German post-communists profit—could also boost the reputation of those old 'exclusive forms of solidarity' (Srubar 1994, p. 217) on which basis a collective self-definition, which might help to quench conflictual dynamics of social integration, would again have a chance to succeed.

CONCLUSION

In Grunthal, in any case, the village peace has been disturbed. But apart from these local conflicts, minds meet in a commonly shared resentment which decisively changes the old definitions of inside and outside. The external space is now occupied by West German agents whereas the older regional institutions and agents of the socialist state have joined the ranks of 'good neighbours'. The deepest contempt of both the local community and the PDS, however, is reserved for those who deserted the party either due to moral or opportunistic reasons. Stigmatized in social life by one side as turncoats, and quasi-blacklisted occupationally on the other by West German administrators, the party-quitters are the greatest losers of that which once began as a peaceful revolution. 'Gorbachev', stated a former teacher and leading party executive, 'who had put the whole thing in motion and whom you admire so terribly, could not even, because of his political biography, become a mail carrier in Germany. But who cares? Life goes on.'

REFERENCES

Adler, Frank, 'Soziale Umbrueche', in Reissig/Glaessner (ed.), *Das Ende eines Experiments* Umbruch in der DDR und deutsche Einheit (Berlin: Dietz Verlag, 1991).

Bergmann, Theodor, 'The Re-privatization of Farming in Eastern Germany', in *Sociologia-Ruralis*, vol. 32, 1992.

Berking, Helmuth and Sighard Neckel, 'Aussenseiter als Politiker. Rekrutierung und Identitaeten neuer lokaler Eliten in einer ostdeutschen Gemeinde', *Soziale Welt*, 42, H.3, 1991.

——, 'Die gestoerte Gemeinschaft. Machtprozesse und Konfliktpotentiale in einer ostdeutschen Gemeinde', in Stefan Hradil (ed.), *Zwischen Bewusstsein und Sein*, Die Vermittlung 'objektiver' Lebensbedingungen und 'subjektiver' Lebensweisen (Leverkusen: Leske & Budrich, 1992).

Der Spiegel, No.33/1994.

Elias, Norbert and John L. Scotson, *The Established and the Outsiders*, London, 1965.

Engler, Wolfgang, *Die zivilisatorische Luecke. Versuche Ueber den Staatssozialismus*, Frankfurt/M., 1992a.

——, 'Individualisierung im Staatssozialismus', in Verhandlungen des 26. Deutschen Soziologentages in Duesseldorf. Frankfurt/M., 1992b.

Inhetveen, Heide, 'Fabrik in der Krise—Krise im Dorf?', in *Pro Regio*, H. 14, 17–28, 1994.

Mayer, Karl Ulrich, 'Die soziale Ordnung der DDR und einige Folgen fuer ihre Inkorporation in die BRD', in *Biss public*, 11, Berlin, 1993.

Mayer, Ulrich, Heike Solga, 'Mobilitaet und Legitimitaet. Zum Vergleich der Chancenstrukturen in der alten DDR und der alten BRD oder: Haben Mobilitaetschancen zu Stabilitaet und Zusammen-bruch der DDR beigetragen?', *KZfSS*, 2, 46, 1994.

Neckel, Sighard, 'Das lokale Staatsorgan. Kommunale Herrschaft im Staatssozialismus der DDR', in *Zeitschrift fuer Soziologie*, 21, Heft 4, 1992.

Niethammer, Lutz, 'Volkspartei neuen Typs? Sozialbiographische Voraussetzungen der SED in der Industrieprovinz', *PROKLA*, 20, Heft 4, 1990.

Niethammer/v.Plato/Wierling, 'Die volkseigene Erfahrung. Eine Archaeologie des Lebens in der Industrieprovinz der DDR', Berlin, 1991.

Offe, Claus, 'Capitalism by Democratic Design?', *Social Research*, vol. 58, no. 4, 1991.

Pollack, Detlef, 'Das Ende einer Organisationsgesellschaft: Systemtheoretische Ueberlegungen zum gesellschaftlichen Umbruch in der DDR', *Zeitschrift fuer Soziologie*, 19, Heft 4, 1990.

Srubar, Ilja, 'Variants of the Transformation Process in Central Europe. A Comparative Assessment', *Zeitschrift fuer Soziologie*, 23, Heft 3, 1994.

Sztompka, Piotr, 'Civilizational Incompetence: The Trap of Post-Communist Societies', *Zeitschrift fuer Soziologie*, 22, H.2, 1993.

Thaa, Winfried, 'Mehr als Adaption und Regression. Ueber die Auswirkungen der Herbstrevolution von 1989 auf die Entwicklung der Demokratie in Deutschland', *Deutschlandarchiv*, Jg. 24, Nr.8, 1991.

6

The Dynamics of Bureaucratic Rule in Pakistan
A Personal View

TASNEEM AHMED SIDDIQUI

Once in a while I visit Islamabad to keep myself abreast of the latest scams and political shenanigans. There I meet fellow bureaucrats who are never content with any regime, in spite of all the powers and perks they enjoy. I hear gossip about grades distribution, suspensions, and out of turn promotions—a game Islamabad-based friends play so zealously that it seems an all-consuming activity. I also encounter shrewd dealers who finally have risen to the highest level of their incompetence and been commensurately rewarded.

Having a non-governmental organization (NGO) link too, I often meet other NGO chiefs. Innumerable workshops, training programmes, seminars, and symposia are in progress in Islamabad on any given day addressing an imposing array of subjects from 'Local-Local Initiative' to 'Global Governance'. Mostly, these NGO leaders anticipate the imminent demise of the government with relish and imagine they have the sure cures to this beleaguered nation's problems. Yet they share many weaknesses with the state they so righteously deplore: dependency on foreign assistance; lavish expenditure on overheads; lack of transparency; fixed notions about what Scott calls 'high modernist' development; and an inordinate fondness for borrowed ideas.

One day I had lunch with a research student in the coffee shop of the only five-star hotel in Islamabad (always teeming with foreign consultants, con men, budding and burnt out politicians, and surveillance staff) where we discussed Karachi's situation. She duly took notes as if I had all the answers. I discussed our system's inability to manage a megalopolis, especially a lack of public investment resulting in near collapse of civic services and in higher unemployment. Former president Zia-ul-Haq's brutal rule (1977–88) promoted a poisonous legacy of divisiveness, bigotry, and militancy. Islamization was used unabashedly as a political weapon. state sponsored divisiveness spurred the rise of combative groups who claimed access to power on the basis of ethnicity, clan, and region. In housing we had a backlog of 6.5 million units. Half of the population lives in bare one-room tenements with an average density of eight persons.[1] Our involvement in the 1980s Afghan war brought the twin menace of drugs and guns home.

Some parts of our cities, and the living styles of our elite, can beat western standards, but many Pakistan citizens are literally living in the eighteenth century, sans sanitation, sans drinking water, sans roads, sans proper housing. We have the state-of-the-art medical facilities for a few, but no health coverage for the millions; centres of excellence in engineering, business administration, and information technology, but no primary schools for half the children. At the policy-making level there is emphasis on short-term, simplistic solutions for complex problems. But the silver lining is that civil society in Pakistan is getting organized, although it is still at the nascent stage and has a long way to go before it proves to be a countervailing force to a corrupt and inept system.

Yet, in spite of random snipers and killings, Karachi was a bustling city. An atmosphere of insecurity, uncertainty, and fear existed, but schools and universities were open; cinema halls and theatres were full; business and trade was thriving; construction activity continued unabated and there was an upswing in real estate market. This demonstrated the great potential of Karachi and the resilience of the population. It was this dignity and courage of ordinary people that held out hope. I hardly finished speaking when two young men from a *katchi abadi* (squatter settlement) in Islamabad came looking for me and asked me to visit their *basti*. They needed my advice. We agreed to go with them. From the rarefied atmosphere of a posh hotel to a katchi abadi was quite a change and we both had an eye-opener.

These people migrated in the mid-1960s and were kept in camping areas where they improvised their shelter. Even after three decades this settlement, numbering 1,200 houses and 8,000 people, lives in constant danger of eviction. In spite of living near the planned urban area, they have no electricity, no sewerage, no roads, and hardly any drinking water. There are no facilities for health and family planning. There was one three-room primary school. This school's plight reflects Pakistan's excessive centralization of authority, inability to deliver social services, and the inherent flaws of a 'high modernist' development strategy.

This school represents thousands more which lack the basics.[2] What is most striking is that it exists in the heart of Islamabad which is packed tight with an oversized education ministry, numerous international organizations, political parties of all hues and colours, and a plethora of NGOs. How do the children of this primary school feel when they see brand new BMWs and shining Mercedes cruising past them? NGO*wallah*s sometime visit but they arrive in imposing land cruisers too. The children cannot help but compare these expensive show pieces with their school buildings and the dirt floors they sit on. What conclusions must they be drawing about the state, and indeed society, from what they experience?[3] Structural changes in society are badly needed. But the elites have neither the desire nor the capability to change the status quo, mainly because it suits them. What, to take an infamous phrase, is to be done?

LOOKING BACK

I joined the Civil Service of Pakistan in November 1965. Pakistan was ruled by the civil-military-landlord triumvirate but, to a young man, everything seemed to be working well enough. I thought that most government servants were honest, intelligent, and dedicated people. Improvements were sorely needed but things could improve with better organization if only 'stupid' politicians were not trying to interfere. And how could the illiterate masses understand the intricacies of public administration? If political parties gave a free hand to bureaucracy, everything would be just fine.

Many idealistic young officers in the Civil Service went as field officers to remote areas, often enduring considerable hardships, to deal with the problems of the population. The presidential election of 1964 and the September war of 1965 provided the backdrop of my joining the service. A severe disenchantment by the middle classes with General Ayub Khan's rule, and the dismal 1965 war further estranged East Pakistan from West Pakistan's elites and slowed the pace of economic development. At the same time, people in smaller provinces, especially Sindh and Baluchistan, rankled against the continuous centralization of authority in Lahore and Islamabad. The 'One Unit' slogan, they thought, was devised unfairly to divert their resources to Punjab. My experience in Sindh and Baluchistan, as a young field officer, showed all too starkly that the bureaucracy there actually was in league with the landed aristocracy, and both were assiduously and expertly protecting their interests.

The army supported the system behind the scenes and was assured its pound of flesh. Officers commonly displayed a woefully false sense of superiority. There were a few who were level-headed and responsive to public needs but they were certainly exceptions. Eccentrics and dimwits had their own, far higher, quotas. Collectively, the civil servants were arrogant, indifferent, bound by precedents, inward-looking, and rigid. Landlords, though denied a formal role in the decision-making process, enjoyed a free hand in running roughshod in their domains. In Sindh a cozy partnership between the bureaucracy and the feudal masters became the corner-stone of the system, and justice, so far as the poor were concerned, was absent. Ayub Khan maintained close links with big landlords. In hunting season they competed to invite him to their grand estates.

I went to East Pakistan in June 1969 for a two-year stint. During those turbulent days I witnessed the abysmal conditions in which the majority of East Pakistanis lived; saw the failure of a military-bureaucratic system to rule, and finally, observed from very close quarters the limited thought processes of West Pakistan elites, especially when exercising power. I served there at the tail end of ballyhooed 'decade of development' of the 1960s, whose chief exponent was the Harvard Development Advisory Service Mission, strategically located in the Planning Commission. They urged that industrialists in Pakistan (who lacked the characteristics of an entrepreneurial class and, at best, were mostly robber barons) be given state support: cheap loans, protection from foreign competition, low wages for labour, tax holidays, raw materials at cheap rates, and machinery imports with reduced import duties. If all these favours were granted, the Harvard Group foretold, industrialists would reinvest profits, rates of saving will sky-rocket, and the country will reach Walt Rostow's vaunted take-off stage. Having generated finances and industrialized the country after absorbing the 'surplus labour', the niggling little matter of income maldistribution can then be tackled and everybody be made happy—the 'trickle down' theory.

THE TRICK OF TRICKLE DOWN

By the 1970s aggregate output surely rose, but benefits were not 'trickling down'. Not only was there continued unemployment, underemployment, and low productivity in rural areas, but high rates of unemployment and underemployment persisted in the cities too. Migrants came but jobs were not to be had. Instead of reaping the benefits of the rapid growth, the poor in Pakistan beheld only abject poverty. The fact that about 75 per cent people depended on agriculture and that a sustained industrial growth was not possible unless this rural sector was improved, was totally ignored.[4]

The paradox is that Pakistan enjoyed growth at unprecedented rates anyway. The official gross national product (GNP) figures showed an annual growth rate of 5 per cent in the 1960s although the proportion of our population below a fixed acceptable minimum standard of living did not fall appreciably, if at all. Michael Lipton at the time cited Pakistan as an egregious example of growth without poverty alleviation. The chief economist of the Planning Commission invoked Keynes' 'foul is fair' comment that, like it or not, it was initially the inequality of the distribution of wealth that made possible accumulations of wealth and later social improvements. The Harvard Development Advisory Service Mission obligingly echoed this hoary wisdom.

Yet industry always had a high import content and there was no integrated technological cycle to sustain development. To quote Lipton, industry in Pakistan is an 'exotic, artificial, and fragile plant' that survives largely by protection, and at the expense of farmers, consumers, and national efficiency. It is fragile, owing to its dependence on the very agriculture whose growth it stunts by its demands for skills, capital, incentive, and enterprise. Our planners and bureaucrats focused attention on high tech capital-intensive industries that employ minimum number of people. This is happening in a country where the rate of unemployment is about 20–25 per cent.[5] Agricultural prices stayed stagnant, inherited holdings were fragmented, and desertification occurred as water logging and salinity claimed 40,000 hectares of arable land every year. Between 1951 and 1981 the per capita cropped area dropped from 0.46 hectare to 0.31 hectare. At the same, the 'Green Revolution' introduced mechanization, fertilizers, and irrigation. Every tractor introduced made 13 people jobless; while the higher intensity of farming and the higher yields created on average two new jobs per tractor. A new class of absentee landlords was created. Quite an achievement.

What came of this smug high modernist strategy? Mahbubul Haq at the end of the 'development decade' conceded that the country's wealth was concentrated in the hands of 22 families who owned 80 per cent of the banks and 95 per cent of the insurance companies. The poor had become poorer. In 1969 Ayub Khan's government was toppled by mobs rioting in the streets, and Mahbubul Haq safely repaired to the World Bank while the Harvard Advisory Group too left for greener pastures. The state became top heavy. Did the planners really think that Pakistan could attain a 'take off' stage with its feudal structure intact?

THE BENGAL TRAUMA

Since the country was ruled by elites based mainly in West Pakistan, the political process was stifled and rigged. Bengalis saw that the benefits of development systematically eluded them. Neither public servants nor landlord-politicians could begin to fathom the deepening political alienation. The Awami League victory in the last elections in an undivided Pakistan in 1970 was not to the ruling clique's liking and so a vicious military action was launched which ended in a humiliating surrender to the Indian Armed Forces in December 1971. Any mention of this ignominious event is religiously avoided in military establishments. I saw all this with my own eyes. It was openly said at the time that the Bengalis were an inferior race and should be taught a lesson.

The insight I had during 1969–70 was that unless there was a decentralization of authority, the federal structure would remain vulnerable. People should be allowed to manage their own affairs. They may commit mistakes but would improve through trial and error. The use of force is no answer to the lack of experience in self-governance. Without real participation even the best development programme fails. I came back to West Pakistan in July 1971 and had a chance to work in Sindh in the fields of district management, industry, taxation, and urban development.

Sindh had more than its share of changes because of its special demography and dichotomous set-up: an archaic feudal stronghold in the rural areas and the domination of a rising middle class of non-locals in the urban centres. With a high rate of population growth, spread of education, high rate of unemployment amongst the educated youth and the 'media revolution,' things had drastically changed in rural areas. Overweaning power in the hands of top civil servants and increasing gap between the rich and the poor stirred strong populist feelings. Bhutto sensed the rebellious mood of the people correctly and his new Pakistan Peoples Party stridently stood for wealth redistribution, land reform, and nationalization. In the initial two years, delivery of services indeed improved. But it soon became clear that the military and the bureaucracy were in only temporary tactical retreat in the aftermath of the East Pakistan debacle. Bhutto deployed populist slogans only to grab power. Nationalization of big business and educational institutions, which was welcomed initially, proved disastrous. Even the land reforms, which, if honestly implemented, could usher in a new era of prosperity, only became a tool to harass opponents, as in the case of Zimbabwe today.

Working as a field officer in Sindh during Zia's period I saw the frustration and anger mounting against insensitive military rule. I could also see that state institutions seriously had weakened. Consequently, most government programmes did not reach the poor. Whether it was rural water supply, a basic health unit or a primary school, priorities were determined by the local power elites, who hogged most of the benefits. Even the rural credit schemes were exploited by landlords using the national identity cards collected from their illiterate and subjugated 'serfs.' Most government programmes failed because the potential link between the communities and higher-order institutions was never developed. There was a vital 'missing link' in the organization of development. The bureaucratic superstructure became powerful, and as a natural corollary, the local government and its allied institutions became weak.

The colonial bureaucratic system Pakistan inherited was designed to serve a rural economy. It maintained law and order, collected revenue, and delivered needed services. The landed gentry remained over-represented in the assemblies, but the functions it performed have been taken over by *arthi*s, middlemen, commission agents, financiers, and transporters. As a result of rapid urbanization, and the state's incapacity to provide infrastructure and services to the burgeoning population, new forces emerged. Call them the mafia, middlemen or whatever, but the fact is that at the turn of the century, 70 per cent of the economy in the bigger cities of Pakistan became 'informal' and controlled by groups outside the government.

Another important phenomenon ignored by planners, economists, and politicians is that a large segment of population has emerged in urban Pakistan which is neither poor nor middle-income. They are the third generation of kathchi abadi dwellers and are more demanding. They need services. They want a share in running the government. They have their own expectations and aspirations. They resort to violence when the state fails to respond to their genuine demands. That 25 per cent of Pakistanis live in squatters slums or sub-standard housing is little concern for planners. Yet housing is the basic requirement for all economic activity. It is the starting point for a person to organize his actions, stabilize 20 per cent of the total population. The rest are lower middle classes and the poor. While the bulk of this class has an average household monthly income of Rs 2,500 or less, about one-third of our total population is living below poverty line and barely surviving. They include the 'wretched of the earth' who hardly have any assured cash income. Most poor people take consumption and production loans and become bonded labour.

Any programme to meet the shelter needs of the low-income groups either does not reach the target groups or they cannot retain the benefits because the planners are woefully ignorant about the sociology of these groups. They follow the planning standards of the First World. Our professional groups always prefer engineering solutions for social problems. Thus we find housing units without occupants, infrastructure without users, basic health units without doctors and medicines, and beautiful primary school buildings sans teachers and pupils. There is a backlog of about four million houses in the country.[6] In Karachi, Lahore, Quetta, and Faisalabad, there is a phenomenal increase in the number of katchi abadis. Here I found an opportunity to work in a social sector and devise, through much trial and error and attentiveness to the target populations, some useful solutions.

'REGULARIZING' THE POOR

Since I work for squatters, I will write about urban areas, but this does not mean that this schema will not apply to rural areas. In Karachi 40 per cent of the population lives in squatter settlements and another 20 per cent in sub-standard areas. When the poor people come to the cities, they purchase land from land-grabbers illegally. They build their houses; they construct the sanitation system on self-help, self-managed basis. They send their children to private schools which charge high fees. They do not depend on the government health system, because it hardly exists, and if it does, it hardly provides any service. If you go to low-income areas, you can see that the state hardly exists there. From solid waste management to road maintenance to water supply to sewerage and street lights, nothing works. This is the state of affairs as far as low-income people are concerned. When conditions become unbearable, poor people organize themselves and try to solve some of the problems

The emergence of katchi abadis was the result of our development strategy. People migrated to the cities but no housing was provided. Therefore they had to squat in the city centre, using all open spaces, then they had to grab land—I prefer to call this grabbing 'self-allocation' because state agencies were of no use to them. So, when government institutions do not work, the land mafia developed in Karachi to provide, at an inflated price, land, and services. The 'informal' sector is like a parallel government. But our planners have the perception that poor people are too poor to afford any housing or services. If you provide technical assistance, they would refuse it. This myth has been proved resoundingly wrong. The rich also forget that the poor people provide services to cities like Karachi. If there were no squatter settlements, cities like Karachi and Lahore would not function for even a day. If you take a look there you will find artisans, skilled persons, plumbers, fitters, foremen, office staff, assistants, clerk, drivers, and other indispensable people.

In October 1985 I was appointed Director General of the Hyderabad Development Authority (HDA), a job everyone avoided. The HDA was a small but problematic organization. HDA launched several ill-conceived housing schemes. The method was that state land was earmarked for schemes advertised in the media. The applicants were required to give 25 per cent of the cost as down payment. Because of the huge backlog in housing, and also because higher income groups see investment in real estate as a safe bet, applicants far exceed plots available. Balloting is resorted to. Afterward, successful bidders are asked to pay another 25 per cent. As the development of infrastructure takes eight to 10 years, naturally no one takes residence. On the other hand, katchi abadis were taking care of the housing needs of the poor. Something was wrong somewhere and this needed to be sorted out.

I began to discuss these issues with the members of HDA staff. Some were young, dynamic, and truly professional in their approach. They were open to new ideas and were not yet deeply entrenched into the 'system'. A small study group was formed to address the problem of providing shelter. We came to the conclusion that if the government could adopt the procedures followed by the successful 'informal' sector, then perhaps some solution would emerge. In a way, it was formalizing the informal sector. We selected a sector to carry out an experiment and called it the 'incremental housing development'. Only the basic objective—making land accessible to the poor—was clear, otherwise everything was trial and error. It was a learning process.

The biggest problem was reaching the targets groups. Initially people would come, look at unserviced plots, and go away. Many considered the area unsafe and uneconomical, as it was about 12 kilometres away from the city centre. We were very clear about the kind of people we wanted to attract: shelterless needy families who would move in immediately and start building houses incrementally. They would get services as the settlement grew. Cost recovery would be linked with provision of services. The concept was new in the public sector and therefore, we had few takers. We used several methods: carrying out surveys of the needy; personal contacts; making announcements in the mosques. We were groping in the dark. But one day we found that a group of 50 to 60 families came from the interior of Sindh in bullock carts, with all their belongings and squatted in a corner of the scheme without permission. We knew at once that they were not going to go back. They were the genuine needy. So they became our target group and taking our cue from them, we developed the concept of 'reception area', which is a sort of a filtering process and now forms the most important part of our procedures.

The settlers first needed an access road and drinking water. Soakpits were constructed for sewerage disposal. The houses were to be built by the people themselves. The formal building laws were not applicable and land-use was flexible. We had started the scheme without any formal approval, and the staff worried about future trouble over bending the rules. So we invited the chief minister to inaugurate the scheme. Thereafter we contrived to present it to the HDA's governing board for approval as a fait accompli.

We overcame many obstacles because of the commitment of the staff, and because the people started organizing themselves. Here the role of development authorities should be clearly understood. They either provide built-up units or announce schemes for fully-serviced plots. Their job is over as soon as these units/plots are allocated. But in 'Khuda-ki-Basti' we stayed on and got involved with the setting up of schools, clinics, and provision of other social sector activities, first through NGOs and then government agencies. Then we wanted to sound out planners, architects, and other professionals about our methodology. Few paid any attention. Some said that at best it was an aberration: it was highly personalized (meaning my person) and possibly could not be sustained. Others, especially the director generals of other development authorities accused us of creating katchi abadis under government tutelage—what we came to call 'regularizing' settlements—and insisted that it should be stopped.

Our team comprised government servants who were subject to the vagaries of the service. In order to be able to extend the concept and sustain the scheme, we created an organization 'Saiban' and got it registered as an NGO. Saiban's charter included replication of incremental housing schemes and dissemination of information. We wanted to prove that the scheme was sustainable and could be implemented elsewhere. In 1995, the scheme was replicated on four acres of Gothabad land and at Taiser Town, Karachi in collaboration with Malir Development Authority. In this scheme, out of 1750 plots, 1,300 were occupied by 2002 and the township was thriving. The Capital Development Authority in Islamabad and the Quetta Development Authority got in touch with us for launching similar schemes in their jurisdiction.

In this model, a very low down payment (Rs 1,000) is required. Development is incremental. Initial services are limited to the absolute minimum; at the start, only communal supply and public transport are provided. Only in the longer run, house-to-house water supply, sewerage, road paving, electricity, and gas will be provided as the allottees pay instalments. Only the layout of the scheme is fixed otherwise no standards are prescribed as to the plan of the house. The allottees are encouraged to innovate and improvise. The critical factor is guaranteed and assured title to the land. Once people have that, it is amazing how resources are pooled by the family to invest and gradually make a respectable structure.

Second, just as is the case of illegal developments, the time-lag between allotment and occupation has been eliminated. Development takes place while the allottees are residing in the scheme. The allotment procedure is crucial. To exclude speculators, a reception area is provided on site where the shelterless family is registered for the allotment only if it brings all its members and belongings. A regular plot is allocated if they stay in the reception area for about a week. The allottees must live on their plot from the first day otherwise it can be given to somebody else. As soon as the first 50 families occupied plots, supply of water through tankers and transport was arranged. Soon after mosque, schools, and mobile vans for primary health care were organized through NGOs. The scheme is sustainable because the community is involved from the planning stage to the execution of development work, maintenance, and cost recovery. The community is organized at block level (that is, about 200 houses).

Separate accounts, maintained for each block, are jointly operated by the block's nominee and HDA project manager. Block residents indicate their priority for desired services in open meetings. If enough money is available in a block's account estimates are prepared by HDA's technical staff and a contractor is appointed from amongst the community. Since the community is involved in the supervision and the community contractor works on marginal profit (there are no kickbacks), development cost is reduced by about 25 per cent. The block organization is responsible for maintenance of services, conservancy, and action against defaulters and absentees. Their services are also used for disbursement of small loans for house improvement and income generation. An attempt has been made to enhance the institutional capacity for meeting the housing and development requirements of the urban poor so the investments and policies are channelled to those in need.[7]

IMPLICATIONS FOR STATE AND SOCIETY

This experiment demonstrates that even without basic changes in the power structure of society, without changing the unequal relationship between government and slum dwellers and even without a programme in favour of the 'wretched of the earth', development authorities can assimilate the role of the 'informal' sector as a reform strategy. A prerequisite for a successful programme is popular involvement at all stages. The top-down approach has failed to deliver goods. Needs are not prioritized by the intended beneficiaries. Since the would-be beneficiaries are not involved in these decisions, they are hesitant to contribute any resources, nor do they want to play any role in their maintenance. The effective stake of international monetary agencies in local development can never exceed that of the communities themselves.

Fortunately, the government is ready to accept alternative models, provided they are tested. We need not confront the system unnecessarily. It is easy to say that the government is corrupt and the politicians are incompetent, and what we need is a revolution. But are we ready to work to solve basic problems? Are we ready to carry out the much-needed research and then implement the models? Are we ready to lobby for acceptance at the appropriate level? If so, the government is likely to change its methods sooner or later. The model we have developed in Sind Katchi Abadi Authority (SKAA) is that smaller things, for example the internal sanitation system, can be taken care of by the community (helped by the NGOs and professional groups). But, for the external work and the costly disposal system, the government has to play its role. The government's responsibility is reduced by half.

When 40 per cent of the population do not own land legally, the state exchequer neither receives the cost of development, nor do the utility agencies receive users' charges. The incidence of corruption is high. Daily wage earners cannot afford to visit their offices for months to get a connection. So they take it illegally and pay the linesmen and valve operators at fixed rates. They are accused of not paying, but are paying more than what is due and are being exploited in the bargain. In the process, the government agencies are getting poorer, while its functionaries are becoming richer.

The costs of failure to accommodate our less fortunate members are tremendous. Utility organizations run huge deficits and proper development cannot be undertaken (not that the rich industrialists, cinema owners, ice factories, marriage halls or influential bigwigs do not steal electricity or the labour unions do not force the management to pay fake overtime or inflated medical bills, or the top notchers do not take hefty commissions on new contracts). The entire burden is shifted to the consumers who pay their bills. The same applies in the case of shelter. If the poor migrants could get a small plot of land, they would improvise a house with their own resources, building as they live there. They are also ready to pay.

Our state is highly overcentralized. Local government bears major responsibilities but, with few exceptions, has no administrative, financial and technical capability. We have to redefine the role of various actors: government, private sector, communities, politicians, professionals and bureaucrats, and their relationship with each other. We can focus our attention on issues which will restore confidence in the state without involving major financial outlays. People want security of life, fair play, and justice. They also want sound infrastructure, a reasonable price level, and an enabling environment where they can work and prosper. So far we have failed. Unless we accept communities as equal partners in the process of development and start a participatory mode of governance, our problems will not go away.

Autonomy should be the pillar of our new mode of governance. Provinces should have all the powers of a federating unit. Elected local government should be accepted as third tier of the government and be provided constitutional protection. It should be given more powers and arrangements should be made to increase administrative, technical, and financial capacity of local bodies. Currently there is adversarial relationship between politicians and the bureaucracy. But it should not be forgotten that bureaucracy is the instrument through which public policy is formulated and plans implemented. After defining the role of public servants, and settling the rules of the game, they should be allowed to operate without interference. There should be an independent authority empowered to look into the grievances of public servants who think they have been victimized for not obeying illegal orders. The Planning Commission should be converted into a research and evaluation organization. It should come up with meaningful recommendations to improve the institutional, managerial, and organizational capability of government agencies to deliver social services.

Privatization is no panacea. There are areas where government must play its role, otherwise poorer segments of the population will be hard hit. The role of the private sector, government, and the public should be clearly spelled out and partnerships established to achieve better results. Certain responsibilities, especially in the field of primary education, basic health and family planning can be shared by communities. Bigger things can be taken care of by the government. Support organizations, NGOs and CBOs can also play a major role in organizing and training the people. The government cannot run away from its basic responsibilities. Unless the intervention is that of a political nature, all the good efforts of philanthropists and the NGOs will not be able to prop up the crumbling system.

Democracy is not only about elections, assemblies, and formation of cabinets. Far from it. Democracy is a way of life. Its prerequisites are courage to listen to a differing point of view; tolerance in matters relating to culture, religion, language; acceptance of rule of law by everyone—big or small; a free press; independent judiciary and strengthening of institutions. When we use the term civil society, it does not merely mean the NGOs, CBOs, and support organizations.

In its wider meaning it includes the middle class intelligentsia. Do we have an articulate, independent, non-partisan, tolerant, intellectual community which could help foster and sustain a healthy debate on social and economic problems that the country faces? The situation may appear dismal but in recent years there has been a proliferation of new organizations headed by social activists.

Working as director general of squatters improvement authority, I have seen this phenomenon taking shape especially in low-income urban areas. Due to long periods of martial law and incompetence of political parties to keep pace with changing ground realities this new class of young activists is emerging. They are not only organizing people, but also helping them to understand the fact that things will not improve unless they make the state accountable for its acts of omission and commission. It is vital that professionals follow suit and use the political and social space available to develop home grown solutions. It also remains to be seen how they develop liaison with the working classes and the peasantry. It has happened elsewhere that civil organizations and social activists developed alternative approaches to solve problems and lobbied for their acceptance.

CONCLUSION

Pakistan is a 'failed' state. Pakistan is ungovernable. The government is dysfunctional. Chattering classes and armchair intellectuals in Pakistan offer a grim picture of institutional collapse.[8] Even senior bureaucrats and policy makers in informal settings say likewise. For the majority of Pakistanis deteriorating law and order, high cost of living, public servants' highhandedness, corruption, and rising unemployment are great concerns.

Governments in most Third World countries are autocratic, corrupt, and incompetent, but the impotence of the state has opened room for elaboration of new civil-state relations. We need to understand how states in the Third World are changing in capabilities, functions, and strategies. But we will understand very little if we capitulate to faddish pronouncements about the imminent end of the state. During Zia's reign, the state unleashed a reign of terror on political activists who opposed it. But now when we have a state that has allowed comparative freedom of the press and provided ample space to activism, its writ does not run. It can neither maintain law and order, nor collect taxes. It cannot even provide rudimentary services. During the last 54 years, the state has gone from an intolerant, repressive institution to a weak, paternalistic, supportive, and reasonably tolerant entity.

We must understand that the state is not one monolithic body. When forces within the state attempt to flex muscles—like the recent attempts by Pakistan Railways to clear their land of illegal low-income settlements—people have found enough support elsewhere within the state to stall, if not stop such attempts. Today a military government (which normally moves towards concentration of authority) is trying to overhaul the state apparatus and has announced a devolution plan. But if the exercise is to be meaningful the principles for reform need to be clearly spelt out on decentralization of political authority; social and civil rights; and the role of the state. In order to gain responsive services, the establishment of empowered local governments, access to information, accountability, and flexibility have to be ensured.

Pakistan's real assets are its people. If the government is dysfunctional, people try to move forward. If the government faces economic fiasco at macro level, things at micro level show vibrancy. If this process of change continues, a day will come when the emerging classes which have come into existence as a result of a new economic situation will be reflected in state institutions and the changes they seek will be institutionalized.

NOTES

1. 67 million people even today are without safe drinking water and as many have no access to health facilities; 89 million are deprived of basic sanitation; there are 740,000 child deaths a year, half of them linked to malnutrition. Maternal mortality is as high as 1600 per 100,000 births. Only a small portion of money we have spent in social sector has reached the target groups. Most of it has either has lined the pockets of consultants, contractors, and engineers or has simply been wasted. This is evident from the number of rural water supply schemes not operating, basic health units, rural health centres, community halls lying vacant or converted into guest houses or cattle-yards, and primary school buildings existing on paper.
2. 32 per cent of primary schools in Punjab alone are without shelter while 39 per cent are running in single rooms.

3. The immediate problem is economic. After debt servicing, defence, bureaucracy, and a pot pourri of subsidies, government is left with less than 15 per cent of resources for needed infrastructure and services. But even this money is misallocated, wasted or devoured by corrupt, inefficient and unimaginative public servants. The common peoples burden is increasing. Indirect taxes constitute 83 per cent of revenues while deficit financing accelerates inflation. The tax base cannot be widened. The rich refuse to pay the taxes commensurate with their incomes because they have the power: the poor cannot pay, because they are too poor.

4. What about the 'Green Revolution'? Agricultural growth doubled or tripled, but the main beneficiaries were big landowners. Small holders suffered because they did not have the resources to purchase expensive inputs like fertilizer, HYV seeds and pesticides. Big landowners found it profitable to evict sharecroppers and start using agricultural machinery or engage wage labourers. Non-farm jobs were hardly sufficient to absorb these landless tenants.

5. During the mid-1970s oil boom in the Gulf states, hordes of unemployed were exported to the United Arab Emirates (UAE) and Saudi Arabia. That eased the job market and we started earning about two billion US dollars annually. Some money was invested in land and small businesses in Central Punjab, Azad Kashmir and parts of North-West Frontier Province (NWFP). Thus, in some areas we see the emergence of peasant proprietors who own economic holdings, and replace farmers who own very small pieces of land due to fragmentation of holdings. In *mandi* towns we see a large number of small entrepreneurs who have invested money in cottage and small size industries. But this phenomenon has not been widespread.

6. Annual incremental demand of about 0.5 million units continues—50 per cent families live in one-room tenements with family members ranging between eight to 15. Urban centres are growing at the rate of around 5 per cent as against the national growth rate of 3.2 per cent. Both rural and urban areas are badly deficient in basic infrastructure. Only 40 per cent people have access to potable water while sewerage services are available only to 20 per cent people.

7. According to World Bank research (Housing for Low-Income Urban Families) the first round effects are the direct increments to income and employment generated by construction activity. The rate of employment creation in housing construction is higher than that for manufacturing and close to that for the economy as a whole. In Pakistan, the income multiplier of housing construction is estimated at two and 14 additional jobs are created for every US\$ 10,000 invested in housing. Income generating schemes (which are mostly family enterprises) have also been started in the scheme by providing small loans ranging between Rs 1,200 to 25,000 without any collateral. Rs 1,101,000 has been disbursed to 85 persons so far. These

family enterprises have provided regular income to 115 persons, one-third of them female. The regular repayment of these 'insecure' loans is over 80 per cent.

8. Everyone knows how the rich and the affluent middle classes in Pakistan live. There are two nations in Pakistan living side by side. The rich have a separate system for everything, from birth till death. They have separate schools. Their children do their O-levels and A-levels and they even have their separate colleges and universities. They have their own transport. Every family owns one or more cars. They have separate residential areas. When they fall ill they are looked after by the private health system.

7

Face to Face with the Indian State
A Grass Roots View

Philip Oldenburg[1]

I meet this American government, or its representative, the State government, directly, and face to face, once a year—no more—in the person of its tax gatherer; this is the only mode in which a man situated as I am necessarily meets it... [He is put in jail for a night for refusing to pay poll tax.] I saw that the State was half-witted, that it was timid as a lone woman with her silver spoons, and that it did not know its friends from its foes, and I lost all my remaining respect for it, and pitied it. [On being released from jail he joins a huckleberry party and soon] was in the midst of a huckleberry field, on one of our highest hills, two miles off, and then the State was nowhere to be seen.

—Henry David Thoreau, *Civil Disobedience*

Theories of the state carry with them, with a greater or lesser degree of openness, an idea of the state as a visible thing: how 'large' it is, whether it is 'growing', whether it is 'strong', whether it can enforce 'its will', and so on. Caveats about the dangers of reification abound (for example Nordlinger 1987) but the State as Metaphorical Person marches on. I adopt that practice to ask: Does the state in India look different when viewed from below, from the perspective of a state in India (Uttar Pradesh or UP) and a district in UP(Ghazipur) than when it is viewed as 'The' Indian State? Is its shape and character, and its personnel, and its mode of functioning so different that our understanding of what 'the state' is has to be questioned?[2]

If we are looking at the boundary-markers of the state, as well well as its capacity, its autonomy, and its legitimacy, we must at some point assess those features of the state. 'Assess' rather than 'measure', because, quite apart from the difficulty of deciding what the appropriate units of measurement might be, in my experience the data we would need do not exist.

But clearly we must try to assess where the boundary markers are—where the state ends and civil society begins—if only to discover just how amorphous the state might be. We need to know how the state, *qua* its administrative and elected officials, is linked to the citizenry, in terms of the power it wields (capacity, autonomy) and the support it enjoys (legitimacy). These assessments must be based on some idea of what the state actually does for, and to, its citizens. If it turns out that the state differs in how it looks from the grass roots as opposed to the more common top-down view, we may want to think again about what the state 'is'.

In this exploratory essay it will not be possible to cover the full range of state activity at the grass roots, and so I have selected for study some of the major departments at three levels of India's federal system, those that touch a very large proportion of the population on a regular basis. I have, chosen some central government ones (postal services, banking), and some of state government (police, education, health), and one that is a mixed bag of state government administration and central government programmes (rural development). This also takes account of departments that are placed in the three broad realms of state activity: the *core* of state functions (which I take to include the judicial system, taxation, and preserving independence); the set of *service* functions (providing health care, education, communication, transport, etc.); and the most recent layer of *transformational* functions (industrial and agrarian development, redistribution policies, etc.).

Somewhat arbitrarily, I will illustrate the problems in 'defining' the state on the ground by looking at education, health, and postal services; problems in measuring what the state actually does by looking at the police, savings, and rural development programmes; and problems in assessing how citizens view and judge the state, by by considering all these departments and relying particularly on a public opinion survey conducted by the UP Evaluation Wing for the State Planning Institute.

My grass roots perspective comes mainly from data collected in 1992 in Ghazipur District, in eastern UP. I also draw on research done in Meerut, Bahraich, and Lucknow districts in 1980–1, when I was studying the land consolidation programme (Oldenburg 1987; 1990; see Ghate 1984 for Ghazipur).

Who is 'part of' the state and how many of them are there? The state is not just an institution composed of roles, but a conglomerate of units in which people are employed. The indicators used commonly to measure the size and growth of the state are numbers of people employed and expenditure. But by simply adding everyone up, are we not obscuring an interesting distinction between those who in some sense are the state (decision-making authorities in core ministries and departments, at one end of the spectrum) from those who are simply state employees? Especially those at one remove, like the contract day labourers the Railways employ, or the office boy of the UP state public sector Textile Corporation?

We must not exclude such people from being part of the state, since the perception of many citizens are moulded by the gate-keeping office boys who may demand bribes and often act as intermediaries with their bosses. (I am not so sure about the day labourers.) My preference is to be inclusive: anyone employed by the state directly is part of the state—but how significant a part remains a separate question. I have had, it should be said, a great deal of difficulty in finding precisely how many persons the state employs, directly and indirectly, and even more, how much they are paid in the aggregate.

The grass roots perspective alerts us to another dimension of the problem of who to count as constituting the state: how to deal with part-time employees. Consider the post office at the district level. The postal services consist of regular department and 'extra departmental' employees, with nearly 300,000 in India in 1990, compared to slightly fewer regular employees. Most of the former are employed in the countryside. In Ghazipur, there were 339 regular employees and 801 'extra departmental' employees. While the latter, persons who deliver mail in the area of the branch post office (typically in a village setting) and the mail peon (who brings the mail bag to the branch post office) have civil service rights, they are expected to work only three to five hours, six days a week, and thus are expected to have other sources of income.[3]

The branch postmaster, who is a regular department employee, must be a resident of the village where the branch post office is located and is required to have an independent means of income, with the idea that he will not be tempted to embezzle the fairly large sums he handles on a regular basis—postal money orders, savings bank deposits, as well as stamp money. Village postmaster is still a prestigious job, and people mobilize high-level politicians to get the post; in UP, they are also believed to 'invest' thousands of rupees to be appointed.[4]

There are ways of recouping that investment, though not necessarily in ways that seem most obvious. The east UP villagers I spoke with said that postal employees did not demand a cut, or even a tip, when cash from a money order was handed over; only a few claimed that 1 to 2 per cent as tip was expected. I was told that blatant embezzlement and fraud is comparatively rare.

But the branch postmaster *can* make money by using the cash he receives for a postal money order to build up a revolving fund out of which he lends money at interest: he will tell the recipient that the entire amount did not come, or he will claim that the recipient was not to be found, and he will use the money for a day—a practice not unlike that of banks who delay the crediting of checks after they are cleared.[5] The village postmaster, then, is a somewhat ambiguous figure, if we want to count up state officials: he is likely to be a landowner or a shopkeeper and a moneylender (not exclusive occupations), as well as a political figure with connections to one party (cf. Gupta 1995, p. 384). When the villager hands his savings to him, does the villager see 'the state' or a 'local notable' or simply 'Ram Das'?

Most state employees who are working part-time are not doing it legally, however. School teachers are a good example. Although, in an interview, the Ghazipur District Inspector of Schools denied vehemently that government school teachers neglected their classes in order to teach in their own (private) schools or give tuitions,[6] villagers complained that teachers in fact did not attend classes and did their own work: typically, farming their land (for similar illustrative evidence, see Dreze and Sen 2002, p. 158 and Srivastava 2001, p. 299). According to the District Inspector of Schools, 75 per cent of the teachers work within walking distance of their home village and rarely move, although the rules say they must be posted more than 20 kilometres away from their permanent residence (Uttar Pradesh government 1986, vol. 2, p. 240). One villager I spoke to fondly recalled his experience when he and his fellow students reported to the teacher at the tube well of the teacher's field—and was taught while the teacher irrigated his crop. There is of course no way of estimating how much time teachers actually spend on their teaching duties, but given their generally low pay, it is hard to believe that many teachers are making a living working full-time simply teaching at school (see also Drèze and Sen 2002, p. 158).

Government doctors in the countryside also are de facto part-time employees of the state (see ORG 1988). Although in the three Ghazipur Primary Health Centres (PHC) observed in that study, at least one doctor was present daily for four-and-a-half hours, and patients' waiting time was only five minutes after the initial rush, the implication is that doctors are as likely to be absent as present on duty. The UP Commission on District Level Administration notes that 'on surprise visits [we] have *usually* found doctors absent', an impression buttressed by the opinions of the various public representatives they surveyed (Uttar Pradesh government 1986, vol. 2, p. 255; emphasis added).

PHC doctors—indeed, virtually all doctors employed by the government—usually set up a private practice. There were complaints I heard that doctors referred patients who had come to the PHC to themselves after hours, so that they could charge fees (and, it was alleged, sell the medicines they were supposed to distribute at no charge), leaving patients too poor to pay few options. The UP Commission on District Level Administration records similar complaints about hospital doctors. The corruption of the subordinate medical staff is notorious at all levels, to the point where, the Commission claims, 'because of continued posting in the same hospital for decades together, [they] browbeat doctors and usually in collusion with some unscrupulous doctors harass poor patients for their selfish ends' (Uttar Pradesh government 1986, vol. 2, pp. 252, 254).[7]

One could interpret the rural health programme as a *de facto* joint sector operation, with government employment providing the financial cushion and thus incentive for doctors to go out into the countryside to set up their practices. Many PHC (frequently housed in inadequate buildings and poorly equipped) are located well off the beaten track where doctors would normally be unlikely to set up shop. Streefland (1991, p. 70) writes 'Several times [in fieldwork in Gujarat] I encountered health staff who had clearly found their niche in a peripheral place and did not want to move. . . . The doctor even said that the peripheral nature of his PHC enabled him to carry on a private practice on the side.' If 'fees' are demanded outside the PHC for medical services that are supposed to be provided free at the Centre, it may not be obvious to the patient that they are bribes.

Village teachers and doctors are figures who must look half public/ half private in the eyes of citizens, employed by the state part-time and thus included in government, but also using their government employment as a base from which to build a private enterprise. How do we count them? How many state medical personnel are to be found at the grass roots? Should we try to calculate 'full-time equivalent' teachers and doctors?

Collecting data on persons employed by the state government in Ghazipur—let alone verifying it—is a difficult job. My effort to get precise figures ended when I was told that I would have to visit all the offices of the departments to get them—with no guarantees at all that such data would be readily available or considered to be public. Even where there is departmental data, they are problematic. For example, the number of primary and intermediate school teachers in Ghazipur is a fact that was hard to pin down. The District Inspector of Schools told me it was 5,502, while another official source says 8,429 (Uttar Pradesh Directorate of Education 1990, pp. 79–81). Data on employment at the state level also is not readily available. The official statistical handbook of UP does not report the numbers of any department employees except education and health. I was unable to find data on the amounts expended on salaries.

These difficulties of definition and data were brought home to me when I attempted to add a local Indian dimension to one vivid portrait of the state that relies on a measure of employees: the 'Mend or Maim' figure in the 'Harmworkers and Healthworkers' map in *The New State of the World Atlas* (Kidron and Segal 1987). It shows the (black) silhouette of a soldier looming over the (white) silhouette of a doctor, portraying the number of military personnel for every 100 doctors, dentists, and trained nurses. We can set out similar data for three levels of the state in India (see Table 7.1).

TABLE 7.1 'HEALTHWORKERS' AND 'HARMWORKERS' IN INDIA

	Armed forces	Healthworkers	Teachers
India (1984)	1,120,000	294,700	3,997,000
Uttar Pradesh (1990)	100,297	42,680	461,000
Ghazipur (1990)	1,068	1,409	8,429

Sources: for India, Sivard (1987, p. 44); for UP and Ghazipur, *Crime in India* 1990; Uttar Pradesh government 1991, p. 263; Uttar Pradesh Directorate of Education (1990, pp. 79–81); Uttar Pradesh Planning Department 1991, vol. 2, p.131.

Note: 'Armed forces' are: military personnel for India; police for UP (including armed police); and police for Ghazipur (although they are mainly unarmed). Paramilitary forces concerned with quasi-military functions and riot control numbered some 500,000 in 1992 (International Institute of Strategic Studies 1993–94), which probably should be added to the armed forces figure (145,000 more than the above figure in 1990). 'Healthworkers' are 'physicians' for India; 'medical officers' and 'nurses, midwives' employed by the UP government for UP; and 'doctors and paramedical workers' employed by government for Ghazipur. 'Teachers' are teachers at all levels, including those working part time for India; and primary and intermediate school teachers (government and private 'recognized') for Ghazipur and UP.

The notes to the headings and the sources trumpet the care with which this table must be viewed: every figure in it rests on weak foundations and most are non-comparable. Nonetheless, the shift in character of the 'portrait' of the Indian state that emerges looks right: from the outside, the 'harmworkers' loom larger;[8] from inside, in UP, and from below, in Ghazipur, education and health emerge as more significant. The ratios (making guesses about paramilitary forces and adding them in to the India figure) of 'harmworkers' to 'health and learning workers' moves from 1:2 to 1:5 to 1:9 as we move toward the grass roots perspective, from 'India' to 'UP' to 'Ghazipur'.

A grass roots perspective on just who 'is' the state suggests a state with blurred boundaries, and one that has a more intimate connection with its citizenry than a top-down view would have it (cf. Gupta 1995). Those who are part of the state are, at the grass roots, often one's next-door neighbour, a person who as often as not works for both the state and privately, often mixing the two. And in terms of what is done, more likely to be at least supposed to provide a benefit, rather than regulate or coerce.

WHAT DOES THE STATE ACTUALLY DO?

There is no doubt that, no matter how we finally decide to draw boundaries around the state and count its employees, it has, in India, expanded in the sectors of society with which it deals; in the number of programmes implemented in those sectors; and in the money and human resources mobilized. There is considerable doubt, however, on the effectiveness of state action, and study after study speaks of failed programmes. Most of those assessments, to be sure, speak of the failure to reach goals set by the programmes, rather than an absolute failure of literally nothing being accomplished (for example, Weiner 1991). Does our assessment of what the state actually does, and what it has managed to achieve, alter as we move from an all-India, to a UP, to a Ghazipur perspective? I will consider problems of interpreting data we commonly use, and of sorting out overlapping functions of the state.

MAINTENANCE OF LAW AND ORDER

The maintenance of law and order lies at the core of the state's goals. The general (or at least rhetorical) view is that the state has not only failed in this area, even worse, it has acted to impose order on the mass of the citizenry on behalf of the elite interests that control it, while the law provides little or no recourse to the weak. Scholars like Atul Kohli (1990, p. 6) have typically used the degree of violence as an indicator of the degree of order. And official data on riots is used as an indicator of political violence. Kohli uses the 'Crime in India' data on riots (with a reference to Nayar 1975), to underpin these assertions, a graph of 'riots per million population' from 1955 to 1985.[9] I have updated the figure (Figure 7.1), using the same source. Kohli's chart (of the years 1955–85) shows an unambiguously rising line, due in part to what turned out to be mistaken estimates by government officials for the 1983–5 data; the expanded data present a very different picture. Figure 7.2 shows the number of riots per 100,000 population in Ghazipur. These data suggest that at the very least we should be very cautious about saying that there has been an enormous deterioration in the law and order situation.

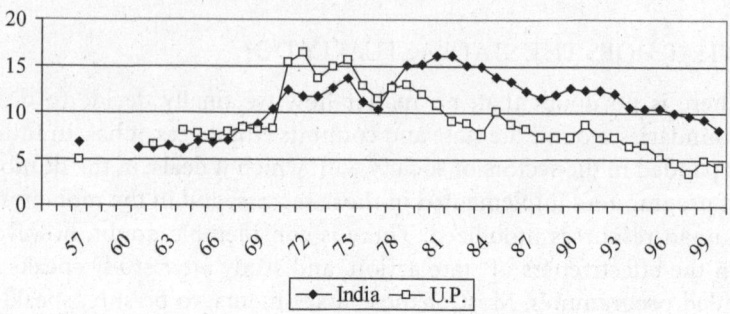

FIGURE 7.1 'VOLUME'/'RATE' OF RIOT CASES

Source: Government of India, Ministry of Home Affairs, *Crime in India* (1956, 1964–99): 'volume' and 'rate' (the changeover in term occurs in 1992) are defined as cases per 100,000 persons, with population mid-year estimates from the Registrar General of India. The volumes containing the 1957-9 data (and the 1963 UP data) have proven to be elusive.

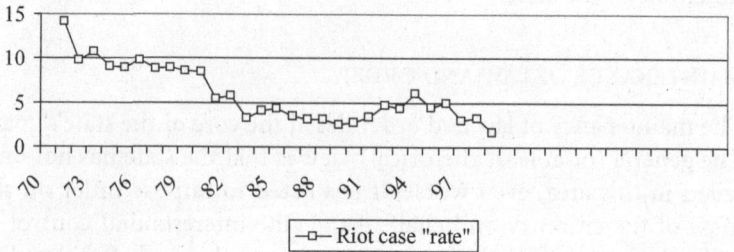

FIGURE 7.2 RIOT CASE 'RATE', GHAZIPUR DISTRICT, 1971-99

Source: Government of India, Ministry of Home Affairs, *Crime in India* (1971–99). District-level data are presented as raw numbers; I have calculated the riot case 'rate' using a rough estimate of each year's population of Ghazipur, based on Census of India data.

But is the incidence of 'riot' a good indicator of political violence? 'Riot' cases are registered under Section 146 of the Indian Penal Code that apply to 'unlawful assembly' of 'five or more persons'. Indeed, about five people are arrested for each case of riot registered.[10] There are probably many more riots than there are cases registered, but there is no estimate of just how large the shortfall is.

There is a more important problem with using 'riot' as an indicator of state performance in the law-and-order arena. The riots that are counted are not the large-scale (especially Hindu-Muslim) battles that make newspaper headlines, but rather what are better labelled brawls. I was able to obtain a breakdown of riots by type at the state and district (see Tables 7.2 and 7.3). Both police officers who provided these numbers indicated to me that they were not comfortable with them. Clearly, the motives are hard to discern for a police officer recording a case in many cases, which accounts for the large numbers classified as 'enmity' or 'other'.

TABLE 7.2 'RIOT' CASES IN UP

	1987	1988	1989	1990	1991
Communal	54	24	67	239	137
Industrial	33	26	23	40	12
Agrarian	462	418	356	411	413
Caste	125	82	55	144	13
Subtotal	674	550	501	834	575
Total 'riot cases'	7,748	7,873	8,431	9,146	9,305

Source: U. P. State Crime Records Bureau records [interview, July 1992]

TABLE 7.3 'MOTIVES' FOR RIOT, GHAZIPUR DISTRICT

'Motive'	1988	1989	1990	1991	1992	Totals
Communal	0	0	0	0	0	0
Caste	0	0	0	0	0	0
Industrial	0	0	0	0	0	0
Enmity	1	1	0	0	16	18
Property dispute	3	2	5	3	3	16
Illicit relationship	0	0	1	0	0	1
Agrarian	1	11	1	0	2	15
Other reasons	12	0	4	3	6	25
Total	17	14	11	6	27	75

Source: Superintendent of Police, Ghazipur. The figures for 1992 are up to August, and may represent the increased registering of crime due to the zeal of the SP.

It is important also to look at the level as well as the trend line: 16 cases of riot per 100,000 population (at the all-India peak) can be interpreted to mean that in a town of 100,000, say, or a set of 100,000 person villages, an average of one brawl per week occurs, usually because of a property dispute. Even if this is a severe undercount, it does not suggest mayhem breaking out. And yet one cannot dismiss the general belief that the law and order situation is not good.

If what we want to use is the level of violence rather than 'political' violence, to evaluate the extent to which law and order is maintained, the 'murder case rate' is a much more reliable statistic.[12] Arguably, there should be some relationship between the general level of violence and murderous violence. A senior officer in Delhi thought that the number of cases significantly understated the number of murders only in Punjab and Bihar.[13]

The data for India, UP, and Ghazipur are graphed in Figures 7.3 and 7.4.

On the surface, these graphs do not suggest a trend trend towards iincreasing violence. It is, however, a shaky inference that the state is maintaining order. If the state were truly failing to maintain law and order, might that not be reflected in just such a decrease in the murder *case* rate, as local power holders make sure that murders they commit are *not* registered? (A contrary bias would come from powerful men to filing false cases of murder against enemies—political, economic,

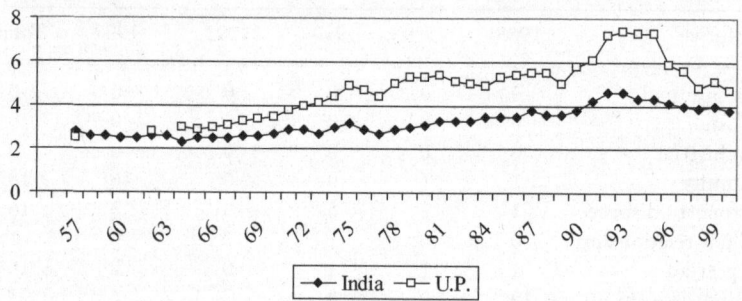

FIGURE 7.3 'VOLUME'/'RATE' OF MURDER CASES

Source: Government of India, Ministry of Home Affairs, *Crime in India* (1956, 1960, 1964–99): 'volume' and 'rate' (the changeover in term occurs in 1992) are defined as cases per 100,000 persons, with population mid-year estimates from the Registrar General of India.

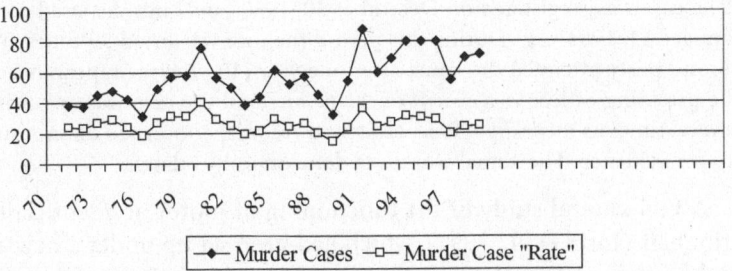

FIGURE 7.4 MURDER CASES IN GHAZIPUR, 1971-99

Source: Government of India, Ministry of Home Affairs, *Crime in India* [1971–99]; my calculations of estimated yearly population figures and murder case 'rate' from Census of India data. The 'rate' is here defined as 'cases per million population' for ease of graphing. Note missing data for 1983.

or family.) Or, might not murders be increasing recently because of changing social or economic conditions, rather than because the state has an effective police force and judicial system that deters murderers? One cannot sort this out using government statistics. We have to investigate systematically what goes on at the grass roots in a substantial, representative, set of places. Indeed, Krishna (2002, pp. 115–40) has convincingly used survey methods to measure the degree of communal harmony in what are probably representative villages (and to explain their variation).

Turning from 'order' to 'law', let us consider the judicial system, which, taken as a whole, is often seen as a solid pillar of the Indian state. If one looks at the higher judiciary, that is not unreasonable. If one considers the judicial system at the district and village levels, however, the picture changes (see Moog 1997; Krishna 2002, pp. 130–4). In 1988, for example, there were more than 10 million *criminal* cases pending before the courts in India, 94 per cent of them in magistrates' courts. Of the 233,404 cases pending in the high courts, 29 per cent had been there for less than a year; 19 per cent for one to two years; 14 per cent for two to three years; and up to 4 per cent for eight or more years.[14]

The record of civil cases must be much, much worse. In one example recounted by the UP Commission on District Level Administration (Uttar Pradesh government 1986, vol. 1, p. 169), the experience of litigation at the grass roots becomes clear:

[The case was] registered on December 30, 1980 [and] not disposed of till January 12, 1984]. . . . During this period the case was listed 39 times. The second party attended the court after one year [10 *peshies* (appearances)], the presiding officer was absent on 11 *peshies* and the case was adjourned several times as the *lekhpal* [keeper of land records] concerned did not turn up for evidence. The actual work was done on only 3 dates.

A very careful study of the functioning of motor accident claims tribunals (Joshi et al., 1991), which had been set up under a new 'no fault' compensation law to get compensation to victims quickly—— that is, when they needed it—shows that the tribunals adopted unnecessary procedures, were unable to get witnesses produced, and were also insufficiently staffed and of insufficient number to get the job done. The delays in getting compensation were enormous: in Madras, the city with the best record of the six studied, only 60 per cent of the claims were settled within one year.

SAVINGS SCHEMES

As another example of what a state actually does, let us briefly examine the mobilization of savings. This reveals another not uncommon feature not normally captured by all-India data: the varied agencies all doing the same thing (without coordination), a state housing a set of autonomous competing agencies. As noted above, the post office handles a set of savings schemes for the finance ministry of the Government of India. (Publicity for those schemes is handled by the state government, by the 'small savings officer'.) Another official in Ghazipur who promotes savings is the district savings officer (of the Government of India), promoting programmes such as the 'Women's Local Savings Scheme' in which an educated unemployed woman takes an agency to promote household savings by women.

This does not exhaust the state's involvement in savings: there are 167 bank branches in the district, including the public sector banks, regional rural banks, and district cooperative bank. There is a District Credit Plan formulated and supervised by the lead bank of the District, a plan in which targets for agricultural loans under the Integrated Rural Development Programme (IRDP) and similar activities are set and appraised. Between these institutions and the village moneylender there can be a number of informal finance organizations, some of which are also run under government regulation.[15]

RURAL DEVELOPMENT

The various programmes for rural development that have been implemented make an impressive list: the community development programme of the 1950s (literally visible in Ghazipur in the form of very large government tube well/water tank installations); food for-work programmes and 'intensive' (or 'integrated') agricultural development programmes, etc., in the next decades and in recent years, the *Jawahar Rozgar Yojana* (Jawaharlal Nehru Employment Plan) (JRY) and the IRDP.[16] While there are comparatively few state employees, the amount of money poured into the system is considerable—and just how much actually reaches the villager is an interesting question. A surprising number of people in Ghazipur quoted (with relish) Rajiv Gandhi's remark that 'of the 100 rupees for agricultural development sanctioned by Delhi, only 15 reach the intended recipients'.[18]

THE JAWAHAR ROZGAR YOJANA

Announced by Rajiv Gandh in April 1989, the JRY is a rural employment programme that was widely criticized in public and contemptuously dismissed in private as an election gambit pure and simple. The talk of scholars, administrators, activists concerned with rural development, in 1991–2 at least, when I was paying close attention, was of the enormous corruption in the programme, and its failure to deliver the benefits it promised. The paradigm remark was 'the JRY is supposed to build roads but the roads that are built exist only on paper'.

Rural roads have been, indeed, a major portion of the 'assets' created by the JRY, along with housing for the 'weaker sections' under the *Indira Awas Yojana* (Indira Gandhi Dwelling Plan), and wells under the 'Million Wells Scheme'.[20] Other 'assets' include trees planted under social forestry programmes, school buildings, sanitary latrines, 'works benefiting scheduled castes and scheduled tribes', and, of course 'other works'. The major difference in this programme, compared to earlier rural employment programmes, was that 'the major portion of the financial allocation is given to the *Gram Panchayats* [village councils] for planning and execution.' (PEO 1992, p. 27) In practice, this means the *pradhan* (elected leader) and the *panchayat* secretary.

In assessing the first 20 months or so of the programme in the sample *panchayats*, the PEO noted that the scheme 'did not provide employment to the extent expected' (PEO 1992, p. 15). Further, the 'quality of the assets created was not up to the mark in a majority of cases (56 per cent). Those were either of average or poor quality.' (ibid., p. 27). And they found that the maintenance of the 'assets' was rarely 'good'.

In Ghazipur, many people told me that the JRY had been used by the pradhan and the panchayat secretary to enrich themselves and favour their supporters. A village activist, a harijan,[21] told the story of how his pradhan (also a harijan) diverted the programme that was to build brick houses, starting with the poorest people (those with shacks). Instead, the pradhan got his supporters' houses (which were of mud) built first. 'Nothing happens when we make a complaint', the activist said, and then proceeded to tell me how the complaint of his small organization got the district development officer to come to investigate, with the result that he ordered a couple of houses built for those who had only shacks.

But there are those who think the JRY is a good programme. The discussion I had (April 1992) with an assistant development officer posted in Varanasi on a visit to his home village bears reporting in some detail. The man, who impressed me as extremely knowledgeable and thoughtful, presented his views forcefully. He told me that a lot of the JRY money went to the pradhan and the panchayat secretary, the proof being that panchayat secretaries used to come into the block headquarters on broken-down bicycles, but 'now 75 per cent come on motorcycles'. He estimated that the two officials 'ate' Rs. 50,000 to 150,000, taking a commission of 25 per cent at a minimum, and probably 30–40 per cent. 'Now,' he said, 'pradhans have just as bad a name as government servants. We are honest until we get the opportunity to steal.' But, he said, corruption has not overwhelmed development programmes; the benefits outweigh the corruption. And, he pointed out,

Even though in JRY 25–30 per cent was eaten, 70–75 per cent got to the village. Before, the commission eaten [by the whole development hierarchy, which is by-passed in JRY] came to 60 per cent. True, the paunch of those with fat bellies has gotten bigger, but at least the hollow-stomached man has filled out. Most of the poverty is in the villages and now they are eating [twice a day]. Because [JRY money] went direct. There are roads built. Roads now are also reaching the hamlets [*bastis*]. To improve JRY we need audits, estimates, open village assembly meetings: then [the programme would be] much better and without corruption.' [22]

We shall return to underline one point made here: the stream of benefits from government is siphoned off by those upstream of the beneficiaries, but what matters most to villagers is perhaps how much reaches them, not how much has been siphoned off, which sum they are unlikely to know or be able to find out. It should be said also that villagers admitted that not all pradhans and panchayat secretaries were corrupt—though no one was prepared to give me an estimate of the percentage that are honest.

When we return to the PEO report with this in mind, it becomes less surprising to learn that 89 per cent of the 600 beneficiaries surveyed declared that the assets created were 'useful', with the 11 per cent who disagreed divided fairly evenly between those who lived too far away from the asset, those who thought them 'substandard', and another section who thought they were not 'permanent' (PEO 1992, p. 30). On the other hand, only 15 per cent said that 'JRY scheme is good/beneficial for the community'. (ibid., p. 45). A decade later, according to Krishna (2002, p. 44), '[Rural employment schemes] have come to form a part of normal life for the ordinary villager. Nearly half of all villagers [surveyed by Krishna in the late 1990s in Rajasthan and Madhya Pradesh] depend on such employment for at least one month every year merely in order to make ends meet.'

The state as seen from the grass roots thus seems to do more than the view from other vantage points would at first blush suggest. Still, the evaluation of state accomplishments by those 'above' the local level is usually very poor (a good example would be Brass 1994).

ASSESSING THE STATE: CITIZENS' VIEWS

How do the citizens at the grass roots assess the government's record of rule? One occasionally hears a voice of dissent among the constant litany of complaints. When I asked one substantial farmer and leader of the village how much government had contributed to development, he said emphatically: 'There is need for the government. We could in principle make our own arrangements, but we couldn't in reality. The government must make the arrangement. . . . These difficulties with government are due to government doing more things.'[23] The question is, how (un)representative a view is this?

In the area of delivery of services to rural areas, we fortunately have some data from a remarkable opinion survey done by the UP government in 1988, as part of its preparation for the eighth five-year plan.[24] This survey was intended to measure the knowledge and approval of programmes that come under the planning process, agricultural and social services, particularly. Respondents were also asked for the opinion of the causes of the lack of success of programmes. There were interesting though not very major differences in the opinions of 'common' (*samaanya*) villagers versus 'elite' villagers; I will therefore report mainly on the former category.

The survey covered 20,000 (male) respondents in 2,000 village of the state (excluding the hill districts), plus 5,000 'elite' villagers. I believe this was a carefully conducted, properly formulated survey —but since I was not able to discuss how it was done with those who carried it out, I treat its results with some caution, especially since the questions were undoubtedly put by people seen as 'from government'. (We should not assume that this would result in responses favourable to the government programme. It has been my experience that villagers are quite willing to present to government officials an honest, and even at times overly critical, assessment of programmes.)

When asked 'what in your opinion is the most important benefit of the plans started by the government',[25] 70 per cent nominated 'growth of agricultural production'; 47 per cent said 'improvement in [people's] financial condition'; 44 per cent said 'lessening societal differences'; 43 per cent 'advance of education'; 35 per cent 'spread of facilities for well-being' (whatever that might mean); 20 per cent 'improvement in hospital and health facilities'; 18 per cent 'lessening of unemployment'; 9 per cent 'lessening of the number of the poor'; 8 per cent 'improvement of other agricultural things' (veterinary services, for example); and 7 per cent said 'lessening population growth'. This is a rank order that might well be replicated by an expert familiar with UP, I would think. Note that there is no statement here of how much benefit there was, and also that the question assumes that benefits exist.

When asked why the plans failed, 69 per cent of the villagers said they were not properly administered, with the remainder saying that 'people didn't help', and that the plans were badly made. The remedy for the failures favoured by 53 per cent was increased allocations of money, while 27 per cent favoured increased efficiency, and 20 per cent the association of the village assembly. Again, these appraisals seem eminently *sensible*. That is, I do not think answers to please the government were being supplied or what was being measured was something else like 'alienation from the government'.

Except for adult education, Table 7.4 reveals a startling success rating for government programmes. IRDP is called successful by 64 per cent! (If we polled a sample of senior administrators in Delhi and Lucknow, or a group of scholars of rural development, what figure would we come up with?)

Similarly, the level of satisfaction reported in Table 7.5 is much higher than the conventional wisdom of the knowledgeable elite: would they believe that more than three-quarters of the population are at least satisfied with health services?

TABLE 7.4 LEVEL OF KNOWLEDGE AND EVALUATION OF SUCCESS OF PARTICULAR PROGRAMS, 'COMMON' VILLAGERS, RANKED IN ORDER OF 'SUCCESS'

Program	Percentage of Respondents who	
	Know of it	Rated it 'successful'
Child immunization	92	75
Integrated Rural Development	94	64
Free (well) boring	88	63
Compulsory primary education	82	59
Cooperative sector loans	89	58
Indira Dwelling Plan	82	51
Special employment programmes	73	48
Improved animal breeding	75	47
Biogas plants	99	43
Pulse and oilseed production	63	41
Adult education	78	20

TABLE 7.5 LEVEL OF SATISFACTION WITH SOCIAL SERVICES
(Elite Class, Percentages)

Service	Very satisfied	Satisfied	Not at all satisfied
Primary education	14	48	38
Health services	6	71	23
Drinking water	15	60	25
Village housing	8	44	48
Scheduled Caste welfare	22	52	26

The finding (Table 7.6) that villagers see improvement in education coming from a disciplined work force rather than from bricks and mortar is also important (and note that this survey was done after the politically salient 'Operation Blackboard' [intended to improve the physical endowments of schools]—from this evidence, not a good symbol).

TABLE 7.6 REQUISITE REMEDIES FOR THE PROGRESS OF PRIMARY EDUCATION

Remedy	Percentage Placing in First Rank	
	Elite class	'Common' villager
Making sure teachers attend as they should	69	65
Construction of buildings for existing schools	45	43
Appointment of sufficient numbers of teachers	27	29
New schools should be opened	23	30
Provisions for proper seating	21	19
Provision of blackboards and other materials	16	14

My previous experience in studying land consolidation (Oldenburg n.d.; see also 1990) had prepared me for these findings, because that programme very clearly was carried out, by and large, according to the rules, and brought farmers enormous benefits. On the whole, the state has, to a greater degree than is visible from Delhi, delivered the goods.

CONCLUSIONS

When I studied land consolidation in 1980–1, I spent most of a year observing the process, mainly sitting in various villages. On the whole,

I did not see much of 'the state' other than the land consolidation officers: the postman and schoolteachers occasionally, a veterinarian doing artificial insemination once, a few politicians and government officials (home on holiday) from time to time. But the state was clearly all around me, in the electric lines, roads, schools, and primary health centres. And in the absence of villagers about once a month in one village—because many of them were accused of inter-caste rioting, and were in court (the case was invariably rescheduled for hearing). Krishna (2002, p. 43) provides an impressive list of the 'barriers erected by the state'—permissions and licences—that the farmer has to get past in Rajasthan. In this grass roots view, the Indian state is an exasperating state, an inefficient state, but not a particularly oppressive one.

Notwithstanding the difficulty with obtaining valid data illustrated above, there is no doubt that the state reaches into the farthest corners of Ghazipur and touches the lives of a a large number of Ghazipur's people, in significant ways. That being so, we can say that the same is true for the overwhelming majority of UP's inhabitants, and for the citizens of India. Indeed, as Gupta (1995, p. 378) claims: 'Everyday interactions with state bureaucracies are to my way of thinking the most important ingredient in constructions of "the state" forged by villagers and state officials.' I have not attempted to show changes over time, but my sense of my Ghazipur data is that the state continues to expand and fill new roles. The programme to create STD/ISD booths through state initiative and licencing (and not without corruption, of course) is a visible sign of the spread of the state.

The state is clearly shot through with corruption; each one of the programmes favourably evaluated by villagers in the survey has huge amounts of money sucked out of them. How can they then be favourably assessed by villagers? Perhaps we neglect the other side of the equation—work done without corruption. The UP Commission on District Administration (1986, vol. 1, p. 367) puts it well: 'Instead of work culture, a graft culture has been created. . . . It is not that there are no honest public servants. There are many honest government servants and they are in all departments and at all levels but their number is declining.' I have explored elsewhere (Oldenburg 1987) the paradox of a largely honest and well-administered programme in UP that is believed by almost everyone to be totally corrupt.

Another possible reason for a favourable evaluation is that the leakage of funds because of corruption is not seen as theft of the citizens' money by villagers. Corrupt bureaucrats and politicians are not 'stealing our tax money'; rather, the state is a lumbering, clumsy behemoth on (and in) which various parasites are living, sucking the blood-flow of funds away, sometimes weakening the state to the point where very little gets done. And while villagers recognize that they ought to be getting the full benefit of state programmes, and get justifiably very angry for the callous treatment they all too often receive in government offices and in hospitals and police stations and the like, they also in a strange way do not condemn the parasites on the state for their behaviour in the same way that one hears in Delhi. Dealing with the nurse who refuses to treat patients without a fee is a bit like dealing with the floods of the Gangesa, and many feel they would do the same had they the chance. So what actually reaches the village—a road built, a doctor attending the clinic—is counted as a service deserved, and appreciated, but not one already paid for. In a sense, that is the essence of the state's con game.

Obviously, many people who live in the more tax-infested cities, or the educated, are not taken in by the con. And yet, they tend not to see themselves as responsible for the state's behaviour, but rather portray themselves as victims of its indefensible actions. When I investigated the 'folklore of corruption' in Delhi and Meerut (less formally in Delhi, to be sure; see Oldenburg 1987), 1 was struck by the contrast: one villager said to me (I give the gist here), 'of course government officers take bribes, because we are greedy to get against-the-rules things done, and they are so poorly paid that we can make them very tempting offers.' But in Delhi, people who paid bribes for improper or even illegal things—jumping the queue for getting a sleeping berth on the train, paying less wealth tax, etc.—invariably blamed the officials for accepting their bribes, and justified their own actions with the time-honoured 'well, everyone does it.' The paradoxical hypothesis this suggests is that the legitimacy of the state is most severely questioned by those who have in fact benefited most from it (the urban elite) and assessed far more favourably by those who have suffered from its inaction.

The state that exists at the grass roots is a loosely coordinated conglomerate of disparate departments, politicians, and half-public half-private service providers. This is clearly not the same 'state' that theories or even generalizations about the state consider, the ones that focus their attention on the state in its country-wide and international arenas. While this essay has largely dealt with what the state 'is' or 'looks like', our theories seek to explain what happens to the state and why (does it grow and why?) and what explains its relationship to the world beyond its country's borders, and to its society (and how those change over time, and why).

Coercion is central to most of our definitions of the state, but the Indian state's exercise of coordinated and irresistible domination seems less convincing from a grass roots perspective. The state is a thing to be avoided or kept at bay, or a cow to be milked. And yet it is domesticated in some sense: its employees are familiar (sometimes literally relations or classmates or friends), but more important, its routines are so old—one is tempted to say ancient—that nothing the state does ever surprises anyone. Its functioning involves a convoluted and hard-to-follow set of procedures, but that mystery is not one of a state behind high, blank, and forbidding walls. The large number of persons half-in, half-out of the state in the purely political realm—the political workers of the politicians (who act, or claim to act on their behalf), as well as officials—also serve to mute the threat of use of force that the state undoubtedly holds in reserve. So too does corruption: threats can be literally bought off.

The degree of autonomy of the state (let alone whether a state is 'autonomous' or not) also looks more problematic from this level. Propertied or otherwise powerful classes or groups may exercise significant influence over certain segments of the state, and very little over others. There are sections—postal services, for instance—which seem unlikely candidates for capture, as they provide service so diffuse and operate with such an entrenched routine, it would be hard to imagine just what the capturing group would change in their functioning. Other sections have been in some sense captured by certain interests—the public distribution system by the retailers of sugar and kerosene, for example—but there is no evidence that those people have extended their control beyond that beachhead (and why should they?). To a certain degree the state retains autonomy due to its being at least minimally coordinated—all its parts are recognizably 'Government'—while civil society in places like Ghazipur certainly is uncoordinated, even though notables exist and exercise power. But it remains to be seen whether on balance the state 'is' autonomous or not at the grass roots (or whether its autonomy is increasing or not).

The grass roots is also the level at which the state looks most impervious to regime change; it is here where the most obvious offices and activities unchanged from colonial times are to be found. Iltudus Prichard's marvelous satire, *The Chronicles of Budgepore*, written more than a century ago, remains one of the best guides to the Indian state at the district level today. As Kohli (1987, p. 29) puts it (though not in the context of the colonial rule-independence transition): 'Regimes can come and go but the basic state type does not alter easily.' He continues by noting that regime changes are not likely to alter the two fundamental characteristics of Third World states— they seek development and this development is based on private property.' This too is consonant with the grass roots view.

Whatever people at the grass roots may feel about who pays the salaries of state officials and for the building of electric lines and roads and schools, a not insignificant part of that money comes ultimately from the mass of the citizenry. Excise and customs get passed down, usually invisibly, to the consumer. The money deposited in savings accounts helps finance the state, and even some user fees pay at least some of the cost of the services provided (for example postal services). Many state officials may supplement their income by 'renting out' public goods under their control, but the state at the grass roots is still largely financed by legitimate means. The Indian state does not float above its society, drawing most of its sustenance from flows of aid or the mining of natural resources or even enclave industries like tourism. The Indian state is deeply rooted in its society, and as the character of the Indian economy changes, it is likely that taxation will be brought more directly home to more and more citizens, and they will demand, more and more, value for *their* money.

There is even evidence for suggesting that the state in India at the grass roots has been accorded legitimacy by the citizenry. Concluding their introductory summary of the papers of an important work on the *Everyday State*, Fuller and Harriss (2000, p. 14) state: '[The] bold 'claim that the impersonal norms and values of the modern state have been widely internalized by ordinary Indians—lower-level bureaucrats, local politicians and ordinary citizens alike —is one that the material in this volume largely supports.'

There is a tendency to discount the parts of the state that loom so large at the grass roots: the state that 'really counts', in this view is the part with military forces and a parliament and a senior civil service, all linked to large-scale industry and other corporate entities. And certainly when the country is threatened—by war, a deep economic crisis, nationalist upsurges and the like—the characteristics of that state are critical. But in non-crisis, dull, routine business-as-usual functioning of the state, the literally millions of interactions it manages at the grass roots count for a great deal in under girding its legitimacy and in helping us understand what it does and does not accomplish.

NOTES

1. This essay is part of a larger project focused on delineating the grass roots foundations of state legitimacy in India. Almost a year's research in 1991–2 in India was funded by the American Institute of Indian Studies and the Fulbright programme, for which I am very grateful (and which does not implicate them in any way with my findings as presented here or anywhere else). Although a full decade has passed since this fieldwork, recent efforts to update the material suggests that the conceptual issues have still not been resolved; so the exploratory nature of the essay is thus meant very seriously. Earlier versions of this essay were presented at the Association for Asian Studies Annual Meeting in 1993, and at the Delhi University Political Science Department in 2003. I am grateful to John Echeverri-Gent, Prabhu Ghate, Ronald Herring, Satyajit Singh, and others for their comments; the responsibility for what is here remains mine alone. Long discussions over some two decades with George Mathew have influenced my understanding of government at the grass roots in ways too numerous to mention. A slightly different version of this essay appears in L.C. Jain (ed.), *Decentralisation and Local Governance: Essays for George Mathew* (New Delhi: Orient Longman, 2005).

2. I take 'the state' to be an institution that encompasses both bureaucracy and political authorities; particularly at the grass roots level, political authorities expend all their influence on policy implementation, and the line of separation between 'administration' and 'politics' is constantly breached by politicians and bureaucrats alike.

3. The source of most of my information on postal services comes from interviews with senior postal officials in New Delhi, and from the annual reports of the Post and Telegraph Departments

4. Jeffrey and Lerche (2000, p. 98) provide the precise figures (tens of thousands of rupees) for typical government jobs 'on the market'.

5. The amounts of money are not trivial: 80 million rupees in money orders were paid out on average every year in the late 1980s in Ghazipur. A low estimate (to take into account money orders paid in the urban areas), would be that each village branch office on average distributed 130,000 rupees annually. 90 million rupees were paid out annually in Ghazipur for at least a few years after 1987–8, as savings certificates were discharged.

6. He did note that students enrol in government schools while actually studying in private schools because the government school is too far away, but you must be enrolled in order to take examinations. Srivastava (2001, p. 303) supports this point. Drèze and Sen (2002, pp. 146–8) show clearly how inflated official enrollment figures are, relying various survey and census data.

7. According to an all-India survey on corruption, conducted for Transparency International by ORG-Marg research in 2002, the health sector was the most corrupt department, with 11 per cent of the respondents reporting the need to bribe doctors to provide medicines and to provide proper health care (the *Indian Express* 18 December 2002). See also Drèze and Sen 2002, p. 202; Gupta 1995, p. 387.

8. Sivard (1987, pp. 48–9) reports that per capita expenditure on the military in India in 1984 was eight dollars, compared to eight dollars for public expenditure on education and two dollars for public expenditure on health. This expenditure data on the military and on health, from an earlier year, is what is mapped in *The New State of the World Atlas*.

9. Kohli (1990, p. 7) apparently agrees with Nayar's argument on why the overall riot figures can be 'used to gauge public protest and political violence', but Nayar simply says that since 'the statistics do cover violence directed against public authority and are, as impressionistic evidence suggests, sensitive to changes in public protest or political violence, they can be usefully employed as an indicator for such protest and violence' (Nayar 1975, p. 17). 1 am not so sure.

10. There were an average of 95,655 cases registered annually in the 1985–99 quinquennium, and 586,032 persons arrested. The eighteenth century Riot Act in England required 12 persons (Oxford English Dictionary).

11. According to a number of senior police officials who have dealt with the data in Delhi, and senior officials of the UP police (a total of 8), interviewed in 1991–2.

12. N.S. Saksena, a former and much respected police officer, and a major analyst of police policy, however, claims that non-reporting and other

factors make the 'murder case rate' is only a third of the actual murder rate (Saksena 1992).

13. Data prepared by the Bureau of Police Research and Development, March 1992.

14. A fine study is Bouman (1989); see also Ghate (1992).

15. Tiwari (1990) studies just rural employment programmes. I present the array of initials: RMP (1961–9), CSRE (1971–4), PIREP (1972–6), FFW (1977–80), NREP (1980–7), RLEGP (1983–87). And that is just central government schemes. In September 2001 the successor of the Jawahar Gram Samriddhi Yojana (JRY) (Jawaharlal Nehru Village Prosperity Plan) was merged with the Employment Assurance Scheme to form the Sampoorna Grameen Rozgar Yojana (Whole Village Employment Plan).

16. This is an 'average' of how the remark was quoted to me, by the District Magistrate and the Chairman of the Zilla Parishad (District Council) and others. I attempted to discover the source of this statistic; I was told that Rajiv's speechwriter believes it came from a planning commission study.

17. Programme Evaluation Organization, Planning Commission, Government of India, *Jawahar Rozgar Yojana—A Quick Study, 1991–92* (New Delhi, 1992). The evaluation relied heavily on an extensive survey of a sizeable sample of villages from around the country.

18. That is, an 'ex-untouchable'. The word *harijan* was used by Gandhi and means 'people of god'; it was used by this man to refer to himself, although in other parts of India the preferred word is 'Dalit' (oppressed) (Interview, April 1992).

19. This is my recollection—written down an hour or so later—of his remarks, which were of course in Hindi. I am completely confident that I have correctly conveyed his basic points, but the text may not be verbatim, and I have erred on the side of literal translation. See Gupta (1995, p. 390) for very similar statements by villagers in western UP.

20. Again, this is my recalled translation of his remarks.

21. I am grateful to officers of the Planning Institution of the UP government, particularly K.K. Bakshi and Lakshmi Narain, for conveying the results of this survey to me.

22. The translations from Hindi are, by and large, my own. The language used was clear and simple, which is one of the reasons I have some confidence in the survey results.

REFERENCES

Bouman, F.J.A., *Small, Short, and Unsecured: Informal Rural Finance in India* (New Delhi: Oxford University Press, 1989).

Brass, Paul R., *The Politics of India Since Independence,* The New Cambridge History of India IV–1, Second Edition (Cambridge: Cambridge University Press, 1994).

Drèze, Jean and Amartya Sen, *India: Development and Participation* (New Delhi: Oxford University Press, 2002).

Fuller, C. J. and John Harriss, 'For an Anthropology of the Modern Indian State', in *The Everyday State and Society in Modern India*, C.J. Fuller and Veronique Bénéï (eds), (New Delhi: Social Science Press, 2000), pp. 1–30.

Fuller, C. J., and Véronique Bénéï, (eds.), *The Everyday State and Society in Modern India* (New Delhi: Social Science Press, 2000).

Ghate, Prabhu et al., *Informal Finance: Some Findings from Asia* (Hong Kong: Oxford University Press, for the Asian Development Bank, 1992).

Ghate, Prabhu, *Direct Attacks on Rural Poverty: Policy, Programmes and Implementation* (New Delhi: Concept, 1984).

Government of India, Ministry of Home Affairs, *Crime in India* (1956, 1964–99).

Gupta, Akhil, 'Blurred Boundaries: Tthe Discourse of Corruption, the Culture of Politics, and the Imagined State', *American Ethnologist* vol. 22, no. 2, 1995, pp. 375–402.

International Institute of Strategic Studies, *The Military Balance 1993-1994* (London: Brasseys for the International Institute of Strategic Studies, 1993–4).

Jeffrey, Craig; and Jens Lerche, 'Dimensions of Dominance: Class and State in Uttar Pradesh', *The Everyday State and Society in Modern India*, in C.J. Fuller and Veronique Bénéï, (eds), (New Delhi: Social Science Press, 2000), pp. 91-114.

Joshi, G.P., B.S. Bedi, and T. Chakroborty, *Functioning of Motor Accidents Claims Tribunals* (New Delhi: Bureau of Police Research and Development, 1991).

Kidron, Michael and Ronald Segal, *The New State of the World Atlas* (New York: Simon and Schuster, 1984).

Kohli, Atul, *The State and Poverty in India* (Cambridge: Cambridge University Press, 1987).

———, *Democracy and Discontent* (Cambridge: Cambridge University Press, 1990).

Krishna, Anirudh, *Active Social Capital: Tracing the Roots of Development and Democracy* (New York: Columbia University Press, 2002).

Moog, Robert S., *Where Interests Are Supreme? Organizational Politics in the Civil Courts in India*, AAS Monograph Series No. 54 (Ann Arbor: Association for Asian Studies, 1997).

Nayar, Baldev Raj, *Violence and Crime in India* (Delhi: Macmillan, 1975).

Nordlinger, Eric A., 'Taking the State Seriously', in *Understanding Political Development*, Myron Weiner and Samuel P. Huntington, (eds), (Boston: Little, Brown, 1987).

Oldenburg, Philip, 'Shared Decisions: Participation in Program Implementation and Legitimacy in India'. Unpublished ms., n.d.

———'Middlemen in Third World Corruption; Implications of an Indian Case', *World Politics*, vol. 39, no. 4 (July) 1987, pp. 508–35.

————, 'Land Consolidation as Land Reform,' *World Development,* vol. 18, no. 2 (February) 1990, pp. 183–95.

Operations Research Group (ORG) *India Population Project-II in Uttar Pradesh; Volume II, Case Study of Nine Selected PHCS* (Baroda: Operations Research Group, 1988).

Planning Evaluation Organization (PEO), Planning Commission, Government of India, *Jawahar Rozgar Yojana—A Quick Study,* New Delhi, 1992.

Prichard, Iltudus, *The Chronicles of Budgepore* (Delhi: Manohar, reprint of 1870 edition, 1972).

Saksena, N.S., 'Hold Police Chiefs Accountable for Excesses', the *Indian Express,* 6 April 1992, p. 9.

Sivard, Ruth Leger, *World Military and Social Expenditures 1987-88* (Washington: World Priorities, 1987).

Srivastava, Ravi, 'Access to Basic Education in Rural Uttar Pradesh.' in *Elementary Education in Rural India: A Grassroots View, Strategies for Human Development in India,* Volume 2, A. Vaidyanathan and P. R. Gopinathan Nair, (eds), (New Delhi: Sage, 2001), pp. 257-319.

Streefland, Pieter H., 'Management and Utilisation of Immunisation and Oral Rehydration Therapy in Rural Gujarat', in *Managing Rural Development; Health and Energy Programmes in India,* Hein Streefkerk and T. K. Moulik (eds), Indo-Dutch Studies on Development Alternatives 7 (New Delhi: Sage, 1991), pp. 50–78.

Tiwari, R.K., *Rural Employment Programmes in India: The Implementation Process* (New Delhi: Indian Institute of Public Administration, 1990).

Uttar Pradesh, *Sankhayaka* [Statistical] *Diary,* 1991.

————, Report of Commission on District Level Administration (T.N. Dhar, Chairman) 3 volumes, 1986.

————, Directorate of Education, *Uttar Pradesh main shiksha ki pragati* [*Progress of Education in UP.*], Allahabad, 1990.

————, Planning Department, *Draft Eighth Five Year Plan (1992–1997),* 3 volumes, Lucknow, 1991.

Weiner, Myron, *The Child and the State in India* (New Delhi: Oxford University Press, 1991).

EXPERIENCING THE STATE FROM OUTSIDE:
PSYCHIATRY, FILM, AND ART

8

Experiencing Care
Psychotherapy and NHS Mental Health Reform in Britain

NICHOLAS TEMPLE

This essay examines the organizational upheaval occurring in the British National Health Service (NHS) as a result of the Conservative government's market-oriented policies from 1989 until 1997 and afterward by the impact of the new Labour government. The Conservative government's introduction of an 'internal market' imposed major changes upon all NHS institutions. Market radicalism, as Will Hutton terms it, was brought to bear on what was the core element of the Welfare State established in 1948 by Clement Attlee's Labour government (Hutton 1995, pp. 151–60).

After the election of Tony Blair's Labour Party in May 1997 a number of Tory measures were reversed but a further round of reorganization, along some of the same lines, also took place (Hutton 2000, p. 42). Blair, for instance, carried on the Tory policy of financing private hospitals that are leased back to the public sector (*The Guardian*, 9 August 2001).[1] The impact of these changes was heightened by the fact that the Labour government expressly was elected to prevent further deterioration and perhaps a collapse of a highly valued NHS, which had been an important issue during the campaign. This period of change in the NHS, generated by rival parties in control of the British state, provides an interesting study of how mental health professionals adapted to rapidly shifting agendas of the state, which aimed to alter dramatically the structure and character of British medical and, more specifically for our purpose, mental health care.

These profound changes—profound even though stopped short of total privatization—in the NHS are examined below from the perspective of the Tavistock Clinic, an NHS mental health clinic and training centre based in London. The Clinic has always had a strong psychoanalytic tradition, which is unusual among NHS mental health services, and has long engaged in psychoanalytically oriented studies not only of individual disturbances and growth but of institutional and organizational processes. Hence, unlike many other mental health institutions, which are concerned exclusively with dealing with individual levels of pathology, many Tavistock staff were accustomed to analysing and operating at the collective level of behaviour, action, and motivation.

HISTORY OF THE TAVISTOCK

Since the Second World War the Tavistock has been a major centre of expertise in institutional and group dynamics, in large part inspired by the Kleinian psychoanalytic work of Wilfred Bion. The study of unconscious processes in organizations and in society always has been an important part of the Clinic's work. As a result, it is an institution which is well situated so as to develop a valuable perspective on, and critique of, the effects of changing government policies on NHS hospitals and clinics, and particularly on the organization of clinical services and health professions. The Clinic's role as the largest mental health training organization in Britain necessarily gives it a strong interest not only in accomplishing its immediate clinical and training tasks but also a more strategic concern regarding the future shape of the delivery of mental health services in the NHS, and the consequences for staff, patients, and society. It should be noted that its premier status among such facilities also placed the Clinic in a relatively advantaged position during the transitional period.

The Tavistock Clinic nevertheless had a strong attachment to the values of the NHS since it was set up in 1920, after the First World War, out of a concern to provide appropriate psychological treatments for mental illness, using approaches which had begun as a treatment for shell shock and war neurosis. This approach to treatment was radical, in the context of asylum-based psychiatry of the day, and heavily influenced by psychoanalytical ideas. The Clinic also had an egalitarian aim of providing psychotherapeutic treatment for ordinary people who did not have the wealth to pay for private psychiatric treatment. The result was an emphasis on the primary value of meeting patients' needs, without having to stint on appropriate treatment because of concern for any given individual's ability to pay.

THE FOUNDING OF THE NHS

The NHS was set up 5 July 1948 by a Labour government, as part of the new Welfare State. The NHS, which was planned by the Beveridge Report (a best-seller) during the Second World War, had the distinction of being 'the only service organised around an ethical imperative', as Klein observes. 'Its proclaimed aim is to achieve equality in the distribution and use of health care'. The wish to develop an organized health and welfare system derived much of its impetus from the national experience of the War, which had strengthened collective and cooperative structures in society. The preceding social insurance scheme established in 1911 by Lloyd George had covered 30 per cent of the population (Widgery 1988, p. 15). There was a strong idealistic motive, as evidenced by the Labour victory in 1945, to improve society following the many hardships and sacrifices of the war period, and employ collective measures to do so (Sked and Cook 1993, p. 18). Hence, the Welfare State was established to provide a fairer distribution of health and welfare services and to alleviate the great inequalities that existed between different social classes and in different parts of the country (Titmuss 1964; Frazier 1984). The Tavistock Clinic, which provides psychiatric and mental health services, had been an enthusiastic participant in the formation of the NHS because its values dating from its foundation were so strongly in line with the social ethos of a national health service, of promoting good quality health care for everybody.

In the first 40 years of its existence the NHS proved to be successful in delivering good quality medical care funded by national insurance and central taxation. The cost to the state and the taxpayers was reasonable while the service was mostly free at the point of delivery to the patient. The NHS was widely used by all sections of society and was not just a basic 'welfare system', as in the USA, designed (after Medicaid and Medicare legislation passed in 1965) to provide a minimal safety net for those who could afford nothing else. In 1987 Britain spent a smaller proportion of gross domestic product (GDP) on health than all but four of the Organization for Economic Cooperation and Development (OECD) countries while providing good care (Gilmour 1992, p. 154). The commitment and devotion of its staff to the ideals of the service, where wage and salary levels were relatively modest at best for professional staff and badly underpaid at worst for lower ranks, were a vital part of its success. The medical profession, ninety per cent of whom had originally opposed the setting up of the Health Service on the grounds that it was a tyrannical socialist measure, had been won over with financial and contractual concessions by the 1948 health minister, Aneurin Bevan, so that the British Medical Association (BMA) eventually became a strong supporter of the service (Klein 1995, p. 45; Eckstein 1958). Bevan's compromise with the BMA—especially with the senior consultants and the Royal College—provided for 'consensus management' by local health authority administrators and by physicians, and allowed the latter to earn salary plus fees (or fees alone) as independent contractors rather than become 'salaried civil servants'.

The NHS professions and workforce strongly defended the service against the Thatcher programme of reforms. One reason for the exceptional staff loyalty was that the NHS was so successful at training to high standards. Most of the staff, from nurses to the most advanced medical scientists, are trained within the service where a group who already to a large degree are self-selecting absorb a common ethos, carry out common tasks and unique research, and form lasting relationships. A number of doctors also owed their opportunity to enter the medical profession to Attlee's educational reforms and had benefited from the time they were children from lifetime access to the NHS (Widgery 1988, p. xiv). Medical schools were run as joint ventures between the universities and the NHS. The NHS thus was able to be a leading force in research and development in medical science and clinical practice. It encouraged commitment and a sense of vocation in its staff and it managed to remove at least some of the socially patronizing attitudes and hierarchy of values, based on class. It formed one of the most effective parts of the Welfare State set up after the Second World War and gained political support from all parties—if grudgingly in some cases—because it was so highly valued by the electorate.

From the start the NHS developed ways of rationing limited resources by the use of waiting lists (which became a major media issue later as budgets were squeezed while public expectations rose) but this was accepted because it was experienced as a fair system in which the staff were doing their best to provide for all. Waiting lists, within reasonable limits, were regarded as a responsible way of dealing with a shortage of resources and patients could not easily jump the queue and gain favourable treatment ahead of others. No citizen was excluded or need fear bankruptcy due to treatment costs, as is the case in private systems. Although from the start there arguably was what the Hutton Commission calls an 'accountability deficit' with respect to wider public rather than just ministerial oversight, the NHS also allowed for some corrective feedback and input through 206 local health councils in England and Wales, 16 similar bodies in Scotland and four in Northern Ireland (Hutton 2000, p. 4).

IMPACT OF NHS REFORMS BY THE CONSERVATIVE GOVERNMENT

The Thatcher government came to power in 1979, according to a former cabinet minister, 'somewhat on the defensive over health'; Tories rarely mentioned the Service except, in some cases, to pledge not to cut resources (Gilmour 1992, p. 151). Nevertheless, a White Paper in 1979 diagnosed present levels of 'public expenditure as being at the heart' of Britain's economic difficulties. Accordingly, in 1982 the Tory Party's Central Policy Review staff issued a report urging that the state funding of higher education be ended, social security be slashed, and NHS be put on a totally private insurance basis. When this report was leaked to the *Economist*, the subsequent furore elicited a mollifying promise from Prime Minister Margaret Thatcher that 'The National Health Service is safe with us' (Young 1993, p. 310). Instead of pressing for abolition of the NHS the Thatcher government resorted to underinvestment: expenditure certainly continued to rise but not so as to match rising costs in the health sector. Shortages of specialist nurses (because of low wages), lack of beds (because of closures in certain regions and urban areas), and lengthening waiting lists for surgery became chronic problems. Health expenditure rose from 15.2 billion in 1979 to 20.5 billion in 1988 but a House of Commons Social Service Committee estimated that the NHS still was underfunded by almost 2 billion pounds (Gilmour 1992, p. 153). Complaints about hospital services burgeoned: 16,000 in 1983 to some 44,000 in 1991 (Klein 1995, p. 228). Meanwhile the government pressed ahead with other aspects of its programme: tax cuts, utility privatization, deregulation, and defence spending.

In her first two terms Thatcher had wanted market reforms in the NHS but deemed it 'too sensitive a topic to expose to the electorate' (Gilmour 1992, p. 155). However, ancillary NHS services, such as catering, laundry, and maintenance, were privatized (Sked and Cook 1993, p. 482). In her third term (1987–90), an emboldened premier went ahead with an internal market in health care, creating an allegedly arm's length division between purchasers (health authorities and general practitioners) and providers (hospitals). The Conservative argument was that this would promote efficient use of resources by introducing a competitive market to remove the complacency that they imputed to the state-funded service. Each purchaser would be responsible for setting contracts with providers who would be required to compete for work, thus raising efficiency. (Klein finds that few purchasers altered their standing arrangements with nearby providers, who enjoyed obvious advantages in expertise and information [1995, p. 205].) The Thatcher policies were based on her wider project of promoting free enterprise and dismantling welfare, which was seen to stifle enterprise and independence.

This analysis was partly justified by economic stagnation but it also seemed to contain an extreme hostility against the Health Service as a humane organization, which recognized the need for appropriate dependency. 'Dependency culture' was an epithet in the Tory vocabulary, which made few distinctions among kinds of dependent situations. Yet the Welfare State that Thatcher regarded as a socialist relic actually was, as a Tory 'wet' critic, who harks back to Elizabethan Poor Laws, points out, 'in reality a traditional and civilized concern for others, which had the most respectable roots deep in the history of England'—whatever their shortcomings and mixed motives (Gilmour 1992, p. 108; Frazier 1984, pp. 31–55).

The NHS had, until the Thatcher period, retained the ethos of the Welfare State, with its roots in the post-war period of reparation and reconstruction and—with the exception of physicians retaining a right to see private patients—resisted the commercialization of medical care. One result of this was that generally the service was economical compared with health systems based on private medical practice. US costs typically were nearly double those of the UK, despite tens of millions of Americans lacking adequate or any coverage. Even among other 'mixed' systems Britain performed well. In the mid-1980s Britain spent 5.9 per cent (5.3 per cent public and 0.6 per cent private) on health compared to France with 9.1per cent (6.5 per cent public and 2.6 per cent private), West Germany with 8.1per cent (6.4 per cent public and 1.7 per cent private) and Italy with 7.2 per cent (Gilmour 1992, p. 154). Paradoxically and implausibly, one of the main arguments used by the government to justify the reform of the NHS was that it was too costly and inefficient, which was the argument also used to justify privatization of publicly owned utilities such as water, electricity, and rail transport, which was occurring at the same time. However, the 1989 White paper on health was a foregone conclusion inasmuch as 'not only the judge, the jury, and court of appeal but even the witnesses were all Thatcherites' (ibid., p. 155). Hence, the internal NHS market, authorized by the National Health Service and Community Care Act, began to be implemented in April 1991.

Was the Service too expensive and inefficient? Advances in medical treatment, many of which were pioneered by the NHS, such as organ transplantation, infertility treatment, plastic surgery, and many new drugs, led not only to higher costs but to increased expectations from patients about the standard of care which should be available. (There also were more elderly to care for while unemployment rising to three million carried adverse health consequences with it.) This led to a much repeated and questionable assertion by Tory critics that the government could not afford to pay these increased costs from taxes, and therefore an unspecified degree of private provision for health care should be made. Those statements were repeated widely in critical forums and often went unchallenged in media debates despite the fact that the NHS plainly delivered the nation's health care at a much lower cost than many western countries. It is true that in the first 10 years of Thatcher's government the cost of running the NHS rose 157 per cent, but the cost of private medical insurance rose 267 per cent 'despite the commercial sector work load being confined largely to low-cost routine procedures' (ibid., p. 150). Neither statistic, of course, was a pleasing one. So the Conservative Party set out to demonstrate that the Welfare State was an exorbitantly expensive burden on the country, making it uncompetitive and further making individuals dependent on the state, undermining their motivation for work and enterprise.

According to the Conservatives' argument, it was morally and practically necessary for every individual to be self-reliant and provide more from their after-tax incomes for their own health care. They pointed out that conditions had changed dramatically since the Second World War; generally people were far better off and social inequality was less extreme, or visible, than it had been. Klein pertinently points out that the post-war NHS relied on 'interlinked and mutually dependent beliefs about the nature of society, about the role of the state and about the relationship between professionals and those who need their services' (Klein 1995, p. xii). The Tories claimed that social conditions had shifted to a degree that demanded NHS changes which are designed to reduce pressure on the public purse. Indeed, Conservative policies contributed to a reversal of even the faintest egalitarian trends by granting tax concessions to the better off and maintaining low wage levels for others. They cut the highest marginal rate of tax from 83 to 40 per cent, the corporation tax from 52 to 33 per cent and the top rate of inheritance tax from 75 to 40 per cent (Hutton 1995, p. 11). The basic rate of income tax was cut from 33 to 25 (and then 22) per cent but flat-rate National Insurance contributions were raised considerably and the regressive value-added tax (VAT) shot up from eight per cent in 1979 to 15 per cent in the 1980s and again in 1991 (to pay for the Poll tax fiasco) to 17.5 per cent. The already affluent did very well while more of the tax burden, which rose under the Tories from 34 to 39 per cent of GDP, was shifted to the less well-heeled.

A steady reduction in the resources made available through the Welfare State was another way in which the poorer sections of society lost out during a period of aggregate economic growth. Government members and spokespersons frequently expressed and celebrated its wish to restore British society to the Victorian values of thrift and hard work. Unfortunately, it also seemed to be encouraging a rapid return to the accompanying Victorian conditions of gross social inequality, with great wealth set alongside dire poverty.

The NHS was continually criticized for what Tories portrayed as its inherent inefficiency, stifling bureaucracy, and relatively weak management. It was charged that the service was run largely for the benefit of the staff and that its overall productivity needed badly to be improved. The government promoted a monetarist world view which was hostile to state provision, even in health and social welfare, and tended to idealize private health care, despite the ample evidence that private health care systems were more expensive and delivered poor service or no service at all to less well-off people. If the empirical data and the rational case for a marketized health service collapses so completely under scrutiny, then one may justifiably look elsewhere for the underlying motives for this radical policy change.

While there surely was a need for some reform in the Welfare State and in the NHS after nearly 50 years, as indeed the Black Report and its follow-up *The Health Divide* (1982) argued earlier, the experience of NHS staff was that they were enduring an unfair and counter-productive attack on the service and upon its proven values and effectiveness. They beheld a government hurriedly putting its new scheme into action without first conducting a pilot study of any kind. The vast majority of staff, who were strongly committed to the service, were dismayed by what seemed to be unjustified and insensitively conducted upheaval. In a skewed media climate (with 70 per cent of newspapers owned by Conservative supporters), and given the reality of cabinet government power in Britain, any opposition to change was easily dismissed as hidebound resistance or characterized as clinging to comfortable state-funded conditions in which the staff organized the service to suit themselves, putting the interest of patients in second place after their own (Marsh 1991, p. 337). Hence, a government elected with a minority of the vote nonetheless promoted privatization of utilities, health marketization, and the disastrous poll tax, despite all these measures being opposed consistently by large majorities of the public.

Still, the British public apparently were slow to understand what was happening. Many citizens had been swayed by the government's argument that the Health Service could become more efficient by using the same or less resources, and still be preserved. This course of action was supposed to limit increases in 'unneeded' public expenditure and allow further tax cuts, which were popular, especially so with the higher income Conservative party constituents who stood to benefit the most. Given the Conservative diagnosis of the NHS as being afflicted by institutional sloth and needing many layers of 'fat' cut from its allegedly swollen budget, a decisive portion of the public—at very least, the 43 per cent who voted Tory in 1983 and 1987—were eager to believe that they could have lower taxes and receive the same or better services from the state.

The key change was the wholesale introduction of the language, calculations, and methods of business into the organization and management of the Health Service. Government ministers proclaimed that this bracing change in managerial style would result in the NHS being run just like any competitive commercial business. This outcome, if it was desirable or attainable, was never possible because the government always kept close central control over the activities of the new NHS Trusts and they were not in fact allowed to operate like independent businesses, as their finances were tightly controlled.

The resulting system arising in the early 1990s was in practice a centralized bureaucracy which employed the language and rhetoric of business but was tightly controlled by government. As Klein puts it, 'all lines of accountability run firmly and unambiguously toward the centre' (1995, p. 203). These were conditions under which any commercial business would find it hard to manoeuvre or even survive, since expansion was not possible within limited budgets and money would not be allowed to be carried over from one financial year to the next. As 'perks' the Trusts were indeed allowed to own their own land and buildings, borrow money, and treat as many private patients as they wished. But the government enforced a strained situation in which every Trust, no matter how well run, operated with very limited financial reserves. The government imposed financial limits to control expenditure and opted deliberately not to fund inflation, so that there was continued downward pressure on resources for the NHS. From 1951 to 1985 alone the number of hospitals already had fallen from 3,027 to 2,341 hospital beds from 546,000 to 404,000 and the average length of stay dropped precipitously (Widgery 1988, p. 29). This accelerating trend tempted or forced more people into the private insurance sector; privately insured citizens rose from 5.1 million in 1986 to 6.5 million in 1991.

The new market ironically required a large management force to operate it and a large expenditure on IT staff and equipment to provide the necessary numerical analysis. This increase in management and administration was considerable. From 1989 to 1993 alone NHS administrative staff rose 116,000 (14.7 per cent of all NHS employees) to 135,000 (17 per cent of the total) while the staff of the supervising Department of Health went up by a quarter (Klein 1995, p. 204). In many new NHS Trusts more than a 100 per cent increase in management staff occurred. In the Tavistock there was a 300 per cent increase in management and financial staff as the market system came into play. Formerly, NHS administrative costs comprised 3 to 4 per cent of total health expenditure as compared to 21 per cent in the private American system (Gilmour 1992, p. 158). Matching the American system therefore meant adding many hitherto unnecessary costs. The elaborate cost-accounting of the new schemes required more managers (versus medical care personnel and researchers), more monitoring staff, and many other hidden administrative costs. Paper work burgeoned; patient care was hardly calculated thereby to improve.

At a late stage of this reorganization process, in 1996 and 1997, as reforms took effect, the wider citizenry, always suspicious, became acutely aware that the Health Service was under severe threat because they directly experienced its diminishing resources and an increasing reduction of standards, particularly the poor quality of nursing, arising from low wages and lowered requirements. It became increasingly clear to a worried electorate that the government's reforms were likely to make the NHS similar to the American private health system, that is an impoverished system operating at a minimum level, which operated as a low level safety net, which desperate patients would only resort to if there was no alternative. Early evidence pointed to the prospect of a two-tier system soon operating in which there would be an expansion of private health care to provide for those able to afford it and a relegation of poorer people to the public sector. This heightened awareness in the electorate, which was reflected in the media and in opposition party statements, challenged further weakening of the Health Service although the Tories were reelected in 1992 despite grave public mistrust of their handling of health care (Butler and Kavanagh 1992, pp. 122, 268). A 1994 survey would find that 75 per cent of the public believed the Tories ultimately wanted to privatize the NHS (Klein 1995, p. 240).

NHS decline became a major political issue, although it still remained vulnerable in a financial regime which, while maintaining nominal levels of funding, cut back investment each year. The Labour Party and the Liberal Democrats argued that the NHS was no longer safe in Conservative hands and the electorate became aware of the serious erosion of the state pension, so that those who had paid in to it all their working lives were no longer able to rely on the state pension to provide fully for them. In essence, the British state was quietly trying to back out of the social bargain it had sustained since the 1940s.

One clear conclusion drawn on the basis of consistent first hand experience in the Tavistock and throughout the NHS was that the Thatcher reforms were aimed at dismantling the ethos which bound the NHS together. This apparent attack on a proven institution, constructed for the social good and drawing upon altruistic motives, inevitably was perceived by healthcare professionals in the Tavistock to be based on a panoply of destructive and envious motives on the part of those in control of the state. The obvious goal was that the health service was to be dismantled in favour of a profit-driven system. By the end of the 1990s, British healthcare funding would slide to the bottom of the OECD rankings (Hutton 2000, p. 2).

The inception of the NHS market in 1991 caused a great deal of concern among the staff of the Tavistock that the animating social and clinical values of the organization were going to be destroyed and replaced with those of a competitive business. The incorporation of the Tavistock into an NHS Trust was feared to result in damage to a well tested system of clinical work and of training. The professional staff of the Clinic viewed this incipient clash of values in the alien context of a new management style in the Health Service which wished to impose rules and ways of functioning that appeared arbitrary rather than well reasoned. It was clear that consensus management (that is, a decision-making process worked out largely between health authority administrators and NHS physicians) was rapidly going to be removed, to be replaced by a line management system in which anxiety and responsibility deliberately were projected downwards through the lower levels of staff. Accountability was emphasized, but this was to be a form of accountability exclusively to management, and not to customary professional structures and values. Many staff expressed scepticism as to whether this was really the way in which any efficient modern enterprise could operate. In the initial shock about the government's reforms there was widespread fear that the ethos of the Tavistock Clinic was under an overwhelming attack that it might not survive. At a collective level this belief stirred a fear of being conquered or overwhelmed and a reluctance to find new strategies to survive. One question was whether the traditions of high quality clinical work and research could be adapted successfully to the new regimen and whether the institution was robust enough to adapt and survive with its founding values more or less intact and how to go about doing so. A widely heard and cautionary metaphor at the time was that of the staff portrayed as the 'Polish Cavalry', referring to the brave Polish army with its outdated tactics and techniques which were to prove no match for the swarming German Panzer Divisions which conquered and pillaged the country virtually overnight.

Locally these issues came to a head over the question of whether and how the Tavistock Clinic, together with the Portman Clinic, should become an NHS Trust and take its place in the new and peculiar NHS market. At the time the government indicated that it was offering a choice, but it soon became evident that there was in fact no choice, since institutions that did not become Trusts would inevitably be taken over by a larger Trust. The Tavistock therefore took the decision to apply to be a Trust, but in the first instance the application was turned down because of the problem of the Clinic's large amount of training activity which did not fit easily into the notion of a market strictly for clinical services.

The professional staff displayed anxiety that the methods of a multidisciplinary professional organization were to be replaced by 'line management' basing its operational practices on the management of a factory or a government department, which were thought particularly ill-suited to an institution devoted to healing and research. This new managerial system seemed to the staff to be profoundly inimical for a centre in which each individual therapist must take full responsibility for their own work with patients. Staff were well aware of the unfortunate example of the social work profession in Britain, whose professional work had been weakened by a line management system which took away the individual social worker's responsibility for their work and attempted to organize it according to guidelines and procedures dictated by the local borough council. This remote and distant method of dealing with clinical anxiety quickly lead to a weak and demoralized profession with a poor capacity to cope with difficult human situations. In many subsequent enquiries into social work individual professionals often were blamed for events beyond their control or inherent in the alienating settings that the line management system had generated.

In order to establish the NHS market it was necessary to divide the NHS organizations into two groups: one group, the purchasers, were given the responsibilities of buying the services of the second group, the providers. In the Tavistock's case the purchasers were usually the existing District Health Authorities, who had previously been responsible for administering a whole health district, that is, administering health services for a population of about one to two hundred thousand people. (Groups of GPs also were given Fundholder contracts, with similar responsibilities which likewise militated against the principle of pooling risks.) The second group, the providers, consisted of groupings of hospitals, clinics, and community services now organized into NHS Trusts. The NHS Trusts had budgets of approximately £60 to £100 million, and in the NHS market this was derived from the cumulative contracts with the purchasers to provide clinical services. The theory of this budding NHS market was that the shrewd purchasers would be able to demand high quality service as a condition of the contract and the providers accordingly would compete to offer the very best service at the lowest price.

There was a considerable upheaval in the NHS reorganization to form the Trusts. There were four 'waves' of Trusts. At first there was a suggestion that hospitals and clinics had a choice as to whether they became NHS Trusts or not. Hutton reports that in a survey of 185 NHS Trust chairpersons that 62 were Conservative councillors, former Tory MPs, Conservative workers or had strong links to the party—and almost three-quarters were business men and women (Hutton 2000, pp. 38–9). Viewing this, Hutton saw a return to nineteenth rule by an oligarchy of unelected conservatives discharging public duties.

The Trusts were expected to balance their books at the end of the financial year and were not allowed to carry money over from one financial year to the next. Those who faltered or failed financially were liable to be taken over by another larger, more successful Trust. The new market atmosphere led to competition between Trusts so that there was a marked diminution of cooperation between clinical services, and even a reluctance to help patients from other areas on the grounds of clinical need. Critics pointed out that cooperative planning and economies of scale among the various organizations were inhibited by this new arrangement. There was a worrisome trend of differences emerging in medical treatment, depending on the status of the GP, the pricing policy of the local hospital and its capacity to gain private finance so that poorer districts 'suffer disproportionately' (ibid., p. 112). Well-situated Trusts endowed with large property holdings and with the ability to attract private patients were encouraged, in effect, by this new system to 'cherry-pick' the lowest-cost patients and offload the poorer and high-cost ones onto other health authorities (ibid., p. 41). These predictable trends flew in the face of the values, however imperfectly realized, of universalism and equity of access which were at the heart of the NHS.

The Tavistock and Portman Clinics together formed the Tavistock and Portman NHS Trust. When the original NHS system was modified to become the 'managed market', it appeared in practice to be a peculiar hybrid between a competitive market and a state-controlled system in which the government set clear rules for the amount of money in the system and what degree of competition was allowed. The Tavistock Clinic's own experience was that very few of the contracts with health authorities were radically altered from previous patterns although a great deal of time was taken up in negotiating these contracts. Usually the result was to arrive at a situation which generally continued the status quo, in which the new contract allowed for the same amount of clinical work that had previously been provided for that area. In relatively few cases was there a reduction in the contract. In fact, overall there was a gradual increase in the availability of resources for the new Tavistock and Portman NHS Trust, which had enjoyed a very good reputation with purchasers. This stemmed particularly from the training contract which accounted for over 60 per cent of the income of the Trust, and was able to increase gradually since paradoxically the negotiation of this large national contract proved to be much less difficult than the negotiation of the smaller Health Authority clinical contracts.

CHANGES BY LABOUR

A new Labour government was elected in May 1997. With the new government, the process of reform continued but the survival of the NHS as a public entity was no longer in doubt. The NHS was a major issue in an election in which the Tories were soundly defeated. The Labour government likewise has been keen to maintain a firm control on costs, while pressing to improve the quality of services (for example, a new Institute for Clinical Excellence) as they have done in all public services.

The Labour government's election commitment was that it would abolish the NHS internal market and that it would shift responsibility for deciding on how Health money was to be spent in contracts towards general practitioners. These promised items were relatively slow to be put into place and during the first two years of this government the changes were relatively limited. The major change has been the abolishing of the extra-contractual referral system, by which patients could be referred out of a contract for specialist treatment. This system, though complicated, actually had benefited the specialist services of the Tavistock Clinic because it enabled new services such as the Learning Disability Service and Gender Identity Service to start up, funded by referrals from outside normal contracts and from a wider area of southern England than was covered by the usual London-centred clinical contracts for the Tavistock.

A total reversal of Conservative policies, however, was not in the offing. The new Labour government and health minister largely continued the same method of management and of cost-benefit measurement—measuring costs without accounting for benefits—that had been developed during the Conservative years (ibid., pp. 1–42). It constantly initiated new policies and ideas and distributed these ideas rapidly to all NHS workers and Trusts. The experience remained that of being in a highly centralized system in which new directives and guidelines are passed down rapidly from unheeding authorities. Many of these have not been worked out in detail and it appears that new initiatives are taken before it was quite clear how they are actually going to work in practice. This type of 'reform on the hoof' has proved very difficult for those who are responsible for implementing the organizational changes.

The Labour government did allow some increase in NHS funding. However, these increases did not initially benefit the ordinary services because it is mostly earmarked for special projects and new initiatives without being put into the mainstream of basic services, which is so important to maintain the standard and quality of the service. (In March 2000, however, Prime Minister Tony Blair promised a 6.1 per cent annual NHS increase in real terms over four years.) On assuming office the government reorganized the NHS into some 480 Primary Care Groups (PCGs), 400 Primary Care Trusts (PCTs) and 99 health authorities, all affixed to what the Hutton Commission calls a system of cost accountability suited to 'bureaucratic control and blame-allocation, not democratic partnership'—or the primacy of patient care (ibid., p. 20). Indeed, the government has been preoccupied with trying to improve the quality of the service and their principle method of doing this, so far as some dismayed recipients could see, is to issue a large number of directives and guidelines. The Labour changes do not seem to correct the problem of 'postcode prescribing', that is, people receiving levels of care relative to the resources in their local area.

The White Paper (*The New NHS—Modern, Dependable*, 1997) has introduced the new idea of Clinical Governance which is an attempt to improve the quality of clinical services by requiring Trusts to be accountable for the quality of clinical work alongside financial good management. Yet Clinical Governance is a jargon term which few in the Health Service so far have understood very well but it seems to consist of a number of areas related to the quality of clinical work, including clinical audit, continual professional development, evidence-based medicine, staff assessment and performance reviews.

While this initiative may act to improve the overall quality of the service, it does appear to run the risk of being another centralized directive and set of guidelines rather than something which has been genuinely grown out of an intimate understanding of the problems of the NHS. It tends to be treated cynically or by those with ambition to progress in the system with a glib acceptance, which means that it runs the risk of having a relatively superficial effect. The Hutton

Commission judges that the top-down and exclusively cost-conscious orientation of present management also has 'reduced independent public input to the vanishing point' (ibid., p. 33).

It is interesting to compare the two governments in charge of the British State in their effect on the NHS. Both are reforming governments wishing to create change and both have a tendency to want to direct in detail, in a commanding manner, without much reference to what the actual situation on the ground might be. This may be rather the way of commanding an army: orders come from on high and the staff are required to follow them regardless. The problem about this for a health service is that staff are required to have initiative and a capacity to take responsibility which may be undermined by exactly this kind of overbearing centralist government.

DISCUSSION

The changes which occurred during these reforms of the NHS can be examined from a psychoanalytical perspective. This view is sharpened by the fact that the whole organization and structure of the Tavistock Clinic was, in common with all other hospitals and clinics, the subject of the government's changes. It is sharpened all the more when considering that while one NHS patient in three is mentally ill, one-seventh of the health budget is allocated toward their care (Widgery 1988, p. 82). It is possible to demonstrate how the government's policies, which continually changed, had an impact on the daily life of the Tavistock as a clinical and training institution.

From a psychoanalytic point of view this type of institution may be seen to grow out of a reparative motive in a society which has been involved in a period of destructiveness in war. Fomari (1966) and Glover (1947) have described how war is the expression of national destructiveness projected onto the enemy. At an unconscious level the setting up of the Welfare State and NHS can be seen as evidence of a nation-wide reparative and integrating movement as a response to the guilt engendered by the destructiveness of the war at home and abroad. At a conscious level the British felt it was a morally just war which they had fought to save Europe, and did not acknowledge the part they had played in allowing the conditions for the war to have developed during the period following the First World

War. Nor did they acknowledge any sense of guilt which might have followed the destruction of the enemy. The great cultural, scientific, and economic achievements of Germany had been brought to ruin. There had been controversy about the destruction of German cities by bombing, which some argue was more to do with revenge than the need to win the war.

There are many ways in which the recent rounds of changes could be understood, but a consistent theme has been a contempt for dependency, which was characterized as a bad moral state. It was deemed not possible for a wealthy country to afford to spend a reasonable percentage of GNP on healthcare, including psychiatric and social work services. Healthcare was to be rationed according to an individual's financial resources. There was a resurgent identification of poverty as a sin in itself. One important aspect of this is the return to the situation in which the poor are to blame for their poverty and the rich are virtuous. This identification of need or vulnerability as badness certainly fits with the drive for the reduction of NHS provision especially for the more vulnerable population of poor, elderly, mentally ill and long-term care patients.

The shifting of economic power from the poorer members of society to the well off was considerable during this period. Tax cuts have most benefited the wealthy and have given little benefit to those on low incomes. A close examination of this situation leads to consideration of the politics of greed and envy since the electorate acceded to cuts in the NHS and Welfare State because of being offered a reduction in tax, overlooking the fact that every individual may become vulnerable, needy or sick and find themselves without the resources to provide for their healthcare.

There is an historical comparison between the weakening of the NHS and the privatization of many publicly owned institutions with the enclosure of common land in the eighteenth and early nineteenth centuries. The enclosures were the expropriation of large tracts of commonly used and shared land by individual landowners, leaving a significant proportion of the rural population impoverished and destitute (Fraser 1984, pp. 1–3). The reason given for the enclosure of the common land was similar to that which justified the reform of the NHS, that the land was being used inefficiently by the commoners and it would be brought into efficient use by the individual landowner. The underlying motive, however, was that of the redistribution of wealth from the poor to the rich. Health care in itself was not really the issue; egalitarian access to a non-profit provision of care was.

Both these processes have at their root the wish to steal resources and attack dependency to fulfill greedy wishes while, at the same time, attributing badness and weakness to those who are vulnerable or needy. This moral atmosphere has pervaded the NHS changes, often taking the form of blaming NHS staff for wasteful or indulgent use of resources, exactly as if they were identified as being themselves dependent and needy like the patients who they cared for. Professionals remarked that they often experienced this antagonistic attitude in their contacts with ministerial staff. Ironically, in the public sphere, these reforms clearly operated as a 'blame diffusion' mechanism to enable those in control of the State to elude responsibility for inadequately running and funding the NHS (Klein 1995, p. 206).

Examining the changes which occurred during the 'reform' of the NHS from a psychoanalytical perspective leads to the conclusion that there was an attack on the need for dependency. This view was sharpened by the fact that the whole organization and structure of the Tavistock Clinic, in common with all other hospitals and clinics, was a subject of the government's changes. In this changeover the Tavistock was a relatively privileged institution yet for the most part the staff remained deeply concerned about, and resistant to, the tenor of the reforms by a state remarkably out of tune with public sentiment and with the founding public purpose of the NHS.

NOTE

1. Tony Blair promised 13 billion of private capital in NHS over 2001–4 and to build 93 new hospitals by 2010. 'In every Private Finance Initiative hospital building, so far, beds and jobs have been cut to generate income and profits. There are 29 of them.' *The Guardian*, 21 June 2001.

REFERENCES

Department of Health, *The New NHS—Modern, Dependable* (London: The Stationery Office, 1997).

Bendix, R., *Work and Authority in Industry: Ideologies of Management in the Course of Industrialization* (Berkeley: University of California Press, 1956).

Black, D., *Inequalities in Health: The Black Report* (London: Penguin, 1983).

Butler, D and D. Kavanagh, *The British General Election of 1992* (London: Saint Martins Press, 1992).

Eckstein, H., *The English Health Service* (Cambridge, MA: Harvard University Press, 1958).

Fornari, F., *Psychoanalysis and War* (Bloomington: University of Indiana Press, 1966).

Frazier, D., *The Evolution of The British Welfare State: A History of Social Policy Since the Industrial Revolution* (London: Macmillan, 2nd edition, 1984).

Gilmour, I., *Dancing With Dogma: Britain Under Thatcherism* (London: Simon & Schuster, 1992).

Glover, E., *War, Sadism and Pacificism: Further Essays on Group Psychology and War* (Edinburgh: Hugh Paton and Sons, 1947).

Hutton, W., *The State We're In* (London: Jonathan Cape, 1995).

———, *New Life for Health: The Commission on The NHS* (London: Vintage, 2000).

Klein, R., *The New Politics of The National Health Service* (London: Longman Press, 3rd edition,1995).

Marsh, D., 'The Media and Politics', in *Developments in British Politics*, Patrick Dunleavy, Andrew Gamble, Ian Holliday and Gillian Peele (eds), (London: Macmillan, 1991).

Sked, A. and Chris Cook, *Post-War Britain: A Political History 1945-1992* (London: Penguin, 4th edition, 1993).

Titmuss, R., *Essay on The Welfare State* (London: Allen & Unwin, 1964).

Webster, C., *The National Health Service: A Political History*, Oxford: Oxford University Press, 1998.

Widgery, D., *The National Health: A Radical Proposal* (London: Hogarth Press, 1988).

Young, H., *One of Us: A Biography of Margaret Thatcher* (London: Pan, Final Edition, 1993).

9

In Cahoots?
Cinema, Cynicism, and Citizenship

JOHN KURT JACOBSEN

'Combining good picture-making with good citizenship'.

—Warner Brothers motto in 1930s.

President Nixon: Espionage and sabotage is illegal only if against the government. Hell, you can espionage and sabotage all you want, unless you use illegal means . . .Can I get away with it?

John Dean: I don't think we'll get away with it forever.

—White House tapes, 14 May 1973[1]

Does cinema shape the way citizens experience the state? Can mere movies alter the way we see the world? Examples seemingly run riot. D.W. Griffith's *Birth of a Nation* in 1915 swayed many Northern urban audiences with its racist take on the Reconstruction era.[2] His reactionary classic helped to revive the Ku Klux Klan in the South where overwrought patrons shot screens full of holes to protect the virtuous white heroine from her wicked black pursuer.[3] (*Mississippi Burning* more recently informed young moviegoers that the FBI were the heroic vanguard of the 1960s Civil Rights movement!)[4] Attending armistice celebrations in 1918 Erich Von Stroheim, who often played arrogant Hun officers, was stoned by a likewise literal-minded mob and fled.[5]

German minister for Public Enlightenment and Propaganda Joseph Goebbels admiringly thought Eisenstein's *Battleship Potemkin* a Marxist call to arms if there ever was one, able to transform any audience 'without firm ideological conviction' into bands of dedicated

Bolsheviks.[6] (His opinion was widely shared for the film was also banned in Britain, France, and in many US states.)[7] One only needed Nazi equivalents. Leni Riefenstahl's *Triumph of The Will* (1935) would exert just the right impact, although her epic celebration of the fascist ethos hardly would have been possible before Hitler became chancellor.[8]

Riefenstahl was more a consecrator than a creator of power. All these directors were acutely attuned to the flow of potent (and congenial) ideas in their respective political cultures, so one ought to be cautious in assigning much influence to film makers—even if they themselves often are not. As dissent arose against the Vietnam war—because irrational citizens thought the government was lying to them and to itself—Hollywood lobbyist and Lyndon Johnson aide Jack Valenti, reminiscent of the comically overconfident producer in *Wag The Dog*, asserted that the administration storyline could be precisely pitched to resume fooling most of the public all of the time: 'We simply aren't doing our propaganda job right in this country.'[9]

This essay explores how recent Hollywood films, whether caustic critiques or Capraesque treatments of politics, exploit conspiratorial themes and cultivate cynicism about the state, particularly its role in controlling the socio-economic 'system'. The degree to which films shape, and are shaped by, the expectations of cinema-goers is a perennial question, especially in cultural studies. Ultimately, film makers must play upon attitudes, values, and discourses that already exist (however they originated), whether these amount to a taste for vengeance, a fear of 'difference' or, indeed, a thirst for social justice. Even Hollywood cannot prosper from creating a totally cynical world on screen where everyone is out to get or gang up on everyone else.[10] I also compare Hollywood films to European examples to illuminate what differences exist as to how these cinemas reflect and inflect state-citizen relationships.

Unlike fringe film makers (who, despite striking rebel poses, are usually desperately eager to 'break in'), Hollywood denizens occupy high income brackets ordinarily associated with conservative views, though not always of a traditional kind. The entertainment industry these days seems to favour a libertarian stance that reconciles an urge to justify doing what they please with the task of shielding their generous fees from government wastrels.[11] Still, Hollywood films

consistently have exhibited the deepest distrust not only of governments but of *all* large organizations. Mass market films such as
Chinatown, Robocop, Silkwood, China Syndrome, Rollerball, and *Alien*
and its sequels, to name but a few, have been hostile toward the
spectre of private governance and its ardent irresponsibility for
anything but its own bottom line. Tyranny, as film makers since the
days of Columbia Studio's Harry Cohn appreciate, is hardly the
exclusive prerogative of public authorities.[12]

I use 'Hollywood' as a convenient term for major American-based
studios and production companies. The definition improves
somewhat on others that go so far as to refer to all 'the film industries
of the English-speaking world'.[13] The typical Hollywood film in the
late 1990s reputedly costs 50–60 million dollars and must earn twice
that to move into the black—if creative bookkeeping falters so as to
allow a taxable profit. The pecking order is usually, but not always,
the producer, director, major actors, and their agents. Actors, if
sufficiently 'bankable', wield the clout to package the elements of a
film. So too can some directors. Way down the line, film critics,
ranging from the 'quote whores'—who strew superlatives freely in
exchange for top billing in industry ads—to the most abstruse
deconstructionists in the most obscure journals, rarely wield the
fabled thumbs up or down power.

What injects a degree of artistic latitude into a notoriously venal
industry obsessed with risk-free sequels and remakes is the
disquieting truth that, really, 'nobody knows anything' about making
a surefire hit film.[14] The studios glom on to outsiders whom they
hope represent the next money-spinning new wave and so
remarkable mavericks do get chances to revitalize genres: the western,
the detective film, romantic comedy, war films and so on. The
development of genres, Slotkin observes, is 'driven not only by social
and cultural change but by the specialised discourses of artists and
producers who work in that form and by institutions that control
the production and distribution of their artefacts'.[15] Small-scale film
makers—a Woody Allen, John Sayles, Jim Jarmusch or, until the
success of *Platoon*, Oliver Stone—willing to toil at Hollywood's edge
to reach niche audiences exert more personal control, as do those
few who parlay clout from commercial mega-hits into an occasional,
deeply personal project such as *Schindler's List*.

EATING LUNCH IN HOLLYWOOD

Prior to the 1960s the institutionalized obstacles to the film makers' personal visions—if indeed they had any—included the Office Production Code administration and the Office of Censorship (1922) which was first headed by Willie Hays, a former postmaster general who in an earlier capacity in the industry had hired gangsters to bust film unions.[16] (Rogin too notes the decidedly 'fascist sympathies of the Hays/Breen Production Code Administration' during the pre-War years.)[17] These intra-industry organizations—used to pre-empt meddling from womens' group and religious organizations—exerted firm control to insure that feet were kept chastely on the floor in boudoir scenes, that 'crime does not pay' messages at least nominally prevailed, and that any expression of discontent with the market ethos be erased.[18]

No industry has been simultaneously so arrogant and so easily spooked by pressure groups. In the approach to American entry in the Second World War, many 'Spanish Civil war films were shelved, the story of *Black Fury* was gutted to make coal company management seem less repressive than it really was and no film was made dealing with the rise of Hitler and Mussolini for fear of cutting off Italian and German markets'; the filming of Sinclair Lewis' *It Can't Happen Here* was scuttled despite a $200,000 payout because of pressure mustered by Babbitts across all the Main Streets of America.[19] In this regard Hollywood ironically reacted to the darker side of its own invention of a benevolent small town America replete with white picket fences, grannies in white aprons, and white townspeople who were the collective soul of common sense.[20]

Hollywood itself was constructed on the basis of interlocking and competing conspiracies of an albeit open and (usually) legal kind. Those not involved in such a group strive mightily to insinuate themselves into one in order to become a player themselves. Deals get worked out among 'cabals' of investors, studios, agents, and even some genuine artistically driven people willing and able to integrate the commercial dimension into their work. The title of a best-selling memoir by a studio executive captures the flavour of this cloistered insider-style influence: '*You'll Never Eat Lunch in This Town again*.'[21] Hollywood, of course, has long been accused of conspiring against America in a long litany of tirades bursting with not-so-genteel anti-

Semitism until the 1940s and, after Auschwitz, by critics—including Jewish neo-conservatives—incensed at the industry's inveterate disregard for what they deem to be heartland values.[22]

CONSPIRACY, PARANOIA, AND APPLE PIE

Conspiracy is an 'illegal, treasonable, or treacherous plan to destroy another person, group or entity' and 'an agreement manifesting itself in words or deeds and made by two or more persons confederating to do an unlawful act or use unlawful means to do an act which is lawful.' A conspiracy, it is vital to point out, also merely may be 'a striking concurrence of tendencies, circumstances or phenomena as though in planned accord.'[23] Curiously, these definitions imply—as Richard Nixon noticed—that so long as technical legality is observed one may set out to destroy any other person, group or entity in order to promote one's interests.

The real culprit, according to Edward Shils and many like-minded scholars, was a 'populist radicalism' propelled by lower class ignorance and resentment so that a belief in a 'conspiratorial complex of politics and society has become one of the commonplaces of modern fanaticism.'[24] But it is worth noting that 'nothing entirely prevents a sound program or a sound cause from being advocated in a paranoid way,' as Hofstadter more judiciously observed.[25] 'Style has to do with the way in which ideas are believed and advocated rather than with the truth or falsity of their content.' In other words, the paranoid style can occasionally be correct: sometimes there really is a 'they' who are out to get you. Certainly there were European Jews in the 1930s and even early 1940s who were accused of behaving in a paranoid manner with respect to Nazi intentions. (We have no clinical word for the antonym of paranoia—for a pollyanna-ish insistence that all is well when it is quite otherwise.)[26] One ought to bear this point in mind particularly when examining Oliver Stones' passionate cinematic expeditions later.

Conspiracy manias seem to erupt in America every half century or so, rather like long cycles in economic theory (though no one, to my knowledge, has tried to make the connection). In the late eighteenth century Freemasons were presumed to be scheming to strangle the new republic in its crib; in the nineteenth century papists were plotters of choice although ample room must be made for what abolitionists beheld as a slave holders' conspiracy too; at century's end agrarian populists espied conspiracies of international bankers; after the First World War munitions makers and Reds shared this clandestine stature; and after Hiroshima and Nagasaki the culprits dwindled down to just the Reds who, however, nestled under every bed.[27]

The key characteristic of a 'paranoid style' is not that one sees plots afoot here and there but that the observers posit 'a vast insidious, preternaturally effective international conspiratorial framework' as the motive force of history. Hofstadter and Shils root this fantasizing in 'a conflict between secrecy and democracy', which creates fertile ground for covert mischief—from Nixon's plumbers (whose clumsiness gave rise to the single redemptive scene in *Forrest Gump*) to Ollie North's White House basement antics—and for exaggerations of their actual escapades, to the extent that that was possible.[28]

An industry boasting a long history of blacklists hardly need be persuaded that conspiracies exist. Conglomerization, concentration, and conspiracy to restrain trade is an old Hollywood tale, complete with sequel. In 1938 the Justice Department sued the majors—Paramount, Loews, RKO, Warner Brothers, 20th Century Fox, Columbia, Universal, United Artists—'for combining and conspiring to restrain trade in the production, distribution and exhibition of motion picture.' The suit culminated in 1948 with dissolution of studio ownership of the majority of theaters and their practices of block booking and price-fixing. (About 440 films were made in 1946 and most were commercially successful due to these cozy arrangements.)[29] The advent of television supplied the coup de grace. By the 1990s, however, a reconcentration was under way so that a handful of giants control television broadcasting as well as film studios. 'Companies are concerned about controls over cellular communication, digital television, satellite networks and ability to market products abroad.'[30] In the 1970s, according to a former executive's estimate, 'between 30 per cent and 50 per cent of what was seen on prime time television was created, owned and controlled by independent creator/entrepreneurs', a figure closer to 10 per cent today.[31]

The first blacklists appeared virtually with the first camera placement and were compiled to thwart union organizing.[32] The same local motivation helped propel anti-communist drives from 1947 onward, and took a more durable form in the backlot-built, macho ideology of former actor and FBI informer Ronald Reagan.[33] Reagan's ascent to the presidency signaled the triumph of—even if it did not single-handedly create—a dangerous notion that the myths produced by mass culture were 'an adequate substitute for actual historical and political action in authenticating the character and ideological claims of political leaders.'[34]

To defeat Upton Sinclair in the 1934 California Governor's race, Hollywood moguls had helped bankroll a $10 million campaign. Apart from uppity employees, the studio heads fretted over the threat of anti-Semitic corporate buccaneers or the state taking it all away. Appeasement was a favoured option in Hollywood as elsewhere. In 1940 Burton Wheeler's ICC Senate subcommittee sallied forth to grill an industry allegedly teeming with Jews and liberals for encouraging an end of neutrality while Martin Dies intrepidly steered HUAC against what he saw as a plot by rich Jews to seize the government with the aid of 150,000 Spanish mercenaries invading through Mexico together with a homegrown strike wave synchronized to ruin a stock market that Dies (who once called Shirley Temple a communist dupe) evidently believed only made WASPs rich.[35] Pearl Harbour interrupted all these proceedings.

HUAC descended again on tinseltown in October 1947.[36] Chairman Parnell Thomas asserted, among other things, that the 1946 film *Crossfire*, because it implied America suffered from a not insignificant degree of anti-Semitism, was distinctly un-American.[37] When Congress cited the Hollywood 10 for contempt, a 'secret conclave' of producers obligingly met at the Waldorf Astoria to institute loyalty oaths and a blacklist.[38] Right wing publicity-seekers completely cowed the film industry, though there was little cowing left to do.[39] Liberals, let alone Communist Party (CP) members, were always a distinct minority. Sidney Buchan, author of the unlikely Stalinist diatribes *Mr Smith Goes To Washington* and *Here Comes Mister Jordan*, was a communist. Other CP members authored the subversive masterpieces: *Abbot and Costello Meet Frankenstein*, *Sweetheart of the Campus*, and *Charlie Chan's Greatest Case*.[40] The notion of reds hypnotically indoctrinating Americans through film was by itself ridiculous—control always rested elsewhere—unless one understood that the crusaders were profoundly anti-liberal too.[41] The League of Women Shoppers made HUAC's list, implying that informed consumers were as great a danger to their idea of America as were Soviet spies. For a good 'summation of what the situation of communist writers was vis-a-vis the motion picture industry.writers,' a blacklisted writer recalled CP leader William Z. Foster's words:

You can't really do very good work in this industry because they won't let you. But you can prevent them, if you know how to it, from making really anti-black, anti-woman, anti-foreigner pictures. You can prevent them from making anti-human pictures, and that really is a very worthy thing to be doing. You can also make straight entertainment in which no important issues are involved. This can be done very easily.[42]

One may wonder what 'good work' Foster had in mind if he had his own way, but another blacklisted writer drolly observed, 'Boy meets girl (thesis), Boy loses girl (antithesis), Boy gets girl (synthesis). Marxism, for me at least, has a lot to do with good story structure.'[43] The many ironies accompanying McCarthyism's long and poisonous fade-out were sometimes bemusing ones. When two blacklistees entered prison they found former HUAC chair Parnell Thomas already doing time there for taking kickbacks. In a filmic riposte *The Manchurian Candidate* (1962) the dithery McCarthy-ish senator picks the number of commies infesting the State Department off a catsup brand label. The sly thesis was that McCarthy inflicted so much damage that he must be a Soviet agent.[44] That same year *Doctor Strangelove* fastened on a fear of fluoridation as the thermonuclear *casus belli*. Not so preposterous were the revelations to come of the Pentagon papers, Watergate, the Church Committee hearings, Iran-Contra, and other clandestine shenanigans.

NARRATIVE CONVENTIONS: 'SEE WHAT THE BOYS IN THE BACKROOM WILL HAVE'

Hollywood narrative requires flesh and blood villains, not cold mechanisms or institutions. The rationale is that audiences cannot get much satisfaction watching a stake pounded through the heart of the imperial presidency or Wall Street, and, anyway, everything must be explained simply lest audience leave unhappy. So politics and economics must always intersect in highly melodramatized backroom deals. From *Mr Smith Goes To Washington* (1939) through *Dave* (1993) Hollywood correspondingly peddled the tenuous remedy that one only needs virtuous persons, not reformed structures. In Frank Capra's affirmational and ill-remembered *Mr Smith* the title character wound up hopelessly ensnared in a frame-up until a knave's fit of conscience, not the system, saved the day, which is not very much to pin democratic faith on. (The FBI thought *Mr Smith* 'possibly subversive' most likely because he endorsed 'looking out for the other guy'—an aspect of the American dream not mentioned much anymore.)

The Capra formula thrust naive intruders into politics to get roughed up, wise up, enact a reform, and get out. And it endures. The hero of *Dave* is an identical stand-in for a comatose President whose reptilian chief of staff brags he can have any 'ordinary citizen' snuffed. Dave outwits all his adversaries but rides off into the sunset lest he suffer the fate of Willie Stark in *All The King's Men* who started out a well-meaning reformer but is twisted over the long run into a demagogue 'manipulating them hicks.' The *Godfather* trilogy—not ordinarily thought of as political films—also wriggled out of the narrative straitjacket when depicting Michael Corleone succeeding his father the Don with the best intentions to 'go legit' yet be driven by systemic exigencies of mob life to become just another murderous, soulless hood. The narrative convention is cynically contradictory: only ordinary heroes can tame the political system, but the system corrupts them in the long run.

Conspiracy stories are alluring, in part, because they build on resonant experiences about who you know being what mostly matters. Since the rise of the yuppie, people once disdained as 'climbers' (or in even ruder terms) came to be admired instead for their deft 'networking' skills. So ingrained is this savviness that those who act on it would be offended if accused of behaving cynically, for in the contemporary context it is not the action but those who rudely identify the action who must be the cynics.[45] Curiously, those in occupations that are most reliant on tiny decision-making circles—academics, journalists, politicians, etc.—thrash the hoi polloi most harshly for suggesting any such things exist.

Yet, in different contexts, French economic planning was depicted cheerfully as 'conspiracies in the public interest'[46] and 'crisis of democracy' proponents—in a report to the Trilateral Commission, no less—waxed nostalgic about an idyllic era when a few tycoons, Wall Street lawyers, and politicians pretty much ran policy as they saw fit—and urged a restoration.[47] A Scottish political economist, who is held in the highest esteem by many of Oliver Stone's critics, long ago observed that merchants seldom meet together but to conspire to raise prices or otherwise to harm the common good. As Robert Reich wryly but ruefully put it after his eye-opening spell in Clinton's cabinet, a 'conspiracy is a coalition that you are not part of.'[48]

One might well define conspiracism tongue-in-cheek as everyday experience, only extrapolated too far and fervently into the body politic. Buffs who deny every accident, every random act, every bad move, and every stupid decision do indeed slip into daft realms. Most Americans were suckered by the emotive myth of Vietnam MIAs, which Hollywood happily exploited, and many people believe that the Feds for some mystifying reason conceal UFO contacts, which *Men in Black* made good fun of.[49] Sane citizens, and an Attorney General too, believe in satanic child abuse networks for which no iota of physical evidence exists. Heeding E.M. Forster's wise advice: 'Only connect'—they connect recklessly. One pundit issued the pursed-lipped verdict that we are witnessing 'an explosion of democratically validated credulity.'[50] But another way of conceiving it is that—just as analysts say of children—citizens, when carefully kept out of the loop and/or systematically 'disinformed', are bound to be good observers but bad interpreters. Too often, though, the difference between looniness and truth might as well be a coin flip.

In 1998 *Time* reported that 34 per cent believe a right wing conspiracy was behind the relentless assault on President Clinton.[51] The next month a news item revealed that a major Republican fund-raiser spent $80,000 to orchestrate sexual misconduct allegations against Clinton, including 'gifts' to two Arkansas state troopers and their lawyer plus planting the story in the *American Spectator*.[52] The Starr investigation resulted. Asked if he was part of the 'vast right wing conspiracy' Hilary Clinton decried, this fund-raiser, a Chicago investment banker, replied, 'No. I don't believe in conspiracies, right or left. People with common thoughts and goals work in the same direction.' Just so.

What then are citizens to make of insider trading legerdemain, a Savings and Loans scandal that dwarfs all the welfare cheats who ever existed or ever will, old boys networks of Fortune 500 'downsizers' frolicking in the Bohemian Grove, lieutenant colonels running illegal ventures from the White House basement, a growing gap between the rich and not only the poor but middle too, the rare non-millionaire who runs for national office and one plainly moronic millionaire who became vice-president? The problem is that all the plausible explanations do not seem a far cry from such venerable scapegoats as the Elders of Zion, the Masons or the British Foreign Office. One reporter dubs this jittery state of perceptual affairs 'fusion paranoia':

At its broadest level fusion paranoia is entirely rational. There is a governing elite. It's interests and values are often radically different than those of ordinary citizens, and this elite does indeed work to advance those interests and values in antidemocratic fashion. 'People talk as though our government had been taken over by alien beings,' Kettering President David Mathews writes. 'Many Americans don't believe they are living in a democracy now! . . . they don't believe that the average citizen influences, much less rules . . .' Eventually, as a matter of degree, 'healthy mistrust and conspiracism meet.[53]

Where the thin line between healthy mistrust and conspiracism is drawn depends on how facts are linked and inferences drawn. In this regard Oliver Stone has been characterized as 'traditional in narrative strategy' but 'postmodern in his relationship to objective knowledge,' where 'post-modern' is synonymous with careless.[54] Stone's 'presidential' films, with their blends of innuendo and evidence, have connected powerfully with audiences and reaped scathing ripostes too.[55] Here I am less concerned with the accuracy of theses or evidence advanced by his films than with the impact they exert, and the reasons why.

JFK: 'ROUND UP THE UNUSUAL SUSPECT'

For all its dazzling editing *JFK* garnered its dramatic appeal by making Kennedy a martyr for the values of a decade that, culturally speaking, had not even started yet. Stone consciously represents many contemporaries who in the 1960s experienced a state whose benign character soon had to be repudiated as a parental and media fiction.[56] Jim Garrison's (Kevin Costner) climactic court room soliloquy roils with this elegaic, and far from unprecedented, loss of innocence: 'Going back to when we are children we thought justice comes about automatically. It just isn't true . . . We want the country back, it still belongs to us.'[57] The extremely unusual quarry in *JFK* is not Clay Shaw but the 'system'—a system which an SDS leader once urged his generation of dissidents to name if they were to hope ever to tame it.[58]

JFK ignites with a quote that Americans of just about any political stripe can applaud: 'A patriot must always be ready to defend his country against his government.' There ensues Eisenhower's farewell address on the 'unwarranted influence' of the military-industrial complex and then a radiant JFK taking office, infuriating the right by calling off air strikes at the Bay of Pigs and complaining that the CIA manoeuvred him into the fiasco. Audiences can only surmise that the JFK who set out to 'pay any price, bear any burden' is, after the Cuban missile crisis, a distinctly chastened New Frontiersman.

The apparent trump-card footage is a Cronkite interview on 2 September 1963 of Kennedy, proud creator of the Green Berets and deployer of 16,000 troops already, saying that 'unless a greater effort is made by the [South Vietnamese] government to win popular support I don't think the war can be won out there. In the final analysis, it's their war.' Next comes a clip of his concili-atory American University speech on the cold war and a shot of a grieving black woman after his assassination: 'He did so much in this country for colored people. Why? Why?' (What?, is the better question for this fundamentally reactive president.)[59] This sequence buttresses Stone's theme that it has been downhill for democracy ever after.

Stone's *bete noire* Warren Commission, as Stanley Karnow attests, had a 'dual mandate,' and not necessarily in this order: (1) get the facts of the assassination and (2) 'dispel rumors that, according to Allen Dulles, might interfere with the functions of government, at home and abroad.'[60] (Lyndon Johnson feared JFK was killed by a communist conspiracy or else a right wing one designed to blame communists.)[61] With dramatic license in hand Stone takes film-goers on a controversial dot-connecting ride through the murky minutiae of the assassination. The film essentially turns on establishing the unlikelihood of a single assassin—for example, who on earth can fire three bolt action shots in 5.6 seconds accurately with a Mannlicher-Carcano—and posing cogent motives for an alliance of high echelon officials and lowlife hoods to kill a president and, what's more, believe they can get away with it.[62]

Garrison sifts through a sleazy procession of characters: corrupt lawyers, Birchers, spooks, gun-runners, smugglers, drug dealers, and riff-raff. Mobster Johnny Rosselli, for example, turns up here as he did in Hollywood in the 1950s as the mafia liaison, and in Nixon's saga too. A former FBI agent who threw a Miami party where he introduced Roselli to the CIA agents mounting Operation Mongoose was asked why he did so: 'It was logical. I'm having a party. Johnny is in town. I invite him over.'[63] Hey, it's just another get-together of all the goodfellas. The temptation for a movie director to overplay such a strange but strong hand is irresistible. Would LBJ bother to plot to kill Kennedy because of a budget cut affecting a Texas company contract to dredge Cam Ranh Bay? Did Oswald give Soviets the exact data needed to shoot down U-2 pilot Gary Powers and thereby ruin the planned Summit in 1960? The degree of Kennedy's own implication in the assassination of Diem also is unclear (although Nixon tried to uncover or else invent such links).[64] Stone stretches it; he need not have.

In the pivotal Potomac Park briefing with a 'black ops' military officer, Garrison gasps: 'I never knew Kennedy was so dangerous to the establishment.' (Nor, one must add, did anyone else.) But in a virtuoso denouement the black ops man recites a deadly accurate list of American covert escapades: Greece, France and Italy in the 1940s, recruitment of 'rat line' Nazis for sabotage in Russia and Eastern Europe, interventions in Iran and Guatemala and on down to Operation Mongoose to kill Castro—which, if anything, the Kennedys seem to have intensified. Which parts of this recitation are paranoid? Stone's *JFK*, however, 'wanted to end the cold war in his second term, stop the moon race, cooperate with the USSR, refused to invade Cuba in 1962, pull out of Vietnam' and cut military budgets. Hence, he had to be rubbed out. 'The organizing principle, Mr Garrison, is war.' The distance between Stone's lurid evidence and the actual gamut of covert actions is at this point frightfully small, even if his portrait of Kennedy is questionable.

Karnow, an establishment-based critic of *JFK*, admits supplying the anecdote of a Christmas Eve 1963 gathering where Johnson blurted the promise 'Get me elected and then you can have your war,' as related to Army chief of staff General Harold K. Johnson.[65] (Stone's film implies that LBJ said it *before* Kennedy was killed.) Karnow dismisses this outrageous remark as LBJ characteristically telling everyone what they wanted to hear. He also denies that anything JFK said 'even remotely envisioned scuttling Vietnam'—which does not wash either. Kennedy's NSAM 263, Karnow says, aimed to cut a thousand US troops with more reductions in the offing so as to encourage Diem to behave leniently toward dissidents—an utterly unlikely course for so intractable a regime. No one can have an ESP fix on Kennedy and how circumstances would have swayed him had he survived, although Robert McNamara asserts Kennedy would have gotten out.[66] Even radical scholars, who are least likely to fall under Camelot's spell, are divided over Kennedy's intentions on Vietnam and his realistic policy latitude.[67] Stone has a point, even if a wobbly one.

The upshot of the park briefing, though, is that Dallas was 'a coup d'etat. A murder planned at the highest levels of our government. Covered up all the way to LBJ and Hoover.' The pertinent, and apparently exhaustive, questions are: 'Why was Kennedy killed?; Who benefited?; Who has the power to cover it up?' Good questions, but the answers do not clinch the case. This seductive deductive technique laced British MI5's appraisal of another spot of bother in 1963: 'Who had suffered from the Profumo affair ?: MI5 and the Conservative Party. And who had benefited?: Harold Wilson and the KGB.'[68] Ergo, the KGB engineered the scandal to bring its minions in the Labour Party to power. This dyspeptic style of reasoning appeals precisely because it leads wherever one is inclined to go. More to the point, though, if this is the best that the cream of British intelligence can come up with, one can hardly sneer at Stone or his audience for doing likewise. Stone's one sound assertion is that no one in authority had much interest in addressing these particular questions at all. A pair of political scientists, who very much reflect the typical critiques of Stone, sniffed at his 'paranoid message.'

The story, moreover, need never end. If evidence appears that refutes the conspiracy, the suppliers of the discrediting material will themselves be accused of being part of the conspiracy. The paranoid explanatory system is a closed one. Only confirmatory evidence is accepted. Contradictions are dismissed as being naive or, more likely, part of the conspiracy itself.[69]

What one gathers from this smug logic—and bad psychology—is that anyone introducing evidence that attributes a significant political event—how about the assassination of Diem, or Archbishop Romero, or Rosa Luxemburg?—to organized action is by definition clinically paranoid. It would appear that paranoid systems are not the only kind that are closed. The charge of conspiracy-mongering has always been a favourite ploy to divert attention from genuinely problematic practices. In Kennedy's era, for example, defence spender extraordinaire Senator Henry Jackson liked to label accusations of military mismanagement and waste as the 'largest version of the devil theory of history.'

'Conspiracy is not the answer', Richard Barnet (a former Kennedy aide) responds.[70] 'The sad truth is that it is not even necessary.' Barnet cites Harold Talbott's role in steering defence spending under Ike, Roswell Gilpatric guiding the TFX contract to General Dynamics in Kennedy's time (which Seymour Hersh rashly attributes instead to a blackmail scheme),[71] David Packard's defence-dependent business and his association with Robert McNamara, Gulf & Western's links to LBJ and Cyrus Vance, and McDonnell Douglas' connections to Clark Clifford, Stu Symington, and James Webb. 'When one scores five out of five, desultory muckraking becomes structural revelation,' Barnet notes. 'All the biggest corporate winners have powerful political contacts at high level in the government and the democratic party. This does not signify corruption so much as the realities of the military-industrial system.'[72] These sort of commonplace arrangements are what Stone cinematically, feverishly, ultimately is getting at.

Stone's film, like the earlier *Executive Decision* (1973) and *Parallax View* (1974) invited derision particularly for portrayal of the grooming of a fall guy for a risky plot that beggars most B-movie imaginations, and the scorn seems warranted—until one pauses to note that during Watergate this was the first and foremost strategy to which the embattled White House resorted to defend itself. Nixon combed his administration for 'a guy who will take the rap, take the heat, and will not speak.'[73]

That the bulk of attacks on *JFK* came from the right and on *Nixon* from the left is perhaps too pat a dichotomy, but seems basically correct.[74] Stone went easy on Nixon to heighten drama, side-step polemics, propitiate Hollywood narrative rules and to pursue instead a big game hunt for the 'system' that Nixon served. When Garrison likens Kennedy to a 'dying king'- an image wildly out of place in a plea for democracy—the silliness of it will be mitigated by the shape of sordid things to come. 'Do you realize the responsibility I carry ?' Kennedy wisecracked during the 1960 campaign. 'I'm the only person standing between Nixon and the White House.'

NIXON: 'WE HAVE TOO MANY ENEMIES'

'Every historically based film in the history of the medium has utilized dramatic license and speculation, including documentaries,' Stone writes in his own defence. 'That's the nature of the art.'[75] Nixon is elevated to the stature of poignant figure in a Shakespearean tragedy not because this is who he was but because it makes for an intriguing, if sublimely hackneyed, story of an 'immensely intelligent and gifted man, but one who carried within him the seeds of his own destruction.'[76] Here is the opposite of the 'good king' myth embodied in *JFK*, and opposite in every way. As Garry Wills perceptively wrote of Nixon:

Self-government' is primarily a personal morality in America, not a political philosophy. If we do not 'govern ourselves' we shall need a king to govern us, like recalcitrant, ancient Israel. But if we govern ourselves—our appetites, our desires—then democracy is safe. Thus does our individualism reduce social problems always to the level of personal morality, to things outside the scope of legislation. No one can make life better for others except those others themselves. A man can be self-made only by himself. . . . Turning the job over to government is a confession that one needs government, an admission that self government has failed. As Nixon likes to put it, people do not become great by what government does for them but by what they do for themselves.[77]

Stone's 'dying king' imagery, in this light, takes on an unintended but sharp significance. Kennedy, though a pragmatic centrist in terms of his times, still stood within the New Deal legacy of Democratic Party politics. Whatever their many shortcomings, the Democrats were still, in part, the party of the helping hand to the 'common man' as a matter of right, as a matter of what TH Marshall called social citizenship, which both Jack and Robert Kennedy were moved to recall during their eye-opening Appalachian journey into 'the other America' during the 1960 primaries.[78] The 'dying king' imagery mingles with the ebbing of a New Deal-style political vision.

Nixon delves into the 'mystery' of the man via flashbacks of his arid family life. 'Can you imagine what he would have been had he been loved?' asks Kissinger, of all people. The trouble with so empathetic an approach is that the new tapes exhibit a Nixon who matched his vilest image, who should have been wheeled out of the White House in August 1974 like another infamous Anthony Hopkins character, Hannibal Lecter. The real Nixon yearned for a 'new McCarthy', tapped the Greek junta for slush fund cash and wanted to revive HUAC in order to leak to it whatever malicious tales his cronies dreamed up.[79] Nixon had a taste for old vintages too. When Charles Colson suggested televising such hearings, Nixon burbles: 'It's better than nothing. But you know what's going to charge up an audience. Jesus Christ they'll be hanging from the rafters . . . Going after all these Jews. Just find one that is a Jew, will you ?'[80] Martha Mitchell got it in one: 'Dick Nixon is as misunderstood as a fox in a hen house.'

Nixon knew that LBJ had bugged his go-between Anna Chennault for damning evidence that he had urged Thieu in 1968 to stall peace talks in anticipation of better terms once Nixon was elected.[81] The publication of the Pentagon papers tarred the entire Executive branch for its instinctive deceitfulness, in effect, for treating the American public as the primary enemy, which Nixon would have continued. No individual's privacy may stand in the way of secrecy. 'I'm not so interested in Ellsberg', Nixon fumed, 'but we have to go after everybody who's a member of this conspiracy.'[82] What is most striking in the tape transcripts is that no phrase pops up more often than Nixon moaning that he was 'up against a conspiracy' even as he waged illicit warfare on the home front via the Huston plan, IRS investigations and the plumbers.[83] Two explanations immediately vie for attention: either Nixon was floridly paranoid or else, rather more disturbingly, he was soberly appreciative that these forms of action were the customary ways of doing things in the groups with whom he consorted. More conspiracies were generated in the Executive branch—and in subsections of it against each other—than against it.

Stone targets personified symbols of the 'system' in three scenes. Two occur at a tycoon's redoubt where in November 1963 his host, urging Nixon to run, hints that a Cuban thug present will take out his rival. Then in 1972 these same magnates try to intimidate him. Nixon did indeed meet a band of oil barons—among 200 other guests—at a Dallas fete two days before the assassination and abundant oil money always, but not exclusively, stoked his campaigns ever since his notorious Senate race against Helen Gahagan Douglas.[84] Stone suggests not that Nixon was a ragged little instrument of the oil industry—for he stands up to the oil men in one scene—but that the smoke-filled rooms matter a great deal, which may not seem out of line to anyone knowledgeable about the relation between money, lobbyists, and electoral politics in America.

A third crucial scene occurs at night after a peace demonstration on 8 May 1970 at the Lincoln memorial where a student protester and the weary and momentarily vulnerable president have a fictitious exchange, though upon an actual occasion:[85]

YOUNG WOMAN: You don't want the war. We don't want the war. The Vietnamese don't want the war. So why does it go on?

Nixon hesitates, out of answers

YOUNG WOMAN: Someone wants it . . .(*a realization*). You can't stop it, can you. Even if you wanted to. Because it's not you, it's the system. The system won't let you stop it.

NIXON: There's a lot more at stake here than what you want. Or even what I want . . .

YOUNG WOMAN: Then what's the point? What's the point of being president. You're powerless.

The girl transfixes him with her eyes. Nixon feels it. The nausea of the Beast makes him reel. The students press on him from all sides.

NIXON: (*stumbling*) No. No. I'm not powerless. Because . . . because I understand the system. I believe I can control it. Maybe not control it totally. But . . . I can tame it enough to make it do some good.

YOUNG WOMAN: It sounds like you're talking about a wild animal.

NIXON: Maybe I am.

This beast, for Stone, is not a 'committee of the whole and entire bourgeoisie' but a crazy-quilt patchwork of state agencies and private interests which in the aggregate cannot even control itself.[86] One wonders how many critics really would disagree with that capsule characterization. Finally, for what looks like the sheer fun of it Stone speculated that a second tape with eighteen and a half missing minutes intact did him in; a deeper layer of surveillance, unsuspected even by Nixon, nails him. His last thoughts are completely in character.

NIXON: Things won't be the same after this. I played by the rules, but the rules changed right in the middle of the game. . . . There's no respect for American institutions anymore. People are cynical, the press—God, the press—is out of control. People spit on soldiers, government secrets mean nothing. . . I pity the next guy who sits here.[87]

Figures in power, and serving it, usually regard legitimacy as if it were an either/or phenomenon, so that a disillusioned public must hurtle from pure trust to cynicism, with no intermediate point along the way to display a reasonably sceptical sensibility about politics. Hence, Nixon, ruminating on his garden variety *realpolitik*, asks contemptuously: 'How do I explain that on TV to a bunch of simple minded reporters and weeping mothers?' Yet Nixon and his kindred spirits cannot bring themselves to imagine a citizenry sporting a critical appreciation of their elites' limits, foibles, and fast ones— perhaps because it would be more threatening to their range of action than shoulder-shrugging cynicism. In the end Stone at least spares us a *Richard III* nocturnal visit by wraiths. 'History will treat you far more kindly than your contemporaries,' Kissinger comforts him. This feature film, for the reasons shown, certainly did.

Conspiracy themes, to be sure, have been played for their slapstick potential too. A cabbie in *Conspiracy Theory* asserts with comic illogic that the militias really are the UN troops they fear are invading America and that Oliver Stone is a magnificent disinformation agent planted to distract us from the real rascals. *Men in Black* spun out a conspiratorial extravaganza extending to the ends of the universe. *Canadian Bacon* and *Wag The Dog* acidly satirized leaders resorting to the diversionary theory of war. *Air America* harked to CIA operations in Southeast Asia in aid of US-sponsored forces, partly by hauling around heroin. A related rumor became a provocative sub-plot in *Panther* ghettoes, many blacks suspect, are being suppressed via an FBI plot to flood them with narcotics. The worrisome underlying judgement being made here is that, for all the concern demonstrated by the State: 'they would have if they could have.' In 1997 president Clinton apologized for a 40-year experiment in which the United States Public Health Service misled and left untreated nearly 400 syphilitic blacks, which left a 'legacy of distrust that hindered doctors' ability to treat blacks for AIDs or HIV.'[88] Bigots, however, always take plausibility several addled and self-advantageous steps further; a Nation of Islam spokesperson opined the AIDs epidemic was 'a result of doctors, especially Jewish ones, who inject AIDS into blacks.'[89] Xenophobia kicks in too. *Rising Sun* told westerners that the Japanese—prior to their massive financial reverses—were achieving world domination in good old yellow peril fashion.[90]

FOREIGN PLOTS: GENTLEMEN DO READ EACH OTHER'S MAIL

How does European cinema treat the conspiracy theme? The UK film *Society* (like the American low-budgeter *They Live*) explained crass behaviour by the privileged strata through a devastatingly simple device: what Galbraith calls the 'fortunate fifth' are really disguised extraterrestrial aliens wholly disdainful of humanity. So that's it. Europeans, perhaps for lack of a Hartzian liberal tradition, seem less perturbed by conspiratorial themes. In *A Very British Coup* (1988) the 'old Labour' leader Harry Perkins becomes prime minister to enact a programme the rabid tabloids dependably denounce 'as nearly

Marxist as makes no difference.' The myriad schemes to thwart him are a sardonic meditation on the thesis of a capital strike, and work off of both documented and reputed incidents. Perkins matches wits with ruthless local honchos, foreign investors, and disapproving Yanks and it's regarded as plain old politics in a class-ridden society: 'They are the opposition. It's their duty to plot against me.' Perkins gamely observes. 'And it's my duty to plot against them.' As it happens, author and Labour MP Chris Mullin, was 'singled out for his perpetual vendetta against British security arrangement' in a subversive surveillance newsletter run by a retired intelligence operative, which perhaps is indicative of the thickness and tone of his own MI 5 file.[91]

Ken Loach's *Hidden Agenda* (1990) was sparked by MI 5 hijinks against Prime Minister Harold Wilson in the mid-1970s and by the John Stalker affair in Ulster in the mid-1980s. A British police chief, appointed to investigate the RUC for evidence of a 'shoot-to-kill' policy, finds himself thwarted at every turn.[92] As in actuality, smear tactics finally led to his replacement. Later, the attorney general admitted that the Stalker/Sampson inquiry demonstrated that the RUC conspired to pervert justice but because of 'national security' no one was prosecuted.[93] A subplot derives from MI 5 activity after being told by the CIA counter-intelligence chief, who later (or, more likely, earlier) went insane, that Harold Wilson was a Soviet agent.[94] What seems clear is that a significant faction—probably a vast majority—in MI 5 thereafter worked to undermine Wilson. Here, the state, as defined by privileged elites in secret agencies, toils to deceive citizens for a higher purpose that predictably coincides with their self-interest.

Costa-Garvas' *Z* targeted the 1967 Greek Colonel's coup. Since the civil war the Army, by the most scrupulous scholarly accounts, had made something of a 'habit of military conspiracy.'[95] By the 1960s the 'virtual monopoly of power enjoyed by the right, with the backing of their foreign allies, could now only be maintained by the most outrageous manipulation of democracy itself.'[96] Hence, in an opening scene an officer prattles fascistically against the virus of dissent. The opposition leader is killed—based on an actual political murder— by men whom an investigator finds are linked to the police and Army.[97] The plotters are nabbed but ultimately instigate the coup on the pretext of saving Greece from Commies. In reality 'there was no communist plot,' says a British scholar, 'although the colonels believed, no doubt sincerely, that there was one.'[98] What, one may ask, does sincerity have to do with it? In these particular states, as films present them, and at these junctures, respect for the rights of others was 'proportionate to the degree of threat that one can plausibly conjure about them.'[99] While it may be cynical to say all states immutably behave this way, is it a cynical or is it a democratically responsible act to argue that this behaviour is sometimes, even often, the case?

Cynical thinking, as Sloterdijk writes, 'can only arise when two views of things become possible: an official and an unofficial one, a veiled view and a naked view, one from the standpoint of the heroes and one from the standpoint of the valets.'[100] The state, in this sense, gave birth to cynicism, and cynicism in turn to conspiratorial speculation. But if cynicism is defined as 'a hard-boiled, shadowy cleverness that has split off courage from itself, holds anything positive to be a fraud, and is intent only on somehow getting through life,' then so far we have gathered an incomplete menu of public responses.[101] Our standard discourse resists imparting any meaning other than cynicism to what Stone or Costa-Gavras might welcome as a relinquishing of credulity, and regard as a jump-off point toward a more effective evaluative role by citizens in political life.

CONCLUSION: BOWLING ALONE, PLOTTING TOGETHER

The framing of political legerdemain in terms of 'conspiracies' stems partly from narrative conventions requiring easily identified heroes and villains, partly from an underlying cultural distrust of centralized organizations, and partly from the personalized (and occasionally idiosyncratic) expressions of these forces by film makers. There is an aesthetic pleasure too. Nothing is more satisfying for the moviegoer or the crackpot or the counterintelligence agent than to transform a disparate succession of genuinely seamy events into a seamless web.

A fundamental 'paradox of the paranoid style', as Hofstadter noted, 'is the imitation of the enemy'—and, moreover, an enemy that authorities often invent or purposefully exaggerate.[102] Secret police always impose their petty imaginations on rebels: whether fabricating the Protocols of the Elders of Zion, Jewish-Bolshevik plots, IRA 'holy wars', a 'fifth man' in Britain, or Moscow gold funding western protest groups. The Chicago conspiracy trial in 1969–70 was orchestrated by a government that at that moment was conducting vast illegal surveillance schemes because its functionaries needed to believe that isolated agitators were to blame for widening public disaffection. When such 'inventions' suit the interests of authorities we safely can ascribe the dominant motive to the predilections of those in power to abuse it, not to mass psychopathology.

Who then is more inclined to conspiratorial thought: authorities nestled in State agencies or guests on the Jerry Springer Show? It may be too close to call. In a richly sardonic sense popular conspiracy theories, as Shils noted, were a democratic advance in that, since the turn of the nineteenth century they 'deprived the upper classes of their monopoly on conspiratorial hallucination'—but only their monopoly, not their predilection.[103] Fuelling conspiracy theories is, of course, a fear of unaccountability, of invisibility, of malevolent indifference. Does not the secrecy of the state always trump the privacy of the individual? Since the Kennedy era Americans, as Slotkin accurately writes, 'have not recovered their faith in the most fundamental principles of national ideology : the belief that American democracy offers effective means for expressing the will of the people through political action, and the belief in personal and national progress.'[104]

If soldiers in the past were used as guinea pigs, as indeed they were, they may reasonably consider whether they have been again (in the case of gulf war syndrome).[105] If a government discriminated against class, racial or creedal groups in the past, it is worth re-examining assurances in place that it will not do so again, or in a different manner. If a state covered up its illegal activities in the past, it is highly likely to do so again. This experiential 'storage' of distrust ought to be differentiated from reports of crop circles, alien abduction, and sightings of Beelzebub in the neighbour's unkempt back yard.

Analysts rarely inquire into the sources of the tensions that they say spur conspiracizing.[106] In the United States, for example, the 'implicit social contract is gone.'[107] The wonder is that in an era of growing gaps in income and wealth, job insecurity, stagnating living standards for the 'lower' 80 per cent, an 'end to welfare as we know it', finicky HMOs and other 'tensions' that more people do not resort to untethered conspiratorial explanations. Certainly, one prescription is arraying institutional arrangements to bring about less secrecy so that conspiracy is less often a reasonable hypothesis. For all the cool, go-along-to-get-ahead cynicism pervading daily, and especially middle class professional, life these films perform the democratic service of flushing out for examination the substantial basis for ordinary citizens' fear that they will have nothing left to say in the body politic except, like the accused assassin in *JFK*, the sorriest words of all: 'I'm just a patsy'.

NOTES

1. Stanley Kutler (ed.), *Abuse of Power: The New Nixon Tapes* (New York: Free Press, 1997), p. 229.
2. The blackfaced actor swigged hydrogen pyroxide so that he literally foamed at the mouth. The film was banned in several Northern cities, including Chicago and Newark. Leon F. Litwack, 'Birth of A Nation', in *Past Imperfect: History According To The Movies*, Mark C. Carnes (ed.), (New York: Henry Holt, 1995), p. 140.
3. Kenneth T. Jackson, *The Ku Klux Klan in The City, 1915-1930* (Chicago: Ivan R. Dee, 1992, 2nd ed.), p. 3. and Allen W. Trelease, *White Terror: The Ku Klux Klan Conspiracy and Southern Reconstruction* (Baton Rouge: Louisiana State University Press, 1971), p. 421. Griffith's view of the audiences was that 'What these horny-handed sons and daughter of toil wanted was a full-course thrilling feast of tragedy and comedy, not delicate tragedy but raw blood, not witty comedy but slapstick.' Karl Brown, *Adventures with D. W. Griffith* (London: Secker & Warburg, 1973), p. 65.
4. See J.K. Jacobsen, 'Mississippi Burning', the *Guardian*, 15 January 1989. Also David Garrow, *The FBI and Martin Luther King* (New York: Norton, 1981).
5. Kevin Brownlow, *Hollywood: The Pioneers* (London: Collins, 1979), p. 248.
6. Quoted in Audrey Salked, *A Portrait of Leni Riefenstahl* (London: Jonathan Cape, 1996), p. 112.
7. Tom Dewe Matthews, *Censored: The Story of Film Censorship in Britain* (London: Chatto & Windus, 1994), pp. 40–1.
8. Riefenstahl declined Party funding but, with Hitler's imprimatur, she had no trouble raising cash, thereby avoiding interference by Goebbels who had taken a dislike to her. The film was distributed though the Nazis who 'provided the setting and every facility possible' in filming the 1934 Nuremberg rally. David Stewart Hull, *Film in The Third Reich* (Berkeley: University of California, 1969), p. 75.

9. Memo to President Johnson, April 1965. Cited in Tom Wells, *The War Within: America's Battle Over Vietnam* ((Berkeley: University of California Press, 1994), p. 29. Valenti encouraged Federal assistance for John Wayne's *The Green Berets* because 'Wayne's politics were wrong, but insofar as Vietnam is concerned, his views are right. If he made the picture he would be saying the things we want said.' Lawrence W. Suid, *Guts and Glory: Great American War Movies* (Addison-Wesley, 1978). pp. 221–2. Valenti was president of the Motion Pictures Association of America until his resignation in July 2004.

10. '[I]t is becoming increasingly difficult for modern man to entertain any ideals whatsoever', Jules Henry writes. 'Yet this condition is impossible for him to confront; for even the most calculating (non-criminal) among us tremble at the thought that everybody else should be equally so.' Jules Henry, 'Values: Guilt, Suffering and Consequences' in *On Sham, Vulnerability and Other Forms of Self-destruction* (New York: Vintage, 1973), p. 118.

11. For example, one can tune into the weekly HBO programme of American comedian Bill Maher (formerly host of ABC television's' Politically Incorrect' until he was dumped for a 9/11 remark the Bush junior White House disliked) to watch him working this vein.

12. As a critic observed: 'it is not only political arrangement which need sustained and convincing criticism, but also the exercise of arbitrary power in all walks of life—in factories, offices, schools and wherever else power affects people's existence. The notion that the battle for democracy has already been won in capitalist democratic systems, save for some electoral and constitutional reforms at the edges, simply by virtue of the achievements of universal suffrage, open political competition and regular elections is a profoundly limiting and debilitating notion which served conservative forces extremely well, and which has to be exposed and countered.' Ralph Miliband, 'Reflections on the Crises of Communist Regimes', in *After The Fall: The Failure of Communism and the Future of Socialism*, Robin Blackburn (ed.), (London: Verso, 1991), p. 13.

13. George MacDonald Fraser, *The Hollywood History of the World* (London: Harvill Press, 1996), p. 3.

14. William Goldman, *Adventures in The Screen Trade* (New York: Simon & Schuster, 1983), p. 124.

15. Richard Slotkin, *Gunfighter Nation: The Myth of The Frontier in Twentieth Century America* (New York: Atheneum, 1992), p. 7.

16. Dan Muldea, *Dark Victory: Ronald Reagan, MCA and The Mob* (New York: Viking, 1986), p. 26.

17. Michael Rogin, *Black Face, White Noise: Jewish Immigrants in The Hollywood Melting Pot* (Berkeley: University of California, 1996), p. 209.

18. In 1930 Hays had commisioned a Jesuit priest to write a doctrine of ethics for the Production Code Administration. Thomas Schatz, *The Genius of*

The System: Hollywood Film-making in The Studio Era (New York: Pantheon, 1989), p. 167.

19. Larry Ceplan and Steven Englund, *The Inquisition in Hollywood: Politics and The Film Community, 1930-1960* (Garden City, NJ: Anchor Books, 1980), p. 304.

20. Neal Gabler, *An Empire of Their Own: How The Jews Invented Hollywood* (New York: Crown Publishers, Inc., 1988), p. 118. Garry Wills asks where we 'find the ideal of participatory democracy in our decentralized past? In the East remembered by the older characters in Marquand, Auchinloss, Cozzens? In the South of Faulkner, or Tom Wolfe? The lingering Pennsylvania of John O'Hara? The Chicago of Upton Sinclair, or Midwest of Sinclair Lewis? The SouthWest of Edna Ferber? The Northern California of Steinbeck? Any attempt to capture the folkways of our local centers has told a story not of participatory democracy, but of closed social corporations, the rules of climbing in them quite rigid, the pinnacle of power monopolized by various social and business combines.' *Nixon Agonistes* (New York: Signet, 1964), p. 463.

21. Julia Phillips, *You'll Never Eat Lunch In This Town Again* (London: Mandarin, 1991).

22. 'The dream factory has turned into the poison factory.' See Michael Medved, *Hollywood vs. America: Popular Culture and The War on Traditional Values* (New York: HarperCollins, 1992), p. 3.

23. *Webster's Third New International Dictionary* (Springfield, Mass: Merriam-Webster Inc., 1986), p. 485.

24. Edward Shils, *The Torment of Secrecy* (New York: Free Press, 1956), p. 30. Michael Rogin demolished Shils' characterization of the social base of McCarthyism in his *The Intellectuals and McCarthy: The Radical Spectre* (Cambridge: MIT Press, 1967).

25. Richard Hofstadter, *The Paranoid Style in American Politics and Other Essays* (New York: Vintage, 1964), p. 5.

26. See Bruno Bettelheim, *Surviving and Other Essays* (New York: Vintage, 1980), pp. 246–57.

27. Hofstadter, *Paranoid Style*, pp. 9–11. Hofstadter takes care to say that he lifts a term – 'paranoid'—from clinical use and applies it to very different purposes. For him it is the 'use of paranoid modes of expression by more or less normal people that makes the phenomenon significant' (p. 4).

28. Ibid., p. 16

29. Leonard Quart and Albert Astor, *American Film and Society Since 1945* (London: Macmillan, 1984), p. 10. Also Schatz, *Genius of The System*, p. 9.

30. *Chicago Tribune*, 26 May 1997.

31. Jerry Isenberg, 'The Exterminators', the *Nation*, 8 June 1998, p. 34.

32. The Screen Actors Guild was formed in 1933 in response to studio demands for 20 to 50 per cent pay cuts. Moldea, *Dark Victory*, p. 59.

33. On FBI informer 'T-10' see Garry Wills, *Reagan's America* (London: Heinemann, 1988), pp. 151–60.

34. Slotkin, *Gunfighter Nation*, p. 644.

35. Gabler, *An Empire of Their Own*, p. 352.

36. The Hollywood 19 in 1947 were Albert Maltz, Alvah Bessie, John Howard Lawson, Ring Lardner, Jr, Herbert Biberman, Lester Cole, Adrian Scott, Samuel Ornitz, Edward Dmytryk, Dalton Trumbo, Bertolt Brecht, Waldo Salt, Gordon Kahn, Irvin, Pichel, Robert Rossen, Howard Koch, Richard Collins, Lewis Milestone, and Larry Parks, and Abe Polonsky. The first 10 constitute the Hollywood 10, after Brecht skedaddled to East Germany. Jules Dassein maintains that it 'was [a] ridiculous idea that they were writing Communist propaganda or subversive stuff. . . . It was not that at all, but that the organization of the [Screen Writers] Guild demanding rights and better financial arrangements with people . . . this was impossible for management to accept.' Interview in *Tender Comrades: A Backstory of the Hollywood Blacklist*, Patrick McGilligan and Paul Buhle (eds), (New York: St Martin's Press, 1997), p. 211.

37. Schatz, *Genius of The System*, p. 443.

38. McGilligan and Buhle, *Tender Comrades*, p. xviii. Eight of the 10 cited for contempt had been Communists, if often only briefly. 10 of the 19 were Jews.

39. As a studio executive put it: 'We're sure of Lassie. Lassie can't go out and embarrass the studio. Katherine Hepburn goes out and makes a speech for Henry Wallace. Bang! We're in trouble. Lassie doesn't make speeches'. Greg Mitchell, *Tricky Dick and The Pink Lady: Richard Nixon Versus Helen Gahagan Douglas: Sexual Politics and The Red Scare, 1950* (New York: Random House, 1998), p. 63. The Lassie TV series, in fact, was a haven for blacklisted writers. A common joke was that there were more aliases than fleas on Lassie during the blacklist era. See Ceplan and Englund, *The Inquisition in Hollywood*, p. 407. While blacklisted, both Dalton Trumbo and Ned Young won screenwriting Oscars under their aliases.

40. Ellen Schrecker, *Many Are The Crimes: McCarthyism in America* (Boston: Little, Brown and Company, 1998), p. 317.

41. 'We are less interested in a film that has communist content, when a few hundred people will come to see it. We are more interested in an ordinary John-and-Mary picture where there is only a drop of progressive content.' HUAC spokeman quoted in Bruce Crowther, *Hollywood Faction: Reality and Myth in The Movies* (London: Coliumbus Books, 1984), p. 71.

42. 'Alvah Bessie Interview', ibid., p. 103. Also Ceplan and Englund, *Inquisition in Hollywood*, pp. 299-323.

43. 'Robert Lees Interview', McGilligan and Buhle, *Tender Comrades*, p. 422.

44. The view that McCarthy also came out of the American Committee for Cultural Freedom project eventuating in James Rorty and Moishe Decter's

volume *McCarthy and The Communists* (Boston: Beacon Press, 1954) On the post-Korean War brainwashing panic which inspired the film see John Marks, *The Search for The 'Manchurian Candidate': The CIA and Mind Control* (Berkeley: University of California, 1987).

45. It is even more likely that the worst cynic, as Freud had written of the worst egoist, 'is the person to whom the thought has never occured that he might be one.' Cited in Alice Miller, *The Drama of Being a Child* (London: Virago, 1987), p. 12. Also Peter Sloterdijk, *Critique of Cynical Reason* (London: Verso, 1988), p. 5.

46. Andrew Shonfield, *Modern Capitalism* (New York: Oxford University Press, 1965).

47. See Huntington's essay 'The United States', in *The Crisis of Democracy*, Michel Crozier, Samuel Huntington, and Joji Watanuki (New York: New York University Press, 1975).

48. Robert Reich, *Locked in The Cabinet* (New York: Knopf, 1997), p. 48.

49. See Bruce Franklin, *MIA, or Mythmaking in America* (New Brunswick: Rutgers University Press, 1993), Susan Katz Keating, *Prisoners of Hope: Exploiting the POW/MIA Myth in America* (New York: Random House, 1994) and Arnold Isaacs, *Vietnam Shadows* (Baltimore: John Hopkins University Press, 1997), pp. 103–36.

50. Michael Ignatieff, *London Review of Books*, 17 July 1997.

51. *Time*, 9 February 1998, p. 63.

52. *Chicago Sun-Times*, 31 March 1998. Also Lars-Erik Nelson, 'Whatever Happened to Whitewater?', *New York Review of Books*, 13 August 1998.

53. Michael Kelly, 'The Road to Paranoia', the *New Yorker*, 19 June 1995.

54. Robert A. Rosenstone, *Visions of The Past: The Challenge of Film to Our Idea of History* (Cambridge, Mass: Harvard University Press, 1995), p. 235.

55. On Stone's earlier films see J.K. Jacobsen 'Talking Through the Long American Night', the *Guardian*, 15 February 1989, and 'Born on the Fourth of July', *Chicago Reader*, 12 January 1990.

56. See Kenneth Kenniston, *Youth and Dissent: The Rise of a New Opposition* (New York: Harcourt, Brace & World, 1971).

57. In the Weimar Republic too an analyst finds George Grosz 'provides the slogan of the epoch: "the rage at having been deceived".' Sloterdijk, *Critique of Cynical Reason*, p. 410.

58. Carl Oglesby, 'Liberalism and the Modern State', in *The New Radicals*, Saul Landau and Paul Jacobs (eds), (New York: Random House, 1966).

59. JFK's civil rights record was hardly commendable. His administration often regarded King's movement as a 'nuisance'. Taylor Branch, *Parting The Waters* (London: Macmillan, 1989), p. 744.

60. Stanley Karnow, 'JFK', in Carnes, *Past Imperfect*, p. 272.

61. Michael R. Beschloss (ed.), *Taking Charge: The Johnson White House Tapes* (New York: Simon & Schuster, 1997), pp, 31, 46, 55, and 64.

62. J. Edgar Hoover gave LBJ off-the-cuff assurance that one could easily get off three shots in three seconds. Ibid., p. 55.

63. Seymour Hersh, *The Dark Side of Camelot* (New York: Little, Brown, 1997), p. 160.

64. Nixon wanted Howard Hunt to forge cables implicating Kennedy directly in Diem's assassination. See Kutler, *Abuse of Power*, p. 34. Also see 'Nixon Wanted to Show Up JFK and Wouldn't Let It Go', *New York Times*, 28 February 1999.

65. Karnow, 'JFK', in Carnes, *Past Imperfect*, p. 273.

66. Robert McNamara, *In Retrospect* (New York: Times Books, 1995), pp. 61–2. On Kennedy's Honolulu press conference on 14 November see pp. 86–7.

67. For a trenchant rebuttal see Noam Chomsky, *Rethinking Camelot: JFK, The Vietnam War and US Political Culture* (London: Verso, 1993) and, for a favourable view, see the third chapter in Michael Parenti, *Dirty Truths* (Seattle: City Lights Books, 1996). Stone relies on John M. Newman, *JFK and Vietnam: Deception, Intrigue and The Struggle for Power* (New York: Warner Books, 1992).

In the middle ground, reflecting on the Bay of Pigs, Laos, Berlin, the Cuban Missile Crisis and Vietnam in the early 1960s, Howard Margolis, who worked for MacNamara in the Department of Defence, said 'it seemed to me striking, the extent to which Kennedy was prudent not to make the kind of commitment that Johnson, everybody, I think, thinks, tragically, did make under conditions vastly more favourable . . . one of the lessons of it was, who the president is makes a difference. I certainly would not claim that had Kennedy lived, we would not have gotten involved in America's troops fighting that war, but certainly the basis was laid to leave the president's options open.' In John Prados and Maragaret Pratt Porter (eds), *Inside the Pentagon Papers* (Lawrence, Kansas: University Press of Kansas, 2004), p. 28.

68. David Leigh, *The Wilson Plot: The Intelligence Services and the Discrediting of a Prime Minister* (London: Heinemann, 1988), p. 87.

69. Robert S. Robins and Jerrold M Post, 'Political Paranoia as Cinematic Motif: Stone's JFK'. Paper prepared for American Political Science Association meetings August/September 1997 Washington D.C.

70. Richard Barnet, *The Economy of Death* (New York: Athenium, 1969) p. 60.

71. Hersh, *Dark Side of Camelot*, p. 151. The TFX (or F-111) was purported to be an all-service all-purpose aircraft but was plagued with technical difficulties and cost overruns that tripled the price of each plane from the original estimate of just under three million dollars. Three of the first six dispatched to Vietnam crashed within weeks. The charge of blackmail certainly does not explain Nixon's subsequent staunch support for the plane. See I.F. Stone, 'Nixon and The Arms Race: The Bomber Boondoggle',

in *Polemics and Prophecies 1967-1970* (New York: Vintage 1973), pp. 169-89.

72. Barnet, *The Economy of Death*, p. 124.
73. Kutler, *Abuse of Power*, p. 98.
74. Frank Beaver, *Oliver Stone: Wakeup Cinema* (New York: Twayne Publishers, 1994).
75. Eric Hamburg (ed.), *Nixon: An Oliver Stone Film* (New York: Hyperion, 1995), p. xvi.
76. Ibid.
77. Wills, *Nixon Agonistes*, p. 533.
78. Richard C. Reeves, *President Kennedy: Profile in Power* (New York: Simon & Schuster, 1993), p. 251.
79. Kutler, *Abuse of Power*, p. 19. Peter Murtagh of the *Guardian* cites evidence that the Greek Intelligence Agency KYP gave illegal donations to Nixon camp via businessman Tom Pappas. 'Given that the KYP was heavily funded by the CIA, such a donation raised the extraordinary possibility that US taxpayers money was effectively laundered through domestic and foreign intelligence agencies to influence a presidential election.' *The Rape of Greece: The King, The Colonels, and The Resistance* (London: Simon & Schuster, 1994), p. 205. Greek investigative journalist Elias Demetracopolous 'told [Larry] O'Brien about the Pappas money and urged the Democrats to use the information against Nixon. It was O'Brien's office that Nixon's burglars raided in June 1972 during his re-election campaign, and Demotracopoulos believed they were looking to remove evidence as well as any available dirt Nixon could use against the Democrats', p. 205.
80. Kutler, *Abuse of Power*, p. 20.
81. Ibid., pp. 175–6, 196. On these contacts see see Daniel Schorr 'Nixon's Secrets', in Hamburg, *Nixon*, p. 11; and Jeffery Kimbel, *Nixon's Vietnam War* (Lawrence, Kansas: University of Kansas Press, 1998), pp. 56–62.
82. Ibid., p. 16.
83. Ibid., p. xviii.
84. Mitchell, *Tricky Dick and The Pink Lady*, pp. 124, 234.
85. Eric Hamburg (ed.), *Nixon* (London: Bloomsbury, 1996), pp. 131–2. In the wake of the Cambodia 'incursion' and the killings of students at Kent State and Jackson State, Nixon did go to the Lincoln memorial between 4 and 5 AM on 8 May 1970 where he spoke with student protesters. Kimball, *Nixon's Vietnam War*, p. 218.
86. 'The Beast became a metaphor for the darkest organic forces in American cold war politics: the anti-communist crusaders, secret intelligence, the defense industry, organized crime, big business . . . a headless monster that does not know it exists.' Christopher Wilkinson, 'The Year of the Beast', in Hamburg (ed.), *Nixon*, p. 59.
87. Ibid., p. 205.

88. Alison Mitchell, 'Survivors of Tuskegee get Apology from President Clinton', *New York Times*, 17 May 1997.
89. Sander Gilman, *Sexuality* (New York: John Wiley & Son, 1989), p. 325.
90. J.K. Jacobsen, 'The Japanese are Coming, the Japanese are Coming', *The Guardian*, 10 July 1993.
91. Dorril, *The Silent Conspiracy*, p. 31.
92. Ibid., p. 90. For John Stalker's version see *Stalker* (London: Harrap, 1988). Also see Mark Urban, *Big Boys' Rules* (London: Faber and Faber, 1992).
93. *Political Killings in Northern Ireland* (London: Amnesty International, 1994), p. 9. In addition to a *de facto* 'shoot to kill' policy, there was also official collusion with Loyalist paramilitaries. Amnesty International found that authorities failed 'to take effective measures to stop collusion, to bring appropriate sanctions against people who colluded, or to deploy resources with equal vigour against both Republican and Loyalist groups that pursue campaigns of political murder', p. 6.
94. Peter Wright, *Spycatcher: The Candid Autobiography of a Service Intelligence Officer* (Toronto: Stoddart, 19987), pp. 364–9. Leigh noted that Wright himself was one of the people convinced Wilson was a spy. *The Wilson Plot*, p. xii.
95. C.M. Woodhouse, *The Rise and Fall of The Greek Colonels* (London: Grafton: 1985), p. 5.
96. James Pettifer, *The Greeks: The Land and People Since the War* (London: Penguin, 1993), p. 16 and, on the American role in events see Murtagh, *The Rape of Greece*, pp. 20–44, 86–125.
97. The film replicates the murder of the popular left wing deputy Grigorios Lambrakis in 1963. 'Interview, Constantine Costa-Gavras', in *Art, Politics, Cinema: The Cineaste Interviews*, Dan Georgakas and Lenny Rubenstein (eds), (London: Pluto Pres, 1984), pp. 4–5.
98. Woodhouse, *Rise and Fall*, p. 19. Costa-Gavras later attracted flak for overstating American involvement in the death of Charles Horman in his film about the 1973 Chilean coup, *Missing*, which enabled indignant critics to miss the point about the actual extent of the US role there.
99. Dorril, *The Silent Conspiracy*, p. 48.
100. Sloterdijk, *Critique of Cynical Reason*, p. 240.
101. Ibid., p. 546. Also see Richard Stivens, *The Culture of Cynicism: American Morality in Decline* (Cambridge, MA: Blackwell, 1994).
102. Hofstadter, *The Paranoid Style*, p. 32.
103. Shils, *The Torment of Secrecy*, p. 30.
104. Slotkin, *Gunfighter Nation*, p. 653.
105. For a different view see Elaine Showalter, *Hystories: Hysterical Epidemics and Modern Cultures* (London: Picador,1997), pp. 133–43.
106. Ibid., p. 23.
107. Reich, *Locked in the Cabinet*, p. 12.

10

Forest of Logos
Empire of Signs

PATRICIA BICKERS

When New Labour swept to power in Britain after a landslide victory on 2 May 1997, the Prime Minister elect, Tony Blair, announced in his characteristic evangelical style that 'A new dawn has broken and it is wonderful. This is a new era in politics in Britain. We are the people's party.'[1] And so it came to pass, the people saw that it was indeed wonderful. In the days that followed a succession of the great and the good filed into No.10 to be photographed mingling with politicians, among them high profile figures from the arts and media—instantly dubbed 'Labour Luvvies' or 'Bollinger Bolsheviks' by the popular press—some of whom had actively campaigned on New Labour's behalf. The guests included Sir Richard Attenborough and Sir David Puttnam (now respectively Lords Attenborough and Puttnam), representing the film industry, as well as Noel Gallagher from the pop group Oasis (bad boy Liam Gallagher was notably absent) and other luminaries from television and the visual arts. After 18 years in the wilderness it seemed as though the arts were finally to receive the recognition they craved.

The issue had never been simply one of funding; it was also one of perception. Successive Conservative governments had come increasingly to view the arts, and indeed the entire public sector, merely as a drain on the public purse. Labour, on the other hand, while in opposition and even before the transition from 'Old Labour' into 'New Labour', had begun to represent the arts in more bullish terms as the 'creative industries', redefining state subsidy as a long-term investment rather than a short-term hand out. The idea of the arts as 'creative industries' had in fact originated in 1988 with a report backed by the then Arts Council of Great Britain (ACGB) and its secretary general, Anthony Everitt, entitled, *The Economic Importance of the Arts in Britain*, published by the Policy Studies Institute. The report, written by John Myerscough, was commissioned against a background of unprecedented State hostility to the arts from the then Tory government under Margaret Thatcher. This was reflected not merely indirectly in the form of swinging cuts to arts funding, but directly through her government's policy of forcing through the closure or merger of fine art courses and departments in London, a policy carried out by the appropriately named National Academic Board (NAB) set up in 1987.[2] In this as in so many other areas of policy, most notably the National Health Service, Thatcher and her advisers were prepared to think the unthinkable. She and her government abandoned post-war consensus politics which, vis à vis the arts, meant the liberal if somewhat paternalistic conception of the arts as intrinsically a Good Thing for society that it is the duty of the State to protect by acting as guarantor of artistic freedom. Enshrined within this concept was the so-called arm's length principle, whereby the government devolved the actual funding and administration of the arts to quasi independent bodies such as the ACGB or the London Arts Board (LAB). Art education had similarly enjoyed a high degree of autonomy in the postwar period, as had the nationwide network of art schools that operated outside of both the secondary school and university sectors. However the setting up of NAB marked the jettisoning of the Pevsnerian doctrine that had obtained in art schools at least since the 1960s, according to which Fine Art was not only the foundation of all the visual arts but that their study represented the best kind of liberal education. Now all the talk was of the necessity to teach 'transferrable skills' that would be recognised in the job market. In effect, what Thatcher's government advocated was a return to the policy of design-linked-to-industry that lay behind the setting up of art colleges, or 'schools of design' as they had originally been designated, in Britain in the nineteenth century.[3] The Government's action was prompted not only by a deep-rooted conservative suspicion of art and art schools—and all who taught in them—but also by an overriding faith in business as the model of good practice (so-much-so that captains of industry and business moguls, such as Jocelyn Stevens, who became rector of the Royal College of Art, were foisted upon art institutions in an effort to 'knock them into shape', with disastrous consequences).

At the time I was a visiting lecturer at St Martin's School of Art, famous now chiefly for its fashion course but previously known primarily for its fine art courses—notably its Advanced Sculpture Course, once hailed by no less an authority than American critic Clement Greenberg, the most powerful critic of the day, as 'one of the prides of England'.[4] Despite the opposition of staff and students, St Martin's was eventually forced as a result of NAB's findings to merge with four other London art colleges to form the London Institute which today is fighting for university status in an effort to compete for the attentions of private sponsors who tend, it seems, to favour institutions with supposedly more academic credentials. Against such a background it was no wonder that, when drafting his report on the arts for the Arts Council, Myerscough sought to speak in a language that the Tory government—and more particularly the Treasury that regarded the arts as an economic black hole—would understand. However, the report cut no ice with the government and it was left to the opposition to seize upon it and to implement it when it came into office. Meanwhile, as a result of NAB's activities, Design and Media courses sprang up to replace or, in some cases, to disguise former Fine Art courses that dare not speak their name.[5]

That the new government had fully embraced the new terminology was signalled by the publication, barely one year after coming to power, of a smart little book titled *Creative Britain*, by the newly appointed Secretary of State for the arts, Chris Smith. (In one of those unhappy coincidences, given the role spin was to play in New Labour's first term of office, the brightly-coloured paper cover sported not one but two of Damien Hirst's circular 'spin paintings' respectively titled, *beautiful, all round, lovely day, big toys for big kids, Frank and Lorna, when we are no longer children*, 1998, on the front, and *beautiful snail crunching under the boot painting*, 1996, on the back.) Inside the book was replete with comparative tables for the projected Compound Annual Growth Rate of the respective industries, drawn up by the 'Creative Industries Task Force' in consultation with Spectrum Strategy Consultants, to make the case for regarding the visual arts as economically viable. In the

Summary Map of the Creative Industries, things looked good for the art industry which, at £3.8 billion compared favourably with the Fashion (£1 billion), Film (£3 billion) and Computer Games industries (£1.8 billion), though the picture would have looked a little less rosy had art not been linked to the antiques industry.[6] But whatever the new government might have intended to signal by its adoption of the term 'creative industries', this kind of language struck some observers as downright Stalinist. Others, such as John Tusa, director of the Barbican Arts Centre in London, merely saw it as symptomatic of the 'dumbing down' of the arts.

Whilst it is customary to refer to all aspects of movie-making collectively as 'the film industry', and to refer to the world of popular music as 'the music industry', extending the use of the term 'industry' to cover classical music and fine art was tantamount to reducing them to the same level. This, at least, was the view expressed by Tusa: 'At a certain stage the arts are creative in a different way", he stated, picking his words carefully, 'Critics of the creative industries are always branded elitists, but you have to stand up and say the arts are different.' All arts are equally creative but some are more creative than others, in effect. Tusa spelled out his concerns in his snappily titled book, *Art Matters*: 'I'm worried about the Prime Minister because he is signalling that Oasis is as important to Britain as opera; that chat shows are as important as novels; and that television soap operas are more valuable than live theatre.'[7] This was hardly the Camelot of the Kennedy era when Pablo Casals played at the White House, he might have said. In fact, there was a similar outcry when the Beatles were awarded MBEs under another Labour Prime Minister, Harold Wilson, in the 1960s—as much in recognition of their contribution to the Exchequer as to culture. Tusa's view can be seen as an extension of an ongoing debate that is probably as old as Modernism in the visual arts and that is generally referred to in art critical shorthand as the 'high/low' debate. It was most clearly articulated by Greenberg in his seminal essay, 'Avant-Garde and Kitsch', published in the *Partisan Review*, significantly in the year that war broke out in Europe in 1939.[8] Indeed, Tusa's language is strikingly similar to Greenberg's definition of 'kitsch': as 'popular, commercial art and literature with their chromeotypes, magazine covers, illustrations, ads, slick and pulp fiction, comics, Tin Pan Alley music, tap dancing, Hollywood movies, etc., etc.'[9] A former Marxist, Greenberg became a confirmed Modernist and an unabashed formalist (and *therefore* an elitist) precisely because it was a term of abuse equally in Stalin's contemporary Soviet Union and Hitler's National Socialist Germany. As Donald Kuspit famously argued, and Eva Cockcroft later demonstrated, Greenberg's promulgation of formalist aesthetics in opposition to Soviet Socialist Realism and Nazi art, on the one hand, and Regionalism, its US equivalent on the other, together with his later championship of Abstract Expressionism, chimed with Cold War rhetoric that pitted creative freedom and individualism in the US and the West against cultural repression and conformity in the USSR and the rest of the Eastern bloc.[10] To all intents and purposes, the state and the artistic community in the West appeared to be speaking the same language.

This apparent consensus came under pressure in the 1960s. The advent of Pop Art, with its apparent celebration of the kind of popular culture that was anathema to Greenberg and his followers (because the art failed to distinguish itself from other objects in the world, a Brillo box from an artwork, for instance), put the cat among the pigeons.[11] However, broadly speaking, for postmodernist critics the central issue was no longer the existence or otherwise of some quasi-metaphysical abstract quality, discernable only to an elite, that is intrinsic to art objects and that distinguishes them from mere objects. Of more pressing concern was the extent to which apparently extrinsic matters such as context and audience reception affected or even effected meaning in art. It was this characteristic of the new art—that it required an audience's direct engagement with it in order to exist in any meaningful sense—that Greenberg acolyte, Michael Fried, not only identified but notoriously stigmatized as 'theatrical'.[12] Art was getting down and dirty, reaching out to the people, as it were—apparently just like New Labour whose watchwords were to be 'accessibility', 'cultural diversity' and 'social inclusion'. This is not to suggest that the self-styled 'people's party' of government was taking a sophisticated postmodern stance vis à vis the relationship of the (visual) arts to society in general and to culture in particular. Rather it is to suggest that there was a similar coincidence of rhetoric, as had existed between the language of formalism and Cold War rhetoric in the USA, that New Labour was quick to seize upon and to apply in a way that caught most of the art world napping. New Labour's hostility to the arts took a different turn from that of the Tories under Margaret Thatcher, but it was no less hostile for that. Tusa was right to sound the alarm, but he did so in conventional, sub Greeenbergian 'elitist' terms that rather missed their mark: what was at stake was not whether Oasis is as important as opera but the very survival of art as a distinct kind of practice that creates a critical space like no other. Frederic Jameson had already drawn attention to the 'logic' of post-modernism which, in his view, should be imagined in terms of 'an explosion: a prodigious expansion of culture throughout the social realm, to the point at which everything in our social life—from economic value and state power to the very structure of the psyche itself—can be said to have become cultural in some original and yet untheorized sense.'[13] Government policy was to attempt nothing less than the absorption of art into culture and culture into politics. But I am getting ahead of myself.

In the first heady days of the New Labour government, it was a relief to me to hear the arts spoken of as if they no longer required special pleading but were part of a creative continuum that could contain widely differing practices and their different constituencies. At the same time such rhetoric also seemed to suggest a new perception of the possible role of the arts that chimed with what many of us who were actively involved in the arts actually wanted from the State, namely recognition of their social and economic as well as, for want of a better word, aesthetic value. According to this view, State funding represented an investment of the kind that governments make in other industries and that might include an equivalent to money for R&D—research and development—in the arts that had also been so neglected under the previous Conservative governments. (There were even some for whom the government's extension of the term 'Industry' to include the visual and other arts had a pleasing ring to it echoing as it does, albeit faintly, the utopian rhetoric of the early Russian Constructivists who, following the Revolution, saw an integrated role for the arts in the building of a new society). Even those who expressed reservations about the term 'industry' being applied to their art could see the advantages to them of the change in language in terms of making a case for continued funding. In the euphoria of the moment, and while still under the impression that the 'arm's length' principle was inviolable, no one was yet thinking about what in the long term the government might want in terms of a direct, as opposed to indirect, return on its investment.

There was another immediate change in rhetoric that seemed even more indicative of a fresh appreciation of the arts on the part of the new government: this was the banishment of the conservative—in every sense—word 'heritage' from the title of the ministry responsible for the arts (and tourism, which it took over from the Department of Trade and Industry [DTI], linking the two in an obviously strategic way) and its replacement by the European-sounding word 'culture'. Henceforth the ministry would be known as the Ministry of Culture, Media and Sport. Many of us in the art world, myself included, applauded the change, not least for its inclusiveness; the new ministry conjured up an image of the golden age of France's culture ministry under the glamorous Jack Lang. Whereas in Britain the arts brief is generally regarded by politicians as the equivalent of a posting to the Russian Front in the Second World War (and indeed few come back from such a posting with their career prospects enhanced), in France they take the arts more seriously. Not only had Lang been tipped for the post of prime minister under president Mitterand but when Pierre Beregovy pipped him for the post, he was given additional responsibility for education, a highly regarded office (indeed, France's former Prime Minister, Lionel Jospin, was a former Minister for Education). This would seem to confirm Deke Dusinberre's summarization of the relative attitudes to the arts of French and British governments in comparison also with American administrations: 'By and large, Britons vaunt their heritage, Americans advertise their moral rectitude, and the French flaunt their cultivation'. However, things seemed about to change since New Labour's Secretary of State for Culture, Media and Sport, Chris Smith, actually seemed to want the job. Though Dusinberre went on to warn that 'Eurocomparisons should be wielded with care, so that issues of substance can be disentangled from issues of symbolic import', in 1997, symbolism mattered as we in the arts tried to interpret the signals being sent out by the new Government.[14]

New Labour's enthusiasm for all things European and cultural, for instance, was further signalled by its hosting of the EU summit in London in 1997. Presumably to distance itself yet more from the 'heritage' tag so much associated with its predecessors, it eschewed traditional venues such as Chequers or Clarence House in favour of a modern, or rather postmodern one: Canary wharf located in London's Docklands. Bemused commentators, while grasping the message that was being sent out nevertheless wondered at the choice of venue, associated as it was with eighties greed and corruption (the developers, Olympia & York, a Canadian property company, had gone bust amid rumours of corruption concerning the role of media tycoon and Tory Party contributor, Conrad Black). Did this mean business as usual? Was the pro-European stance merely a pose? Already, to the disappointment of the arts and other sectors, the new government had elected to stay within the public spending limits set by the outgoing Tory administration and had gone out of its way during its election campaign to assure the city and the traditionally Tory-sympathizing Confederation of British Industry (CBI) of its business-friendly intentions. (This was one of the more practical outcomes of the New Labour government's much-vaunted Third Way or neo-social democratic philosophy launched in a semi-religious spirit of 'reconciliation'.)[15]

Arts commentators, however, were unsure whether to be gratified or amused by the somewhat last-minute decision to trick out the suite of rooms in the best of British contemporary art and design. There was a scramble among government advisers and commercial dealers, anxious to make the most of an unprecedented promotional opportunity, to pull together an exhibition featuring the work of so-called yBas, or young British artists, so named by Simon Ford after the series of chauvinistic exhibitions of 'Young British Artists', held between 1992 and 1995, at the private gallery of the collector and dealer Charles Saatchi (one half of the Saatchi & Saatchi advertizing company retained by the Tory Party and responsible for the notoriously damaging slogan 'Labour isn't working' during the 1979 election campaign won by Margaret Thatcher).[16] Word was sent out, for example, that a print of *The Great Bear*, Simon Patterson's 1992 reworking of the London tube map described by art pundit, Matthew Collings, as 'an icon of 90s art', was required for the conference room as soon as possible.[17] (The work has since been acquired for the government art collection and, at the time of writing, hangs in No.10.

The work was on view during a visit by the Chinese premier in 1998; he was presumably not made aware—assuming that anyone had previously noticed their presence—of the fact that the names of prominent Chinese dissidents, and members of the pro-democracy movement who took part in the Tiananmen Square demonstration, had been inserted on the 'Sinologues' line on that part of the Dockland Light Railway labelled 'under construction'. Tricky stuff, is this contemporary art.) While some took heart from the government's desire to embrace the new, others mocked their sudden conversion to contemporary art and saw behind it mere sloganizing: New art for New Labour. In the words of one commentator, the summit became 'shorthand for the government's entire arts policy: "anything modern and British".[18]

This episode represented the birth of the 'Cool Britannia' phase that presaged the government's full-scale attempt at rebranding Britain. Twenty-four-year-old wunderkind, Mark Leonard, of the Demos research group was charged with the task. Leonard, described in the *Sunday Times* as too young to have been 'contaminated' by Old Labour, had impeccable New Labour credentials: his father is a former Labour MP and member of the Fabian Society committee while he himself was brought up in Brussels, speaks three languages and is a fervent Europhile. In addition, according to Quentin Letts, he had other advantages from the government's point of view. Firstly, he was employed by an independent research group and not, therefore, funded by the taxpayer; secondly, not being an elected MP his opinions could not be directly attributed to the government. He was thus licensed to think and to advise the government accordingly.[19] The result was a report entitled, *Britain: Renewing our Identity* published in 1997, in which he identified 'five "stories" of British identity: a belief in Empire, great institutions, fair play, industrial might and the English language', all of which he declared officially dead. By implication he simultaneously consigned to the dustbin of history the Tory vision of Britain memorably evoked by John Major in his nostalgia for warm beer, cycling spinsters, and long evening shadows on the cricket pitch.

However, contrary to popular perception the slogan 'Cool Britannia' did not originate with 'the commissar of cool', nor did it emanate from New Labour's image-makers at Walworth Rd, a fact which the government has recently been at pains to point out—since, that is, the backlash against 'Cool Britannia'.[20] In fact, the slogan predated New Labour's electoral triumph by a year. It was invented by Sarah Moynihan-Williams, an American solicitor living in London, and was the winning entry in a competition to name a new flavour of ice cream for Ben & Jerry's. The prize was a free trip to America, coupons for 100 tubs of ice cream and the opportunity to ride a chariot around the Royal Albert Hall dragging a 10 feet inflatable ice cream tub for the launch of the new flavour.[21] This story is irresistible for a number of reasons, not least because it is symptomatic of the government's increasing reliance on image over content, of an administration that, in former Conservative leader William Hague's single most telling tilt against Blair, is 'all spin and no substance'. But it is also irresistible for its rich metaphorical resonance, particularly the fact that the slogan, like so much of New Labour policy that was to follow, originated from an American source.

It could almost be said that New Labour's appropriation of contemporary art and popular culture in the first months of its administration was sanctioned by American cultural commentators in the first place. First *Newsweek* and then *Vanity Fair* declared that Britain was again hip and that London, 'the world's coolest city', was 'swinging' once more.[22] Even before Noel Gallagher accepted the invitation to No.10, in fact in the month before New Labour's victory in the polls, his brother Liam had appeared on the cover of *Vanity Fair*, with his then wife Patsy Kensit, lying in bed and wrapped in the union flag with the banner: 'London Swings Again!' The 'again' clearly referred to the 1960s, when London first swung, while the special pull-out section represented Britain as a land of nobs, yobs and yBas, titled models, and bad boy pop stars. As with so many attempts to conjure up the spirit of the so-called 'Swinging 60s', this one failed to recognize the political realities and complexities both of the present and of the 1960s period—so brilliantly captured in Richard Hamilton's excoriating image *Swingeing London* in1967. This was equally, if not more the case, with the exhibition "Brilliant!" New Art from London', held at the Walker Art Center, Minneapolis, on 22 October 1995.[23] This American-curated exhibition was intended as a follow up to 'London: The New Scene', staged at the

Walker 30 years earlier in 1965. Inexplicably, at the private view extras got up as British Bobbies and Horse Guards in joke-shop costumes handed out Altoids™throat pastilles to the guests, presumably because they are considered by Americans to be typically British (and because the weather is so bad we always have colds). However, none of the British contingent had ever heard of them, which is not surprising because they are in fact manufactured in America. The hype surrounding the exhibition, and some of the texts in the accompanying 'fanzine' style catalogue (whose cover by Mat Collishaw comprised a black and white photograph of Bishopsgate in the City of London after the IRA bombing in 1996), shamelessly presented a stereotypical and unrepresentative view of the British, in particular the London, art scene. This clichéd view—one that has more to do with heritage than culture—is all too reminiscent of the conservative image of Britain and it is to New Labour's credit that it actively sought to update it. However, the implication that real change could be effected merely through rebranding by means of slogans and advertizing did not augur well. In time the slogan 'Cool Britannia' came to haunt the new government the way the reviled 'Back to basics' campaign had the old.

So much for spin, what of the substance of New Labour's policy towards the visual arts? The government seemed determined to hit the ground running and implement as many of its election promises—or pledges, in New Labour's preferred parlance—as possible. The first port of call for any incoming arts minister is the Arts Council. Under the Tories, the ACGB grant had been repeatedly slashed, culminating in a 7 per cent cut in real terms in 1994 that was to be followed by a further cut of 12 per cent over the following three years. In protest Everitt resigned as secretary general and, in a valedictory published in the *Guardian*, wrote 'The Arts Council of Great Britain's life is drawing peacefully to its close'.[24] In March of the same year the ACGB was indeed dismantled, as part of the most radical overhaul of the Council since its inception, and replaced by four devolved national Arts Councils in England (ACE), Northern Ireland, Scotland and Wales, while new Regional Arts Boards (RABs) were set up in England to cover London, the South East, South West, North East and North West respectively. Since Tory governments are not generally known to favour devolution of any kind, the suspicion was that these far-reaching changes were intended to reduce the Arts Council's central role with a view eventually to abolishing it and ultimately public funding for the arts altogether. The Arts Council has always had its critics on all sides: while the press and conservative critics constantly accused it of being elitist and of supporting worthless, wasteful, self-indulgent art, to those who depended upon it for all or some part of their funding it was often perceived as being bureaucratic, unwieldy, and timid. In the years leading up to the 1997 election, the Arts Council's efforts to appease its critics, both at central and local government level, led to new directives whereby grants to institutions were increasingly tied to highly laudable, socially relevant, practical issues such as the provision of disabled access or educational facilities, the provision of which many considered to be more properly the direct responsibility of local government. As it was, the need for art galleries and museums to service and staff these new facilities spread their ever-diminishing funds even more thinly. Nevertheless, it would still probably be true to say that few of the Arts Council's critics envisaged—much less advocated—its abolition. The reasons are partly historical: the Arts Council is one of those postwar institutions, like the NHS, that the British consider to be both sacrosanct and indelibly British. In fact, however, the Council for the Encouragement of Music and the Arts (CEMA), as it was originally known when it was set up 'to prevent cultural deprivation on the home front' in 1939, was not only modelled on President Roosevelt's Federal Arts Program of the Works Progress Administration, set up in response to the Depression, but was founded by the Board of Education with a grant by the American-based Pilgrim Trust.[25] After the war, its successor, the entirely publicly funded ACGB, was set up as part of the Welfare State: 'to develop and improve the knowledge, understanding and practice of the arts and to increase the accessibility of the arts to the public.'[26]

Ironically it was to be a Labour government, albeit a New Labour one, which was openly to abandon the cherished though much abused 'arm's length' principle—a principle that like so many dearly held British constitutional principles—was unwritten and therefore not ultimately binding. Initially the government signalled its intention by making the secretary general of the Arts Council a direct, as opposed to indirect, political appointment. Dubbed one of 'Tony's cronies' by the press, Gerry Robinson was a media tycoon who had little patience with the public sector and who correspondingly set about reforming ACE immediately. Again ironically, given that New Labour was in favour of (limited) devolution for Scotland and Wales, this involved re-centralizing its organization, wresting power away from the regions (a process still underway). Anyone who thought that public funding for the arts would be significantly increased and that the era of private and corporate sponsorship of the arts was effectively over was also soon disabused of such misconceptions. Even before the Government made public its commitment to all the 'Ps' of privatization, as in Private Finance Initiatives (PFIs) and Public/Private Partnerships (PPPs), it was clear that once again, New Labour was building upon rather than dismantling previous Tory initiatives. In 1984, inspired by American models such as the Business Committee for the Arts (BCA), the Tories had set up the Business Sponsorship Incentive Scheme (BSIS) administered by the Association of Business Sponsorship in the Arts (ABSA). The idea was that grants to Arts Council clients would henceforth be contingent upon their ability to secure 'matching funding' by entering into sponsorship partnerships with the private sector; BSIS's task was to match clients with potential sponsors and to encourage business to participate in such schemes—hence the forest of logos that was to spring up around every artistic venture in the following years.[27] The process of blurring the boundaries between the public and private sectors had begun in earnest. As Chin-tao Wu has pointed out in her major new study of corporate art sponsorship in the 1980s, the relations between public policy and business sponsorship in Britain became so close that, 'in 1991 the [then] director of the Association of Business Sponsorship of the Arts (ABSA), Colin Tweedy, went so far as to suggest that arts sponsorship was one of the cornerstones of Thatcherism.'[28] This was despite the fact that things got off to a bad start when the inaugural director of ABSA, Nicholas Wood, was found to be rather less accountable than the good old Arts Council. He was indicted, and later convicted, for fraud and sentenced to 18 months imprisonment in 1994. Nevertheless, the Tory government remained committed to its policy of weaning the arts off public subsidy and pursued American models with renewed zeal. Unfortunately, public art institutions in Britain were ill prepared to tackle the private sector, BSIS and ABSA notwithstanding. Neither the tax incentives available in the USA nor the infrastructure were in place to fill the hole left by cuts in public funding. This remains the case under New Labour: comparison with the fundraising capacity of the Metropolitan Museum New York, for instance—which in 2001 employed some forty fundraisers as compared with Tates Britain, Modern, Liverpool and St Ives which in the same year collectively employed some 15 fundraisers—reveals the glaring disparity between them.[29] In addition, there is not the collector base for contemporary art here nor a tradition of patronage of new art such as exists in the USA or Germany—Charles Saatchi being the notable and highly problematic exception.[30] The competition to attract business and corporate sponsorship has begun to drive curatorial policy in ways that bring evermore diminishing artistic or creative returns. It is no secret that sponsors want exposure and that means attracting the mainstream media; this often requires that the art and/or the artist(s) be headline-grabbing or at least media-friendly which, in turn, attracts further sponsorship.

In the light of this unequal situation, the mind boggles at the thought of the resources, in terms of time and effort, deployed to raise the money for Tate Liverpool's first Biennale which took several years to plan and finally took place in 1999. A list of the sponsors involved gives some idea:

In the press material, the twenty-six sponsors were divided into two groups:

thirteen national sponsors, subdivided into:

Principal Sponsors and Supporters:

Bloomberg News

followed by, in alphabetical order with logos:

Afoundation
The Arts Council of England
Citibell Network Partner
The City of Liverpool Leisure Services Directorate
Foundation for Sport and the Arts
The Granada Foundation

Jupiter
Littlewoods, the Littlewoods Organisation plc
Liverpool Hope University College
Northwest Arts Board
PH Holt Charitable Trust
Tate Liverpool
Walton Group plc

Thirteen (main) international sponsors, listed without logos (alphabetical by country):

Australia Council for the Arts
Arts Victoria, Australia
International Cultural Relations, Department of Foreign Affairs and International Trade of Canada
Canadian High Commission UK
The Danish Contemporary Art Foundation
AFAA (Association Française d'Action Artistique), Ministère des Affaires Etrangères, France
Ifa (Institut für Auslandsbeziehungen), Germany
The Cultural Relations Committee of Ireland
Conaculta Fonca INBA, Mexico
Fomento Cultural Banamex AC, Mexico
SRE (Secreteria De Relaciones Exteriores), Mexico
Pro Helvetia
The Arts Council of Switzerland

Notably omitted is any mention of the National Lottery, and for good reason since access to lottery money for the arts was limited to capital projects—which translated meant bricks and mortar—rather than much-needed revenue funding or funding for other more controversial and short-term projects such as exhibitions or biennales, the argument being that the use of public money in these instances could not be justified on economic or moral grounds. The introduction of the National Lottery by the Tories in 1994 constitutes the single most significant change in the funding structure of the arts in Britain since the setting up of the Arts Council more than fifty years earlier. It became the Arts Council's primary role to select and administer applications to the Lottery for funding, and ultimately to allocate money to successful applicants.[31] However, governments of whatever complexion suffer from an edifice complex, that is a preference for permanent buildings and monuments by way of a lasting legacy. As a result Britain is now studded with new or refurbished museums and galleries—the most high profile being the behemoth of Bankside, Tate Modern[32]—which their directors cannot afford to run, let alone programme. Since Tate, like the majority of public museums and galleries in Britain, has no significant endowment from which it can draw funds, it cannot purchase significant works for the nation either, one of its reasons for being. Since New Labour, there has been some adjustment to the terms under which institutions may apply for lottery grants but they have been at the cost of those institutions surrendering yet more of their autonomy to the government through its representative bodies such as ACE and regional arts boards such as LAB, recently restyled as London Arts (LA).

And here we come to the crunch: the arts, including the visual arts, were about to experience the state arguably more directly than at any time since the war. Whereas the Tories merely wished to shuffle off responsibility for the arts to the private sector, showing little or no interest in the visual arts in terms of form or content, New Labour was to take an altogether more hands-on approach, the implications of which are only now becoming apparent. We were warned, however. All the signs were there, in apparently benign form, in Chris Smith's vision of 'Creative Britain'. Citing Max Hastings, journalist and former editor of the conservative *Daily Telegraph* and then of the equally conservative London *Evening Standard*, who had written, 'Labour Governments, and especially this Labour Government, are expected to show a sympathy for the arts, an instinctive sensitivity to the vital cause of seeing the largest number of people see the greatest possible number of films, plays, operas, great pictures and great museums', Chris Smith commented smugly: 'Quite so. I could hardly have put it more eloquently myself. The thing that frankly baffles me is how on earth anyone ever developed the misguided idea that we might conceivably have abandoned such a basic tenet of faith.'[33] Baffling indeed, although in the old days it was regarded as an ideological issue rather than as a 'tenet of faith'. Be that as it may, initially Smith's insistence that 'Cultural experience must . . . be available to the many and not just to the few',[34] and his emphasis on 'accessibility' did not cause undue alarm, echoing as it did the Arts Council's original mandate 'to develop and improve the knowledge, understanding and practice of the arts and to increase the accessibility of the arts to the public.' Who could quarrel with such a manifestly equitable policy?

Many interpreted Smith's apparent reiteration of this mantra in the most obvious sense to mean that New Labour was utterly committed to free entry/access for all to all public museums and galleries. If public money, via the National Lottery, was to continue to be used to build or extend public museums and galleries then clearly it must be the duty of any government to ensure that the public has free access to those same institutions. For many, this was axiomatic. However, not only did this turn out to be a somewhat simplistic view of government policy, but it also turned out to be one that Smith, as Culture Secretary, had difficulty persuading the Treasury to enable him to deliver, despite extensive lobbying from, among others, Sir Nicholas Serota, director of Tate. In any case, it soon became clear that the government intended to apply the notion of accessibility in a far more instrumental sense by making grants conditional not only on institutions achieving matching funding, as successive Tory governments had required, but on their commitment to and achievement of greater accessibility. But what did the government mean by 'accessibility'? If it meant that art itself must be accessible to the many and not only to the few, then how could or should this be achieved? One way would be to curate popular art shows, but what makes for a 'popular' exhibition and how might that popularity be measured? The other way would be to attract new audiences to art and, sure enough, the government launched another new initiative entitled 'New Audiences for Art', which offered additional funding to organizations which could demonstrate their success in creating such new audiences, thereby putting the government's wider policies of 'social inclusion'— code for reaching poorer communities and ethnic minorities—and urban regeneration into practice. The problem still remained, however: how could such success be demonstrated? The one sure way is to point to the amount of media coverage and to the numbers of people attending shows— the 'bums on seats' argument—but first you have to attract those new audiences, and one way of doing that is to mount popular—or populist—shows. Thus the argument became somewhat circular. It may be the fault of museum and gallery directors and curators that government policy in the arts, as enacted through its various representative bodies, has been interpreted so narrowly and, it must be said, so fearfully. But when both private and public funding for the arts comes with so many strings attached, it is hardly surprising that the public art sector lost its nerve.

The aim of reaching new audiences for art, including the socially excluded, is not only a practical policy but ideologically and in every way a highly desirable one. However, building up audiences must be a long term, ongoing process that can only work if it is part of a wider government social, economic, and educational policy. (If art requires an audience's direct engagement with it in order to exist in any meaningful sense then those audiences must be empowered by both education and opportunity to do so. We surely do not want a return to the nineteenth century paternalistism that held that mere exposure to the arts was somehow 'good for you'; the arts cannot provide a panacea for social ills.) Such a policy needs to be funded, and sponsorship is not the answer because sponsors want quick returns. As it is, the public museum and gallery sector is being used to drive social change by a government that is abrogating its own responsibilities. Now, in addition to trying to attract private sponsorship, museums and galleries are under increasing government pressure to fulfill various and ever more onerous criteria in order to qualify for public funding. Not surprisingly, this leads to a certain degree of schizophrenia within the public sector. In reality, however, it is the smaller or more regional public institutions that are more subject to government directives since they cannot compete with the larger institutions for private sponsorship. The government thus has it both ways: the perceived success of high profile institutions such as Tate Modern—which can attract sponsors—appears to testify to New Labour's 'sympathy for the arts', while smaller, more dependent galleries, especially in the regions, must do the government's bidding. Here, the regional arts boards hold sway, none more so than the LAB/LA, whose cultural commissars have taken the government's obsession with focus groups to new levels of absurdity. Take this section, headed, 'Your Opinion', from the *Visual*

Arts Assessment Form 2001, a confidential report filled out by anonymous LAB appointed Assessors: 'How successful did you think the event was? Did you enjoy this show, would you encourage other people to go? What was good or exciting/weak or poor? With reference to presentation/context/form of the event, how did it compare with other work you have seen? Did you find anything that pleased, angered, inspired, amused, challenged or frustrated you? Did the event raise any issue of which you feel the Board should be aware? Do you have recommendations or suggestions that might be put to the organisation/artist or LAB? Was it possible to gauge how the audience or presenter felt about the event? Did you agree with their views? Was a particular audience being targeted for this show? Did it succeed in attracting that audience?'[35] The implied threat in the question, 'Did the event raise any issue of which you feel the Board should be aware?' is obvious to anyone reading it. Less obvious, however, is the underlying threat contained in the reference to the target audience. This is code for a form of social engineering, whereby poorly-funded public galleries, many of them in deprived areas with large ethnic minorities ('culturally diverse' in New Labourspeak), are being used to apply a quick cultural fix in place of real political solutions to real social problems. At the same time the idea of art as a distinct kind of practice that occupies a critical—critical in every sense—let alone a creative or aesthetic space, is being eroded. This is what I meant by this government's radical agenda that seeks not only to absorb art into culture, but culture into politics. The ultimate effect of this aestheticisation of politics is the erosion of real democracy in favour of its image, all spin, no substance.

*With apologies to MOCA, Los Angeles from whose exhibition, 'A Forest of Signs', the title is derived.

NOTES

1. Tony Blair quoted on the front page of the *Evening Standard*, 2 May 1997.
2. For instance, as a result of NAB's activities, Camberwell School of Art's Fine Art department was closed and five other colleges were merged into the London institute comprising the former St Martin's School of Art, Central School of Art and Design, The London College of Printing, the London College of Fashion and Chelsea School of Art.

3. Unlike the Royal Academy that was set up in the eighteenth century under royal patronage, most art schools in London, such as the South Kensington School of Design—now the Royal College of Art—had been set up in the 19th Century originally as schools of design for the training of artisans to design products for industry. Almost from the first, staff and students fought for the status of schools of fine Art and most eventually succeeded. Many, like St Martin's School of Art, (which was merged with The Central school of Art, Chelsea School of Art, The London College of Fashion, and The London College of Printing to form the London institute), or Hornsey School of Art, now part of Middlesex university, have since been subsumed into larger merged institutes or into the new universities, an initiative again begun under the Tories. See Patricia Bickers, 'The Curse of Academe', in *Research and the Artist: Considering the Role of the Art School*, Antonia Payne, (ed.), (The Ruskin School of Drawing and Fine Art, the University of Oxford, 2000), pp. 50–7 and Quentin Bell, *The Schools of Design, London*, 1963; Christopher Frayling, *The Royal College of Art: One Hundred & Fifty Years of Art & Design* (London: Barrie & Jenkins, 1987). See also Stuart Macdonald, *The History and Philosophy of Art Education* (London: University of London Press, 1970).

4. Greenberg, in a letter dated February 1964 in support of the course that was threatened with closure at the time. Cited by Charles Harrison, 'Sculptures's Recent Past', in *A Quiet Revolution: British Sculpture Since 1965* (London: Thames & Hudson, 1987), p. 30, n. 30.

5. In time, these were to be replaced, at least in my own present institution, the University of Westminster, formerly the Polytechnic of Central London—whose management is ever ready to comply with government directives—by different courses under the rubric of Communication and Creative Industries, in conformity with New Labourspeak.

6. Chris Smith, *Creative Britain* (London: Faber & Faber, 1998), *Appendix*.

7. John Tusa responding to Melvyn Bragg's review of his book, *Art Matters*, quoted by Stephen Moss in, '"Is Melvin taking the side of the arts or is he a government spokesman?"—John Tusa, the *Guardian*, 29 May 1999. 'Melvin' refers to Melvin Bragg, presenter of 'The South Bank Show', novelist and all-round media pundit who was created Lord Bragg and appointed the government's arts spokesman in the House of Lords.

8. 'High and Low: Modern Art and Popular Culture', the Museum of Modern Art, New York, October 7–January 15, 1991. An accompanying book was published entitled, *Modern Art and Popular Culture: Reading in High and Low*, MOMA and Harry N. Abrams, 1990. See review by John T. Paoletti in *Art Monthly*, No. 141, November, 1990, pp. 3–4.

9. Clement Greenberg, 'Avant-Garde and kitsch', *Partisan Review*, vol. vi, no. 5, (Fall) 1939, pp. 34–49, reprinted in F. Frascina (ed.), *Pollock and After: The Critical Debate* (Harper & Row, 1985), pp. 21–34.

10. Max Kosloff, 'American painting During the Cold War', *Artforum*, vol. 11, no. 9, (May) 1973, pp. 43–54 (the essay appeared first in the catalogue introduction for the exhibition, 'Twenty-five Years of American Painting', Des Moines Art Center, 1973); Eva Cockcroft, 'Abstract Expressionism: Weapon of the Cold War', *Artforum*, vol. 12, no. 10, (June) 1974, pp. 39–41.

11. By 1991, when Kirk Varnedoe and Adam Gopnik curated the exhibition of Pop Art, 'High and Low', at the Museum of Modern Art, New York, its critics perceived its agenda to be a reactionary one; while apparently celebrating popular culture, the show in fact represented a last ditch attempt to differentiate Pop Art, in its turn, from popular culture in general and thus to secure its position as 'high' art in the hierarchical Modernist sense.

12. Michael Fried,' Art and Objecthood', *Artforum*, vol. 5, no.10, (June) 1967, pp. 12–23.

13. Frederic Jameson, 'The Cultural Logic of Late Capitalism', from Chapter 1 of *Postmodernism, Or, The Cultural Logic of Late Capitalism* (Durham: Duke University Press, 1991), pp. 32–8, 41–5, 54. Reprinted in Cahoone, Lawrence (ed.), *From Modernism to Postmodernism: An Anthology*, (Blackwell, 1995), pp. 556–72.

14. 'Sticky comparisons?', *Art Monthly*, no.158, (July–August) 1992, pp. 2–5.

15. The Government's intentions have been made good, it seems: a global survey published by Management Today in July 2001, revealed that British chief executives take home an average of £100,000 more than their counterparts in the rest of Europe. One of the beneficiaries at the time of publication was Dianne Thompson, chief executive of Camelot, the company that runs the national Lottery, who was awarded £600,000 in bonuses on July 26, despite declining ticket sales and therefore of revenue. See 'Onwards and upwards: the corporate gravy train has no brakes', the *Guardian* Comment, 27 July 2001. More on the Lottery later.

16. Of which more later. The term 'yBa', first coined by Simon Ford in the pages of *Art Monthly* in 1996, derived from the series of exhibitions of Young British Artists held at the Saatchi Gallery in London between 1992 and 1995 caught on fast. Simon Ford, 'Mythmaking', *Art Monthly*, no. 194, 1996, pp. 3–9.

17. Source: Lisson Gallery, London which represents the artist; Matthew Collings described the work as 'an icon of 90s art in, 'A Guide to Invisible London', the *Independent on Sunday*, 25 September 1994, pp. 32–3.

18. Andy Beckett, 'The myth of the Cool', *The Guardian G2*, 5 May 1998, pp. 2-3.

19. Quentin Letts, interview with Mark Leonard, 'A Mark of Youth', the *Independent on Sunday*, 29 November 1998, p. 13.

20. 'He gave us Cool Britannia and thinks that Prince William should go to the local comp…', ibid.

21. Beckett, 'Myth of the Cool'.
22. *Newsweek*, November 1996; *Vanity Fair*, March 1997.
23. Curated by Richard Flood, '"Brilliant!" New Art from London', was at the Walker Art Center from 22 October–7 January 1996. Arguably, this exhibition set the agenda for successive exhibitions both at home and abroad. I attempted to trace the origins of this constructed, stereotypical view in *The Brit Pack: Contemporary Art from Britain, the View from Abroad*, revised and extended in 'As Others See us: Towards a History of Recent Art from Britain', in *Pictura* Britannica, Museum of Contemporary Art, Sydney, 1997, pp. 65–89.
24. Anthony Everitt, 'Why I Resigned', the *Guardian*, 18 February 1994.
25. Chin-tao Wu, *Privatising Culture: Corporate Art Intervention Since the 1980s* (London: Verso), 2002, pp. 33–4.
26. In 1942 the Trust withdrew money and the new chair, John Maynard-Keynes, according to Wu, concentrated on the 'Best' as opposed to the 'Most' This was succeeded by ACGB, in 1946. Ibid.
27. Ibid., pp. 6, 12.
28. Ibid., Introduction, p. 3. (Taken from Colin Tweedy, 'Sponsorship of the Arts – An Outdated Fashion or the Model of the Future?' *Museum Management and Curatorship*, vol. 10, June 1991, p. 161.) See also p. 81 on the relationship between the BSIS and ABSA and of both with the Thatcher Government and the further blurring of distinctions between the private and the public spheres. Since 1999 ABSA has been known as Arts and Business, ibid., p. 322 n.115.
29. F.T. McCarthy, *The Economist*, 21 April 2001.
    Indeed, Labour took on Tory attitudes to corporate sponsorship of the arts so wholeheartedly, that in *Creative Britain*, Chris Smith trumpets the activities of ABSA celebrating the fact that business donations to the arts in 1997 were at an 'all-time high', totalling some £97m, as compared with £10m 20 years ago (p. 31).
30. See 'Sense and Sensation', *Art Monthly*, no. 211, (November) 1997, pp. 1–10. (Republished in, *Magazyn Sztuki*, no. 18, (February) 1998, pp. 93–101. Also reprinted *Art Planet*, Journal of the Association Internationale des Critiques d'Art, AICA Press, vol.1, 1999, pp. 14–21.)
31. The original frontrunner—indeed the 7–2 favourite—to run the National Lottery was Richard Branson's Lottery Foundation which promised that all profits would be returned to the community. A poll conducted by the National Opinion Poll (NOP) at the time revealed that 72 per cent of the public wanted all profits to go to good causes and that 64 per cent would be more likely to play the game if that were the case (*AM* Editorial No.174, March 1994, p. 22). Peter Davis, Director of Oflot (which regulated the working of the National Lottery) plumped for the 9 - 2 outsider, Camelot, a consortium whose backers included major corporations such as Cadbury

Schweppes, De LA Rue, ICL, Racal and G-Tech (the latter bringing with it American know-how in running lottery schemes) and whose board included the ex-Metropolitan Police Commissioner, presumably there to ensure fair play. Branson's Foundation, on the other hand, while it included on its board arch Tories such as Lord Young, former Trade Minister under Margaret Thatcher, and her champion in the Lords, William Whitelaw, also included the unimpeachable Labour peer, Lord Tonypandy, a former Chairman of the Trades Union Council (TUC), a gesture towards 'reconciliation' that prefigured Tony Blair's 'third way'.

32. Tate Modern was built, or rather re-built, with the support of The Arts Council of England with National Lottery Funds, The Millennium Commission, English Partnerships, Southwark Council, as well as numerous individuals and Trusts, while the launch in 2000 was funded by the Tate 2000 association with British Telecom (BT), supported by *The Guardian* and the *Observer* newspapers, the ubiquitous *Bloomberg News*; Unilever and BP Amoco.

33. Smith, Creative Britain, p. 49.

34. Ibid., p. 39.

35. Other questions included under the section 'Details of Exhibition or Event': 'Was the project successfully communicated? Did you understand the aim of the exhibition? To what standard was the exhibition presented? Could it have been improved? In what way did you find it interesting or not? Who were the artists involved? What artform/materials/equipment was used? Did you think the show demonstrated a development for the artists/ the artform?' This is followed by a section headed 'Interpretative Material' which asks: 'Was there suitable information on the artistic content of the event? i.e., leaflet, text panels, catalogue, other. Was someone available to answer questions? Were they well informed? Was there a chance to participate in any events or talks or seminars? If so did it enhance your experience of the event/exhibition?'.

EMANCIPATORY RESISTANCE

11

Gandhi's Trial and India's Colonial State

SUDIPTA KAVIRAJ

The purpose of this essay is not to throw any more historical light on Gandhi's famous trial after the Non-Cooperation movement was called off following the incident at Chauri Chaura. There are several historical studies of what happened which provide detailed accounts of Gandhi's behaviour at the trial and the legal moves of the prosecution. I wish to pay greater attention to the element of rhetoric, not the statement but the manner in which the statement is made, the elements of drama or theatre in the contest between the colonial state and the most celebrated rebel it encountered in India. A reconstruction of Gandhi's trial would also show us how an historical event is literally 'created' through the deliberate, often opposed, strategies of the actors, their partial fulfilment and frustration, unintended consequences and how as time goes on, it is constituted by the play of historical and subhistorical/mythical memory.

A trial has an astonishing capacity to condense and sum up the relations of the whole political world. Trials bring together those who hold and exercise formal power and those who do not, but seek to organize other elements in society to create an alternative basis of power of their own. Trials are spectacles of power and thus bring to representation not only the material, violent, tangible aspects of political power, but also its ideal, symbolic, and representational forms. These are events in which all sides conspire as it were to make an exhibition of themselves; this is because they are making studied, deliberate statements about themselves and what they stand for. However, despite the inevitable element of spectacle, these are not mock battles but real ones in which the fates of individuals and institutions are sometimes determined with irreversible finality. Thus, under pressure, often the pretences fall away and the real relations of the intricate world of politics show themselves through the fractures of the spectacle itself.

Descriptions of historical events, like any other social fact, depend on discursive and narrative strategies. Various sides to the conflict of the trial come with ideas about what they want this coming event to be. Political trials are, however, peculiar in one respect. Unlike common political events, which are brought into being by inadequately prepared action of contesting sides so that control of events is partly a result of adeptness in responding to surprise, political trials are exceptionally deliberate occurrences. Since they are fixed, anticipated and therefore deliberate—that is, the actors know that a trial is coming, when it will come, and can plan for it in a way which is usually unavailable for other political acts—they usually bring to these particularly well-defined narrativistic strategies.

Human acts are narrativistic in a double sense. Some events are such that stories can be told about them, they are eminently narratable incidents in the lives of concerned individuals and groups. But this sets up an external relation between events that make up human lives and the stories that are told about them. Narratives, it may be thought, are *later* facts, dependent upon the structure of events of which they constitute the stories. But in some cases it appears necessary to look at the relation between narratives and acts in a different way. Because they know stories are narratives told about lives, human beings give their lives a storylike form, living up to various narrativistic standards. Narratives do not relate to lives secondarily, narrativity determines the lives that people live.

Gandhi lived the most narratable of modern human lives in India—the most storylike, susceptible to exaggeration and gossip, to embroidery, to mythmaking. It is capable, in the exaggerating imagination of ordinary people, of touching the edges of the superhuman. Or at least as close as one can come to that in our fallen and regrettably disenchanted age. Of the various forms of narrative, the one that is most adequate for the intensity, condensation, and clarity of punctuation in political life is the dramatic form. This is reflected in our common language; we do not say a political event read or was like a short story or the modern novel, but like a drama. The drama is the most formally adequate to the depiction and, I would suggest, the enactment of the large political acts like trials of leading dissenters. These usually have a clearly understood and designated audience, a theatrical space marked off from the ordinary, insubstantial, unsymbolic space of everyday life. They also generate the intense concentration of expectation and often the enlargement of gestures that drama consists of.

Often a great political event like this is prepared for in advance and reveals the ideological representations of power. The British colonial state had a strongly rationalistic image of itself, and liked to maintain an image of a clockwork world of history, pretending complete mastery of the world including the time and rhythm in which it prosecuted everything. A trial therefore is prearranged, part of an unhurried rationalistic ordering of time which shows both its scruples and its power. Given its ideological image of itself it could not send an assassin to finish off Gandhi stealthily at night. It had to bring him to justice.

The structure of the rationalistic legal regime provides the rebel with two great assets. First it provides him with the opportunity of a spectacle which, however tilted in favour of the state from the start, however unequal, gives him a chance to utilize its implicit and ineradicable dialogic character. The trial is an opportunity for the state to accuse but it is also—inextricably—one for the rebel to answer back. And Indians who opposed the colonial state all implicitly acknowledged this aspect of the legal process. Communists in Kanpur and especially those involved in the Meerut conspiracy cases, revolutionary terrorists during their trials always tried to turn the legal process into an argument between the state and themselves, and to turn the rationalistic format of the legal trial to their advantage.

Like a drama enacted in a theatre, political trials also have audiences which are often clearly designated, and the meaning of the trial as an historical event, at the first level, would be interpreted and read quite differently by the different circles of its viewers. There was, however, something in common, a certain element of overlap between the meanings that they would make of this incident, which would constitute its eventual historical significance. At least three audiences watched Gandhi's trial and tried to fit this new event into the narrative of the history of British colonial rule they had already constructed. Its first audience was British—the administrators and civilians who constituted the colonial regime in India; but behind them stood the larger audience of the British political public with its internal complex layers and structures, of class, access to power, degrees of politicization, and interest in colonial happenings in India.

One important part of Gandhi's rhetorical strategy was his attention to this audience; every single act of his contained an implicit gesture, a reference, an interpretation of itself directed to this audience. Gandhi was a particularly skilful observer of the structures of feeling and affect in British culture, and appealed with rare effect to prevailing notions of 'justice' publicity, fair play in the judicial process. More narrow-minded nationalists often did not understand the historical need for this dimension of Gandhi's acts, why they had to send an unambiguous message to the British public. They thought, sometimes, that this acknowledgment of their historical presence looked very much like an unnecessary deference towards colonial rulers.

Besides the British audience, Gandhi's other predominant audience was the Indian middle class educated elite, an audience which was equally diverse and layered. At one level, this audience included those who had prospered under colonial rule, particularly the professional classes whose scarce skills were remunerated excessively by the emerging structure of modern professions. Their political caution, and their understandable watchfulness about the possibility that the defeat of the British might insidiously translate itself into their dispossession, was reinforced by the caution of the bourgeoisie which supported the Congress. At lower levels of prosperity, this audience, however, also included the voluble, excitable, petty bourgeoisie who already had been mobilized into anti-colonial forms of political action in various ways; terrorism in Bengal, Tilak's extremism, and the stirrings by this time of more a straightforward socialist ideology among the urban lower middle classes. They shared the advantages of culture and articulateness with the upper classes of colonial society, and the degradation of economic and political powerlessness with the poor.

But Gandhi's exceptionalism lay in drawing into politics the masses of the poor, illiterate peasantry, by an extension of its meaningfulness towards them. He had to accomplish that in a society which was in a peculiar historical state. I have argued elsewhere that the cultural peculiarity of colonial India was that, unlike most other societies which, despite their cultural inequalities, function around a core of common sense shared across the cultural hierarchies, it gradually developed two distinct circles of common sense which interpreted most significant things in the social world in radically different ways.

For the western educated middle class, often speaking, when discussing grave and complex things like their politics or their collective historical possibilities in English, the world was a realm of causal and instrumental action. Politics, particularly, was a field of instrumental acts dealing with modern forms of entirely secularized power. It was the domain of calculations, moves, and countermoves, of the instrumental use of the resources of order and disorder at one's command. Peasant groups did not share this entirely secularized, profane, disabused view of political rationality. To them, the world was not a realm of causality alone but also of meaningfulness in everything, thus, even causally efficient acts contained an ineradicable aura of mysteriousness of something larger, of the world's inscrutable design expressed through the small and finite acts of ordinary people.

In this discourse, the language of power was inextricably linked to the language of saintliness. The peasantry are so convinced of the instrumental intractability of the power of established regime, and the ineffectuality of frontal disobedience, that successful defence seems to them always as a miracle. Since defiance against the constituted power of the state, particularly the awesome power of the British colonial state, was itself a miracle, it is not surprising that this fundamentally true sense of the miraculous was embroidered by stories of Gandhi's literally supernatural powers of invincibility. Gandhi's exceptionality consisted in executing his political acts in a way that made sense, albeit, in very different ways, to both these conflicting 'rationalities', being interpretable to both these ways of making sense of the ontology of the political universe.

In every society, social transactions use various types of communicative systems; words and discursive practices are only a small part of them in illiterate societies. Let us call this entire set of communicative techniques a semiotic register. It is structured like a register with communicative forms stretching from bodily gestures, symbolism of clothing and dress, the use of food as language, to the level of words which is divided again into two elementary strata of the spoken and the written. We must consider the ambiguity of the status of the written word particularly because of our natural preference toward its qualities of transparency, fixity, and clarity.

To the illiterate, however, the realm of the written word has just the opposite characteristics of obscurity, falsity, and unreliability; because, above everything else, it was through the written word that the moneylenders and the functionaries of the state imposed incomprehensible and unjust demands on them. It can thus be argued that to those without modern education, the hierarchy of the semiotic register would be the reverse of what it would naturally appear to the educated. The educated would rely, in their most serious transactions, on exchanges of the written word. They would not merely prosecute the action in words, as it happens predominantly in court proceedings, but the activity of interpretation of that single incident, the more complex and fluid business of framing it in credible narratives is also primarily done in words. It is not accidental that the prosecution of politics, as the struggle between the colonial state and the nationalists grew more intense, became increasingly a battle of words, giving increasing advantage to those who could use the written word with great effect.

Gandhi's use of rhetoric is exceptional, I would argue, precisely because he did not, unlike other middle class politicians, abandon the rhetorical resources of the other parts of the semiotic register of Indian peasant society. Dress, language, posture, food, forms of greeting were all laden with meaning, full of rhetorical possibilities. And although Gandhi was a shrewd and prolific user of the discursive in both its written and spoken forms, his success with the larger peasant audience depended, I suspect, on his use of other strata of the semiotic register. It is not that the peasantry was an already constituted audience to which he contrived to appeal by these means; rather, through politics and defiance in the non-discursive language of common peasants, he made the formerly meaningless written exchanges between the Congress and the state, reported in incomprehensible newspapers, meaningful to them and constituted them into an audience.

The trial was an anticipated event, everybody knew when it was going to take place. Thus it gave everybody, all parts of its complex audience, time to fashion their preparatory narrative frames. For the three segments of the audience, it was variously judicial proceedings which would bring the irritatingly difficult rebel to a proper trial, a contest of will and politico-legal skill between the nationalist movement and the colonial state, and a test of the saintliness or the miraculous power of Gandhi. Each side prepared a narrative frame in which the event, before it had even begun, was to be interpreted and fitted into the rest of the narrative structure of historical reality.

For both sides the trial was not just what it was, an everyday courtroom case, but was fated to be metaphorically enhanced. Both sides wanted to show the limits of the possibilities of the political world; for Gandhi it was to show the possibility of transgression of colonial political rules, for the authorities, it was to show that some limits laid down by the law and upheld by the power of the state were not meant to be crossed without severe penalties. It was not the trial of a single man and the decision of a single judge. The entire political world in its central contradiction of the colonial power and political rebellion was condensed into that single theatre.

Gandhi's trial was however more complex than a normal drama, which has a fixed text before it is played. This was more like a historical fact in waiting. Everyone knew that this space in time would be filled by a fact of great historical consequence, but what kind of fact it would be was still indeterminate. In one respect, the political trial is more like a game played between players than a drama in which the roles are predetermined and fixed. Or to continue with the idea of writing, the manner of acting in a political trial is one in which the drama is written and cited at the same time. Both sides come to a political trial with a script for it and the actual event is a contest between the two scripts as the event unfolds.

Gandhi was adept at British law not only in the legality of the judicial process but, what is less often appreciated, also in its theatre. A trial is irreducibly an act of power, despite legal efforts at maintaining formal impartiality. Formally, the jurisprudential system takes a great deal of trouble to ensure against explicit prejudice, that is to see that cases were not prejudged, a principle entirely consistent with the philosophical principles underlying modern citizenship. But in the colonial context, especially in trials like Gandhi's, it is impossible to avoid some subtle prejudgements. It is only the power of the state which can bring somebody to justice. The language of the court proceedings is therefore, not surprisingly, highly unequal.

In legal terms, the accused, is not yet guilty, not even a person against whom there already exists a strong presumption of guilt. He is merely someone against whom a charge has been preferred. In civil cases between individuals who are parties to a conflict, this impartiality can of course be maintained. But a trial like Gandhi's immediately altered this structure of the legal transaction. So language does not give the accused the opportunity that the law in a strict sense does. The entire language of the trial is structured against the accused. The accused must speak to defend himself, which means he must speak after the others. This also condemns him to speak after them in another sense; their pre-emptive statements structure the possibilities of his speech, he can only respond to what they have said. The prosecution has the ineradicable advantage over him of having the power, the honour, the privilege of having the question, of having the beginning, the advantage within the trial, of moving the white pieces.

The accused, by this ritual of legal dialogue, the subtle insertion of sequence, of the relations between before and after, within the formal equality of legal exchange of opinions about the case, is reduced to the permanent inferiority of having to answer in a conversation which has been started by the state. Before Gandhi, there were political leaders or militants who made the judicial proceedings showcases for their own martyrdom. Terrorists condemned to death often made ringing statements of patriotism in the courtroom before they were executed. Not surprisingly, these statements were then turned into material for nationalist mythology. But despite this, martyrdom signalled, against all attempts at transformation of its meaning, an undeniable victory of the state. Gandhi did not move into the 'paradigm', to use Victor Turner's phrase, of this kind of martyrdom. He devised a different rhetorical response peculiar to himself.

Gandhi's case is made fascinating by his understanding and subtlety in using the political theatre of the court. He showed an acute awareness of the theatricality of law, the sense that it is an arena, a stage for high drama in which both sides are obliged to enact an unprepared play, unrehearsed and unpremeditated to a certain extent, because the exchanges are not fixed but strategic. Whoever plays this game better has the capacity to stamp his version on this historical act; from its softness in the present moment when it is still happening, its meaning would harden forever once the exchange is finished. Miraculously, in this case, the historical event came to be determined by Gandhi, not by the judge not the public prosecutor despite the structural dramatic advantages they had over him.

Colonial authorities clearly wanted some political trials to be spectacles because of the importance of the people brought to trial. They understood quite well that politics often works by a fearful process of contagion, or rebellious acts, fear of which makes potential rebels desist from them. Therefore, from the point of view of authorities, the main purpose in the trial of a notorious political leader was not merely to punish *him*, but to reduce his more intangible aura, the first beginning of his myth. Trials, if theatrically effective, would not merely bring strictly and scrupulously proportionate legal punishment for breaking the laws of the colonial state, but would discourage others from taking the same path.

British authorities tried this kind of legal-theatrical reduction of most of their serious opponents—Tilak, Gandhi, terrorists, and communists. Thus, this theatricality actually deals with the problem of political myths. A political trial is not significant for what happens inside it in a secular, demystified, rationalist sense of the term. It is vital precisely because of its symbolic significance its ability to resonate and its ability to speak across the boundaries of that limited situation, in the intimations of universality implicit in its occasion.

Colonial administrators, like other people in power, Foucault's judges or E. P. Thompson's lawmakers, saw trials as dramas of deterrence. They were also spectacles of power; they brought the dissenter, the individual who disobeyed the law, to a place of humiliation where he would be shown as powerless, isolated, and insignificant. It is not the dismemberment of the body that is attempted, but the more effective dismemberment of the image. The theatrical task of the state is to reduce him, through the public porches of the trial, into a common man, whose pretensions of enacting the political miracle of a successful defiance of colonial rule are stripped away. Conversely, Gandhi's task was to show that he could protect the image of a person who showed the possibility of defiance and, through his example, encouraged others to do the same.

But as the conflict and the violence were symbolic rather than physical, as the cuts and thrusts were through concepts and arguments, both sides chose their champion with care. From the point of view of the state, the choice of Gandhi as the victim of its legal punishment was crucial, precisely because of the symbolic structure of the political movement. Nothing short of the defeat of the leader was a full defeat for the movement. It was only when the leader was silenced and reduced to commonness, frailty and anonymity that the movement could be politically embarrassed and concede at least temporary defeat. But these repressive apparatuses of the state often accomplish by their negative acts a complete identification of the leader and the movement.

Gandhi, I would suggest, accomplished something like a complete reversal of meaning in his trial, turning what was meant to be a spectacle of humiliation of the rebel into an embarrassment of the state. He did this through his ability to speak and be meaningful to all three of his audiences; this did not play a mean role in determining the actual nature of the eventual transfer of power. The legal frame which he had to deal with presupposed some principles of the liberal nation state, and by manipulating them, he was able to startle and outmanoeuvre others in the courtroom drama.

Apart from putting the accused in a secondary position by forcing him to answer, the structure of the law also presumes that the power of the state would induce him to plead not guilty, and his rational reaction as the accused individual would be to try to escape punishment. Also, there is a presumption behind all this that the punishment is being inflicted by the state on *behalf* of the society as a whole, of which the accused individual is a part. So the nation-state accepts and owns him as a subject, a citizen in the process of punishing him. Implicitly, behind the legal forms there exists the liberal idea of the nation as a community which owns its members.

As it turned out, the state's preparations actually helped Gandhi. Since the focus was so intensely on him, it offered him a chance to draw upon and put to use the rhetoric of his loneliness to great effect. Starting from his dress, which was a symbol of intransigence, to his deliberate discursive moves, everything was meant to underline his ability to enact defiance. The legal report which with typical blandness, deliberately took away from the theatricality of the occasion said, 'Sir T J Strangman and Rao Bahadur Girdharlal conducted the prosecution, while the accused were undefended.' What the legal report could not say but was clearly implicit in Gandhi's behaviour was his symbolic refusal. By refusing to defend himself, he refused to make the expected countermove in the game of the trial, and rejected the assumptions of the liberal conception of a nation state which were implicit in the legal structure.

Gandhi singlemindedly and systematically disrupted the script of the state for the trial. As the charges were read out, the judge asked Gandhi to plead guilty to the charge or ask to be tried. Gandhi pleaded guilty in a specially difficult way. He not only acknowledged that he wrote the seditious material mentioned in the charges against him, but mentioned several others which were possibly even more inflammatory in their sedition. Since he pleaded guilty, he encouraged the trial judge, C.S. Broomfield, to state that the only matter that was left was sentencing the accused since he pleaded guilty to the charges.

The public prosecutor objected to this abbreviation of legislative procedure and claimed that the charges were not only to be read out, but also fully explained. In the theatre of law, it is of great significance for the prosecuting side to keep control over the proceedings and stick to its proper sequence. Since in this case it was also a contest between the moral claims of the two sides, it was imperative for the state's side to present its argument to the audience outside the court. This explains the public prosecutor's anxiety that the charges were not merely recited but explained, and illustrates the effectiveness of Gandhi's brief but fundamental move to disrupt the formal sequence of the procedure. The power of the state strained to appear justified, to prove itself with compelling arguments of legitimacy in the eyes of both its British and Indian audiences.

The discursive purpose of the trial was to disarticulate Gandhi's argument and establish his image as a lawbreaker, a person who tried but failed to resist the power of the colonial state, which was able, after all, to bring him to trial and send him to prison. The tone of the state, as the representative of the society it protects, had to imply its moral superiority and put the moral blame of causing unnecessary and ineffectual disturbance on the nationalist dissenter. This required, both morally and theatrically, that the accused should act as a rational individual and seek to escape punishment. If he did not do that, if he refused to escape punishment, if he refused his right to be tried this upset the entire dramatic structure of the legal form. Gandhi, in a sense, chose to do the exact opposite of what the law of sedition expected him to do. Though the punishments were draconian, he literally invited them. Given the opportunity to ask for a trial, he spurned it by pleading guilty. He did everything from his point of view to disrupt the script of the state through the prosecutor brought to the trial.

From a narrow quotidian point of view, the outcome of the trial was already decided. It was a foregone conclusion that the colonial authorities would sentence Gandhi and send him to prison. The practical question was how long his sentence would be; and the symbolic question was how the more interesting contest over the 'historic meaning' of the trial would end between the two descriptions that the colonial state and Gandhi brought to it with their different scripts. Gandhi's actions placed emphasis on just the opposite elements in the court; he could not match the state in pomp and pageantry, but he could turn his loneliness and vulnerability into an idea of immense rhetorical and symbolic force.

But the great ingenuity of his exchanges with the law could again be read in two different ways. The middle class Indian audience saw in it the subtlety of his lawyer's mind, and perhaps a degree of courage in standing up to the state's coercive authority. But the peasants could easily see in it a contest with evil and interpret it, in their own way, as a form of saintliness. Saintliness was marked by an improbable extension of subjectivity, subsuming within itself the more inadequate and cowardly subjectivity of others. It was the mark of saintliness to be able to suffer exemplarily. Suffering was the common human fate but exemplary suffering was to suffer without cause. Gandhi also showed his extraordinariness by defying the logic of normalcy in attempting to maximize rather than shorten the punishment he saw coming. To act like that was irrational; but that precisely marked him out as someone who was uncommon, extraordinary and touched by the divine insanity of the saint. This transcended narrow, ordinary, rational calculations and was accompanied by the ability to bear extraordinary sacrifice.

This was an immense exaggeration of the scale of his actions which became larger than life. This was heightened by another rhetorical device Gandhi often used during his trials. During several crises he enjoined his supporters to act with utter and imperturbable restraint, to ensure that not a single brick was thrown at a single policeman. This served two rhetorical purposes. First, it heightened the dramatic sense of his representativeness of the whole nation, his acting on their behalf, and assuming to himself their suffering and anger. It also created a wonderful stillness in the political world providing the perfect frame for his acts inside the court. It was as if the whole stage of India's confusing, chaotic political universe was plunged into darkness with a single circle of light illuminating the courtroom, which meant that his faintest whisper, the smallest possible move he made would not be lost to his audiences. They would stand out in this stillness of all other actions with an unusual, extraordinary clarity. These acts were already on their way to being mythicized.

The way Gandhi moved, both in devising the general character of his movement of non-violence, with the strong and surprising connection between defiance and non-violent resistance against the state, not countering force with force but a moral stance against the state's legitimacy, put the colonial administrators into great difficulty in making their responses meaningful to the audience they feared the most—the one at home. It seemed to leave them with only three options, all less than satisfactory. They could remain passive in the face of Gandhi's constant provocations and appear weak and irresolute. They could try massive repression, but the numbers were large and if the use of force got out of control and slid into excess, they would appear shockingly brutal, creating a dissonance between policing measures of the colonial regime and the rationalist, civilized, self-image of colonial ideology. Alternatively, they could mix restraint with harshness—which is what they eventually did—and managed to appear hesitant and brutal and, worst of all, inconsistent.

On a small scale, this differentiation of approaches could be seen in the responses to Gandhi in the judicial setting itself. The public prosecutor did not lose his nerve and refused to fall into traps constantly sprung by Gandhi's discourse. But soon it was amply clear that Gandhi's discursive moves had had their effect, and driven a clearly discernible line of distinction between the prosecutor and the judge. While the judge was willing to abbreviate the accusation procedures because Gandhi had already pleaded guilty, the prosecutor had to remind him of the 'fullness' of legal formalities and the necessity of an explanation of the charges.

How judge Broomfield behaved in the trial is generally well known, the way he almost conceded to Gandhi the title of saintliness. But that was the end result of the intricate moves and countermoves in the language of legality. The judge's language became increasingly defensive about the sentencing and deferential towards Gandhi, and a tone of fatal ambiguity crept in even when he lay down the procedures of the trial. Gandhi proceeded in his opening remarks, before he read out his prepared sentence, to assume responsibility for the events of Chauri Chaura and Bombay—again an assumption of responsibility for acts that others had done, thus so enlarging his responsibility and making himself, in a sense, their representative by suffering in their place.

I am therefore here to submit not to a light penalty but to the highest penalty. I do not ask for mercy. I do not plead any extenuating act. I am here therefore to invite and cheerfully submit to the highest penalty that can be inflicted upon me for what in law is a deliberate crime and appears to me to be the highest duty of a citizen. The only course open to you, the Judge, is, as I am going to say in my statement, whether to resign your post, or inflict on me the severest penalty, if you believe that the system and law you are assisting to administer are good for the people.

This showed an astonishing alertness about the smallest openings in the legal transactions. For this was a move which could not have been prepared or rehearsed; it was improvised as a reaction to the courtesy with which the judge conducted the proceedings, and in which Gandhi quickly sensed an opening to discomfit the state's discourse. He succeeded at least partially since this introduced a dissonance between the discursive acts of the prosecutor and the judge, and we detect a note of growing moral defensiveness and ambiguity in the judge's behaviour. He said, 'the determination of a just sentence, is perhaps as difficult a proposition as a judge in this country could have to face.' He continued, more famously, to say, 'it will be impossible to ignore the fact that you are in a different category from any person I have ever tried or am likely to try. Even those who differ from you in politics look upon you as a man of high ideas and of noble and even of saintly life.' What is interesting is the ambiguity that creeps into his language in constant qualifications which touch embarrassingly the borders of apology and extenuation. The judge said that he had to deal with Gandhi 'in one character only', he was sentencing him because of 'what appears to him to be necessary in the public interest'; it was 'his duty' to pass a sentence on him, which he evidently did not find agreeable or morally straightforward. Finally, he expressed the hope that it would be possible for the Government of India to reduce the period of the sentence Gandhi would have to serve. Gandhi was sentenced, after this extraordinary display of contrition of the judicial representative of the state, to two years of simple imprisonment on three different counts, six years in all. He had to serve only two years of those six.

But the trial had taken on a completely different meaning from the theatre of humiliation or at least reduction it was meant to be. It did remove the popular leader from his natural position at the head of the movement, away from the admiration of the multitude in public meetings into the unnatural loneliness of the courtroom, and placed him in a position of enormous theatrical inequality—between the pageantry of the court, enhanced by its measured, deliberate, ritualized language of unhurried procedures and his own forlorn existence in the dock. But Gandhi defeated the theatrical script of the trial by finding a way of exaggerating precisely the qualities which the state wished to emphasize—his dress declaring his affiliation to the poor, his vulnerability which only increased the general sense of his courage and spiritual resolution. He undermined the attempt to accuse him and try out his case by the pre-emptive move of pleading guilty and asking for the maximum punishment, denying the functionaries of the state even the luxury of clemency.

Finally, in his short but highly significant exchanges with the judge, he pushed him into the defensive on moral grounds and the judge came very close to acknowledging his saintliness. Of the two scripts which the two sides brought to the trial, surprisingly it was Gandhi's that left its mark on the event, determining its character. The script of the state, despite the considerable advantages of the theatre of law and the first move, was taken apart and reduced to a sense of incoherence. Through the judge it came close to accepting the position of the accused, because he spoke in terms of extenuation and guilt which evinced a sense of great moral unease in front of

Gandhi's complete self-possession. Gandhi had said in 1937 'My writings should be cremated with my body. What I have done will endure, not what I have said or written.' He wanted people to read the texts of his actions correctly, and his actions often exhibited the deliberate construction of texts.

Through the trial of 1922 Gandhi had begun to turn the spectacle of the discursive contests between the colonial state and the nationalist movement against the colonial power. For all sides saw in the trial a sort of victory for Gandhi, a strange frustration of the power of the colonial state, and an odd diminishment of its prestige. The tone of embarrassment that gradually overcame the speech of the trial judge later spread to the public discourse in Britain and, at least to a large segment of the British public, the colonial authority had its legitimacy fatally undermined.

The educated audience in India, except for communists and the extreme left, saw in the trial at least marks of Gandhi's great political ingenuity if not surprising moral force. But the ordinary peasant consciousness happily attributed to him, through popular tales, a miraculous power which even the evident might of the British raj could not contain, curb, or subdue and created the myth of his invincibility. Only Lord Reading, with a foresight and sensitivity typical of the excessively powerful, wrote to his son in understandable relief that Gandhi 'had certainly come to his last ditch politically.' A more careful study of the trial would reveal the exact moves by which the trial of the rebel was turned into something that appeared more like a trial of the state.

12

Experiencing Repressive States in America and the Koreas

BRUCE CUMINGS

The American observed Yi In-dong, a big, heavy-set man with a large head on his shoulders. There was something odd about his big head: it appeared 'slightly twisted in relation to his body'. The American asked if there was anything wrong with Mr Yi's head. In a patois of 'rough worker talk', Yi responded that it had been that way ever since the Japanese tortured him. Sitting next to Yi was Pak Pong-u, to whom the American directed some additional questions. However, right wing terrorists had knocked all his teeth out so Pak couldn't talk very well. The American turned to a third labour organizer, Mun Ûn-chông, who also had a few physical problems. He had been in jail for most of the previous two years, and could not see or hear when he was released. A physician had partially restored his senses, which had retreated when he was 'hung by his heels, given the water cure, beaten, and had his face smeared with a mixture of ashes and human waste'. These union leaders, many of whom had been activists for two decades, told the American that 15,000 of their members had been arrested in the past two years.[1]

In the port town of Samch'ôk on the upper northeast coast of South Korea, the Japanese conglomerate named Onoda had opened a cement factory. Shortly after Emperor Hirohito spoke for the first time to his people on 15 August 1945 and, in a masterpiece of Japanese understatement, averred that the war had developed in a manner not necessarily to the Japanese advantage, a self-governing committee drawn from the Onoda factory workers took over the factory and ran it for the next few weeks, under the leadership of a

Korean who had come to the plant when he graduated from engineering school, Oh Pyông-ho. Around 15 September, an American calling himself Captain Chapman arrived in town, as head of a military government team. Shortly he took over the Onoda housing facilities for his team's headquarters, and said that from then on every important decision at the factory should be checked with him first.

Two months after that the American Military Government issued Ordinance #33, which prohibited self-governing committees at all Korean factories and announced that all former Japanese-owned public and private properties now belonged to the U.S. Occupation—about 3,000 properties, including all the large factories. The Americans appointed a factory manager named Yi Sôn-gûn, who, as it happened, was a close friend of the man advising Americans on such matters, named Yu Han-sang.

The union continued to run the cement factory anyway, in part because the manager, Mr Yi, preferred to stay in Seoul. Although the US Military Government had outlawed this union nationwide, it was still flourishing, as was the self-governing committee at Onoda. So in March 1947, 30 so-called leftists and 'Red elements' were arrested in Samch'ôk, including all the leaders of the factory committee. Engineer Oh Pyông-ho, still a member of the self-governing committee, was one of them. It was these arrests that caused an American named Hugh Deane (a reporter for the *Nation* in the 1940s and an unsung but honest American who died on 25 June 2001), to travel to Seoul in 1947 to interview the union organizers of rough mien and tormented body.

At length, in 1957, Syngman Rhee's government sold the Onoda factory to the fifth Seoul-appointed absentee owner and regime crony, Kang Chik-sôn—for 700 million *hwan*, or about $500,000. This was four years after the US allocated $632,000 in United Nations relief funds to the factory, although the factory had not been much hurt in the Korean War—supplies were pilfered, and the main crane was demolished, but otherwise it was intact. In the 1960s the man tarred as a leftist and 'Red element,' engineer Oh Pyông-ho, was chief cement engineer for all of South Korea.[2]

At about the time when Captain Chapman appeared in Samch'ôk, a different American, Colonel Francis Gillette, appeared in Taegu, a large southeastern city and the seat of government in North Kyŏngsang Province. Taegu had been inhabited by so many Japanese before August 1945, for so long, that it often appeared to be a Japanese city. Col Gillette commanded the 40th Division, source of the 'tactical troops' that Americans used to keep order in southern Korea before the arrival of regular civil affairs of 'military government' teams. Shortly there appeared in his office a man named Yun Il, who said he represented the local Korean governing authority in the province, which had been running things since Hirohito's surrender. Yun Il had experienced the Japanese state not in the streets of Taegu, but mostly from the window of his jail cell—he had been repeatedly incarcerated for resistance to the colonial authorities.

A Thames Television crew found Colonel Gillette residing in California 40 years later and interviewed him about his experience for a British documentary entitled *Korea: The Forgotten War*. I was the principal historical consultant for this film and conducted many of the interviews in the US and elsewhere, but Col Gillette had read or heard about my work, and refused to be interviewed by me. He proceeded to tell the Thames crew that 'You Neal' (in his pronunciation) had barged into his office in Taegu claiming to run the place, but Col Gillette told him in no uncertain terms that he had not arrived with the American army to turn over the reins of government to 'communists.' Yun Il then exclaimed, 'we will bury you' (according to Francis Gillette) and left the office. Yun Il was not a communist. He represented a popular regime of more local backing and legitimacy than any other claimant, as a major rebellion coming a year later demonstrated. Gillette had only arrived in early October, yet already he operated according to intuited Cold War principles, which he reconstructed in this 1986 interview according to a distinctly *ex post facto* narrative (unless he would have us believe that Yun Il invented the 'we will bury you' line, not Nikita Khrushchev at the United Nations in 1959). Instead of the ignorant American that he was, barging into a charged political situation and leaving little but wreckage in his wake, Gillette's reconstruction places him as the prescient agent of a global doctrine two years ahead of its appearance, which (as we now know from any number of American pundits) proved to be the winning strategy of the only morally-defensible side.

In these introductory anecdotes, we encounter human beings who have encountered the State—they have 'seen the State,' after the state has seen them. Among the many virtues of James Scott's recent book, *Seeing Like a State*, is his unwillingness to distinguish between types of modern states. The industrial states were all gripped by 'high modernist ideology', yielding state practices that are best conceived as a strong, one might even say muscle-bound, version of the self-confidence about scientific and technical progress, the expansion of production—the mastery of nature (including human nature), and, above all, the rational design of social order commensurate with the scientific understanding of natural laws.

There is an 'elective affinity' between high modernist ideology and the interests of state officials—whether they hark from formal democracies, like the US in 1945, totalized colonial states like the one Japan bequeathed to Americans in Korea in that same year, or military regimes like the one Captain Chapman represented.[3] I am interested, though, in the self-confident, 'strong, one might even say muscle-bound' exercise of state power. Col Gillette's methods of suppressing dissent or Captain Chapman's disdain for labour unions running factories, are no different in their effects than the policies of the Japanese officials whom they relieved; during a major uprising in the region of Gillette's responsibility in October 1946, one American officer said this: 'We went into that situation just like we would go into battle. We were out to break that thing up and we didn't have time to worry too much if a few innocent people got hurt. We set up concentration camps outside of town and held strikers there when the jails got too full. It was war. We recognized it as war. And that is the way we fought it.'[4]

What unites Chapman, Gillette, and other officers in the occupation is a self-confident certainty that they implement a seamless 'rational design for social order' amid a heterodox reality, and through this optic, Yun Il ends up in the same jail that he exited on 15 August 1945. Furthermore Korean officials from the colonial administration, who on the day these two Americans arrived in September 1945 were typically either on furlough or in jail (instead of 'seeing like a state' they suddenly experience what it is like to have that same gaze fall on them, to be seen by that same state), are retroactively emboldened to resume their duties; two years later,

Hugh Deane is witness to the mayhem perpetrated against labour organizers like Yi In-dong and Mun Ŭn-chŏng, and the head of the American Civil Liberties Union, Roger Baldwin, tours South Korea and denounces an American administration presiding over a country 'literally in the grip of a police regime and a private terror'.[5]

Because of the nature of my early work on Korea, beginning with a dissertation on the US Occupation of Korea (1945–8), it has been my professional fate to experience the American state through a Korean optic, and also to experience the Korean state through an American optic—a state that was, more than any post-war Asian regime, the clear result of American midwifery (not to mention successive decades of support so munificent that only Israel dwarfs Seoul's take from the American treasury). The illegitimacy of this state in the eyes of its own people also spawned a nightmarish history of arbitrary power, popular resistance and resulting political mayhem that lasted from 1945 until the partial democratization of South Korea 50 years later, leaving in its wake multitudes of walking wounded—ordinary people of extraordinary courage, it seems to me, who confronted the state and paid a horrible price for it, but who remain fully human in their capacity for resistance, grit, regeneration, and finally, reconstituted memory. It is their 'unspectacular reserves of resistance,' to use Helmut Berking's phrase, that I am interested in. But I am also interested in a phenomenon of avoidance, which begins with the light hold that such people have on the American mind. This mind seems insatiable in its appetite for horror stories emanating from regimes that the American government, as a matter of high policy, does not like, but curiously uninterested in victims of regimes that the US systematically supports.

INDELICATE EXPERIENCES OF THE STATE

Those of us who study politics encounter human experiences that do not regularly occur in other walks of life: how many people do we know whose heads are (literally) not screwed on straight because of some fiendish torture? The modern state may possess a monopoly on violence, as Max Weber taught us, but who gave it a monopoly on the production of monstrous cruelties that only a deeply sick person could imagine, let alone employ? When a Mafia thug puts a gun to someone's temple and indicates that he will have either a signature or brain matter on the contract in front of him, the thug clearly made an offer that couldn't be refused—and we appreciate the entertainment value of such displays of raw power (if only in Hollywood films). What do we think when established orders of justice do the same thing? Because we are human, we imagine ourselves the subjects of such morbid 'experiences of the State'. I don't like pain and have a low tolerance for physical or mental torment (I would guess I am not alone here), and probably would tell an interrogator what he wanted to hear as soon as my first fingernail was about to be pulled. The kind of things I fret about are box score results from daily baseball games, not an impending torture session where my values will be mortgaged against my tolerance for gallons of red-pepper water force-fed into my stomach; my experience of state torture is limited to audits from the Internal Revenue Service.

So how can we comprehend political prisoners in Rafael Trujillo's jails, who reputedly were terrorized by an albino dwarf with razor sharp teeth named 'Snowball', who transferred his skill in gelding sheep to the same function applied to recalcitrant prisoners?[6] What about jailed anti-Japanese resisters in Manchuria in the 1930s, most of them Korean, who would get dragged over to the headquarters of Japan's biological warfare operation near Harbin, 'Unit 731' (when another human guinea pig died, they would dial up the prison and say 'bring me another communist')? We are all innocent in the face of such fiendish experiences of the state; we cannot imagine how people even live through them (often they don't), let alone retain their own humanity.

Yet I have two friends who fit this description. One is a prominent figure in Kim Dae Jung's government who was tormented by the KCIA in the early 1970s: regime torturers would attach electrodes to sensitive parts of his anatomy, read passages aloud from the doctoral dissertation he had recently completed in a foreign country, 'ring him up' so his shrieks would also terrify other political prisoners in the KCIA compound, and just to complete this Dante-esque circle of torment, they would also ring up his wife (if only on the telephone), and leave the receiver off the hook so she could hear her husband screaming. When I got to know him several years later, I learned that he was unable to fall asleep at night without several stiff whiskies; his wife, a highly-trained concert performer, could not perform anymore because of a psychogenic nervous ailment that left her extremities stone cold. At length both of these torture-induced residues disappeared, the careers of both flourished, and today I know them to be peerless among truly decent, sensitive individuals.

The other person's travails are better known, primarily because they were obviously and measurably worse—if that is a measurement that means anything. Suh Sung's memoir of torment is now available,[7] but the day I first learned about him remains vivid in my mind. I had arrived in Seoul in September 1972 to begin a year of dissertation research, not knowing that the KCIA was cranking up its torture machine at its headquarters on South Mountain. I had an office on the campus of a research centre at Korea University, and was working there in mid-October when a particularly virulent tear gas wafted through the building. I escaped the gas only by bolting in the direction of a distant fence, following a fleet-of-foot female professor; we climbed over the fence only to find ourselves on the roof of a gas station, arriving back on *terra firma* after someone fetched a ladder. The next day a full complement of troops had taken up residence on the main campus quadrangle, after tanks broke through the gates and deposited them there. Dictator Park Chung Hee, it turned out, had issued a 'Garrison Decree' the day before, the first of many subsequent emergency decrees that would mark his determination to be president-for-life.

I relocated my research to a library near Seoul's venerable Independence Gate, and it was there, some weeks later, that I opened a package sent to me by a friend in Tokyo. Inside was a pamphlet showing the ravaged face of Suh Sung, or what was left of it. Half of it was burned off, including an ear that would normally hold his eyeglass frames—so he looped them around his head with a string; behind the glasses were eyes filled with stark-staring anguish and hatred. The pamphlet said that his face had disappeared during the KCIA's 'Genghis Khan torture', involving the use of a charcoal stove. (Later the government claimed that Suh had buried his face in the flaming stove, in a suicide attempt while under torture—hardly a comforting amendment.) I left the research centre and wandered the streets of Seoul all day, wondering what I had gotten myself into, and how the United States could possibly support a regime capable of such things—no matter what the justification. (And the justification was the tried-and-true one that leads most Americans to turn the page and forget about the Suh Sungs of the world; he was—falsely of course—accused of being a communist and a spy for North Korea.) Not a word of criticism came from the Nixon administration as General Park deepened his atrocities during coming years, and a subsequent study by a Senate committee found that Nixon and his henchmen had tacitly aided and abetted the nearly simultaneous martial law administrations of both Park Chung Hee in Korea and Ferdinand Marcos in the Philippines.[8]

On 30 September 1999, a woman named Chôn Chun-ja appeared on the front page of the *New York Times*, dressed as if she were yet another middle-aged and middle-class Korean housewife going shopping. Instead she stood at the mouth of a tall tunnel in Nogûn village, down the road from the town of Yôngdong in South Ch'ung'ông Province. She pointed to a hill where, she alleged, in July 1950 'American soldiers machine-gunned hundreds of helpless civilians under a railroad bridge.' She and other survivors went on to say that they had been petitioning their government and the American government for years, seeking compensation for this massacre; they had been completely stonewalled in both Seoul and Washington. Meanwhile the article also carried the testimony of American soldiers who did the firing, who said that their commander had ordered them to fire on civilians.[9]

The *New York Times* (our paper of record and 'all the news that's fit to print') did not produce this story, but rather front-paged an Associated Press account of the massacre. In subsequent days and weeks it did no follow-up reporting, to my knowledge, except periodically to up-date its readership on what the Associated Press was saying about the reaction in the Pentagon, or Seoul, the announcement of an investigation into the survivor's claims, and the like. It did choose to put on the front page an account that sought to discredit the eyewitness testimony of one soldier, Edward Daily (who apparently was not at Nogûn village on the day in question), ignoring the testimony by many Korean survivors, not to mention the large amount of internal American documentation turned up by the Associated Press team.

In this manner modest American attention came to the Nogûn village massacre because of unusual investigative reporting by the Associated Press, which nonetheless was two years after the radical Seoul magazine *Mal* had first exposed what happened at Nogûn-ri—often called 'Korea's My Lai'. Meanwhile a book published in the US twenty years ago detailed the 'revelation' of a massacre of 1800 people around the same time at Taejôn, a city just north of Nogûn village. In his 1981 book a former U.S. Central Intelligence Agency operative gave witness to the systematic slaughter of political prisoners near Taejôn in the first week of July:

I stood by helplessly, witnessing the entire affair. Two big bull-dozers worked constantly. One made the ditch-type grave. Trucks loaded with the condemned arrived. Their hands were already tied behind them. They were hastily pushed into a big line along the edge of the newly opened grave. They were quickly shot in the head and pushed into the grave.[10]

Again, however, only when the Associated Press developed this story, along with pictures of the massacre, did any attention come to it—and the *New York Times* chose only to run a brief account of the AP story, without the pictures. A psychologist in New York by the name of Do-young Lee got the massacre photos declassified at the end of 1999, and they are dramatic evidence of American complicity in this tragedy—indeed the most striking fact uncovered by the AP, unreported in the *Times*, was that in September 1950 the US Government at the highest level (in this case the Joint Chiefs of Staff) chose to suppress the pictures, never to be revealed until Dr Lee got them declassified. Instead the Pentagon subsidized official histories which blamed every civilian atrocity at this time, including Taejôn, on the North Koreans.

The day after the Taejôn story broke, I got two messages: the first was an anonymous e-mail from a person claiming to be a Korean, who ranted on for two pages about how I would surely go to hell for spouting North Korean propaganda (I had been interviewed the day before by a Seoul newspaper about the Taejôn story); the second was a phone call from an American woman in Los Angeles whose father was one of the 1,800 people slaughtered. In 1947 she was a Korean citizen of the American Military Government, one of six children of a factory owner in a town near Taejôn. He had prospered during the Japanese period, and at liberation thought it desirable to share some of his wealth. He was arrested for giving money to 'Communists' in the raucous summer of 1947 (when hundreds if not thousands of Koreans died at the hands of the Occupation's National Police) and was still in the Taejôn jail in early July 1950.

This woman (a registered nurse) and her four sisters and one brother have never been able to tell anyone how their father died. For half a century they have agonized over the loss of the patriarch of the family, but privately even unto themselves, no one ever talked about it. She was weeping over the phone for half an hour about her experience. Do-young Lee's father also perished in a massacre by South Korean authorities in August 1950, but it was only after years of searching that in 1999 he found 'smoking gun' evidence of similar events. After the war, of course, no one was able to raise such issues, on pain of being jailed and perhaps shot. If the police killed your brother, you were to say it was a communist who killed him. If you wouldn't say that, your entire family would entered upon ROK blacklists that lasted into the late 1980s.[11]

Why did the *New York Times* and other papers find massacre stories fit to print in 1999, but not fit to print at any point after September 1950? Especially when this same paper-of-record had printed so many massacre stories during the early months of the Korean War? In late September 1950 Charles Grutzner, a reporter covering the war for the *New York Times*, probably referred to Nogûn-ri when he said that in the early going, 'fear of infiltrators led to the slaughter of hundreds of South Korean civilians, women as well as men, by some US troops and police of the Republic;' a high-ranking US officer told him of an American regiment that panicked in July 1950 and shot 'many civilians'. John Osborne of *Life* Magazine told readers of the 21 August 1950 issue that American officers had ordered GIs to fire on clusters of civilians; a soldier remarked that 'it's gone too far when we are shooting children'. It was a new kind of war, Osborne wrote, 'blotting out of villages where the enemy *may* be hiding; the shelling of refugees who *may* include North Koreans'.[12]

In some arcane manner, what one could learn from the magazine table of a barbershop in 1950 gets buried for 50 years, only to be disinterred as front-page news. In one sense Korea *is* a 'forgotten war', American reporters of the first rank often know nothing about it. Forgotten, unknown, never-known: and thus Nogûn-ri becomes interesting and salient, because it suggests to reporters of the younger generation not Korea but the Vietnam War and the Mai Lai Massacre—and we thought things like that happened only in Vietnam (and really, only once). So, in this curious American lexicon, civilian massacres—about which one could read in the *New York Times* or *Life* magazine in the summer of 1950—disappear into oblivion because of a false construction of the nature of the Korean War, never to be mentioned again; they are lost for a sufficiently long time, such that that when they reappear, they appear to contradict much of the received wisdom on this forgotten war. But Chôn Chun-ja carried her 'experience of the state' with her continuously from 1950 to the present, retaining in her recurrent denunciations an indelible authenticity—a *will* to tell her story, regardless of the personal consequences.

Barrington Moore once wrote that to sustain state power, people are 'put up against a wall, beaten, shot, and sometimes taught sociology'.[13] The experiences of the state suffered by the likes of Yun Il, Chôn Chun-ja, Oh Pyông-ho, Yi In-dong and the others mentioned above, afford a better education in actually-existing politics than any classroom experience—because they show us human beings at a particular extremity who nonetheless remain human. They survive, they persist, they live, and sometimes they even flourish. Indeed, sometimes they even become heads of state.

THE UBIQUITOUS, OMNISCIENT ORBITAL EYE OF THE UNITED STATES

I am also interested in the construction put on atrocious experiences of the state in the US, where to the majority political culture the experience of politically victimized people cannot be explained by any mainstream American narrative, whether it be the narrative of our organs of opinion, or the narrative of the dominant forms of political science. Of course, if the individuals are victims of stigmatized regimes, above all if it is a communist state, a catastrophic experience will be placed on the front page,[14] and relegated to the inner pages if it is some anachronistic state form (Saudi Arabia cutting off a thief's hand, for example, or another cliterectomy in Sudan).

The memory of such mayhem is lodged in the comfortable mental categories of a demonized political form, a 'North Korea' of the American mind. (It is little known in America, and mostly incomprehensible, that the core leadership of the most reviled contemporary state in the world, North Korea, came from the same political grouping that supplied guinea pigs to Unit 731, namely, colonial resisters in Manchuria.)

If we—that is, Americans of the majority—were somehow the subject of state terrorism, we would 'experience the state' as the worst imaginable violation of our body, not to mention our basic rights. It would amount to an absolute, total outrage, never to be forgotten. If, however, a Korean or a Chilean or a Guatemalan has the same experience at the hands of a state brought into being or sustained by American power, my sense is that the average American—and especially the average government official in Washington—offers to the victim the same indifferent, 'cold gaze' that former West Germans reserve for former East Germans, in Helmut Berking's account. When they are victims of states allied to the US, the tortured victims are so deeply misunderstood as to be displaced persons, prisoners with no names in cells with no numbers (to use Jacobo Timmerman's metaphor), people dislodged from any narrative that an American would construct (outside the tiny circle of human rights activists, of course).

If and when news of vicious tortures should leak out (nearly always in the form of a revelation), the first recourse is to separate Americans from any responsibility for the action; the perpetrators were Chileans or Argentines or South Africans or Koreans. Or you can blame Richard Nixon after his disgrace in 1974; in some circles you can also get away with blaming Henry Kissinger—but not if you want to swim in the American mainstream. Blaming Nixon has many virtues: it excludes the multitude of career officials who serviced authoritarian client regimes on a bipartisan basis for decades; it renders his two nationwide electoral victories in 1968 and 1972 mere aberrations (in spite of 1972 being an historic landslide and Richard Nixon being so clearly a warped personality that a single encounter was enough to raise questions about his mental stability); above all blaming Nixon allows a convenient forgetting of any number of nasty stories emanating from our client regimes.

My strangely-warped perspective, however, is always to remember these stories, to reflect on them, and to find them much more interesting than mimetic and predictable tales of political mayhem emanating from communist states or medieval sultanates (most of the latter, of course, remain staunch American allies). When you pay attention over time, you also typically find out that some American knew all about it—usually the US ambassador or CIA station chief, but sometimes an obscure leaf wafting briefly on the surface currents of history like Col Gillette or Captain Chapman. The global structure of American power since 1945 and its extraordinarily far-flung interests (limited only by the reach of organized states on the planet), combined with truly ingenious intelligence-gathering capabilities (like the National Security Agency's 'Echelon' system, which monitors electronic conversations on a world scale), means that some American somewhere knows what happened around the world, and usually knows it first; no matter where a political atrocity occurred in the 'free world', my research experience and daily reading of the newspapers over many decades has taught me that Americans in official capacities learn *first* about such things (while denying any knowledge to reporters), while only extraordinary diligence makes it possible for people independent of the state to know the same things.

The Center for National Security in Washington, for example, has spent years seeking documents that trace American knowledge of mayhem in South America, from Pinochet's torturers to Argentine butchers to 'Operation Condor', a repellent joint effort against dissidents fronted by the likes of Stroessner's Paraguay. Their evidence led Christopher Hitchens to indict Henry Kissinger as a war criminal,[15] and indeed authorities from Chile and other states have recently been soliciting Kissinger's testimony about political mayhem in the 1970s (unsuccessfully). Kissinger is the prominent example of the truth that some American, somewhere, knows about these things because it their business to know about them, but I always wonder what goes through their minds, how they 'experience' being witting (as the 'intelligence community' would put it) to political mayhem by American-supported states.

Of greatest interest are those Americans who participate in the mayhem themselves. The head of the Office of Strategic Services in war-torn China, Admiral Milton Miles (known as 'Mary' to his friends, a US Navy affectation that bears closer attention) was good friends with T'ai Li, the notorious head of Chicago Kai-shek's secret police, who among other things liked to throw suspected communists into the boilers of steam locomotives. Miles was well acquainted with what went on in Chiang's many torture chambers. After his retirement 'Mary' Miles enjoyed vacations in the Dominican Republic courtesy of Trujillo, reveling in the glamour of El Jefe pulling up to his hotel, tooting the fancy fender horns of his Cadillac limousine, and taking Miles and his wife on tours of the island.[16] A similar American would be William Pawley, an important CIA figure who also linked Asian interests to Central America. Pawley had been a 'Flying Tiger' in China and was Trujillo's advisor on 'mining and oil ventures' for many years, eventually owning large nickle mine concessions in the Dominican Republic. Pawley also owned bus lines in Havana under the Batista regime. In the 1950s he helped the Eisenhower administration overthrow the Arbenz regime in Guatemala, and played an important role in the initial planning for the Bay of Pigs.[17]

With the passage of time such people may seem merely misguided or aberrant, but I think Miles and Pawley were quite typical of the Americans who served their country and a variety of tyrants throughout the twentieth century, going back at least to the American role in chasing Sandino and his guerrillas out of power in the 1930s (and putting Nicaraguan dictator Somoza in power), and forward to the succor offered to Central American fascists like Roberto D'Aubisson in the 1980s, both by the Reagan administration and D'Aubisson's personal friend, Senator Jess Helms. During the first two decades of the Cold War American blacks and other people of colour did not have the right to vote in many states, living under political regimes not so different from presumed 'banana republic' tyrannies in Central America, and subject to routine police tortures of various types, not to mention kangaroo courts set up by whites and, in the final instance, mob lynchings. In retrospect it seems to be a big, qualitative leap from Washington to Santo Domingo or San Salvador, because Americans are encouraged to believe that their leaders take most of their cues from the Founding Fathers. But it was not a big step from Birmingham, Alabama to Santo Domingo.

EXPERIENCING THE INAUGURATION OF THE DISSIDENT

I went to Seoul for the inauguration of Kim Dae Jung, who at the time Engineer Oh was managing the Samch'ôk factory, had his first political experience as a young member of a People's Committee in Mokp'o, a southwest port town at the geographic diagonal opposite from Samch'ôk. I stood there in the tenth row of some 50,000 people arrayed in front of the massive podium, where Kim took his oath of office under a warm, sparkling, cloudless sky that would not return in 10 Korean Februaries. He made a number of unusual pledges, including one to actively pursue reconciliation with North Korea that he assiduously followed thereafter, and for which he won the Nobel Peace Prize in 2000. When he made a highly unusual call for women's rights and equality ('the wall of sexual discrimination in homes, work places and society must be removed'), I was able to appreciate the sound of 100,000 hands left folded. Not a single cheer punctuated the suffocating silence, a reflection of this public democracy having no household or workaday counterpart. But if my ears were left hungry, my eyes had plenty to feast upon, up there on the podium.

Seated next to Kim were two former Presidents, Chun Doo Hwan and Roh Tae Woo. They looked less than resplendent in matching tuxedos, fidgeting and squirming and darting their eyes here and there. Perhaps this unaccustomed nervous tension had something to do with the unlikely event of Kim having pardoned both of them, the first from a death sentence and the second from life in prison, or maybe they were just looking out at a sea of faces and wondering how many of them had been imprisoned during their respective reigns. I reflected back on a pregnant year, 1985, when Chun Doo Hwan had banned the book that grew out of my dissertation, to much applause from my friends and not a little enthusiasm from the publisher since sales leapt ahead on this news (unfortunately Seoul had not yet signed the copyright convention, so I remained dependent on the slim royalties generated in the US).

I had arrived at Kimp'o Airport in February of that year with a delegation of foreigners whose questionable charge was to protect Kim Dae Jung, who was finally returning home from exile in the US, from suffering at Kimp'o what Benigno Aquino had suffered on the tarmac in Manila two years earlier, namely, assassination. I doubted that the garden variety officially-employed thugs with their tan windbreakers and leather jackets who greeted our delegation as we left the jetway were likely to murder Kim, given (again) Seoul's large hold on the US treasury, but I did not expect them to be so stupid as to throw Pat Derian (Jimmy Carter's one-time human rights person in the State Department) rudely to the ground, so she could emit a blood-curdling shriek and then tell all about it on Ted Koppel's *Nightline* a few days later. Then they spirited Kim Dae Jung and his wife away, to parts unknown and fates that could only be imagined. Shortly the airport fracas was resolved thanks to the adept diplomacy of an American friend of mine, Ken Quinones, whom the Embassy had dispatched to meet us, and we motored over to that same Embassy to meet with the Ambassador, Richard Walker.

Dr Walker, known as 'Dixie' to his friends, was part of an odd assortment of Americans whose pedigree included connections to two not entirely incongruent places, Yale University and the Central Intelligence Agency. But let's take our cue from Jack Jacobsen's chapter, and simply assert an odd (if recurrent) coincidence and not a conspiracy, lest someone call us paranoid, and return to the matter below.[18] At the Embassy Ambassador Walker pulled a note sheet from his pocket and began reading to us the latest figures on South Korea's miraculous economic growth, and appeared prepared to do that *ad infinitum* until interrupted by former ambassador to El Salvador Richard White, who said we had come to inquire as to the whereabouts of our charge, Kim Dae Jung, not to listen to economic statistics. The ambassador was not sure where he was, but he was sure he was okay. As I watched him fumbling with his note sheets and trembling in front of us, I remembered that Dixie Walker was one of the first Americans to rush into Chun Doo Hwan's office in the summer of 1980, in the wake of the bloodletting at Kwangju by virtue of which Chun climbed into his presidency, to assure him of American support, or at least Republican American support if Ronald Reagan were elected President. That event duly coming to pass in November, Reagan than sent Dixie to Seoul as his new envoy. Dixie, in turn, refused to receive Kim Dae Jung at the American Embassy at any point before we met with him in February 1985.

I look around the inaugural grounds to see if any of the veteran semi-official thugs, they of the tan windbreakers and leather jackets, are wandering around the inaugural grounds. I do not see any, but I remember another experience with one of their number on a second visit to Seoul in 1985. It strikes me as slightly incredible now, but the KCIA mobilized a virtual brigade of people to follow me around Seoul. One day I left my hotel in mid-morning and walked over toward the centrally-located Choson Hotel, intending to catch a cab and go see some old friends. In a large underground walkway, home to a subway station and many shops, I noticed a man in a tan windbreaker who seemed to be following me. I would walk a bit, pause to look in a store window, and then notice the man doing the same thing, 30 yards behind me. After a few such encounters, I spied an empty hallway leading to a long stairway and bolted down it and up the stairway as fast as I could run. I came out in the driveway of the Choson Hotel and walked into the lobby. I came out a moment later to hail a cab, and saw the man in the tan windbreaker at the head of the stairway, signalling to a waiting black car to pick him up, thus to follow my cab. I gave him a look at my upraised middle finger, and disappeared back into the lobby. I walked quickly through it and into an attached, labyrinthine department store, where I sought to disappear as quickly as possible. A few minutes later I exited a side door and found a cab waiting, took off, and thus succeeded in shucking off my tail, so that I could visit some friends without necessarily getting them into trouble.

I can hear readers laughing as they read this story, for the same reason that I laugh about it in retrospect and enjoyed the chase at the time: as an American I had a citizen's privilege to do such things, and not get the worst 'experience of the state' as my punishment. Had they arrested me, it would have been news. Had they tortured me, the Embassy would have had to protest. Both were no-win propositions. So why waste the time and resources in tailing me around in the first place? I don't know, but it probably has something to do with a large state bureaucracy having too much money allocated to it by the authorities, searching for a function.

My eyes return to the podium where Kim Dae Jung is speaking. Seated close to him is Michael Jackson, in a crimson tuxedo and a flat black hat which, combined with his ringlet sideburns, make him look vaguely Hasidic. The newspapers were full of stories saying Jackson might invest in a theme park in North Ch'ungch'ŏng

Province, then being reinvigorated by a new provincial governor, a Korean economist who had been teaching for years at Rutgers University. Why was it, I asked myself, that the semi-periphery seemed to have become a catchment area for pop-culture stars with careers on the wane in the core? Not far to Michael Jackson's left were seated two other individuals hailing from the Yale-CIA coincidence, James Lilley and Donald Gregg, and close to them was Richard Allen, along with the head of the Heritage Foundation [name] and several of his underlings.

After Kim Dae Jung was unexpectedly elected in December 1997, Richard Allen competed with Richard Holbrooke on the Op-Ed page of the *New York Times* to claim credit for saving Kim's life back in 1980,[19] during the transition from Carter to Reagan and from blood-soaked Kwangju to a new dictatorship. (Chun had arrested Kim on charges of sedition and appeared ready to hang him, blaming him for the Kwangju Rebellion and many other things; among them the indictment mentioned Kim's involvement with that People's Committee back in the port of Mokp'o.) Meanwhile Donald Gregg had long claimed to have saved Kim's life in 1973, when the previous dictator, Park Chung Hee, had arranged for the Korean CIA to abduct Kim from the Tokyo Grand Hotel and to truss him up Mafia-style (chains and concrete boots) for a dip in the Japan Sea. Gregg, who was then CIA station chief in Seoul, claims that he arranged for an American helicopter to buzz overhead while the (KCIA) boat bobbed and pitched around in the choppy waters of the Tsushima Strait, thus saving Kim's life. Who knows if any of these stories are true, and don't wait for the the *New York Times* to get to the bottom of any of them. But what I remember from reading that same newspaper is the evidence its reporters gave forth in 1979-80 as to the systematic aiding and abetting of Chun's rise to power by these very same people—although 'liberal Democrat' Richard Holbrooke was even more active and prominent in enabling Chun's rise to power.[20] We might call this the Korean experience of the American bipartisan state.

A year before Kwangju, in June 1979, I sat cooling my heels in the office of the cultural attaché to the Korean embassy in Tokyo. He had taught psychology in a tiny American college for 17 years, but when his brother-in-law became head of the KCIA, his reward was this post in Tokyo. He was patiently explaining to me why I was denied a visa to travel to Seoul. Actually I had gotten a visa with no trouble from a young clerk in the Korean Consulate in Seattle, but when I tried to board my plane for Seoul at Narita International Airport, another young (Japanese) clerk had spent some panicked period of time looking back and forth at my passport and a large notice with my name on it sitting in front of him, and then in stark fright had told me I had been blocked from getting on the plane to Seoul. That's how I ended up at the Korean Embassy in Tokyo.

The cultural attaché assured me that he would do what he could to get me the visa, this problem was caused by stupid people in the KCIA with nothing better to do, so on and so forth. He said all of this in a very relaxed American manner, in fluent English. Then one of his underlings would come bowing and scraping into the office, and he would sit ramrod straight and treat them like troublesome slaves. As soon as they left, he was back to his relaxed self. (Eventually he got me a three-day visa, and the KCIA relegated itself to following me around everywhere for the full three days. Then in October 1979 his brother-in-law, Kim Chae-gyu, shot the President in the head— not a trifling matter—and so the attaché returned to the US. Last time I heard he was running a vegetable store in New York City.)

Also nearby on the inaugural podium was 'CIA hand' (William Safire's term[21]) and Yale graduate James Lilley, with whom the Reagan Administration replaced Walker as Ambassador in 1986, on the grounds that you needed a savvy operator on the ground in case the CIA's judgment that a revolution was brewing in Seoul might turn out to be correct, and if it didn't, to shepherd the transition from Chun to his handpicked successor, Roh Tae Woo. (Chun had bartered American backing in 1980 for his pledge to make 'the first peaceful transition of power in Korean history.'

Chun retracted the pledge in June 1987, occasioning a popular insurrection. Lilley was in effect the emissary of a National Security Council decisions taken in 1985 which argued that it might be better for Reagan to promote democracy instead of authoritarian dictatorship (Jeane Kirkpatrick's choice up to that point), lest some of our clients lose power altogether. At any point over the past decade Lilley was the usual suspect rounded up by the American media to comment on 'rogue state' North Korea; in my experience he is always referred to as a former ambassador, never the career CIA employee that he was before taking up his ambassadorship.

I look at Roh Tae Woo squirming up on the podium, the 'kinder, gentler' militarist. I remember the blessed event that happened in 1988, not his accession to power but the marriage of his daughter to the son of Sunkyung conglomerate chairman Chey Jong Hyun. Chey was let go from the Chicago economics department back in the 1950s with a terminal master's degree, but by the 1980s he was fabulously wealthy, and became the primary benefactor of the University of Chicago's Korean studies programme. Roh Tae Woo's daughter was then a student at Chicago. We all have our moments of paranoia, as John Kurt Jacobsen notes in his essay, and mine is deeply involved with this blessed event. I began teaching at Chicago in 1987, knowing little about its Sunkyung connection, and one of the first people to ask me to lunch was a person with one of those tell-tale name cards that has only a name and a telephone number. He was heavily involved with providing security for the upcoming Olympics in Seoul, he told me, and toward the end of a long lunch he inquired whether I might want to consult with him and his colleagues. I don't remember if he actually identified himself as a CIA employee, or whether he was merely a security consultant with the CIA. In any case I politely declined, and never saw the man again. But he did tell me quite a bit about the extraordinary involvement of American intelligence in making sure no untoward events marred South Korea's coming-out party in 1988—just another little example of the services Washington provides to its clients.

Some months later a Korean-American student of mine said that in the course of applying for a visa to go to Seoul for the summer, someone in the local Korean Consulate had said I was a really bad guy, and he hoped she was not taking any courses from me at the university. I took umbrage, and asked the University administration to look into the matter. Much time passed without my hearing anything, until one day two FBI agents asked to interview me about my student's experience with the Consulate. For half an hour I explained to them that all members of a Korean Consulate consider themselves to be acting *in loco parentis* with regard to American students having any kind of Korean ethnicity, no matter how remote the Korean extraction, on behalf of the greater good of all Koreans everywhere; and that every Korean Consulate was also the repository of an unknown number of agents employed by the KCIA. I suggested that a good role for the FBI would be to find such diplomats and get them to cease and desist form interference with academic freedom.

The agents then asked me if I knew any North Korean agents in the US. Roh Tae Woo was coming to Washington for a visit, they said, and they were involved in preliminary security checks. I said that in the two decades since I first got interested in Korea I had never found a single person in the US who could qualify, and certainly none in the Korean-American community, with the exception of a shadowy figure whom I once met in New York City and who spoke of the North Koreans as the 'democratic forces'. A Caucasian of indiscernible ethnic or national provenance who wore sunglasses at all times, I had assumed at the time that he was probably working for P'yŏngyang, or for the Russians, or that perhaps he had just seen too many spy movies. They asked me for his name more than once, but if I ever knew it, I certainly couldn't recall it—nor did I want to give it to the FBI, on the flimsiest of evidence.

Then one of the FBI agents said he had been talking to someone at the Korean Consulate, and that person had pulled out what he claimed to be a piece of stationery from my academic department, and said that at the University of Chicago there was a North Korean agent who taught in the very department that used this stationery. Did I know who that might be? I said it would be me, of course, and the FBI could learn a little bit about the McCarthyism that has afflicted South Korea for forty years by thinking about what they were told at the Consulate. I should have denounced them both and thrown them out of my office, but this being the FBI, I politely ended the meeting and called to ask for an appointment with the University counsel. Instead I got an audience with Jonathan Kleinbard, then the primary public relations man for 'town-gown' relations between the University and the public, and especially the vast black public of Chicago's south side.

I knew Mr Kleinbard as a very funny person always ready with a wisecrack, also a Tom Wolfe-style flak-catcher extraordinaire, who had made his periodic bonfire-of-the-vanities encounters with the local South Side citizens a primary entertainment for the faculty. Jonathan asked me how the FBI visit had come about, and to his great credit and my considerable relief, also said I should never allow them into my office again without having the University Counsel present. (No such thing had happened when the FBI had visited me at the University of Washington, after my first trip to North Korea in 1981—and after the FBI had solicited my credit report and bank accounts without my permission). I told him that the FBI had ostensibly called on me to discuss the Consulate's harassment of my student, but in fact had wanted to see my reaction when they told me someone in the Consulate thought I was 'a North Korean agent'. Jonathan burst out laughing, indeed he nearly doubled over and fell to the floor, and by the time he was done I was laughing too, at this 'experience of the American State'. After our meeting, Jonathan got the State Department to threaten the KCIA man in the Consulate with immediate expulsion should he harass my students again, and in the course of this investigation it turned out this was the same agent who was notorious in Chicago's Koreatown for intimidating any Korean merchant who hadn't expressed clear support for the Roh Tae Woo government.

Within a few months I received a notice of an audit of my tax returns from the Internal Revenue Service (I had been audited only once before, in the last year of the Ford administration). Subsequently three of my next four returns were audited at great taxpayer's expense and correspondingly miniscule gain for the government (the last audit took days to complete, I remember it as a thorough root canal of my finances, even delving into the financial support I gave to my mother at the time). The audits ended in late 1992, which happened to coincide with the election of Bill Clinton. Again, I can't claim to have been tortured or more than mildly oppressed by this 'experience of the State', and were I to assert that the American and Korean CIA work closely together, that the FBI men see the KCIA man in the Consulate as their ordinary foreign counterpart, and that the Bush administration initiated these audits because of my encounter with said KCIA and FBI agents, I would instantly run afoul of the peculiar American tendency to attribute paranoia to anyone who claims that two or more people in Washington are working together toward some obnoxious political end. But as I now think about the preponderance of Republicans and the paucity of Democrats on Kim Dae Jung's inaugural podium, I reflect on Robert Reich's comment that a 'conspiracy is a coalition that you are not part of'. And I admit to checking my mail with more than a little apprehension these days, now that another denizen of the Yale coincidence is (coincidentally) our President.

After the post-inaugural 'Blue House' reception we all return to our hotels, and I am standing in front of the Seoul Hilton just as a US Embassy van arrives carrying Lilley, Gregg, Allen, and various other Americans, including a couple of the human rights activists whom you might have expected to see at this inauguration instead of artifacts of the Yale coincidence. While I toyed with shouting 'Boolah-Boolah', Lilley dismounts the van and gives me the same look that I reserve for megalocephalic *cucaracha* roaches crawling out of Manhattan gutters, and keeps on walking. This, a not atypical 'experience of the American State' for me, conjures up the surmise that the mouth Lilley showed me, a jagged and curled tear in the skin above his chin, rimmed by non-existent lips, must inevitably be the distilled residue of centuries of Puritan breeding, in hot pursuit of Nietzsche's 'excision of the senses'. Donald Gregg, however, is a hail fellow well met (or at least has been since he became president of the Korea Society); he greets me jauntily and asks, 'What brings you to Seoul?' 'What else? Kim Dae Jung,' I answer. 'Oh really? Were you at the inauguration?' And with that he looks at me quizzically and walks away, making a mental note not to allow such a thing to happen again.

Richard Allen then steps out of the van, walks up to me and says, 'We seem to have some mutual misunderstandings. We should talk about them some time.' This was the second time in my life that Mr Allen had spoken to me, and both times (separated by many years) he had said the same thing before walking away. This time, I thought, he probably referred to an article of mine where I noted his continuing presence on Justice Department lists of paid agents for the Republic of Korea.[22] Some months later a member of Kim Dae Jung's administration told me that Allen had been getting $250,000 annually from Seoul for many years, but it had been hard to determine what Koreans got in return for their money; some bureaucrats in Roh Tae Woo's government had tried to put a stop to Allen's annual allowance, but General Roh had stepped in to countermand them.

Still milling around in front of the Seoul Hilton, I exchanged pleasantries with some officers of the Heritage Foundation. You might wonder why this group would come halfway around the world to see a dissident get inaugurated, but Kim Dae Jung's assiduous courting of American supporters during his long years in the wilderness included the right wing of the Republican Party, on the pragmatic axiom that if and when he might become president, there was a 66 per cent chance that a Republican would be in the White House (that being the Republican allotment over for the previous three decades, 1968-98). Furthermore the Yale coincidence found part of its function in bridging the moderate and conservative wings of that same party, a function epitomized in the careers of George H W Bush (Yale '48, Skull and Bones '48, and former CIA director for whom the Agency's Langley headquarters is now named, with hard-earned Texas credentials to please conservatives) and George W Bush (Yale '68, Skull and Bones '68, CIA connection unknown or nonexistent, with overflowing, overweaning, all-too-obvious Texas credentials).

Bush the Younger, however, was not just a poor student at Yale but a poor student of the Yale coincidence; when Kim Dae Jung showed up in the oval office in March 2001, President Bush told the South Korean leader that he didn't trust the North Korean leader, Kim Jong Il (inadvertently raising the question, who does?), and argued that the North wasn't likely to keep its agreements. Kim returned home empty handed with his advisors publicly calling the meeting embarrassing and privately cursing the new American president.[23] Some weeks later the Bush administration reversed itself, however, and announced that it would hold talks with the North Koreans. Newspapers reported that a memo from Donald Gregg to former president Bush somehow wended its way to the oval office and turned the new president around on the issue. It was clear during the Clinton administration that an opening to North Korea had bipartisan backing, and Republican Gregg was one of the vocal backers. It is not clear, though, that Kim Dae Jung's assiduous courting of Republicans of both the middle and the right will help him much in the last two years of his term, particularly in regard to furthering reconciliation with North Korea. Republican affinities run in the direction of the old ruling group, the party of Generals Chun and Roh and Park, which hopes to make a comeback in the 2002 presidential elections. That prospect, and the disdain for North Korea felt among rightwing Republicans, will make any progress in reconciling with the North very difficult.

EXPERIENCING THEORIES OF THE STATE

Most of what I have said so far in this chapter would be chucked out of any 'refereed' or 'discipline-conscious' journal of political science, either on the grounds that I have allowed my normative feelings to intrude on the inquiry and that my 'experience' of the Korean and the American state is personal, 'anecdotal,' and *ad hoc* (not to mention *ad hominem*), and therefore idiosyncratic and non-generalizable; or on the grounds that what I have said is not 'theoretical'. Yet the experiences that I have related are all true, they all happened, they recur and repeat themselves in predictable fashion, and they are all the predictable result of a particular structure of international relations, namely, a Korean-American relationship forged in the period 1945–53 that, when all is said and done, has changed very little up to now. But I would be hard put to get this 'experience of the relationship' published in, say, the *American Political Science Review*.

However it so happens that the formulation I just put down resonates with the single most important—or most frequently cited—enunciation of 'theory' in the field of international relations. That theory is 'neo-realism' and its author is Kenneth Waltz. Professor Waltz wants his theories to have both explanatory and predictive power. My theory has explanatory and predictive power (I know more or less what Richard Allen is going to say to me, and why), my experiences are as recurrent as they are predictable, and I can explain them as having a particular relationship to an enduring structure of international relations. But Waltz says theories also must possess 'elegance'. I am not quite sure if my theory is elegant, because I am not quite sure what that means—my experience of the Korean-American relationship has been anything but 'elegant' in the usual sense of the term. 'Elegance in social-science theories,' Waltz writes, 'means that explanations and predictions will be general.' My theory seems to fail the test of elegance in this sense, because it is perhaps not sufficiently 'general', it deals only with Korea and the United States (although I would guess that many scholars in other fields—say, Chilean-American relations, or South African-American relations— would have similar experiences). But let's probe a bit more into what Waltz means. Here is one of his key statements about what a good, elegant theory of international relations should do (I have interspersed numbered points for later discussion):

[1] Within a system, a theory explains continuities. It tells one what to expect and why to expect it. Within a system, a theory explains recurrences and repetitions, not change. [2] At times one is told that structural approaches have proved disappointing, that from the study of structure not much can be learned. This is supposedly so for two reasons. Structure is said to be largely a static concept and nearly an empty one. [3] Though neither point is quite right, both points are suggestive. Structures appear to be static because they often endure for long periods. [4] Even when structures do not change, they are dynamic, not static, in that they alter the behaviour of actors and affect the outcome of their interactions. Given a durable structure, it becomes easy to overlook structural effects because they are repeatedly the same.... A constancy of structure explains the recurrent patterns and features of international-political life. Is structure nevertheless an empty concept? Pretty much so, and because it is it gains in elegance and power. Structure is certainly no good on detail. Structural concepts, although they lack detailed content, help to explain some big, important, and enduring patterns.[24]

Based on this passage I would argue that my experience of the Korean-American relationship has a certain structure that lies behind, or under, or *causes*, the 'recurrences and repetitions' that I have described over the nearly six decades since 1945. The continuities are there, from Col Gillette to Ambassador Walker, Captain Chapman to Ambassador Lilley; 'a durable structure' influences behaviour, but it is easy to overlook that structure because its effects 'are repeatedly the same' (indeed in my career they have taken on the character of Nietzsche's 'eternal recurrence of the same'). Some 'big, important, and enduring patterns' are easily discernible in the relationship between Seoul and Washington: for example, the rulers in Seoul know that no matter what they do, Washington will not cut them off, because whatever they do, their opposites in P'yŏngyang are *ipso facto* worse in American eyes. (One eternal caveat to this point, however, is that should Seoul ever join hands with P'yŏngyang and unify the country against American wishes, then-and-only-then would Seoul be cut off.)

Waltz's statement reads oddly, however. It begins (point 1) with something that would seem to be important, namely an explanatory theory, then quickly dissolves that theory into the mere result of some larger structure. That structure is then termed a system, the words being used interchangeably; the system also appears to do something, but the minute it does anything (or the author thinks it is about to do something), the sense of the passage changes again. At point 2 the passage abruptly conjures up its own interlocutor, as if responsive to some hidden presence, like the off-stage prompter in an opera. At the point where we expect to learn what is it that the theory or the system does, we are told instead what the critics of that structure or theory say: namely, that the theory is either 'disappointing' or that from it 'not much can be learned.' This is supposedly because of two reasons: (1) structure is a static concept and/or (2) structure is an empty concept. Then we read (point 3) that neither (1) nor (2) is 'quite right' (well then, how right are they?), but both are 'suggestive' (of what?). Actually, structures only appear to be static, and that is because they often endure for long periods. Even (point 4) when structures do not change (that is, they are static), they are dynamic (not static), in that they alter the behavior of actors and affect the outcome of their interactions.

I think an example of what Professor Waltz is talking about would be this: A large tiger is sleeping in the jungle with its mouth open, for a long period of time. This is the structure. During that time, a few foraging deer wander along and suddenly give a start at seeing that gaping mouth. The tiger remains asleep and the mouth does not change its position, but the deer scamper away as fast as possible anyway. In other words it is, indeed, possible that a given structure can be both static and dynamic (in Waltz's terms of altering the behaviour of the actors). Now assume that a political scientist is sleeping with his mouth open or closed, and in his dreams he sees that same tiger. The tiger remains stationary or static (sleeping with his mouth open), but the political scientist finds himself drawn toward putting his head in the mouth of the tiger. The tiger keeps on sleeping, but the political scientist puts his head in the tiger's mouth and then wakes up in a sweat, and determines that he has had what is conventionally labelled 'a dark night of the soul.' He keeps this experience secret from his colleagues, or from interfering with his formal models, but he worries nonetheless that it might recur and begins to toss and turn before going to sleep. I hope the reader will keep this last example in mind.

Later on Professor Waltz uses a simile to tell us what 'the system's structure' is all about: 'A political structure is akin to a field of forces in physics: Interactions within a field have properties different from those they would have if they occurred outside of it, and as the field affects the objects, so the objects affect the field.'[25] Any kind of political structure—say, a New England town meeting? It would appear so, since 'structure designates a set of constraining conditions.' What kind of constraints? Would they include the leader of the town meeting not calling on you when your hand is up? Perhaps:

> Such a structure acts as a selector, but it cannot be seen, examined, and observed at work as livers and income taxes can be. Freely formed economic markets and international-political structures are selectors, but they are not agents. Because structures select by rewarding some behaviors and punishing others, outcomes cannot be inferred from intentions and behaviors. This is simple logic that everyone will understand.[26]

I must be a nitwit because I cannot understand the simple logic here. I have never seen a liver up close unless it is already inert and ready to be eaten, but I would guess that no scientist could have told us from looking at a functioning liver, what it is that the liver accomplishes; yet none of us can live without our livers. Scientists can measure their weight and content and their enzyme output, but cannot reproduce either the enzymes or the livers; if they could, we would not have patients with poorly-functioning livers waiting for transplants on a scale of scarcity worth its weight in gold. I have seen a person representing the Internal Revenue Service when I have been audited; indeed, as I said earlier, when I saw him I thought that I was 'seeing the state', and when he audited me I certainly felt that I was experiencing the state. I can 'see' my income taxes exiting from paycheck every month, but I have never seen what exactly they are used for. I have never seen a 'freely-formed economic marke', either, with the possible exception of an agrarian periodic barter market in rural and depressed Korea three decades ago; I gather from Waltz's words, though, that such a market is similar to 'international-political structures'. Both, however, are 'selectors' and not 'agents'. A selector is something that rewards some behaviours and punishes others: in my experience, therefore, an IRS agent should in fact be called an IRS 'selector'. But the next sentence in the passage threw me: I would have thought that a 'selector' who manipulates the pleasure/pain principle would give me enough information to indicate which behaviour might produce which outcome, but we apparently cannot know either the intentionality or the intended outcome of this structure (or selector): 'outcomes cannot be inferred from intentions and behaviors.' I may think that the FBI got me placed on an IRS audit list, but that cannot be inferred from the gumshoes who called me in to inspect my tax returns.

Professor Waltz seeks to clear all this up at the bottom of this same page, by giving an example of 'the simplest case' of the 'socialization' of an individual (which could also be a firm or a state):

A influences *B*. *B*, made different by *A*'s influence, influences *A*. As Mary Parker Follett, an organization theorist, put it: '*A*'s own activity enters into the stimulus which is causing his activity'. This is an example of the familiar structural-functional logic by which consequences become causes.[27]

In search of further clarifying this point, Waltz writes that '*B*'s attributes and actions are effected by *A*, and vice versa. Each is not just influencing the other: both are being influenced by the situation their interaction creates.' Now I think I can grasp this particular point: Dean Rusk draws a dividing line along the convenient axis of the 38th parallel in a place known generally as 'Korea' (although not to Koreans, who call it something else) in mid-August 1945, the consequence of which is that American forces must repress some Koreans while supporting others. Union organizer Yi, Engineer Oh and Kim Il Sung are among those repressed (the US refused to acknowledge Kim's effective rise to power in early 1946, and still does not recognize his regime). Four years later war nearly breaks out along the parallel, as those whom Rusk has supported incessantly attack those whom he has sought to repress. Rusk then decides that should the reverse occur, meaning that those whom the US has repressed were to attack across the 38th parallel, he will call it by the name 'aggression' and take the case to the United Nations (which at the time had a legislature that his president can control better than the US Congress). One year later the reverse does indeed occur and Kim Il Sung invades, seeking to support those who have been repressed and to repress those who have been supported, but above all to erase the 38th parallel as anything other than a longitudinal marker. Thus both Dean Rusk and Kim Il Sung interact with each other (albeit never having met), and both inhabit the general conflict situation known to history as the Korean War.[28]

But in Waltz's account that 'simplest case' is immediately followed by another, perhaps more complex one, which extends the example and 'makes the logic clearer'. Which case? This one is not drawn from the field of physics, the organic function of livers, or the infernal tax collectors, nor is it drawn from organization theory circa 1941, but from a literary example—none other than George and Martha, the academic couple from hell, out of Edward Albee's play, *Who's Afraid of Virginia Woolf*.[29] A 'profound study' of that play by Paul Watlawick and his associates, according to Waltz, concluded that George and Martha are part of a system: 'each acts and reacts to the other. Stimulus and response are part of the story.' Furthermore, 'each is playing a game, *and* they are playing the game together.... These are descriptions and examples of what we all know and experience.'

I do not know about anyone else, but I have never experienced anything like *this*. I have never played a four-person-game with my wife and a junior faculty couple, a drunken one lasting all night long, the young wife herself already a victim of *pseudocyesis* (psychogenic false pregnancy) and the husband already the victim of his inordinate aspiration for tenure, who heedlessly goes upstairs and screws his department chair's wife Martha nonetheless, in a 'game' lubricated with so much drink and male camaraderie that he decides to tell George all about it—and not just about his having bedded Martha, but about his wife's most closely-kept secret (the phantom neonate). George, being a really nice guy, tells Martha in front of the young woman that he *also* knows *all* about it, abruptly shattering her (the young woman, not Martha—Martha enjoys the game too) and sending her husband stumbling into the morning mists to vomit, thus ending the evening—except for the unsettling news that there was a fifth player, the unborn or dead son of George and Martha, and then even a sixth, Martha's father, who was responsible for George getting tenure in the first place.

Somehow I think that the game in *Who's Afraid of Virginia Woolf* would be a difficult game to play or to develop a theory about, let alone to 'game out' along the lines of the (still unsolved) prisoner's dilemma, at least in a manner that would satisfy Professor Waltz. Strangely enough, however, Edward Albee's play does resonate with the professor dreaming that his head is in the mouth of the tiger, or with the experience of the Korean and American states viewed through the Korean optic that I have narrated above. Except that, even though it may seem like we've been peering through the same looking glass, people die. Unlike the pseudocyetic young wife or the phantom boy-child of George and Martha, real people die all the time in the 'experience' of the historically-bound Korean-American relationship.

Every American (and no doubt every Korean) perhaps experiences something akin to the George-and-Martha family trauma in their personal lives, at different frequencies from all the time to rarely (from daily life to once in a lifetime), although perhaps academics know the neurotic culture that spawns Albee's type of behaviour best; in any case this common human experience explains the gripping authenticity of Albee's play, in spite of its ostensible exaggeration. But Americans rarely if ever experience the American State in the same arbitrary way, in which State action *flows from structure* in Waltz's sense, but the action is not mediated by an assortment of founding-father, Tudor-polity myths by which most (white, middle-class) Americans experience their politics, but can only be explained by arbitrary power or *force-majeur*.

In recent years there have been two such national moments, it seems to me, when Americans as a people could experience their State in all its arbitrary and undemocratic power. The first came in early 1991, when the Pentagon closed off even the ubiquituous, orbital, all-seeing television eye that it had employed to tell the story of the air war in the Persian Gulf to the American people, with the willing compliance of major media outlets. No, the ground war was too important even for that highly constrained and limited optic on what the American state was about to do to Iraq, and so the Pentagon declared a media blackout. For many hours there was simply no news, until it became apparent that the ground war had turned into a rout, eventually won by the American armed forces in four days (with the Iraqi Army trying to cut it to three).

The second national moment was more recent, indeed I recall it as if it were yesterday: in early December 2000 I was sitting in a traffic jam that had turned an interstate highway into a parking lot, trying to creep down the expressway just a few exits to meet some friends for dinner. As we sat there unable to move, the radio began reporting a bulletin, which turned out to be the final moment of the 2000 presidential election. For the next half-hour reporters struggled to interpret the meaning of the decision by five Supreme Court justices to award the election to George W. Bush. Had it remanded the affair back to the Florida Supreme Court, or had it countermanded the decisions of that same court? Had it decided to allow vote-counting to continue in Florida, or had the narrowest possible majority of nine people declared Bush president? Slowly it became apparent that five individuals had decided the election for the American people, by arbitrary and undemocratic authority, if not by *force-majeur*. In this manner Americans got a taste of what Koreans experienced for four decades. A scion of the Yale coincidence once again became President, and quickly sent the Korean-American relationship tumbling back to the structural equilibrium that has held sway since 1945.

NOTES

1. 'Notes on Labor in South Korea,' July–August 1947, Hugh Deane Papers.
2. Soon won Park, 'Colonial Industrialization and Labor in Korea: The Onoda Cement Factory' (Harvard East Asian Monographs, 1999), pp. 161–86.
3. James C. Scott, *Seeing Like a State: How Certain Schemes to Improve the Human Condition Have Failed* (Yale: Yale University Press, 1999), pp. 4–5.
4. Quoted in Bruce Cumings, *The Origins of the Korean War*, v. 1 (Princeton: Princeton University Press, 1981), p. 371.
5. Roger Baldwin Papers, Princeton University, box 11, 'Report to Friends', 23 May 1947; 'Civil War', 16 May 1947; 'More Civil War', 17 May 1947.
6. This story may be apocryphal, but anyone who knows the history of Trujillo's regime would also find it eminently believable. After I told Daniel

Chirot this story, he failed to find hard evidence of its truth, for the Trujillo chapter in his book, *Tyrants*.

7. Part of it was excerpted in *The Bulletin of Concerned Asian Scholars* (Spring) 2001, introduction by James B. Palais.
8. Senate study, 1973
9. The *New York Times*, 30 September 1999.
10. Col Donald Nichols, *How Many Times Can I Die?* (Brooksville, Fla: Brownsville Printing Co., 1981), cited in Korea Web Weekly, www.kimsoft.com.
11. The best analysis that I have read of the intense psychological pressures caused by decades of repressed memory in Korea is Seong Nae Kim, 'Lamentations of the Dead: The Historical Imagery of Violence on Cheju Island, South Korea', *Journal of Ritual Studies*, vol. 3, no. 2, (Summer) 1988, pp. 251–85.
12. Grutzner, *New York Times*, 30 September 1950; Osborne, 'Report from the Orient—Guns are not Enough', *Life* (21 August 1950), pp. 74–84.
13. Barrington Moore, *Social Origins of Dictatorship and Democracy: Lord and Peasant in the Modern World* (Boston: Beacon Press, 1966), p. 486.
14. For example a report by a dissident Chinese doctor that valuable internal organs of people executed by the Chinese state were harvested for sale by corrupt prison officials even before the victim was fully dead (*The New York Times*, 6 July 2001.
15. Christopher Hitchens, *The Atlantic Monthly*,
16. On Miles and Tai Li, see Michael Schaller, *The U.S. Crusade in China, 1938-1945* (New York: Columbia University Press, 1979); other vignettes come from my perusal of the papers of Admiral Miles and his wife, held at the Naval War College.
17. William D. Pawley Papers, box 2, 'Russia is Winning', pp.366, and biographical information included therein.
18. Readers who wish to probe a bit further on this point can consult Sigmund Diamond, *Compromised Campus: The Collaboration of Universities with the Intelligence Community* (New York: Oxford University Press, 1992), and Robin Winks, *Cloak & Gown: Scholars in the Secret War, 1939-1961* (New Haven: Yale University Press, 1987).
19. reference to be supplied
20. Holbrooke, 'far too much attention to Kwangjoo [*sic*]'; see also Tim Shorrock's excellent work, based on Freedom of Information Act documents. presented in composite form in 'The US Role in Korea in 1979 and 1980.' www.kimsoft.com/kore/kwangju3.htm (to be supplied)
21. Safire, 'Two Intelligence Slants on China', *International Herald-Tribune* (10 July 2001). Safire referred to an external review commission, appointed by the CIA, which examined 'the most sensitive data' to come to the 'highly classified' conclusion that the CIA suffered from 'an institutional predisposition' to underestimate China's military threat. Included among

the members of this highly secret commission were Lilly, Aaron Friedberg (political scientist from Princeton), and Stephen Rosen (political scientist from Harvard).

22. My article for JPRI.
23. The *Korea Herald*, 13 March 2001.
24. Kenneth N. Waltz, 'Laws and Theories', in *Neorealism and its Critics*, Robert O. Keohane (ed.), (New York: Columbia University Press, 1986), pp. 57–8.
25. Ibid., p. 62.
26. Ibid., pp. 62–3.
27. Ibid., p. 63.
28. Waltz would still have to account for why, in the conventional American accounting of this conflict situation, the drawing of the line, the repression and support, the author of most of the fighting in 1949, and the secret decision to go to the UN that Rusk drew out of that 1949 fighting, are never mentioned.
29. Waltz, 'Laws and Theories', p. 64.

Conclusion
Sovereignty Unbound
Experiencing the State after 9/11

LLOYD I. RUDOLPH AND JOHN KURT JACOBSEN

We conclude this book about experiencing the state not by offering a summary but by writing about how Americans have experienced the state after 9/11. Doing so challenges us to outline an alternative mode of inquiry for studying the state. We conceived the idea of a book of essays about experiencing the state independent of the events of 11 September 2001. The 12 essays for this volume and our introduction to it were written before or outside the purview of the 9/11 attacks. As we worked on the book over the past three years it became increasingly clear to us that the 9/11 event, and how it was rendered, had profoundly altered how Americans and others experienced the state. We asked ourselves, why not write a conclusion that combines a framework for how to study the state with a case study of a history-altering event that may be transforming how Americans experience the state?

We start with our thoughts about an alternative to objectivist methodologies for studying the state. Objectivists start with the question, what *is* the state? We start with the question, what does the state *mean*? The first question can be answered via the objective knowledge that observation is said to yield. The question about meaning can be answered via the subjective knowledge that experience yields. Yet, neither meaning nor facts are transparent; neither is directly accessible. Both are mediated, subjective knowledge by discourse in the public sphere, objective knowledge by theory or paradigms in epistemic communities.[1]

Our case for analysing the state in terms of experiencing it rather than observing it starts with relating experience to subjective knowledge.[2] The relationship between experience and subjective knowledge can be illustrated by a story that James Clifford tells about a Cree Indian. When asked by a Canadian court to tell the truth, the whole truth and nothing but the truth about his people's way of life, he says he is 'not sure that he can tell the truth' but 'I can tell what I know.'[3] Subjective knowledge can be understood as telling what you know about what you have experienced, the kind of knowledge that Aristotle referenced when he spoke about *phronesis*.[4]

We have said that experience helps produce subjective knowledge and that subjective knowledge mediated by discourse in the public sphere helps produce the meaning by which we know the state. In these relationships, discourse plays a crucial role. Our use of the concept, discourse, draws on the importance and consequences that Michel Foucault assigned to it. For Foucault, discourse not only defines meaning but also constitutes relations of power. This is how he put it: 'In any society, there are manifold relations of power which permeate, characterize and constitute the social body, and these relations of power cannot themselves be established, consolidated nor implemented without the production, accumulation, circulation and functioning of a discourse.'[5] It is discourse that creates the systems of surveillance and control and of discipline and punishment that constitute 'relations of power'.

The practice of the post-9/11 Bush administration, which we examine in greater detail below, illustrates how the Foucauldian interactive, mutually determining relationship between discourse and power works. Here is how Mark Danner explained it: Our government officials have been unprecedented in their frankness '... in explaining how they conceive the relationship of power to truth. Our officials believe that power can determine truth, as an unnamed senior adviser to the President explained to a reporter last fall:

We're an empire now, and when we act, we create our own realtity. And while you're studying that reality ...we'll act again, creating new realities, which you can study too ...

The reporter, the adviser said, was a member of what he called 'the reality based community,' destined to 'judiciouly study' the reality the administration was creating. ... [I]t is important that we [the members of the reality-based community] realize that our leaders of the moment really believe this, as anyone knows who has spent much time studying September 11 and the Iraq war and the various scandals that have sprung up from these events—the 'weapons of mass destruction' scandal and the Abu Gharaib scandal, to name only two.[6]

Habermas picks up where Foucault leaves off by theorizing in his concept of the public sphere the context for the 'production, accumulation, circulation and functioning of discourse.' Habermas found a 'public sphere' embedded in and emergent from a wide variety of voluntary associations whose members' 'communicative process . . . is directed at common questions and creates shared discourses. . . .' Despite contemporary inroads on Habermas' conception of rationality wrought by the mass media, he argued that 'in these locations and through these activities . . . educated urban persons who previously led separate lives in private spaces become a public, transcending private preoccupations and addressing common purposes.'[7]

We have already observed that discourse constitutes meaning as well as relations of power. Clifford Geertz agrees that meaning matters; without it we can not make sense of behaviour or events. We can not, for example, read a wink unless we know what it means; is it the result of grit in the eye, a flirtatious intention or, as in the case of Inspector Clouseau, a nervous tic? Is a French schoolgirl's headscarf meant as a fashion statement or as a religious statement? The French state tried to establish a dominant discourse for the meaning of a headscarf when it forbade the wearing of conspicuous religious symbols such as women's headscarves to state schools. A few days before state schools in France were to open in September 2004, kidnappers in Iraq challenged the French state's 'surveillance and control' and 'discipline and punishment' by seizing two French journalists and threatening to kill them if the French state did not rescind its order. Schoolgirls who wore headscarves to school were to be interrogated individually by school officials. What did Muslim schoolgirls who wore headscarves to school in early September 2004 mean by doing so? When those who wore headscarves were asked by school officials about why they had worn headscarves did they give 'sincere' or 'strategic' answers, for example say the headscarves were fashion statements in order to insinuate Islam in France's *laique* schools? Did school officials try to distinguish fashion statements from religious statements and if so did they, in turn, choose to be sincere or strategic in how they interpreted words and deeds?[8] Orhan Pamuk has used the discursive struggle in Turkey over the meaning of the headscarf in his brilliantly achieved novel, *Snow*, in ways that show how central discourse is to relations of power.[9]

At the macro-historical level, too, 'excavated' meaning revealed the relations of power that Foucault says characterizes discourse.[10] In our Introduction we narrated the emergence of the state in European history as an institution and as an object of study. We spoke in the first instance of Richelieu's campaign in seventeenth century France to invent, in the language of state formation, an absolutist state out of the materials of a dynastic and feudal monarchy. We reminded readers of how, in the narrative of state formation in the western world, the absolutist state was succeeded by the modern state, and then the nation state. The essays that followed invoked the high modernist state (Scott, Roy); the totalitarian state (Joo); the developmental state (Brass); the colonial and post-colonial state (Kaviraj, Oldenburg, Siddiqui, Berking); the welfare state (Temple, Bickers); the warfare state (Jacobsen); and the national security state (Cumings). All of these modifying adjectives are tropes for meaning systems, for kinds of subjective knowledge, that epitomize or stereotype the experience involved. The adjectives—high modernist, totalitarian, developmental, colonial and post-colonial, welfare, warfare, national security—invoke a dominant framework, a hegemonic form of life, for the kind of experience and relations of power involved.[11] So too do canonical works of fiction about the state, such as Arthur Koestler's *Darkness at Noon*, Alexander Solzhenitsin's *One Day in The Life of Ivan Denisovitch*, or George Orwell's *1984*.

The attack on the twin towers of the World Trade Center in New York and the Pentagon in Washington changed the way Americans and others experienced the state (in no small part because of the way in which those in charge of the state chose to react).[12] Clichéd as the use of 'post' has become, we think it makes sense to speak of a post-9/11 state world. The change was neither complete nor overnight; it has taken place as meaning and relations of power were contested in public spheres. The changes sought by those in authority in the Bush administration often were questioned but, as time passed, it became increasingly clear that the world after 9/11 can be distinguished from the world before 9/11.[13]

In our analysis we privilege meaning and subjective knowledge over observation and objective knowledge. We shift the emphasis from objective knowledge based on observation to subjective knowledge based on experience to avoid what we have come to think of as the objectivist fallacy. In our view, scholarship based on objective knowledge has limited and in some measure distorted what is known about the state by treating partial and contingent truths as impartial and universal ones.[14] By the objectivist fallacy we have in mind the widely held belief that observation and measurement can be transparent and unmediated. For example, some argue material conditions like level and distribution of income, or place in the scheme of production, determines consciousness and agency. Explanations associated with class and interest group politics often adopt such an objectivist causality by arguing that inequality of income distribution 'causes' political instability and that equality of income distribution promotes stability. Countries or regions within countries with worse Gini coefficients (a measure of income distribution) will experience destabilizing class conflict, while those with better Gini coefficients will experience political stability. Seymour Martin Lipset's well known dictum that the more middle class (that is a relatively equal distribution of income)[15] a country is, the more likely it is to be a stable democracy is an example of the objectivist fallacy.

We speak of the objectivist fallacy because objective determinants are mediated by subjective determinants.[16] Objective determinants on their own and by themselves can not make things happen (even Marx argued that class consciousness was a necessary condition for collective action).[17] Tocqueville used subjective determinants in his *Old Regime and the French Revolution* to explain why, at the time of the French revolution, French peasants revolted and Prussian peasants did not. Objectively, Prussian peasants were serfs, unfree labourers, and their labour and production belonged to their masters; the French peasants were relatively free, with tenancy rights and some access to markets. Going by objective determinants, the oppressed and exploited Prussian peasants, not the relatively free and prosperous French peasant, should have revolted. But meaning, subjective determinants, were what ultimately mattered. Well before rising expectations and relative deprivation became fashionable concepts in the social sciences, Tocqueville used the absence of rising expectations and relative deprivation to explain the quiescence of the Prussian peasant and the presence of rising expectations and relative deprivation to explain the revolutionary activism of the French peasant.

Whether or not one agrees that 'everything changed', after 9/11, the 9/11 attack seems to have become the defining event for experiencing the state in the opening decade of the twenty-first century. America was the epicentre of the event and the place where it seems to have had its greatest effect on collective consciousness. The 9/11 attacks challenged the widely held American view that it was invulnerable to international terrorism. Their impact on America's collective consciousness was conditioned by a synergistic mix of geography and ideology. First, geography. The precarious era during the Cold War when Soviet and American ICBMs were deterred by the fear of mutually assured destruction was quickly forgotten once the Cold War ended. Americans resumed thinking of themselves as occupying a continental bastion protected by two oceans. The oceans had exempted North America from the carnage of the First World War's battlefields, from the devastation wrought by the Second World War's strategic bombing and, it was conveniently believed, made America immune from the reach of international terrorism.

We read *The 9/11 Commission Report* as an officially sanctioned means to make sense of the event.[18] The Commission, in a chapter labelled 'Foresight—and Hindsight', wrote that 'the 9/11 attacks revealed four kinds of failure . . . the first of which was the failure of imagination. . . . Neither in 2000 nor in the first eight months of 2001 [before the 9/11 attack] did any polling organization . . . think the subject of terrorism sufficiently on the minds of the public to warrant asking nor was it an important topic in the 2000 presidential campaign. Congress and the media called little attention to it. . . . While we now know,' the Commission observed, 'that al Qaeda was formed in 1988, at the end of the Soviet occupation of Afghanistan, the intelligence community did not describe this organization . . . until 1999' (341).[19] National Intelligence Estimates command attention at least in Washington but 'none was produced on terrorism between 1997 and 9/11' (343). Despite the best efforts of then

National Coordinator for Counterterrorism, Richard Clarke, a week before 9/11 'the government still needed to make a decision at the highest level as to whether al Qaeda was or was not 'a first order threat'' (343). Geography imagined as a continental bastion protected by two oceans seems to have anaesthetized Americans both in the street and in high office with regard to the threat of international terrorism.

Al Qaeda, on the other hand, experienced the US as very near indeed. 'The United States,' the Commission noted, 'emerged into the post-Cold War world as the globe's pre-eminent military power. . . . America stood out as an object of admiration, envy, and blame. This created a kind of cultural asymmetry. To us, Afghanistan seemed very far away. To members of al Qaeda, America seemed very close. In a sense, they were more globalized than we were' (340).[20]

Second, ideology. Americans' sense of invulnerability was grounded in an ideology of exceptionalism as well as in a geography of oceanic protection. Tocqueville identified the roots of American exceptionalism when he said in *Democracy in America* that 'the great advantage of the American is that he has arrived at a state of democracy without having to endure a democratic revolution; and that he is born free without having to become so.'[21] Americans' sense of immunity was nurtured by their sense of chosen-ness and special calling; they were the heirs of the intrepid band of Puritans who crossed the formidable ocean in search of religious freedom in the new world, a place that John Locke subsequently was to imagine as unmarked nature, empty but fertile.[22] They would establish what John Winthrop in 1630 called 'a city on a hill.' 'For we must consider that we shall be as a city upon a hill, the eyes of all the people are upon us.'[23] In time, the Puritan ethos was said to have become hegemonic; Europe's poor and hungry masses fled to the land of opportunity, learned English and adopted white Anglo-Saxon protestant (WASP) culture.[24] Winthrop's 'city on hill' became the trope of choice for politicians who wished to tell the world that others had it in them to be like America. Ronald Reagan often spoke of America as 'a shining city upon a hill whose beacon light guides freedom loving people everywhere.'[25]

When, on September 20, 2001, President George W. Bush addressed the nation for the first time after 9/11, he solemnly invoked the city upon a hill metaphor to frame the war on terror. It was, he said, a mission blessed by God that the rest of the world must join.[26] The president told the nation and the world that 'America was targeted for attack because we're the brightest beacon for freedom and opportunity in the world.'[27] Some leading scholars and public intellectuals fell enthusiastically in line with President Bush's city on a hill discourse. One was Michael Ignatieff. 'A confident and carefree republic—the city on the hill, whose people have believed that they are immune from history's harms—now has to confront not only an unending imperial destiny but also the remote possibility that seems to haunt the history of empire: hubris followed by defeat.'[28]

Others did not fall in line. Jessica Mathews thought that the most obvious point about 9/11 was that it 'changed the United States far more than it did the rest of the world. It tore away the sense of distance and difference that has enfolded us throughout our history. Some time ago technology and globalization turned that safe and separate 'city on the hill' into an illusion. . . . but it was one we still believed in.' At the same time 9/11 'widened a transatlantic gap' not only in the way Americans and Europeans had come to view international security but also in the way they viewed the threat of terrorist attacks. 'With Europe's long experience of domestic terror attacks, and no illusions of an invulnerable homeland, the events of that day [9/11] could never have held the significance for Europeans that they have for Americans.'[29] Inexplicably, the 1995 Oklahoma City bombing by American domestic terrorists does not seem to have breached the country's sense of invulnerability.[30]

So what significance did the attacks of 9/11 come to have for Americans? How has discourse about the state since 9/11 changed the relations of power? For answers, we look to what has been said in the public sphere by President Bush and members of his administration and by their critics. Paradoxically, we see the discourse about the state after 9/11 moving in opposite directions: on the one hand toward sovereignty unbounded, justified as response to a putative war against terrorism, on the other, toward sovereignty diminished as a result of continued globalization. Pre-9/11 territorially sovereign states were expected to be constrained by balance of power politics,[31] the interdependence and obligations of multilateral institutions, treaties and laws[32] and the power and resources of 'global' and transnational actors and processes.³³

The 'Vulcans' of the Bush war cabinet soon revealed themselves to be strong proponents of unbounded sovereignty.³⁴ Their intentions and plans for a war against Iraq matured before launching a war against the Taliban regime in Afghanistan.³⁵ A 2002 British government memo confirming this US policy orientation, and an accompanying inclination to fix 'intelligence and facts' around it, embarrassingly emerged during the 2005 UK general election.³⁶ Early on their doctrines exceeded those associated with the national security state at the Strangelovian heights of the Cold War struggle against the Soviet Union and 'communism', what Ronald Reagan called 'the evil empire.' Bi-polarity and the deterrence of mutually assured destruction as well as commitments to multilateral institutions and collective security put limits on the doctrines and practice of the Reagan era national security state. James Fallows speaks of the year after 9/11 (2001–2) as 'Bush's Lost Year'; 'by deciding to invade Iraq,' he says, 'the Bush Administration decided not to do many other things: not to reconstruct Afghanistan, not to deal with the threats posed by North Korea and Iran, and not to wage an effective war on terror.'³⁷

For citizens and policy intellectuals alike, the state's shape and character have been naturalized by the teleological perspective of modernization theory, a perspective that depicts the modern state as originating in the seventeenth century absolutist state in Western Europe and culminating in the twentieth century. 'Inside,' the expectation was that nationstate sovereignty would be qualified and limited by a government of laws; 'outside,' in the 'anarchic' space where sovereign states confronted each other, the expectation was that their rivalry would be checked by balance of power mechanisms and by the interdependence and cooperation associated with international institutions.³⁸ According to modernization theory, the twentieth century modern state represents an historical climax; in theory, the state story ends with its realization³⁹ in the modern state, a state constrained outside by the balance of power and inside by the rule of law. But the story of course continues, as the Bush administration's response to the traumatic events of 9/11 reveals.

The experiences of the state portrayed in the 12 chapters of Parts I through IV,⁴⁰ all happened before 11 September 2001. Even in the four years since they occurred the 9/11 attacks can be read as William Sewell read the storming of the Bastille in Paris on 14 July 1789, as a transformative event heralding the onset of the French Revolution. Unanticipated because seemingly uncaused, the event undoes for a time common understandings and expectations about what things mean and how they happen; all is in flux, anything seems possible. For a time, the shape of the future is open to those willing and able to seize the day. Because a transformative event reshuffles the causal deck of cards, it is uncertain how to seize the day but easier to do so.[41]

The Bush administration didnot hesitate to seize the day. It defined the 11 September 2001 attacks on the twin towers of the World Trade Center and on the Pentagon as acts of war rather than as crimes[42] and began beating the drum for a war against terrorism, a war Chris Hedges called against a 'phantom' and a British commentator called a war against an 'abstract noun.'[43] Three days after the attack, on Friday 14 September the President asked Congress to authorize the use of force against those responsible for the terrorist attacks. Unanimously in the Senate and with one vote against in the House of Representatives, the Congress authorized the President 'to use all necessary and appropriate force against those nations,[44] organizations, or persons he determines planned, authorized, committed, or aided the terrorists attacks.'[45] This was *not* an official declaration of war by the Congress as provided for by Article I, Section 8 of the Constitution giving Congress the power 'to declare war'[46] but the President used the vote to speak as though the country had launched a war against terrorism.

Wars are fought between states; one state wins, the other state loses. The Bush administration likened the 9/11 attacks to the attack on Pearl Harbor on 7 December 1941. It was said to be a 'Pearl Harbor-like event.' On 7 December 1941, the naval and air forces of the Japanese state launched a surprise attack on the US Pacific fleet based at Pearl Harbor, Hawaii. The US responded by declaring and conducting war, a war that it won when, on 2 September 1945, representatives of the Japanese state surrendered to representatives of the US state on the deck of the *U.S.S. Missouri* in Tokyo Bay. Because the Bush's administration 'war on terrorism' was being waged against an action, not a state, and an action perpetrated by an amorphous, stateless foe, the war was not subject to victory or defeat.

Thus, the war on terrorism can last longer than the US, role in the Second World War in defeating the (original) axis powers, with little media comment about the unflattering comparison. Chris Hedges put it this way: 'The battle we have begun is never-ending. . . . We have embarked on a campaign as quixotic as the one mounted to destroy us.' But the discourse of war, in Hedges' phrase, 'is a force that gives us meaning;' it evokes patriotism, creates purpose, demands sacrifice and requires discipline. The discourse of war establishes what Foucault calls 'relations of power'. Going to war resuscitated a problematic and failing presidency. With the winds of war blowing strongly at its back, a becalmed and drifting Bush presidency was able to choose a course and, Ahab-like according to critics, pursue it undeviatingly.[47]

In the aftermath of 9/11 the Bush administration's discourse and actions achieved considerable success in transforming the meaning of experiencing the state. It was fairly easy because of bin Laden's presence in Afghanistan to convince the public that the war against its Taliban regime was part of a war against terrorism but the war against Iraq was another matter. As it became clear that there were no weapons of mass destruction to be found and that the alleged link between the Iraq regime and al Qaeda was spurious, the claim that the war against Iraq was part of a war against terrorism lost credibility. Nevertheless, during the run-up to the 2004 election, almost half of the electorate (and three of four Bush supporters) were said to believe that there was such a link. The result was to enable the President to portray the war in Iraq as the frontline of the war against terrorism, and to make the President almost invulnerable to criticisms for the multiple failures associated with the Iraq war. The Bush administration's success in making the war against terrorism the dominant discourse not only saved the administration politically but also served to legitimize its discourse about unilateralism, pre-emptive war, regime change, and homeland security.[48]

Spokespersons for the Bush administration such as Secretary of Defense Donald Rumsfeld and Attorney General John Ashcroft were the vanguard for changing the discourse from multilateralism, collective security, and civil rights to unilateralism, pre-emptive war, regime change, and 'homeland' security. Prior to 9/11 the Bush administration had already begun its turn to hypernationalism and unilateralism by withdrawing from international treaties—from the Kyoto Treaty on Climate Change, from the Anti-Ballistic Missile Treaty, withdrawing the American signature to the treaty establishing the International Criminal Court and attempting to gain immunity from ICC prosecution. The President increasingly presented himself as the commander-in-chief leading a crusade against a newly appointed 'axis of evil'.

Military victory came quickly in the blitzkrieg war against Iraq. Portrayed as a 'war on terrorism' the war cast George Bush as commander-in-chief, a role he tried to use to enhance his political standing. He may have overplayed his hand on May 2, 2004, when he arrived in the copilot's seat of a Navy S-3B Viking that landed on the flight deck off the aircraft carrier *USS Lincoln*. Wearing a green flight suit and holding a white helmet, he stood below an enormous sign hung from the carrier's tower that read 'Mission Accomplished'. 'The picture-perfect landing, covered live on television, marked the latest effort by the White House to showcase Bush as commander in chief.'[49] Just hours later Bush told the nation '… that major combat operations in Iraq have ended.'[50] On the home front and abroad state discourse shifted to patriotism and hegemony; those who were not for the Bush administration were against it, including brash TV comedians.[51] In the eyes of many Europeans, America had become a 'rogue colossus.'[52]

The post-9/11 war on terrorism opened the way for the Bush administration to recast globalization too, from a process whose effect was to diminish state sovereignty to one that enhanced it. Conducting a war against terrorism became a new form of globalization, a form that unbound rather than diminished state sovereignty at home and abroad. The President's new discourse about pre-emptive war warned the country that, 'If we wait for threats to fully materialize, we will have waited too long.'[53] Condoleezza Rice, the National Security Adviser, warned that when you see the mushroom cloud it will be too late. The war on terrorism required the President to wage pre-emptive war. Given Congress constitutional authority to declare war and the country's commitment to collective security and deterrence, a doctrine of pre-emptive war was revolutionary but not without precedent.

President James Polk's pre-emptive war against Mexico (1846-48) provoked first term Congressman Abraham Lincoln to warn that, in the absence of imminent danger of attack, 'no one man should have the power to take the country to war.' Suppose, Lincoln wrote to his law partner back home in Illinois, W. H. Herndon, a president 'should choose to say he thinks it necessary to invade Canada, to prevent the British from invading us, how could you stop him? . . . You may say to him, 'I see no probability of the British invading us' but he will say to you, 'be silent; I see it, if you don't.''

The Constitution gives the war-making power to Congress to eliminate the kingly prerogative to wage power at his pleasure, a prerogative that was 'the most oppressive of all Kingly sources of oppression. . . . [the constitutional convention] resolved to so frame the Constitution so that no one man should hold the power of bringing this oppression upon us.' President Polk had shown, as Arthur Schlesinger, Jr put it, 'that a single man, if President, and backed, as he undoubtedly was, by public opinion, could through unilateral initiative compel Congress to declare war.' President Bush had shown the power of discourse by doing something similar.[54] United Nations weapons inspectors and allies doubted whether Iraq had weapons of mass destruction but the President said the equivalent of, 'be silent; I see it, if you don't.' The President and his willing ally, British Prime Minister Tony Blair, conducted themselves, despite dubious evidence, as though Iraq's President Saddam Hussein, possessed weapons of mass destruction and the President convinced 69 per cent of the country that Saddam Hussein was 'personally involved' in the attack on the World Trade Center.[55]

On 19 March 2003, the President lauched a pre-emptive war. He did so after it became clear that a US-sponsored resolution at the UN Security Council authorizing war against Iraq would not accrue the required support. On 18 September 2004, 18 months later, UN General Secretary General Kofi Annan said America's action was 'not in conformity with the United Nations Charter' and 'raised questions about the legitimacy' of the United States and Britain going to war against Iraq without specific authorization from the Security Council.'[56] In the immediate aftermath of the Iraq war, however, it seemed likely that President Bush would succeed in changing the discourse in America about pre-emptive war from illegitimate to legitimate. Prominent scholars and policy intellectuals, even those on the liberal to left side of the political spectrum, began to rationalize and justify unilateral use of American power in world politics.[57] Running with the hounds of war, Niall Ferguson in his 2004 bestselling *Colossus: The Price of America's Empire*, argued that 'if the United States retreats from global hegemony' the world was likely to experience 'the anarchic nightmare of a new Dark Age.'[58] He welcomed what he identified as American imperialism but found it wanting. It suffered, he said, from 'attention deficit disorder' and lacked the sense of duty and commitment to a civilizing mission (the white man's burden) that characterized British imperialism. Ferguson had held up British imperialism as a model for America in a 2002 book, *Empire: The Rise and Demise of the British World Order and the Lessons for Global Power*, where he argued 'that Britain's colonial enterprise benefited not only Britain's own possessions but much of the rest of the world.'[59] Ferguson would have the world believe that what he calls American imperialism is saving it from the 'anarchic nightmare of a new Dark Age' and, in a return to the spirit of Woodrow Wilson as manifest in the thoughts of Paul Wolfowitz, making the world safe for democracy.

There are ample reasons to doubt Ferguson's claims about the civilizing mission of US imperialism. In the same issue of *Foreign Policy* that carried Ferguson's article on how American power can save the world from a new Dark Age, John B. Judis tells us, in 'Imperial Amnesia', that American power in the form of military interventions in the Philippines in 1898 and in Mexico in 1913 produced violent nationalist resistance rather than grateful democracies and world order.[60] When President George W. Bush, on a six nation Asian tour, addressed the Philippine Congress on 18 October 2003 he told the Representatives that 'our soldiers [in 1898] liberated the Philippines from Spanish colonial rule' and transformed the Philippines into a democracy.[61] America, Bush asserted, was doing the same today in Iraq. Bush's narrative of liberation from imperial rule (or tyranny) followed by democratic self-government follows Woodrow Wilson's sleeping beauty theory[62] of self-determination and democracy: America, the handsome prince, arouses the slumbering maiden with a kiss of liberation. America's Lockean inspired liberal universalism leads it to assume that people are the same everywhere. Underneath, deep down, they know and love freedom in the same way that Americans do.[63] Woodrow Wilson indeed believed that America's participation in the First World War could spur national self-determination and make the world safe for democracy. He especially had in mind the oppressed nations ruled by defeated empires, the Austro-Hungarian and the Ottoman empires. This radiant belief was premised on something like a sleeping beauty theory.[64]

George Bush had a similar shining premise in mind when on 6 November 2003 he told an audience at the National Endowment for Democracy in a speech on freedom in Iraq and the Middle East that 'The United States has adopted a new policy, a forward strategy of freedom in the Middle East. . . . The advance of freedom is the calling of our country. From the Fourteen Points [Woodrow Wilson] to the Four Freedoms [Franklin Roosevelt], to the Speech at Westminster [Ronald Reagan] America has put our power at the service of principle. We believe that liberty is the design of the future, we believe liberty is the direction of history.'[65]

Have American armies in the colonial and post-colonial world been experienced as liberators, Prince Charmings whose sensitive touch awakens a slumbering democracy? After annexing the Philippines and installing a colonial administrator, American military forces waged a brutal war against the Philippine independence movement which the McKinley administration earlier had encouraged to fight against Spanish rule. The war went on for 14 years with 120,000 troops deployed, 4000 US casualties and at least 200,000 Filipino soldiers and civilians killed. According to Judis, democracy in the Philippines has had a hard time taking hold. 'The electoral machinery the United States designed in 1946 provided a democratic veneer beneath which a handful of families, allied with US investors—and addicted to kickbacks—controlled the Philippine land, economy, and society. The tenuous system,' Judis says, broke down in 1973 when Philippine politician Ferdinand Marcos had himself declared president for life. Marcos was finally overthrown in 1986, but even today 'Philippine democracy remains more dream than reality.'[66]

The consequences for experiencing the state of the movement toward establishing discourses of unbounded sovereignty 'outside' and diminished sovereignty 'inside' have been considerable. 'Outside', the discourse and practice of superpower unilateralism, pre-emptive war and using war to bring about 'regime change'[67] challenged the discourse and practice of world order multilateralism and collective security. The Bush administration tore up the scripts that neoliberal institutionalists and constructivists said led to cooperation among sovereign states.[68] 'Inside', the Star Chamber and police state[69] consequences at Guantanamo Bay and Abu Ghraib of the 'war against terrorism' and the practice of homeland security challenged the limits on the arbitrary exercise of power that Carl J. Friedrich identified as the essence of constitutional government.[70] Benjamin Barber put it this way: 'It is hard for the US to be the beacon of freedom that Bush's speech [at the NED on November 6, 2003] celebrated. . . . When it has in many places come to be seen as the maker of war the world most fears. It is hard to lead a global struggle for human rights when the US holds enemy aliens prisoners without rights and when Americans who criticize the preventive-war policy are vilified.'[71]

After 9/11 the Bush administration succeeded sufficiently in changing the discourse and the relations of power to allow the state to launch pre-emptive wars against Afghanistan and Iraq; to hold prisoners in secrecy, without cause, counsel or right to habeas corpus at the US military base at Guantanamo, Cuba; to condone the physical torture and sexual humiliation of prisoners at Abu Ghraib prison near Baghdad.[72] The 'Patriot Act' opened the way to overriding citizens' civil rights in the name of homeland security.[73] Outside, the discourse of unbounded sovereignty challenged world regimes for collective security, environmental protection, and crimes against humanity. Inside, it served to set aside human and minority rights in the name of an amorphous and ubiquitous terrorist threat.

By using the vocabulary of war to characterize the 9/11 attack the Bush administration was able to challenge the dominant discourse about the state. Acts of war are acts of states. States make and wage war. The 9/11 attack was, in International Relations language, authored by an amorphous non-state actor, al Qaeda, a loose network of global operatives working at local levels who share an ill-defined but strongly held world view. According to counterterrorism expert Richard Clarke that world view is 'Islamic Jihadism, which must be defeated in a battle of ideas.'[74] The illusion created by the phrase, a war against terrorism, helped the Bush administration to persuade a majority in the US that bin Laden's al Qaeda and Saddam Hussein's Iraq were joint authors of the terrorist attacks on the US and that, by going to war against the sovereign state of Iraq, it was waging a necessary 'war against terrorism'.

There was an alternative discourse available about the 9/11 attacks. Writing in *The New Yorker* as early as 24 September 2001, Hendrik Hertzberg, for one, argued that al Qaeda was a non-state actor and should be treated accordingly. According to Hertzberg, treating the al Qaeda attacks as acts of war 'is a category mistake. The metaphor of war—and it is more metaphor than description—ascribes to the perpetrators a dignity they do not merit, a status they cannot claim, and a strength they do not possess. Worse,' he continues, 'it points to a set of responses that could prove futile and counterproductive [such as going to war against Iraq in March 2003]. . . . [A] more useful metaphor than war is crime. The terrorists of September 11 are outlaws within a global polity . . . . they do not constitute or control a state. . . . Their status and numbers are such that the task of dealing with them should be viewed as a police matter, of the most urgent kind. As with all criminal fugitives, the essential job is to find out who and where they are.' The British military historian, Sir Michael Howard, made a similar argument. The Bush administration, he said, had made a 'terrible and irreversible' mistake in calling its anti-terrorism campaign a war: 'I can think of no policy more likely, not only to indefinitely prolong the war, but to ensure that we can never win it.'[75]

The political philosopher Anne Norton also questioned whether there could be a war against terrorism. 'War,' she wrote, 'was once a matter of simple questions: who are our friends? Who is the enemy? In this war the enemy is unknown, uncertain. Not knowing the enemy, we cannot know when or how or whether victory will come .... or how the nation can be defended.'[76] Alyson J.K. Bailes added a European perspective. Making war on terrorism she said '... is illogical because it uses methods that work within a 'statist' system of power against opponents who reject that system and who in practice largely escape its disciplines.'[77]

Further compounding the confusion about how to read the 9/11 attacks is the difference between terrorism and terrorist, between the tactic and the adversary. As the 9/11 Commission said, 'Terrorism is a tactic' (363). A war against terrorism can never be won; a war against terrorists might be won. Terrorism in the form of terrorist acts is well nigh a universal phenomenon: assassinations, killing of innocent civilians, the use of violence to intimidate or coerce governments and societies. By mesmerizing people with the threat of terrorism, the Bush administration has been able to frighten the American public and some abroad with a bogeyman of unfathomable proportions. Civil wars, asymmetrical conflicts more generally, often spawn terrorists' acts, acts that have occurred throughout history. As has been frequently said, one man's terrorist is another man's freedom fighter. In order to gain allies in the 'war against terrorism' the Bush administration has been willing to apply the label terrorist to the Chechnyan struggle against the Russian government, the Uighar struggle against the Chinese government, and, despite occasional statements to the contrary, the Palestinian struggle against Israeli occupation.

In treating terrorism as a diffuse enemy rather than as a tactic and by fighting wars against Afghanistan and Iraq in the name of fighting the war against terrorism, the Bush administration has perhaps misled itself and certainly the public about the terrorist threat.[78] The 9/11 Commission saw the threat differently: 'The present transnational danger is Islamist terrorism. . . . Islam is not the enemy. . . . Our enemy is twofold: al Qaeda, a stateless network of terrorists. . . and a radical ideological movement in the Islamic world' (363). The Commission has moved in the right direction but not far enough. The anonymous author (now known to be Michael F. Scheuer) of *Imperial Hubris: Why the West is Losing the War on Terror*[79] gets closer to specifying who and what the 9/11 adversary is about. Anonymous, who has devoted his intelligence career to understanding bin Laden and al Qaeda, asks his readers to enter into the Islamic world of bin Laden and his movement. 'Because of his defense of Islam, personal piety, physical bravery, integrity, and generosity,' bin Laden, Anonymous tells us, 'is seen by millions of his coreligionists. . . . as an Islamic hero, as that faith's ideal type, and almost as a modern day Saladin, determined to defend Islam and protect Muslims. . . . bin Laden certainly is the most popular anti-American leader in the world today. . . . Thanks to the Internet, his words also are available to anyone on the planet with access to a computer, or via the largest

Arabic satellite television channels, Al-Jazirah and Al-Arabiyah.' He represents, according to Anonymous, 'not a failed civilization's envious, resentful and irrational response to a successful, triumphalist West, but a determined resistance to wrongs done and oppressions experienced.'[80] This is a far cry from President Bush's reading of what motivates bin Laden and al Qaeda. In his first major speech after 9/11 on 20 September 2001, he asked, 'Why do they hate us?' He has been giving different versions of this answer ever since: 'They hate our freedoms.' Subsequently he has re-phrased the message: 'They hate us for who we are' and 'They hate us because we are free.' James Fallows has called the President's message dangerous because it is self-justifying and self-deluding; the only thing we have done wrong is to be 'so excellent.' And dangerous because, as Anonymous has argued, 'it reflects so little knowledge of how Islamic extremism has evolved.'[81]

We have tried to persuade our readers that 9/11 was indeed a transformative event for how the American state was experienced at home and abroad. The Bush administration seized the day by launching new state discourses about unilateralism, pre-emptive war, regime change, and homeland security. In so far as the discourses have successfully challenged the dominant discourses of the post-Second World War era, they have changed 'relations of power' and thus the way Americans experience an increasingly, and openly, aggressive and intrusive state. The uncertain effects of America's pre-emptive war against Iraq on American and world opinion and the uncertain longer term consequences of Bush's thin victory in the 2004 presidential election means that the fate of the Bush administration's post-9/11 discourses remains uncertain.[82] Still, by the spring of 2005, according to Harris and Gallup polls, six of 10 Americans regarded the Iraq war as a mistake and 'favor bringing most troops home within a year.'

We have not said anything about how the Bush administration's discourses fared outside the US, particularly in the Islamic world and Europe. However, there seems to be wide agreement that the standing in public opinion of the Bush administration's version of the American state is at a low ebb. The rift between America and Muslim countries and between America and its oldest and closest allies in Western Europe seems deep and problematic for the future effectiveness abroad of the American state. Many have remarked on how quickly the Bush administration drained the huge reservoir of respect and good will that the American state had built up in the half century that followed the close of the Second World War. At home, the 2004 presidential election showed that the country remained divided metaphorically and, to a considerable extent, empirically between the red (Republican) and the blue (Democratic) states, the red states apparently content with the Bush administration and their experiences with the American state, the blue states apprehensive, even alienated.[83] Roughly half the voters at the November 2004 election seems to welcome unbounded sovereignty, undisturbed by its consequences for freedom and security at home and abroad, while the other half finds that unbounded sovereignty has made them less free and less secure at home and abroad.

NOTES

1. For epistemic communities see Peter Haas, 'Introduction: Epistemic Communities and International Political Coordination', *International Organization* (special issue) vol. 46, no. 1 (winter), 1992 pp. 1–35. The term, paradigm, was coined by Thomas Kuhn in his transformatory book, *The Structure of Scientific Revolutions* (Chicago, IL: University of Chicago Press, 1962). Kuhn argued *inter alia* that facts and methods exist in the context of paradigms, the dominant theories that define epistemic communities. Science was cumulative *within* epistemic communities but was not cumulative across them over time because 'scientific revolutions' displaced regnant paradigms. Stephen Toulmin modified Kuhn's view of scientific change by showing that the anomalies that Kuhn argued led to scientific revolutions more often than not led to incremental change rather than to the radical displacement of an earlier paradigm or theory by a later one. For a recent version of the Toulmin perspective see his, *Return to Reason* (Cambridge, MA: Harvard University Press, 2001), particularly Chapters 7 and 11, 'Practical Reason and the Clinical Arts', and 'The Varieties of Experience'. Paul Feyerabend attempted to 'reconcile' these views in his own flamboyant way in his 'guerrilla war' theory of paradigm change. See John Kurt Jacobsen, *Dead Reckonings: Ideas, Interests, and Politics in the 'Information Age'* (Atlantic Highlands, NJ: Humanities Press, 1997), pp. 3–24.
2. Lloyd Rudolph and Susanne Hoeber Rudolph make the case for the validity and importance of subjective knowledge in Political Science in 'Engaging Subjective Knowledge: How Amar Singh's Diary Narratives of and by the

Self Help Explain Identity Politics', *Perspectives on Politics*, vol. 1, no. 4 (December) 2003, pp. 681–94. The epistemology of subjective knowledge involves telling what a speaker—or writer—knows about what he or she has experienced. His or her knowledge is situated and contextual; his or her voice is located in time, place, and circumstance. 'The epistemology of subjective knowledge,' the Rudolphs write, 'stands counter to that of objective knowledge—i.e., knowledge based on a view from nowhere, unmediated, transparent observation generated by unmarked and unencumbered observers' (p. 682).

3. James Clifford, 'Introduction: Partial Truths', in *Writing Culture: The Politics and Poetics of Ethnography*, James Clifford and George Marcus (eds) (Berkeley, CA: University of California Press, 1986), p. 8.

4. More can be said about the contrast between subjective knowledge and objective knowledge but we think it best not to burden the text with a distinction that is not central to the argument about experiencing the state so we have confined it to this note.

   Unlike the objective knowledge called for in telling the truth, the whole truth and nothing but the truth, the Cree Indian's knowledge is situated and contextual; his voice is located in time, place, and circumstance. The epistemology of subjective knowledge stands counter to that of objective knowledge—i.e., knowledge based on a view from nowhere; unmediated, transparent observation generated by unmarked, unencumbered observers. James Clifford describes the Cree hunter's concept of truth as 'rigorous partiality'. Rigorous partiality recognizes and validates the situated, inflected nature of truth. Rather than denying or repressing the sociology of knowledge, rigorous partiality self-consciously acknowledges that context shapes why and how knowledge is acquired and what it is taken to mean. Clifford's claim for rigorous partiality is consistent with Hans-Georg Gadamer's hermeneutic stance in *Truth and Method* (New York: The Seabury Press, 1975), that the scientific ideal of objectivity is compromised by personal experience, cultural tradition, and prior understandings. Partiality also signifies that which is not whole, complete or being carried to completion. 'Rigorous partiality' makes the epistemological claim that knowing the whole truth is a capacity not given to mortals. The best they can strive for is partial truths. In this sense subjective truth is rigorously partial and contingent, not impartial and objective.

   For Aristotle on *phronesis* see *The Nichomachean Ethics* (Hammondsworth: Penguin, 1976), 1140a24 – 1140b12. For a contemporary application, see Bent Flyvbjerg, *Making Social Science Matter* (New York: Cambridge University Press, 2001).

5. Michel Foucault, 'Lecture Two: 14 January 1976', *Power/Knowledge: Selected Interviews & Other Writings, 1972 -1977*, Colin Gordon (ed.), Colin

Gordon, Leo Marshall, John Mepham, Kate Soper (trans.), (New York: Pantheon Books, 1980) 93.

6 . Mark Danner, What Are You Going to Do With That?' *The New York Review of Books*, 23 June 2005, p. 53

7. The 'original' German version of Jurgen Habermas' version of a public sphere was published in 1962 under the title *Strukturnwandel der Offentlichkeir*. It narrowly focuses on political associations and features strongly rationalist and speech-act oriented dimensions. The 1962 book was published in English as *The Structural Transformation of the Public Sphere*, trans. by Thomas Burger and Frederick Lawrence (Cambridge, MA: MIT Press, 1989).

Habermas, who appeared at a panel on his work in 1989, had expanded his horizons to include associations with mainly social ends. The institutional core of 'civil society' is constituted by voluntary unions outside the realm of the state and the economy and ranging from churches, cultural associations, and academies to independent media, sport and leisure clubs, debating societies, groups of concerned citizens, and grassroots petitioning drives all the way to occupational associations, political parties, labour unions, and 'alternative' institutions. Craig Calhoun (ed.), *Habermas and the Public Sphere*, (Cambridge, MA: MIT Press, 1996), p. 253.

For Habermas' later view of the public sphere see his, 'Further Reflections on the Public Sphere', in Calhoun (ed.), *Habermas*, p. 422.

8. See Elaine Sciolino, 'Hostages Urge France to Repeal Its Scarf Ban', the *New York Times*, August 31, 2004.

9. Orhan Pamuk, *Snow*, trans. Maureen Freely (New York: Alfred A. Knopf, 2004), p. 22.

10. On this apt metaphor see Foucault's *The Archaeology of Knowledge* (New York: Routledge, 1972).

11. We do not think of 'experiencing' the state as a passive activity; it is shaped *inter alia* by social position, interests, values, resources, and even by the unconscious. The same 'stimulus' does not engender identical 'responses'; it will be interpreted, Merleau-Ponty argues, according to what it signifies in the situational context for the perceiver. Maurice Merleau-Ponty, *Structure of Behavior*, trans. Alden L. Fisher (Boston, MA: Beacon Press, 1963), p. 45. 'A human being does not only have a hand and a heart', Crozier observed of lower participants in formal organizations. 'He also has a head, which means that he is free to decide his own game. This is what almost all proponents of human relations theories, as well as their early rational proponents, tend to forget.' Michel Crozier, *The Bureaucratic Phenomenon* (Chicago, IL: University of Chicago Press, 1967), pp. 158, 162.

12. Indeed, some noteworthy citizens wonder aloud whether it really is their state any longer. Michael Moore's bestseller *Dude Where's My Country* (New

York: Warner Books, 2003) was a comical expression of an underlying widespread concern as the Bush agenda unfolded. Eminent commentators of the calibre of Fritz Stern have gone so far as to speak of worrisome parallels of Bush's America to Weimar Germany.

13. Members of the Project for the New American Century (PNAC—for details see note 3 were waiting for a 'catastrophic and catalyzing event—like a new Pearl Harbor' that would mobilize the public and allow them to put their theories and plans into action. 11 September was, of course, precisely what they were looking for. Within days, Condoleeza Rice called together members of the National Security Council and asked them '*to think about 'how do you capitalize on these opportunities to fundamentally change American doctrine, and the shape of the world, in the wake of September 11th."(Emphasis supplied.) Chalmers Johnson, The Sorrows of Empire: Militarism, Secrecy, and the End of the Republic* (New York: Henry Holt, 2004) p. 229.

14. For a recent effort to say what the state *is*, the state as an observed object or idea, see Margaret Levi, 'The State of the Study of the State', *Political Science: State of the Discipline*, Ira Katznelson and Helen V. Milner (eds.), (New York: W. W. Norton/Washington, DC: American Political Science Association, 2002).

Drawing on the literature, Levi says that 'a state is a complex apparatus of centralized and institutionalized power that concentrates violence, establishes property rights, and regulates society within a given territory while formally being recognized as a state by international forums' (p. 40). We wonder if this definition does not represent a contestable aspiration or prescription more than does an essential meaning. Levi goes on to cite favourably Joel Migdal's observation that states have 'insinuated' themselves into the core identities of their 'subjects' via patriotism and nationalism, opening the way, in our view, to a broad space for interpreting states in terms of subjective knowledge.

Also contributing to Katznelson and Milner, *Political Science*, Miles Kahler in 'The State of the State in World Politics', takes a more contingent view of the state by embedding it in alternative and sometimes competing epistemic communities, modes of inquiry, and historical contexts. He starts with the view that there is 'a growing awareness that the state has too often been defined as the European state, a species delimited in both time and space' (p. 58) and ends with the view that there are alternative units of analysis, action, and identity. Because Kahler's view is implicitly constructivist, relying as it does on the narratives and discourses of competing epistemes, it more closely approximates our effort to analyse the state via the subjective knowledge gained by experiencing it.

We welcome recent efforts to historicize and culturally contextualize state analysis in *Dynamics of State Formation: India and Europe Compared*,

Martin Doornbos and Sudipta Kaviraj (eds.), (Thousand Oaks, CA: Sage Publications, 1997) and in *The Everyday State and Society in Modern India*, C. J. Fuller and Veronique Benei (eds.), (New Delhi: Social Science Press, 2000). However innovative the mediating epistemes used by the editors and contributors to these two volumes, their analyses remain within the framework of objectivist epistemology.

15. See Seymour Martin Lipset, *Political Man* (New York: Doubleday, 1960), and S. M. Lipset, 'The Social Requisites of Democracy Revisited: 1993 Presidential Address', *American Sociological Review* 59, no. 1 (February 1994): 1–22 for the argument that presence and viability of democracy depends on the existence of a middle class and Lloyd I. Rudolph, 'The Modernity of Tradition: The Democratic Incarnation of Caste in India,' *The American Political Science Review*, vol. 59, no. 4 (December), 1965, pp. 975-89, for a theoretical and empirical critique of Lipset's generalization on the basis of India's experience.

16. See Lloyd I. Rudolph and Susanne Hoeber Rudolph, 'Determinants and Varieties of Agrarian Mobilization', *Agrarian Power and Agricultural Productivity in India*, Meghnad Desai, Susanne Hoeber Rudolph, and Ashok Rudra (eds), (Berkeley, CA: University of California Press, 1984), pp. 281–344, where objective determinants are held to be necessary but not sufficient to explain outcomes and subjective determinants are held to be sufficient to explain outcomes.

17. Of the large literature on the subjective element in historical materialism see, for example, Bertell Ollman, *Alienation: Marx's Concept of Man in Capitalist Society* (New York: Cambridge University Press, 1971) and note the impact of Antonio Gramsci's writings within that tradition.

18. This is not to suggest the report has not been subject to criticism. Googling '9/11 Commission Report' in October 2004 raised 178,000 web pages, many querulous.

19. The Commission's statements about the non-recognition of the Al Qaeda threat begs the question whether it was the public or the specialized agencies supported by tax dollars which should have been dealing conscientiously with the matter. As Richard Clarke tacitly conceded and former Carter administration national security adviser Zbigniew Brzezinski admitted, the covert state-sponsored cultivation of the Afghan fundamentalist rebel forces in the 1980s provided the fertile ground in which Al Qaeda sprouted and grew, a phenomenon now widely known as 'blowback'. Clarke writes that the Clinton Administration had to badger Bosnian leader Izetbegovic after the Dayton accords to eject a large contingent of 'muj' fighters, renowned for their ferocity and brutality (and links to Al Qaeda) to whom the US turned a blind eye, at least when transported into the Balkans in the early 1990s. Richard A. Clarke, *Against All Enemies: Inside America's War on Terrorism* (New York: Free Press, 2004),

p. 137. See also Brzezinski's interview with *Le Nouvel Observateur*, Paris, 15-21 January 1998, which is translated and posted by the Centre for Research Globalisation at http://www.globalresearch.ca/articles/ BRZ110A.html.

Finally, Chalmers Johnson analyses the phenomenon of 'blowback' in his book of the same title, *Blowback: The Costs and Consequences of American Empire* (New York: Henry Holt, 2000).

20. Page citations indicated in parentheses are from *The 9/11 Commission Report, Authorized Edition of the Final Report of the National Commission on Terrorist Attacks Upon the United States* (New York: W. W. Norton, 2004). Before a defining event such as 9/11, the Commission wrote, signals are 'obscure and pregnant with conflicting meanings.... As time passes, more documents become available, and the bare facts of what happened become still clearer. Yet *how* those things happened becomes harder to reimagine' (339).

    For more on when and why Osama bin Laden and Al Qaeda surfaced as a threat to the US see Chapter 6, 'Al Qaeda Revealed', Clarke, *Against All Enemies*, pp. 133–54. Clarke faults President George W. Bush for failing 'to act prior to September 11 on the threat from al Qaeda despite repeated warnings and then harvested a political windfall for taking obvious yet insufficient steps after the attacks' and for launching 'an unnecessary and costly war in Iraq that strengthened the fundamentalist, Islamic terrorist movement worldwide' (p. 153).

21. The argument for how the circumstances of American exceptionalism played out in American history and politics and shaped American ideology was powerfully argued in Louis Hartz's *The Liberal Tradition in America* (New York: Harcourt Brace and Company, 1955). The Tocqueville quotation is from the prologue of Hartz's book.

22. For John Locke's view of America as an un-marked, empty space see Uday Singh Mehta, *Liberalism and Empire* (Chicago, IL; University of Chicago Press, 1999), particularly Chapter Four, 'Liberalism, Empire and Territory', pp. 115–52.

23. Winthrop was echoing Matthew's account of Jesus' words at 5:14–16: 'You are the light of the world. A city set on a hill cannot be hid, nor do men light a lamp and put it under a bushel, but on a stand, and it gives light to all in the house. Let your light so shine before men, that they may see your good works . . .'

24. A canonical work for the European immigrants to America is Oscar Handlin's *The Uprooted* (New York: Grosset & Dunlap, 1951). The assimilation story is classically told in Milton M. Gordon, *Assimilation in American Life* (New York: Oxford University Press, 1964). The narrative of assimilation is convincingly challenged in James Morone's *Hellfire Nation* (New Haven, CT: Yale University Press, 2003). Earlier, Nathan

Glazer and Daniel Patrick Moynihan's *Beyond the Melting Pot* (Cambridge, MA: MIT Press, 1970) had challenged the assimilation thesis and Nathan Glazer's *We Are All Multiculturalists Now* (Cambridge, MA: Harvard University Press, 1997) made the case against it by depicting a pluralist America.

25. Center for Media and Democracy, 'America is a shining city upon a hill', Disinfopedia, http://www.disinfopedia.org/wiki.phtml?title=America_is_a_shining_city_upon_a_hill.

26. For the Puritan origins of America's unreflective self-righteous apprehensions of the foreign 'other', and its dark consequences, see Richard Drinnon, *Facing West: The Metaphysics of Indian-Hating and Empire Building* (Minneapolis, MN: University of Minnesota Press, 1980).

27. Kimberly Winston, 'From Theological Tenet to Political Password: Three of the Democratic candidates have already pitched their audiences some version of the 'City on the Hill' speech'. *Belief. Com*, http://www.beliefnet.com/story/139/story_13917_1.html as cited by Center for Media and Democracy, 'America is a shining city upon a hill', Disinfopedia, http://www.disinfopedia.org/wiki.phtml?title=America_is_a_shining_city_upon_a_hill.

28. Michael Ignatieff, 'The American Empire: The Burden', the *New York Times Magazine*, 5 January 2003, p. 52.

29. Jessica Mathews, 'September 11, One Year Later: A World of Change', *Policy Brief*, vol. 18 (Special Edition August), 2002, pp. 1, 8–9.

30. On the Oklahoma City bombers see Garry Wills, 'The New Revolutionaries', the *New York Review of Books*, 10 August 1995.

31. The doctrine and practice of balance of power is central to realist and neo-realist theories of and explanations for international relations understood as the relations among sovereign states. Leading books included Hans J. Morgenthau, *Politics Among Nations*, rev. 6th edition (New York: Knopf, 1985); Kenneth N. Waltz, *Theory of International Politics* (Reading, MA: Addison-Wesley, 1979); Stephen M. Walt, *Revolution and War* (Ithaca, NY: Cornell University Press, 1996), where the theory of band-wagoning was added to that of balancing; and John J. Mearsheimer, *The Tragedy of Great Power Politics* (New York: Norton, 2001), where balance of power theory is supplemented by theories of deterrence.

32. For an overview of neoliberal views of interdependence and cooperation see Robert O. Keohane, 'International Relations, Old and New', in *A Handbook of Political Science*, Robert E. Goodin and Hans-Dieter Klingenmann (eds), (New York: Oxford University Press, 1996) pp. 462-76 and Joseph S. Nye's *The Paradox of American Power: Why the World's Only Superpower Can't Go It Alone* (New York: Oxford University Press, 2002), where Nye introduces the concept of 'soft power'.

33. The case for why and how economic globalization should diminish state

sovereignty by replacing it with market forces is made *inter alia* by Thomas Friedman in *The Lexus and the Olive Tree: Understanding Globalization* (New York: Farrar, Straus and Giroux, 1999) and, more recently, by Jagdish Bhagwati, *In Defense of Globalization* (New York: Oxford University Press, 2004). Friedman and Bhagwati see the benign face of globalization. State sovereignty, except for the protection of property and the enforcement of contracts, tends to interfere with efficient working market forces. The dark side of economic globalization, a view that sees the losers and the victims of global power and interdependence, can be found, *inter alia*, in the work of Joseph E. Stiglitz, *Globalization and Its Discontents* (New York: Norton, 2003); George Soros, *George Soros on Globalization* (New York: Public Affairs / Perseus Books Group, 2002); Teresa Brennan, *Globalization and its Terrors* (London: Routledge, 2002) and, from a former adviser to Margaret Thatcher, John Gray, *False Dawn: The Delusions of Global Capitalism* (New York: New Press, 2000).

For how transnational civil society diminishes state sovereignty see *inter alia* Susanne Hoeber Rudolph's introduction, 'Religion, States, and Transnational Civil Society', in *Transnational Religion and Fading States*, Susanne Hoeber Rudolph and James Piscadtori (eds), (Boulder, CO: Westview Press, 1997).

34. The term 'Vulcan' is taken from the title of James Mann's *The Rise of the Vulcans: The History of Bush's War Cabinet* (New York: Viking Press, 2004). Mann has closely examined the past words and deeds of Bush's foreign policy team for evidence about the ideological predispositions, past experiences, and mindsets as well as the contingent circumstances that made it possible for, in the words of reviewer Stephen Holmes, Dick Cheney, Donald Rumsfeld, Paul Wolfowitz, Condoleeza Rice, Colin Powell, Douglas Feith, Richard Armitage, Stephen Hadley, and 'Scooter' Libby, 'to hijack the country's reaction to 9/11'. 'Unfortunately for us,' Holmes concluded in May 2004, 'we have only begun to witness the consequences of this ghastly misuse of unaccountable power.' The contingent circumstances include a few conservative Congressmen's ability to block Tom Ridge's nomination as Secretary of Defense on the 'immaterial reason that he was wobbly on abortion.' Stephen Holmes, 'The National Insecurity State', the *Nation*, 10 May 2004, http://www.thenation.com/docprint.mhtml?i=20040510&s=holmes.

35. According to Chalmers Johnson, 'Ever since the first American war against Iraq, the Gulf War of 1991, a number of the key people who planned and executed it in the White House and the Pentagon wanted to go back and finish what they had started.' From 1992 to 2000, when they were out of power, 'they drafted extensive plans for what should be done if the Republicans retook the White House. In the spring of 1997, they organized themselves as the Project for the New American Century [PNAC] and

began vigorously for aggression against Iraq and the remaking of the Middle East.' Key players in the PNAC included William Kristol, Elliott Abrams; Paul Wolfowitz, John Bolton, Richard Perle, Dick Cheney, L. Lewis Libby, and Stephen Cambone, all persons involved in the transformation of the US government that occurred after 9/11. See Chalmars Johnson, *The Sorrows of Empire: Militarism, Secrecy, and the End of the Republic* (New York: Henry Holt, 2004), pp. 227–8. Richard Clark in *Against All Enemies* tells a similar story; see particularly p. 264.

36. Bush 'wanted to remove Saddam, through military action, justified by the conjunction of terrorism and WMD,' the high level British government memo said. 'But the intelligence and facts were being fixed around the policy [and it] seemed clear that Bush had made up his mind to take military action, even if the timing was not yet decided.' The news of the memo was published in the London *Sunday Times* 1 May 2005.

37. In early 2002 the US and the Northern Alliance 'had beaten the Taliban but lost bin Laden.' The choice became to go after bin Laden, work on the reconstruction of Afghanistan, and attend to nuclear proliferation in the two other axis of evil states, North Korea and Iran, or shift the emphasis on the putative 'global war on terror' 'somewhere else.' According to James Fallows, the choice had already been made. During top level meetings at Camp David immediately after the 9/11 attacks, 'Paul Wolfowitz forcefully argued that Saddam Hussein was so threatening and his overthrow was so 'doable,' that he had to be included in the initial military response.' Colin Powell prevailed in his insistence that Afghanistan had to be first; 'the American people just aren't going to understand if you don't do something in Afghanistan right away,' he is reported to have argued. 'But Afghanistan first did not mean Afghanistan only.' On 17 September 2001, Richard Clarke reports that his pre-9/11 memo on anti-terror strategy had only one amendment, 'the addition of a paragraph asking the Defense Department to prepare war plans for Iraq.' James Fallows, 'Bush's Lost Year', *Atlantic*, no. 68 (October) 2004.

    Jane Mayer's account in 'A Reporter at Large: The Manipulator', of how Ahmad Chalabi pushed a tainted case for war provides a detailed picture of Paul Wolfowitz and other 'Vulcans'" commitment to an Iraq war. The *New Yorker*, 7 June 2004, pp. 58-72.

38. For the theory and practice of sovereignty 'inside' and 'outside' the state see R. B. J. Walker, *Inside/Outside: International Relations as Political Theory* (Cambridge, UK: Cambridge University Press, 1993). For the conceptualization of cooperation in the context of international society, i.e. a society of states, see Hedley Bull, *The Anarchical Society: A Study of Order in World Politics* (New York: Columbia University Press, 1977).

39. For the teleology of the modern nation state embedded in modernization theory see Robert Nisbet, *The Quest for Community* (New York: Oxford

University Press, 1953), especially Chapter 7. Some of this thinking can be traced back to Hegel's universal progress of spirit institutionalized in the state. Historicizing the state not only gives it a career but also a discursive space and a constructed character. Those who find modernization theory or the end of history view plausible might accept that the modern state culminated in its post-1945 version of the welfare/warfare state.

40. The topics Parts I through IV are 'Experiencing High Modernist States in America, India and Russia'; 'Experiencing the State From Below in Village Germany and India and Urban Karachi'; 'Experiencing the State From Outside: Psychiatry, Film and Art'; and 'Emancipatory Resistance.'

41. William H. Sewell, Jr, 'Historical Events as Transformations of Structures: Inventing Revolution at the Bastille', *Theory and Society*, vol. 25, no. 6 (December), 1996 pp. 841–81.

42. See Hendrik Hertzberg, 'Tuesday, and After', *Politics: Observations & Arguments, 1966 -2004* (New York: Penguin Press, 2004), pp. 604–6, for the disputed decision to choose war rather than crime to define the meaning of the attacks.

43. Terry Jones, 'Why Grammar is the First Casualty of War', *Daily Telegraph*, January 12, 2002.

44. Note the ambiguity of the word 'nation'; a nation is not a state but may be a people or an ethnic group, linguistic or religious group. In domestic and international law, wars are declared and waged against states.

45. The resolution is quoted in Chris Hedges, *War Is a Force That Gives Us Meaning* (New York: Anchor Books, 2003), p. 5. The only dissenting vote in the House was by Barbara J. Lee, a Democrat from California. She warned that military action could not guarantee the safety of the country and that 'as we act, let us not become the evil we deplore.' Hedges warns against going to war 'not against a state but against a phantom. The *jihad* we have embarked on is targeting an elusive and protean enemy' p. 4.

46. 'The Founders were determined,' Arthur Schlesinger, Jr writes, 'to deny the American President what Blackstone had assigned to the British King— 'The sole prerogative of making war and peace.' …. As Madison put it in a letter to Jefferson in 1798: 'The constitution supposes, what the History of all Govts demonstrates, that the Ex is the branch of power most interested in war, & most prone to it. It has accordingly with studied care vested the question of war in the Legislature". Arthur M. Schlesinger, Jr, *The Imperial Presidency* (Boston: Houghton Mifflin Company, 1973), pp. 3–5.

47. After the attack on Pearl Harbour and the declaration of war that followed, President Roosevelt quickly united a badly divided nation. The Bush administration successfully used the trope of war to gain and consolidate power. Having subsumed the Afghan and particularly the Iraq war to the

war on terrorism, it remains to be seen as of spring 2005 whether the Iraq war will sustain or undermine support for the Bush presidency.

48. On 20 October 2003, the Bush administration began to institutionalize discourse control. A 'far reaching study' conducted by the National Defense University at the request of the plans and policy branch of the Joint Chiefs of Staff produced a proposal to create a 'director of central information.' The director would have responsibility for budgeting and 'authoritative control of messages'— across all the government operations that deal with national security and foreign policy. The study was presented to a panel of senior Pentagon official and military officers, including Douglas J. Feith, the under secretary of defense for policy. Feith's shop had already created an Office of Strategic Influence whose aim was 'perception management.' The *New York Times*, December 13, 2004.

49. CNN reported that 'the exterior of the four-seat Navy S-3B Viking was marked with 'Navy 1' in the back and 'George Bush Commander-in-Chief' just below the cockpit window. On the plane's tail was the insignia of the squadron, the 'Blue Wolves.'" CNN.com, Commander in Chief lands on USS Lincoln. 2 May 2004. http://cnn.allpolitics

50. The account of the president's arrival on the Lincoln can be found on CNN.com Commander in Chief lands on USS Lincoln. 2 May 2004. http://cnn.allpolitics.

51. Bill Maher lost his nightly ABC programme 'Politically Incorrect' in 2003 after the White House objected to certain tart criticisms he made.

52. The phrase is taken from Mathews, 'September 11, One Year Later', p. 8.

53. George W. Bush, 'President Bush Delivers Graduation Speech at West Point', The White House, http://www.whitehouse.gov/news/releases/2002/06/20020601-3.html.

54. Despite the cautionary example of how President Johnson, also using faulty intelligence, stampeded Congress into voting for the 1964 Tonkin Gulf Resolution, Congress on 14 September 2001 authorized the President to use all 'necessary and appropriate force' against those who committed terrorist attacks. Chris Hedges warns that Congress authorized a war 'not against a state but against a phantom. The *jihad* we have embarked on is targeting an elusive and protean enemy. The battle we have begun is never-ending.' Hedges, *War is a Force*, p. 4.

55. The 69 per cent figure is from Schlesinger's *American Presidency*, p. 34. For narratives of the why and how the Iraq war came to pass see Chapter 2 'Eyeless in Iraq' (pp. 21–44), and Chapter 10 'The Iraq War' (pp. 145–71) in Ivo H. Daalder and James M. Lindsay, *America Unbound* (Washington, DC: Brookings Institution Press, 2003).

The official statement of the preemptive war doctrine appears in *The National Security Strategy of the United States of America*, a White House document issued in September 2002. It argues that 'the United States can no longer rely on a reactive posture as we have in the past. The inability to deter a potential attacker, the immediacy of today's threats, and the magnitude of potential harm that could be caused by our adversaries' choice of weapons, do no permit that option. We cannot let our enemies strike first.' Quoted in Schlesinger, *American Presidency*, p. 24-5. Condoleeza Rice put it melodramatically when she remarked that when you see the mushroom cloud it will be too late.

Richard Clark reports that Paul Wolfowitz was deeply committed to the view that Al Qaeda terrorism was state sponsored and that the sponsor was Saddam Hussein's Iraq. He has Wolfowitz saying to him, 'You give bin Laden too much credit [for the 9/11 attacks]. He could not do all these things like the 1993 attack on New York, not without a state sponsor....' I could hardly believe it but Wolfowitz was actually spouting the totally discredited Laurie Mylroie theory that Iraq was behind the 1993 truck bomb at the World Trade Center, a theory that had been investigated for years and found to be totally untrue.' Clark, *Against All Enemies*, pp. 231–2.

56. Patrick E. Tyler, 'U.N. Chief Ignites Firestorm By Calling Iraq War 'Illegal'', the *New York Times*, 17 September 2004. On 21 September, in a follow up of the press conference on 16 September where he criticized US unilateral action in Iraq, the Secretary General, Kofi Anan, opened the annual meeting of the UN General Assembly with a plea for bounded sovereignty in the form of greater observance of international law and the rule of law: 'Those who seek to bestow legitimacy must themselves embody it, and those who invoke international law must themselves embody it. . . . Every nation that proclaims the rule of laws at home must respect it abroad,' he said, 'and every nation that insists on it abroad must enforce it at home.' Warren Hoge, 'Annan Reiterates His Misgivings About Legality of War in Iraq', the *New York Times*, 22 September 2004.

57. See Stephen Eric Bronner and John Kurt Jacobsen, 'Dubya's Fellow Travelers: Left Intellectuals and Bush's War', *Logos: A Journal of Modern Society & Culture*, (Fall) 2004, http://www.logosjournal.com/issue3.4.html.

58. The quote is from Niall Ferguson, 'A World Without Power', *Foreign Policy*, (July-August) 2004, pp. 32/37 The New Dark Age would reverse what, for Ferguson, are benign effects of globalization ('raised living standards throughout the world') and produce 'economic stagnation and even depression.' A world without a 'hyperpower' would experience 'waning empires. Religious revivals. Incipient anarchy. A coming retreat into fortified cities.'

Ferguson's *Colossus: The Price of American Empire* (New York: Penguin Press, 2004) urges the US hyperpower to stop being a reluctant empire. He suggests that a US that embraced empire could save the world from a descent into a new Dark Ages and, like Rome and Britain, bring order and civilization. Power shocks and awes; the natives obey and learn. Ferguson seems oblivious to the response to American military power, nationalism, extremist religious fundamentalism, and escalating use of violence against civilian populations (sometimes called collateral damage).

59. Ernest R. May, review of *Colossus: The Price of American Empire,* by Niall Ferguson, the *Times Literary Supplement,* 16 July 2004, p. 11.

60. Judis' article 'Imperial Amnesia' appeared in *Foreign Policy* for July/August 2004. It anticipated the arguments advanced in his subsequent book, *Folly of Empire: What George Bush Could Learn from Theodore Roosevelt and Woodrow Wilson* (New York: Scribners, 2004).

61. Commenting at the time on the U.S. intervention in the Philippines, Mark Twain differed radically from President Bush's account of America's motives and conduct. After musing upon General MacArthur's (father of Douglas) order to kill all wounded Filipinos, Twain writes in 'To the Person Sitting in Darkness':

Having now laid all the historical facts before the Person Sitting in Darkness, we should bring him to again, and explain them to him. We should say to him: 'They look doubtful, but in reality they are not. There have been lies; yes, but they were told in a good cause. We have been treacherous; but that was only in order that real good might come out of apparent evil. True, we have crushed a deceived and confiding people; we have turned against the weak and the friendless who trusted us; we have stamped out a just and intelligent and well-ordered republic; we have stabbed an ally in the back and slapped the face of a guest; we have bought a Shadow from an enemy that hadn't it to sell; we have robbed a trusting friend of his land and his liberty; we have invited our clean young men to shoulder a discredited musket and do bandit's work under a flag which bandits have been accustomed to fear, not to follow; we have debauched America's honor and blackened her face before the world; but each detail was for the best. We know this. The Head of every State and Sovereignty in Christendom and ninety percent of every legislative body in Christendom, including our Congress and our fifty State Legislatures, are members not only of the church, but also of the Blessings-of-Civilization Trust. This world-girdling accumulation of trained morals, high principles, and justice, cannot do an unright thing, an unfair thing, an ungenerous thing, an unclean thing. It knows what it is about. Give yourself no uneasiness; it is all right.'

Mark Twain, 'To the Person Sitting in Darkness', *The Portable Mark Twain* (New York: Penguin, 1977), pp. 611–12.

62. We have adapted the sleeping beauty theory of democracy from Ronald Suny. See his *The Revenge of the Past* (Stanford, CA: Stanford University Press, 1993).

63. A major poll in the Middle East and Arab states shows that public opinion there appreciates freedom, would like more of it, and admires American

ideals, but resents and resists American power and cultural imperialism. See James Zogby, 'It's the Policy Stupid', Media Monitors Network, http://www.mediamonitors.net/zogby49.html. The Zogby report, 'America as Seen through Arab Eyes: Polling the Arab World after September 11th' is available at http://64.233.167.104/search?q=cache:jKJJ7YjbqFQJ:www.cato.org/events/gulfwar2/zogby.ppt+%22Zogby%22++%22april+2002%22&hl=en. A Defense Science Board report that became available on the web in November and was reported on in the *New York Times* of 22 November 2004 took the view that 'Muslims do not 'hate our freedom,' but rather hate our policies.' 'When American public diplomacy talks about bringing democracy to Islamic societies,' the report continued, 'this is seen as no more than self-serving hypocrisy.'

64. As the second World War ended, Franklin Roosevelt's similar liberal universalist anti-colonial stance was invoked, futilely, by Ho Chi Minh in an appeal to the United States.

65. George W. Bush, 'Bush Discusses Freedom in Iraq and the Middle East', The White House, http://www.whitehouse.gov/news/releases/2003/11/20031106 -2.html.

66. Judis, 'Imperial Amnesia', pp. 50–2.

67. The Bush administration capitalized on the fear and disorientation of the post-9/11 moment to extend and deepen its unilateralism and to initiate and launch the doctrine of preventive war. America's 'victory' in the Cold War had left it the only superpower. Its military power was unchallengeable. The new strategic doctrines made interdependence, deterrence, and balance of power redundant or obsolete. In the first war against Iraq, George Herbert Walker Bush sought UN as well as Congressional sanction to undo Iraq's invasion and occupation of Kuwait. He led a broad coalition that included *inter alia* Iraq's Arab and Muslim regional neighbours. Having failed to gain the UN Security Council support for attacking Iraq, the second Bush administration acted unilaterally with 'coalition of the willing' acolytes. It was the first application of the pre-emptive war doctrine President George W. Bush unveiled on 1 June 2002 when he spoke at West Point's graduation exercises. George W. Bush, 'President Bush Delivers Graduation Speech at West Point', The White House, http://www.whitehouse.gov/news/releases/2002/06/20020601-3.html.

68. For a helpful review of the literature on neoliberal institutionalism and constructivism see Thomas Risse, 'Constructivism and International Institutions: Toward Conversations across Paradigms', *Political Science: State of the Discipline*, Ira Katznelson and Helen V. Milner (eds), (New York: W. W. Norton and Company / Washington, DC: American Political Science Association, 2002), pp. 597–623. On internecine conflict over the analytical character of constructivism see John Kurt Jacobsen, 'Duelling

Constructivisms: A Post-Mortem on the Ideas Debate in IR/IPE', *Review of International Studies*, vol. 29, no. 1 (January), 2003), pp. 39–60.

69. For a recent review of threats to civil liberties in 'war time' see Geoffrey R. Stone, *Perilous Times: Free Speech in Wartime, From the Sedition Act of 1798 to the War on Terrorism* (New York: W. W. Norton & Company, 2004).

70. We take the idea that preventing 'the arbitrary exercise of power' is the essence of constitutional government from Carl J. Friedrich's *Constitutional Government and Democracy* rev. ed. (Boston, MA: Ginn and Company, 1950).

71. Benjamin R. Barber, 'Democracy Cannot Coexist with Bush's Failed Doctrine of Preventive War', *Los Angeles Times*, 3 December 2003 (as published by the Global Policy Forum, http://www.globalpolicy.org/empire/analysis/2003/1203democracy.htm). Barber's critique did not prevent President Bush from telling the 2004 annual meeting of the UN General Assembly that 'our world needs a new definition of security. Our security is not merely found in spheres of influence or some balance of power; the security of our world is found in the advancing rights of mankind.' From a partial text of the speech in the *New York Times* of 22 September 2004.

72. There has been extensive news coverage, analysis, and interpretation of the American state's treatment of prisoners at Guantanamo, Abu Ghraib, and, to a lesser extent, in Afghanistan. This is being written at the time of the release of the report, one of numerous reports, chaired by former Secretary of Defense James Schlesinger. According to a *New York Times* editorial of 26 August 2004 ('Holding the Pentagon Accountable for Abu Ghraib'), 'it was clear that the road to Abu Ghraib began well before the invasion of Iraq, when the administration created the category of 'unlawful combatants' for suspected members of al Qaeda and the Taliban who were captured in Afghanistan and imprisoned in Guantanamo Bay, Cuba. Interrogators wanted to force these prisoners to talk in ways that are barred by American law and the Geneva Conventions, and on August 1, 2002, Justice Department lawyers produced the infamous treatise on how to construe torture as being legal. . . . Interrogators and members of military were sent from Afghanistan to Iraq and the harsh interrogations 'migrated' with them.'

On 28 June 2004, the Supreme Court rules on the Bush administration's incarceration of 'enemy combatants' without access to the outside world and without limit of time. These arrangements epitomize how the Bush administration attempted to redefine the American state. It was, in the words of the *New York Times*, 'a radically broader view of government's power to detain people. The administration claimed the right to hold foreign terrorism suspects in indefinite legal limbo in Guantanamo, and to designate American citizens as 'enemy combatants' and hold them for years without access to lawyers.' The court rebuked the administration in landmark decisions. The court made clear that habeas corpus is a core principle of American law that gives anyone behind bars the right to challenge their imprisonment in court. Six months later Britain's highest court, a special panel of nine law lords of the House of Lords, deemed the indefinite detention of foreigners suspected of terrorism without charging them or trying them violated the European Convention on Human Rights. The law lords' decision paralleled that of the US Supreme Court's 28 June 2004. Both the US and the UK governments argued that the courts should have no role with respect to detentions aimed at fighting terrorism.

In a second case the court ruled for Yaser Esam Hamdi, an American citizen who has been designated an enemy combatant. Justice Sandra Day O'Connor spoke for a majority when she wrote that the conditions of Mr Hamdi's confinement were not permissible. Hamdi must be given access to a lawyer, told the basis on which he was designated an enemy combatant, and afforded an opportunity to challenge it before a neutral decision maker. 'Reaffirming the Rule of Law', Editorial, the *New York Times*, 29 June 2004. See also Anthony Lewis' *New York Times* Op-Ed of 30 June 2004, where he argued that the justices had firmly rejected President Bush's 'presumption of omnipotence' and quoted Justice Sandra Day O'Connor's remark that 'a state of war is not a blank check for the president when it comes to rights of the nation's citizens.'

73. The 9/11 Commission was sufficiently disturbed by the danger of the erosion of civil liberties in the quest for security at home that it recommended the creation of a special board to do so. In commenting on the inadequacy of the Bush administration's 'caricature of the 9/11 commission's proposed board', the *New York Times* took the view that 'Mr. Bush has tried to sweep aside the Constitution by declaring selected American citizens to be unlawful combatants and jailing them indefinitely; Mr. Ashcroft's Justice Department produced the appalling memo justifying the torture of prisoners. It was also responsible for, among other things, jailing a lawyer from Portland, Oregon, on charges of international terrorism based on a misreading of his fingerprints and, apparently, on his religious beliefs. The administration set up a detention camp in Guantanamo Bay where minimal standards of justice have been suspended or eliminated altogether.' 'In Defense of Civil Liberties', Editorial, the *New York Times*, 20 September 2004.

Responsibility of senior persons in the Bush administration for what eventuated in the practice of torture and the abuse of prisoners can be found in the documents in Karen J. Greenberg and Joshua I. Dratel (eds), *The Torture Papers: The Road to Abu Ghraib* (New York: Cambridge University Press, 2005). Particularly egregious is the first memo in the book to Timothy Flanigan, Deputy Counsel to the President by John C.

Yoo, Assistant Attorney General, U. S. Department of Justice, Office of Legal Counsel, dated 23 September 2001, entitled 'The President's Constitutional Authority to Conduct Military Operations against Terrorists and Nations supporting them.' Yoo's memo can be taken as the manifesto for sovereignty unbound. Yoo took the view that 'The President has constitutional power not only to retaliate against any person, organization, or State *suspected emphasis* of involvement in terrorists attacks on the United States, but also against foreign States *suspected* [emphasis supplied] of harboring or supporting such organizations', p. 3. After 2003 Yoo returned to his position as faculty member at the Boalt School of Law, University of California, Berkeley. Earlier, he had clerked for Justice Clarence Thomas on the US Supreme Court.

74. Clarke, author of *Against All Enemies: Inside America's War on Terror*, asks in a *New York Times* Op-Ed of 25 July 2004, who the enemy is and what threat does he pose. Terrorism, he says, 'is a tactic, not an enemy.' The threat is from 'Islamic Jihadism', which must be defeated in a battle of ideas as well as in armed conflict.'

75. The essay, 'Tuesday, and After' appeared in the *New Yorker* of 24 September 2001 and was republished in Hendrick Hertzberg, *Politics; Observations and Arguments, 1966-2004* (New York: The Penguin Press, 2004). According to Michael Howard, 'Many people would have preferred a police operation conducted under the auspices of the UN on behalf of the international community as a whole, against a criminal conspiracy, whose members should be hunted down and brought before an international court.' Tania Brannigan, 'Al-Qaida is Winning War, Allies Warned', the *Guardian*, 31 October 2001. 'When responding to the bombs in the Madrid railway system on March 11, 2004, the Spanish authorities and the European Union chose a police approach. It meant concentrating on finding the culprits, capturing them, and eventually, bringing them to court.' Perter Wallensteen, 'Reflection on September 11 and Democracy', in *Developing a Culture of Conflict Prevention*, Anders Mellbourn, (ed.), (Stockholm: Gidlunds, for the Madriaga European Foundation and The Bank of Sweden Tercentenary Foundation, 2004); an Anna Lindh Programme on Conflict Prevention, 2004 edition, p. 65.

76. Anne Norton, *Leo Strauss and the Politics of American Empire* (New Haven, CT: Yale University Press, 2004), pp. 2–3.

77. Allyson J. K. Bailes, 'Terrorism and Conflict,' in *Conflict Prevention* Mellbourne, (ed.) p. 71. Allyson Bailes is the Director of the Stockholm International Peace Research Institute (SIPRI).

78. On the question of what the Bush administration knew, or did not want known, about WMD see, for example, Mark Danner, 'The Secret Way to War', *New York Review of Books*, 9 June 2005. 'Since 'the intelligence and facts were being fixed around the policy' as early as July 2002 (as 'C', the

head of British intelligence, reported upon his return from Washington),'
Danner, among many others, observes, 'it seems a matter of remarkable
hubris, even for this administration, that its officials now explain their
misjudgments in going to war by blaming them on 'intelligence failures'—
that is, on the intelligence that they themselves politicized.'

79. Anonymous, *Imperial Hubris: Why the West is Losing the War on Terror*
(Washington, DC: Brassey's Inc., 2004).

80. Anonymous differs from well-known scholars of Islam such as Bernard
Lewis, Ralph Peters, Malise Ruthven, and Victor Davic Hanson who hold
that
'Bin Laden, his allies, and their goals have been spawned by a 'failed
civilization'—one hostile to democratization, capitalism, and modernity,
save for the tools of war—and that they are driven by both the realization
that Islamic society is dying and a maniacal desire to destroy other
civilizations that are successful and causing the demise of Islam. These
men, the argument goes, recognize this failure, blame it on the West, and
are lashing out with indiscriminate violence to spark an Armageddon-
like battle with Western civilization. This line of analysis takes a brilliant,
calculating, and patient foe like bin Laden and reduces him to the status
of madman, bloodthirsty and irrational' [p.110].
'At this point,' Anonymous says,
'we are faced with the chance to incorrectly answer the question, 'Why do
they hate us?' Do they hate us for what we think and how we live, or do
they hate us because of what we do in the Muslim world? . . . Bin Laden
consistently has put the blame for the decrepit conditions of Islamic
civilization squarely on Muslims themselves. . . . Bin Laden, at the end of
the day, is a happy warrior, a brilliant hunter-killer waging war to achieve
precise, devastating, but limited goals. There is simply no evidence to
support the idea that he is vaingloriously trying to lead the world—
Muslim, Christian, and other—to Armageddon. And it is for this reason
that I, with respect, strongly disagree with those who apply the failed
civilization theory to bin Laden and al Qaeda. An armed patience, and
positive predator always is more dangerous and less prone to errors than
the bomb-throwing madman crazy for revenge' [pp. 114–15].

81. Fallows, 'Bush's Lost Year,' 82.

82. Had 60 thousand votes officially gone the other way in Ohio, Democratic
candidate Senator John Kerry would be President today.
Greg Mitchell, 'Why do Most Americans Feel the 'War is not Worth it'?
Editor & Publisher 29 May 2005.http://editorandpublisher.printthis.
clickability.com

83. While we find the differences between the red and the blue states are
rooted in world view and culture, we do not exclude the influence of
material interest. According to Paul Krugman, the red states, it should be

noted, as of 1999 were subsidized by the blue states at about $90 billion dollars. 'When you do the numbers for red states without major cities, you find that they look like Montana, which in 1999 received $1.75 in federal spending for every dollar it paid in federal taxes. The numbers for [Krugman's] home state of New Jersey were almost the opposite. Add in the hidden subsidies, like below-cost provision of water for irrigation, nearly free use of federal land for grazing and so on, and it becomes clear that in economic terms America's rural heartland is our version of southern Italy: a region whose inhabitants are largely supported by aid from their more productive compatriots.' Paul Krugman, 'True Blue Americans', the *New York Times*, 7 May 2002. Republished in Paul Krugman, *The Great Unraveling: Losing Our Way in The New Century* (New York: W.W. Norton & Co., 2004), 177-9. Also see Thomas Frank's analysis of a form of 'false consciousness' apparently at work in a red state, *What's the Matter with Kansas?: How Conservatives won the heart of America* (New York: Metropolitan Books, 2004).

Contributors

HELMUTH BERKING, Professor of Sociology, Technical University of Darmstadt.

PATRICIA BICKERS, editor, *Art Monthly*, and Principal Lecturer, Art History and Theory, University of Westminster.

PAUL BRASS, Professor Emeritus of Political Science and South Asian Studies, University of Washington.

BRUCE CUMINGS, Department Chair and Gustavus F. and Ann M. Swift Distinguished Service Professor, Department of History and the College, University of Chicago.

JOHN KURT JACOBSEN, Research Associate, Program on International Politics, Economics and Security, University of Chicago.

HUNG MIN JOO, Associate Professor, Korea University, Seoul, South Korea.

SUDIPTA KAVIRAJ, Professor of South Asian Politics, Department of Middle East and Asian Languages and Cultures, Columbia University.

PHILIP OLDENBURG, Research Scholar, Southern Asian Institute, Columbia University.

ARUNDHATI ROY, writer and activist.

LLOYD I. RUDOLPH, Professor Emeritus of Political Science, University of Chicago.

JAMES C. SCOTT, Sterling Professor of Political Science and Anthropology, Institute for Social and Policy Studies, Yale University.

TASNEEM AHMED SIDDIQUI was formerly with the Civil Service of Pakistan where his longest tenure was with the Sindh Katchi Abadis Authority. Subsequently, he has been associated with NGOs such as the Orangi Project and Saiban.

NICHOLAS TEMPLE is Consultant Psychiatrist in Psychotherapy, Adult Department, Tavistock Clinic, UK.